Burlesque Plays of the Eighteenth Century

Burlesque Plays of the Eighteenth Century

EDITED

WITH INTRODUCTIONS AND NOTES BY

SIMON TRUSSLER

OXFORD UNIVERSITY PRESS

LONDON   OXFORD   NEW YORK

1969

Oxford University Press

LONDON OXFORD NEW YORK
GLASGOW TORONTO MELBOURNE WELLINGTON
CAPE TOWN SALISBURY IBADAN NAIROBI LUSAKA ADDIS ABABA
BOMBAY CALCUTTA MADRAS KARACHI LAHORE DACCA
KUALA LUMPUR SINGAPORE HONG KONG TOKYO

First published as
an Oxford University Press paperback
by Oxford University Press, London, 1969

PRINTED IN GREAT BRITAIN
BY RICHARD CLAY (THE CHAUCER PRESS), LTD.,
BUNGAY SUFFOLK

Contents

Acknowledgements

I have been particularly indebted in the preparation of this volume to the limited critical editions of *The Rehearsal* edited by Montague Summers in 1914, and of *The Tragedy of Tragedies* edited by James T. Hillhouse in 1918. John Harrington Smith's prefatory remarks to his facsimile reprint of *Three Hours after Marriage*, published by the Augustan Reprint Society in 1961, helped to determine the edition of that play used in the present collection, as did G. C. Faber's editorial work on *The What d'ye Call it* for his Oxford edition of Gay's *Poetical Works*, published in 1926. I owe seminal debts to V. C. Clinton-Baddeley's *Burlesque Tradition in the English Theatre*, which first directed my interest to the burlesque form, and to Henry Morley's long out-of-print collection of *Burlesque Plays and Poems*—in a battered copy of which I first read (albeit in bowdlerized and textually dubious reprints) several of the plays in the present collection. My gratitude also goes to Miss Wendy Slemen, for transforming texts into typescript, to Richard Brain, of the Oxford University Press, for supporting and encouraging the whole project, to my wife, Glenda, for supporting and encouraging me, and to the staffs and resources of the British Museum Reading Room and of University College London Library.

S. T.

Introduction

Great art has often begun as burlesque. Chaucer's 'drasty rymyng' in the *Tale of Sir Thopas*—'nat worth a toord', as the host succinctly put it—has survived the prolix metrical romances it parodied, just as *Don Quixote* has outlived the hack tales of chivalry which irritated Cervantes into writing it. The scribblers ridiculed by Pope in his *Dunciad* have been condemned to a heavenly Grub Street, their works to the underworld of the annotator's footnotes: and even Richardson's *Pamela* attracts far fewer readers than Fielding's mock-sequel, the tale of the virtuous heroine's chaste brother, *Joseph Andrews*. In each of these cases, a work of literature has transcended its immediate function, to survive not as a burlesque, but as a novel or a poem in its own right. Can there, then, be no such thing as a burlesque in its own right? It is my hope that the plays assembled in the present collection will suggest that there can be, and that a continuing consciousness of a critical as well as an artistic purpose can enliven rather than diminish one's appreciation of this unjustly neglected dramatic form.

Theatrical burlesque is almost as old as the theatre itself. Aristophanes made incidental use of it in several of his comedies, notably in that histrionic tug-of-war between Aeschylus and Euripides in *The Frogs*. The deeds of legendary Greek heroes, reworked in the earliest tragedies of that nation, were vulgarized in the satyr plays which rounded off each dramatist's latest trilogy; and the religious rituals from which English liturgical drama developed in the middle ages suffered the annual indignity of travesty during the Festival of the Boy Bishop. Shakespeare burlesqued the alliterative ranting of bombastic heroes in the character of Pistol, who enlivens the final plays of the first Henrician sequence. He made gentle fun of folk-drama in the Nine Worthies scenes of *Love's Labour's Lost*, and travestied the theme of his own *Romeo and Juliet* in the Pyramus and Thisbe episodes of *A Midsummer Night's Dream*. And he even introduced a rehearsal-play of sorts into *Hamlet*. In none of these cases, however, was the burlesque element more than incidental. And the backbiting between Jonson, Marston, and Dekker, which took dramatic shape in such plays as *Every Man out of his Humour*, *Satiromastix*, and *The Poetaster*, had not really to do with burlesque at all, but with 'comical satire'. The tradition of dramatic satire, as Fielding more satisfactorily dubbed it, is, of course, closely related to that of burlesque, and occasionally overlaps it—but it is, I think, convenient to attempt a rule-of-thumb distinction between the two.

Burlesque, then, is essentially *formal* parody. It makes fun of artistic pretensions—whereas dramatic satire hits at faults and foibles in real life. Such a distinction cannot be applied either prescriptively or absolutely. But it does, for example, help to explain why the burlesque elements of Fielding's *Tom Thumb* are so much more polished and pointed than those of the mock-tragedy and comedy harnessed together in *Pasquin*. For in the earlier play the dramatist's aim had been to ridicule excesses of tragedy-mongering: but in the self-styled 'dramatic satire' he was using the rehearsal-formula merely as a convenient vehicle for an attack on actual, governmental corruption. Dramatic satire is undoubtedly a fascinating field of study: but here it must suffice to distinguish its aims and its methods from those of burlesque, to remark that the form is not represented in the present collection—except in the hybrid *Three Hours after Marriage*—and that it can command no further consideration in this introduction.

Probably the first full-length burlesque play in English was Francis Beaumont's *Knight of the Burning Pestle*, written in or before 1610. But 'for want of judgement,' as its preface put it, 'or not understanding the privy mark of *ironie* about it,' the piece was 'utterly rejected' by its original audience —for though its content was entirely contemporary, its burlesque form was half a century too sophisticated for its time. The play ridiculed grocer knight-errantry—that discovery of the stuff of chivalry in the exploits of city merchants and their apprentices which distinguished, among other pieces, Heywood's *Four Prentises of London*. In *The Knight of the Burning Pestle*, a young lad apprenticed to a grocer and his wife (all three members of the play's own audience) is elevated to heroic rank, and in the play-within-the-play is made to wander from Waltham Forest to Moldavia in promotion of a romantic match. He eventually expires 'with a forked arrow through his head', because no better way can be devised to bring the play to an end—and it was just such arbitrariness of motive and action, with its attendant subordination of probability to dramatic effect, that Beaumont was setting out to satirize. But the 'privy mark of ironie' went unperceived, and burlesque had to await the recognition and appreciation of a more formally-conscious age.

Etymological dictionaries agree in recording the earliest occurrences in English of the words *burlesque* and *travesty* around the middle of the seventeenth century. In France, the two terms—at first virtually synonymous—had already been used to describe the poetic style and subject matter of Scarron, whose *Vergile Travesti* appeared in 1648: and they were soon to be applied to the work of Scarron's English imitators and successors, Charles Cotton and Samuel Butler. The doggerel octosyllabic couplets of the latter's

Hudibras were characteristic of early poetic burlesque—which in the hands of lesser writers than Butler tended to be over-assertive and inconsequential —but it is in fact to the kind of mock-heroic idiom employed by Dryden in *MacFlecknoe* that burlesque drama enjoys a closer kinship, sharing both its pentametric form and its subtler methods of ridicule.

The first theatrical burlesque to reach the stage after the Restoration was Sir William Davenant's *Play-House to be Let* (1663), which pioneered the use of mock-heroic couplets in its fifth-act version of the Cleopatra story. But between *The Play-House to be Let* and *The Rehearsal* (1671) lies the essential difference between travesty and truly *critical* burlesque—the difference between a mere vulgarizing of an elevated or classical theme, and satire purposefully directed against the striking of false tragical attitudes. (Paradoxically, Davenant himself also essayed the new heroic vein, for which presumption he was duly ridiculed in *The Rehearsal*.) Davenant's mock-play, then, foreshadows a tradition of extravaganza rather than of burlesque—a tradition to which Carey's plays, among those in the present collection, in part belong, but which is more often associated with the ephemeral punnings of latter-day pantomime. *The Play-House to be Let* nevertheless occupies a small niche in the gallery of true burlesques for its declared intention of ridiculing 'the actions of the hero' in 'verse burlesque'. With this declaration, the form became self-conscious—aware of its distinctive *function* as a dramatic genre, though not of its ultimate purpose or potential. It was left to George Villiers, in *The Rehearsal*, to begin to realize that potential.

It was the vogue for heroic drama which gave *The Rehearsal* its immediate critical purpose. Most plays actually couched in heroic couplets were first performed in the decades before 1677—at which date Dryden, in *All for Love*, initiated a general return to tragedy's more familiar blank-verse idiom. But the enduring popularity of the heroic plays—and of their characteristic themes, love and honour, in blank-verse dress—ensured the survival of *The Rehearsal*, as of the burlesque tradition it established. Their heroes intended to inspire awe and admiration rather than pity, their language hyperbolic, and their settings gaudily extravagant, heroic plays—hopefully theatrical equivalents to the epic poem—had in Dryden a formidable theorist. But time has justified Buckingham's ridicule, as it has justified those who mocked the new dramatic modes of the eighteenth century—and it was not, in fact, until this classical age of English literature that *The Rehearsal* spawned worthy successors. True, *The Empress of Morocco* travestied Elkanah Settle's heroic drama of the same name in 1673, and two years later its author, Thomas Duffett, essayed in *Psyche Debauch'd* and *The Mock-Tempest* successful burlesques of Shadwell's *Psyche* and of Dryden's adaptation of Shakespeare's romance. But although the dates of these pieces are closely contiguous to that of *The Rehearsal*'s first performance, they proved to be lone imitations.

It is notable that Buckingham's burlesque and *The Mock-Tempest* are alike full-length works: for conciseness, if not brevity, contributes to the making of a burlesque's case, and avoids the danger of labouring its satirical or parodistic points. To sustain a burlesque's impetus for a whole evening is not easy: and accordingly it was not until the *afterpiece* was established as a staple ingredient of a theatre's daily programme—a change which dates from around the turn of the new century—that theatrical conditions were truly ripe for the development of the form. It was no mere coincidence that Gay's *What d'ye Call it* was first staged at Drury Lane in February 1715, as an afterpiece to *Jane Shore*: for this was just two months after the opening of John Rich's new playhouse in Lincoln's Inn Fields had generated a new spirit of competition between the companies, and forced the rival theatre to emulate Rich's institution of a regular afterpiece.

The sorry state of the legitimate drama also favoured the growth of burlesque. In the aftermath of Jeremy Collier's aptly titled *Short View*—a puritanical polemic against the immorality of the English stage, which echoed the feelings of its increasingly middle-class audience—comedy had been purged of its Restoration lewdness. But only in the works of Farquhar— which proved to be the culmination of an older, Shakespearian tradition of comedy, rather than the beginning of a new—was a full-blooded zest for living transfused into the anaemic veins of its morally self-conscious heroes and heroines. The taste was for 'comedies of sentiment', of which Cibber's *Careless Husband* (1704) and Steele's *Conscious Lovers* (1722) are representative examples. These were sentimental indeed, but not at all comic: and they tended to differ from tragedy only in the formal business of their happier outcomes, and in their more commonplace characters and settings. 'Laughing' comedy was out of fashion: but the consequent poverty of the comic spirit presented not so much a *target* for burlesque as an opportunity for it—along with other less regular forms of entertainment—to corner the theatrical market in laughter. It would certainly be fair to assert that almost all plays of comic emphasis (between those of Farquhar and Sheridan) which still merit reading or revival are in one or other of the 'irregular' forms —the forms of farce, ballad opera, dramatic satire, and burlesque. Also remarkable, though less often remarked, is the refreshing frankness with which sexual mores are exemplified in such pieces as *Three Hours after Marriage*, *The What d'ye Call it* and *The Covent-Garden Tragedy*. Coarse the treatment may occasionally seem: but it is surely preferable to the mixture of titillation and trite moralizing which characterizes the presentation of sex in most sentimental comedies.

Sentimentalism itself is ridiculed less in the drama than in fiction and in verse satire—although Gay's *What d'ye Call it* sustains an implicit attack on the false idealization of rusticity. Mainly, it was the pretensions of tragedy which burlesque dramatists were still concerned to expose. Heroic drama continued to flourish: and its original rhymed form is duly burlesqued in *The What d'ye Call it*, *Distress upon Distress*, *Chrononhotonthologos* and *Bombastes Furioso*. Its strutting heroes are also parodied in the last two pieces, as are heroic assumptions in general in the play-within-the-play rehearsed in *Three Hours after Marriage*. But *Tom Thumb* (though it incidentally parodies the rhymed tags which continued to denote scene-changes) and *The Covent-Garden Tragedy* are in blank-verse—and these two burlesques of Fielding's ridicule between them all three major forms of eighteenth-century tragedy. *Tom Thumb* reworks a conventionally heroic sort of theme in bathetic terms: but *The Covent-Garden Tragedy* travesties the pseudo-classical idiom of Ambrose Philips's *Distrest Mother*—an idiom Joseph Addison had attempted with greater (indeed, unique) success in *Cato*. Philips's play had distorted the Andromache legend by squeezing it into the straitjacket of poetic justice— that theory propagated by Thomas Rymer, which demanded that moral propriety rather than probability should determine the outcome of a dramatic action. By his eponymous choice of setting for *The Covent-Garden Tragedy*, Fielding at once debased the classical legend *ad absurdum* and— more to the point—demonstrated poetic justice working in favour of pimps and bawds. Moreover, he made tangential mock of the genuinely new form of domestic tragedy, which recognized the rise of the merchant classes by making tragic heroes of them. George Lillo's *London Merchant* (1731) was a seminal example of the form—and one whose date is significantly close to that of *The Covent-Garden Tragedy*.

After the temporary setback of burlesque during the seventeen-twenties— the heyday of two oddly assorted enemies of legitimate theatre, the Italian opera and the pantomime—it was the unprecedented success of Gay's *Beggar's Opera* in 1728 which created a climate newly favourable to the irregular comic forms: and five of the ten burlesques in the present collection have been culled from the quarter-century which followed Gay's triumph. Pantomime and opera themselves attracted the attention of burlesque writers. Carey's *Dragon of Wantley*, for example, travestied Italian opera, and Fielding's *Tumble-down Dick* made incidental mock of the pantomimic style— though its elements of political satire predominated. But merely to list all the burlesques which proliferated during these years would be at once tedious and impossible—for many plays which were essentially farces, ballad operas, or satires contained elements of formal parody. (The deliberately contrived climax of *The Beggar's Opera* is a case in point.) And fuller considerations of the plays reprinted in this collection will be found preceding their individual texts. One further piece which demands particular mention, however—and whose exclusion requires a word of defence—is Sheridan's *The Critic*, with which the golden age of burlesque reached its culmination in

1779. *The Critic* exists in so many modern reprints that it was decided to exclude it from the present anthology in the interests of making available one of the lesser-known pieces. *The Critic* is, nevertheless, of immense importance in the burlesque tradition. Its form is that of the mock-rehearsal —in this case, of Mr. Puff's play, *The Spanish Armada*. And in this respect, it is similar to *The Rehearsal* itself, to *The What d'ye Call it*, and to the Clinket episodes in *Three Hours after Marriage*—but unlike the later burlesques in this collection, which dramatize a single and consecutive action. Sheridan's choice of the rehearsal formula enabled him to make the kind of references to the state of the contemporary theatre which also enlivened *The Rehearsal*, but which Fielding had to confine to footnotes in his revision of *Tom Thumb*, as did George Alexander Stevens in *Distress upon Distress*. And the metre chosen by Sheridan for his play-in-rehearsal was burlesqued blank verse—a choice no doubt inspired by the pseudo-Elizabethan idiom of the tragedies of Richard Cumberland, who served as a model for Sir Fretful Plagiary. However, *The Critic* is in the tradition of *The What d'ye Call it* and of *The Covent-Garden Tragedy*, rather than that of *The Rehearsal* and *Tom Thumb*, in generalizing its satire, rather than attempting a close parody of particular passages.

It does not seem probable, as some critics have surmised, that this generality of *The Critic*'s satire explains its greater popularity on the stage: for although a recognition of the allusions in, say, *Tom Thumb* does heighten one's appreciation of the play, a lack of acquaintance with Fielding's sources is no real hurdle to its enjoyment—indeed, it generalizes the play's satire by default. No: a simpler explanation for the survival of *The Critic* is its invariable inclusion in complete editions of Sheridan's works—his single burlesque lives on, as it were, by virtue of his success in more regular forms of comedy. *Tom Thumb*, the only play in the present collection which has similarly been made available, other than in scholarly or limited editions (albeit in its later, revised form, often wrongly masquerading under its original title), has also proved a resounding success on the occasions of its revival in university and other 'fringe' productions. Of its new-found stablemates in these pages, only *Distress upon Distress* and *The Rovers* are, as they stand, unsuitable for stage performance. The remaining pieces all seem to me stageworthy—*The Dragon of Wantley* and *Bombastes Furioso* rather less so than the burlesques by Buckingham, Gay, and Fielding, the strangely neglected *Three Hours after Marriage*, and *Chrononhotonthologos*. All provide promising material for amateurs and students, in whose acting styles a measure of skill often combines with a heightened self-consciousness curiously appropriate to burlesque, and also for professionals, who would no doubt relish that counterpointing of styles—and that verging on the edge of ham without quite overstepping its mark—which the form demands.

Certain it is that, with the two exceptions noted, these plays were written primarily to be performed, and can never live so fully on the page as on the stage.

There was little left to be said in the old mock-tragic forms after *The Critic*: and even Sheridan's play, for all its greater polish, lacks the satiric sting which lends a feeling of immediacy to *The Rehearsal* or to *The Covent-Garden Tragedy*. So often had burlesque hit its tragic targets that they were worn away: and in general the form failed to adapt itself to the ridicule of new kinds of theatrical pretension. *The Rovers* is thus unique in its parody of the sentimental-cum-revolutionary drama which flourished in Germany towards the end of the century, and which influenced the development of the melodrama in this country. But the conservative satirists who drafted *The Rovers* were already out of touch with the literary spirit of their times. Rhodes's *Bombastes Furioso* was faithful to the old and now outdated form and subject-matter—and it contributed to that transformation of the mock-heroic burlesque into mere extravaganza, which was to take place during the nineteenth century, and which found its leading exponent in J. R. Planché.

Mock-melodramatists were few: the age was not disposed to formal satire, and melodrama, in any case, contained the essence of its own absurdity—as modern revivals demonstrate. And in the later nineteenth and early twentieth centuries a renewed burlesque impulse flickered only occasionally into life. In *Mr. Punch's Pocket Ibsen*, a series of nutshell-plays culled from the weekly humorous magazine in 1893, F. Anstey pertinently parodied the formal characteristics of the Norwegian master. Bernard Shaw—aptly enough, for a man who recognized in Fielding the greatest practising English dramatist since Shakespeare—attempted one self-contained burlesque, *The Admirable Bashville*, and one in the rehearsal form, which made casual mock of contemporary critics, *Fanny's First Play*. Stephen Leacock published a burlesque scenario of a 'modern problem play', which he dubbed *Behind the Beyond*, and which V. C. Clinton-Baddeley knocked into stageworthy shape. And Nigel Playfair similarly adapted Max Beerbohm's *Savonarola Brown* for the stage. But such pieces were no more than occasional—as are the travesties of fashionable drama and dramatists which feature regularly in contemporary revues, those direct descendants of the old dramatic satires.

The recent renaissance of English drama has, in short, yet to generate its own body of burlesques. Now this is sad, and rather strange. For the mood of present-day drama, in which theatres of the absurd, of cruelty, and of this, that, and the other proliferate, is—as it was in the early eighteenth century—one of generic confusion. Again, there are certain pretensions which demand deflation—as David Halliwell, author of *Little Malcolm*, a few years ago deflated the cult of the director in a joyous entertainment dubbed *The Experiment*. A healthy theatre is a self-critical theatre—even if that health mainly resides, as it did in the eighteenth century, in the very plays which were staging a critical protest against fustian, bombast, and moral hypocrisy. Then, the irregular, satirical forms of comedy flourished, and deserved to flourish. I believe they also deserved to survive. In rescuing ten plays in one of these forms—burlesque—from the oblivion of admitted but allegedly ephemeral merit, it is therefore my hope that their humour, and the moral honesty whence it derives, may prove itself longer lasting than the literary historians like to suggest. There is a certain critical nearsightedness which, in ferreting out every topical allusion, gets the broad outlines of a work out of focus. I think the general reader and the theatregoer are in better positions to see these plays whole, and to place enjoyment before exegesis.

1967   SIMON TRUSSLER

A Note on the Texts

The present volume is intended chiefly for the use of general students of the drama, and for those wishing to revive the chosen plays in performance. But in view of the scarcity or non-existence of reliable modern editions of these burlesques, every attempt has been made to provide texts which will also meet the requirements of serious scholars. Without space in which to justify chosen readings or to indicate rejected alternatives, a definitive collation of early texts has not been attempted: rather, it has been thought preferable to select a single text—usually that of the latest authoritative edition—and to reprint the play in as close conformity as possible to this original. Catch-words and the use of long *s* have been abandoned: but spelling and punctuation have been exactly transcribed—except in a very few cases involving obvious misprints—and the original conventions for the use of italic and for the abbreviation of names have been followed, as has, in general, the layout of the text. A degree of regularization has only been imposed where there are distracting inconsistencies within the original text. Prefatory matter, cast-lists, footnotes, and other non-dramatic appendages, have been incorporated in their correct order, so that each text constitutes a virtually exact reprint of its original.

The text of *The Rehearsal* is that of the third edition of 1675, the last edition authoritatively revised by Buckingham. *The What d'ye Call it* is reprinted from the first collected edition of Gay's works, *Poems on Several Occasions*, published in 1720—and slightly more reliable, in this case, than the edition of 1731 used in G. C. Faber's Oxford edition of the *Poetical Works* (1926). I have, however, followed Faber in adopting the style of the octavo editions of the piece, and so printing the names of its characters as to distinguish the opening and closing scenes from those of the play-within-the-play. And I have concurred with the arguments advanced by John Harrington Smith— in the introduction to his facsimile reprint of *Three Hours after Marriage*— for preferring the text included in the second Dublin edition of *A Supplement to the Works of Alexander Pope*. This edition of the play, although not published till 1758, is probably closest in its act-divisions to the version staged forty years earlier: but typographically it is flawed by inconsistencies, and some conventions have accordingly been regularized in this reprint—notably those governing stage directions and the use of italic.

I have chosen the second edition of *Tom Thumb*: it was published, like the first, in 1730, but it contains substantive additions which are undoubtedly of Fielding's own. It must, however, be emphasized that all editions of *Tom Thumb* differ in innumerable respects from those of the revised *Tragedy of Tragedies*, the version reprinted in most modern anthologies. *The Covent-Garden Tragedy* has been reprinted from its first and only edition, which appeared in 1732. But no such simplicity of choice existed in the cases of *Chrononhotonthologos* and of *The Dragon of Wantley*, both of which plays went into many (and markedly varied) editions. I have used the first edition of the former, printed in 1734, and the twelfth of the latter, which appeared in 1738. Some standardization of conventions has been necessary, and I confess that my choice of editions was only a little less arbitrary than Carey's attention to the printing of his plays.

Distress upon Distress is a reprint of the first London edition of 1752. The text of *The Rovers* is taken from the collected edition of *The Poetry of the Anti-Jacobin* published in 1799: it corrects some serious errors incorporated in L. Rice-Oxley's allegedly verbatim reprint. And the first authorized edition of 1822 has been followed in reprinting *Bombastes Furioso*. For the errors doubtless perpetuated as well as those created, I ask pardon and crave correction.

Finally, a note on notes. Some of these are, of course, the dramatists' own embellishments to their texts. My own few annotations—keyed to the line numbers instead of the symbols used for the mock-annotations, and appearing below a rule when both kinds of note occur on a single page—are not 'to make the commodity swell, and sell better', but to elucidate semantic ambiguities, allusions to places long forgotten or out of fashion, to people whose fame has proved transitory, and the like. I have *not* attempted to pinpoint the sources of parodied lines and passages: the editions of *The Rehearsal* and of *The Tragedy of Tragedies* cited in the Bibliography do so in detail, but to have assembled similar material for the present collection would have extended its length beyond reasonable limits—and suggested possible stumbling blocks to the appreciation of the plays where none in fact exist.

S. T.

THE
REHEARSAL

George Villiers, Duke of Buckingham
1628—1687

Restoration comedy has survived changes of moral emphasis as of theatrical taste, and it still shines as brightly as ever on the contemporary stage. If its light has a certain harshness—playing as it does on sexual gamesmanship stripped of all but its verbal disguise—it must be remembered that the need of its original audiences for some compensatory idealization of human behaviour was met by the writers of heroic tragedy, a form no less popular and no less controversial in its day than the comedy of manners itself. But heroic tragedy has survived only in the controversies it generated—in the critical theorizing which variously justified or abused it, and, of course, in the burlesque play penned by the Duke of Buckingham, possibly in collaboration with a few fellow wits, to expose its pretensions. That play was *The Rehearsal*.

   Though first drafted in the mid-sixties, *The Rehearsal* did not reach the stage till 1671, by which time the heroic dramas of Davenant, Boyle, Dryden, Stapylton, and the Howards had successfully caught and held the public taste. Thus, in Dryden's *Essay of Dramatic Poesy*, Neander—the dramatist's own persona—confidently affirms that 'no serious plays written since the King's return have been more kindly received . . . than *The Siege of Rhodes*, the *Mustapha*, *The Indian Queen*, and *Indian Emperor*'. And only four years later—in the *Essay of Heroic Plays* prefixed to his *Conquest of Granada* in 1672—the recently-created laureate claimed that heroic verse was 'already in possession of the stage', and that 'very few tragedies, in this age, shall be received without it'. Soon afterwards, however, Dryden himself was to abandon the heroic form for good, an intention explicitly avowed in the Prologue to his last rhymed tragedy, *Aureng-Zebe*—and for which *The Rehearsal* must take its share of the credit. This is not to say that heroic tragedy henceforth failed to attract the town—still less to assert that love, valour, and honour ceased to be the chief concern of 'tragic' dramatists, or that their audiences ceased to respond to such ingredients with awe and admiration instead of pity and fear. Nor is it to imply too absolute a connection between Buckingham's successful parody and Dryden's change of heart. But it does sufficiently suggest the *corrective* function of his burlesque, that the grosser absurdities of the heroic idiom could no longer be perpetrated with impunity. And it would at least be fair to say that Buckingham helped to slacken the production of new heroic tragedies, though he failed to stem the popularity of the old.

The Rehearsal was Buckingham's single major contribution to the drama, though his adaptation of Fletcher's *The Chances* is occasionally preferred to its original. A man of incredible virtuosity—political, artistic, and sexual—his part in the history of the period, constantly in and out of royal favour, needs no restatement. He

> Was everything by starts, and nothing long;
> But, in the course of one revolving moon,
> Was chemist, fidler, statesman, and buffoon.

Such, at least, was Dryden's verdict, in the caricature of his enemy as the Zimri of *Absalom and Achitophel*—the poet's revenge for his own portrayal as Bayes in *The Rehearsal*. John Lacy, the comic actor who created the part in Dryden's image, and under Buckingham's own instruction, had many famous successors in the role—Joe Haines, Richard Estcourt, Colley and Theophilus Cibber, and, of course, Garrick, who essayed the part nearly fifty times between 1740 and 1755. This was the period of the play's greatest popularity—a period during which Mrs. Clive also donned the breeches as Bayes, and which witnessed in all some ninety revivals of the piece. As this suggests, the tradition of English theatrical burlesque, in which *The Rehearsal* is the first great milestone, was to be continued in the following century rather than in Buckingham's own. But like all great burlesques, *The Rehearsal* has long outlived the plays it ridiculed, though an acquaintance with them added zest to every allusion for its seventeenth- and eighteenth-century audiences. A scholarly tracing of such allusions—in all, to some seventy different plays—still serves to heighten one's relish for the piece, but is by no means essential to its appreciation. Buckingham's satire is directed not just against particular plays, but against poverty of dramatic conception and poverty of taste: and in this respect the play can safely be left to speak for itself.

THE
REHEARSAL,

As it is now Acted at the

Theatre-Royal.

The third Edition with Amendments and
large Additions by the Author.

LONDON,

Printed for *Thomas Dring*, at the *Harrow* at the
Corner of *Chancery-lane* in *Fleet-
street.* 1 6 7 5.

PROLOGUE.

WE might well call this short Mock-play of ours
    A Posie made of Weeds instead of Flowers;
Yet such have been presented to your noses,
And there are such, I fear, who thought them 'em Roses.
Would some of 'em were here, to see, this night,
What stuff it is in which they took delight.
Here brisk insipid Rogues, for wit, let fall
Sometines dull sence; but oft'ner none at all:
There, strutting Heroes, with a grim-fac'd train,
Shall brave the Gods, in King Cambyses vein.   10
For (changing Rules, of late, as if men writ
In spite of Reason, Nature, Art and Wit)
Our Poets make us laugh at Tragœdy,
And with their Comoedies they make us cry.
Now, Critiques, do your worst, that here are met;
For, like a Rook, I have hedg'd in my Bet.
If you approve; I shall assume the state
Of those high-flyers whom I imitate:
And justly too, for I will teach you more
Than ever they would let you know before: 20
I will not only shew the feats they do,
But give you all their reasons for 'em too.
Some honour may to me from hence arise.
But if, by my endeavours, you grow wise,
And what you once so prais'd, shall now despise;
Then I'll cry out, swell'd with Poetic rage,
'Tis I, John Lacy, have reform'd your Stage.

---

10 *King* Cambyses *vein*] The allusion is to *King Cambyses*, a tragedy written by Thomas
Preston in 1570, notorious for its bombastic strains. Falstaff, wishing to 'speak in passion',
intends to do so 'in King Cambyses vein', in *Henry the Fourth: Part One*, II, iv.

The Actors Names.

*B*AYES.
   Johnson.
Smith.
Two Kings of *Brentford.*
Prince *Pretty-man.*
Prince *Volscius.*
Gentleman Usher.
Physician.
Drawcansir.
General.
Lieutenant General.
Cordelio.
Tom Thimble.
Fisherman.
Sun.
Thunder.
Players.
Souldiers.
Two Heralds.

Four Cardinals. ⎫
Mayor.   ⎬ Mutes.
Judges.   ⎪
Serjeants at Arms. ⎭

Women.

Amaryllis.
Cloris.
Parthenope.
Pallas.
Lightning.
Moon.
Earth.
   Attendants of Men and Women.
     Scene *Brentford.*

Bayes] Played, of course, by John Lacy. It is also known that Cartwright played Thunder and the Second King of Brentford, that Kynaston played Volscius, and Mrs. Reeve Amaryllis.

THE
Rehearsal.

ACTUS I. SCÆNA I.

Johnson *and* Smith.

Johns. HONEST *Frank*! I'm glad to see thee with all my heart: how long hast thou been in Town?

Smi. Faith, not above an hour: and, if I had not met you here, I had gone to look you out; for I long to talk with you freely, of all the strange new things we have heard in the Country.

Johns. And, by my troth, I have long'd as much to laugh with you, at all the impertinent, dull, fantastical things, we are tir'd out with here.

Smi. Dull, and fantastical! that's an excellent composition. Pray, what are our men of business doing?   9

Johns. I ne'er enquire after 'em. Thou knowest my humour lyes another way. I love to please my self as much, and to trouble others as little as I can: and therefore do naturally avoid the company of those solemn Fops; who, being incapable of Reason, and insensible of Wit and Pleasure, are always looking grave, and troubling one another, in hopes to be thought men of Business.

Smi. Indeed, I have ever observed, that your grave lookers are the dullest of men.

Johns. I, and of Birds, and Beasts too: your gravest Bird is an Owl, and your gravest Beast is an Ass.

Smi. Well; but how dost thou pass thy time?   20

Johns. Why, as I use to do; eat and drink as well as I can, have a she-friend to be private with in the afternoon, and sometimes see a Play: where there are such things (*Frank*) such hideous, monstrous things, that it has almost made me forswear the Stage, and resolve to apply my self to the solid nonsense of your Men of Business, as the more ingenious pastime.

Smi. I have heard, indeed, you have had lately many new Plays; and our Country-wits commend 'em.

Johns. I, so do some of our City-wits too; but they are of the new kind of Wits.

Smi. New kind! what kind is that?   30

Johns. Why, your Virtuosi, your civil persons, your Drolls: fellows that scorns to imitate Nature; but are given altogether to elevate and surprise.

Smi. Elevate, and surprise! pr'ythee make me understand the meaning of that.

Johns. Nay, by my troth, that's a hard matter: I don't understand that my self. 'Tis a phrase they have got among them, to express their no-meaning by. I'l tell you, as near as I can, what it is. Let me see: 'tis Fighting, Loving, Sleeping, Rhyming, Dying, Dancing, Singing, Crying; and every thing, but thinking and Sence.   39

Mr. Bayes *passes o'er the Stage.*

Bayes. Your most obsequious, and most observant, very servant, Sir.

Johns. God so, this is an Author: I'l fetch him to you.

Smi. No, pr'ythee let him alone.

Johns. Nay, by the Lord, I'l have him. [*Goes after him.*] Here he is. I have caught him. Pray, Sir, now for my sake, will you do a favour to this friend of mine?

Bayes. Sir, it is not within my small capacity to do favours, but receive 'em; especially from a person that does wear the honourable Title you are pleas'd to impose, Sir, upon this.—Sweet Sir, your servant.

Smi. Your humble servant, Sir.

Johns. But wilt thou do me a favour, now?   50

Bayes. I, Sir: what is't?

Johns. Why, to tell him the meaning of thy last Play.

Bayes. How, Sir, the meaning? do you mean the Plot?

Johns. I, I; any thing.

Bayes. Faith, Sir, the Intrigo's now quite out of my head; but I have a new one, in my pocket, that I may say is a Virgin; 't has never yet been blown upon. I must tel. you one thing. 'Tis all new Wit; and tho I say it, a better than my last: and you know well enough how that took. In fine, it shall read, and write, and act, and plot, and shew, ay, and pit, box and gallery, I gad, with any Play in *Europe*. This morning is its last Rehearsal, in their habits, and all that, as it is to be acted; and if you, and your friend will do it but the honour to see it in its Virgin attire; though, perhaps, it may blush, I shall not be asham'd to discover its nakedness unto you.—I think it is in this pocket.
                                                    [*Puts his hand in his pocket.*

Johns. Sir, I confess, I am not able to answer you in this new way; but if you please to lead, I shall be glad to fo.low you; and I hope my friend will do so too.   67

Smi. Sir, I have no business so considerable, as should keep me from your company.

59 pit, box and gallery] Reputedly a favourite expression of Edward Howard's.

Bayes. Yes, here it is. No, cry you mercy: this is my book of *Drama Common places*; the Mother of many other Plays.   71

Johns. Drama Common places! pray what's that?

Bayes. Why, Sir, some certain helps that we men of Art have found it convenient to make use of.

Smi. How, Sir, helps for Wit?

Bayes. I, Sir, that's my position, And I do here averr, That no man yet the Sun e'er shone upon, has parts sufficient to furnish out a Stage, except it were by the help of these my Rules.

Johns. What are those Rules, I pray?

Bayes. Why, Sir, my first Rule is the Rule of Transversion, or *Regula Duplex*: changing Verse into Prose, or Prose into Verse, *alternative* as you please.   82

Smi. Well; but how is this done by a Rule, Sir?

Bayes. Why, thus, Sir; nothing so easie when understood: I take a book in my hand, either at home or elsewhere, for that's all one, if there be any Wit in't, as there is no book but has some, I Transverse it; that is, if it be Prose put it into Verse, (but that takes up some time) and if it be Verse, put it into Prose.

Johns. Methinks, Mr. *Bayes*, that putting Verse into Prose should be call'd Transprosing.   90

Bayes. By my troth, Sir, 'tis a very good Notion, and hereafter it shall be so.

Smi. Well, Sir, and what d'ye do with it then?

Bayes. Make it my own. 'Tis so chang'd that no man can know it. My next Rule is the Rule of Record, by way of Table Book. Pray observe.

Johns. We hear you Sir: go on.

Bayes. As thus. I come into a Coffee-house, or some other place where witty men resort, I make as if I minded nothing; (do you mark?) but as soon as any one speaks, pop I slap it down, and make that, too, my own.

Johns. But, Mr. *Bayes*, are you not sometimes in danger of their making you restore, by force, what you have gotten thus by Art?   101

Bayes. No, Sir; the world's unmindful: they never take notice of these things.

Smi. But pray, Mr. *Bayes*, among all your other Rules, have you no one Rule for invention?

Bayes. Yes, Sir; that's my third Rule that I have here in my pocket.

Smi. What Rule can that be, I wonder?

Bayes. Why, Sir, when I have any thing to invent, I never trouble my head about it, as other men do; but presently turn over this Book, and there I have, at one view, all that *Perseus, Montaigne, Seneca's Tragedies, Horace, Juvenal*,

97 a Coffee-house] Will's coffee-house, of course, where Dryden regularly held court.

Claudian, *Pliny*, *Plutarch's lives*, and the rest, have ever thought upon this subject: and so, in a trice, by leaving out a few words, or putting in others of my own, the business is done.   113

Johns. Indeed, Mr. *Bayes*, this is as sure, and compendious a way of Wit as ever I heard of.

Bayes. Sirs, if you make the least scruple of the efficacy of these my Rules, do but come to the Play-house, and you shall judge of 'em by the effects.

Smi. We'l follow you, Sir.   [*Exeunt.*

Enter three Players upon the Stage.

1 Play. Have you your part perfect?

2 Play. Yes, I have it without book; but I don't understand how it is to be spoken.

3 Play. And mine is such a one, as I can't guess for my life what humour I'm to be in: whether angry, melancholy, merry, or in love. I don't know what to make on't.   6

1 Play. Phoo! the Author will be here presently, and he'l tell us all. You must know, this is the new way of writing; and these hard things please forty times better than the old plain way. For, look you, Sir, the grand design upon the Stage is to keep the Auditors in suspence; for to guess presently at the plot, and the sence, tires 'em before the end of the first Act: now, here, every line surprises you, and brings in new matter. And, then, for Scenes, Cloaths and Dances we put 'em quite down, all that ever went before us: and those are the things, you know, that are essential to a Play.

2 Play. Well, I am not of thy mind; but, so it gets us money, 'tis no great matter.

Enter Bayes, Johnson *and* Smith.

Bayes. Come, come in Gentlemen. Y'are very welcome Mr.—a—Ha' you your part ready?

1 Play. Yes Sir.   20

Bayes. But do you understand the true humor of it?

1 Play. I, Sir, pretty well.

Bayes. And *Amarillis*, how does she do? Does not her Armor become her?

3 Play. O, admirably!

Bayes. I'l tell you, now, a pretty conceipt. What do you think I'l make 'em call her anon, in this Play?

Smi. What, I pray?

Bayes. Why, I make 'em call her *Armarillis*, because of her Armor: ha, ha, ha.

Johns. That will be very well, indeed.

Bayes. Ay, it's a pretty little rogue; I knew her face would set off Armor extreamly: and, to tell you true, I write that Part only for her. You must know she is my Mistress.   32

Johns. Then, I know another thing, little *Bayes*, that thou hast had her, I gad.

Bayes. No, I gad, not yet; but I'm sure I shall: for I have talkt bawdy to her already.

Johns. Hast thou, faith? Pr'ythee how was that?

Bayes. Why, Sir, there is, in the French Tongue, a certain Criticism, which, by the variation of the Masculine Adjective instead of the Fœminine, makes a quite different signification of the word: as, for example, *Ma vie* is my life; but if, before *vie* you put *Mon* instead of *Ma*, you make it bawdy.   41

Johns. Very true.

Bayes. Now, Sir, I, having observ'd this, set a Trap for her, the other day in the Tyring-Room; for this said I, *Adieu bel Esperansa de ma vie;* (which I gad is very pretty) to which she answer'd, I vow, almost as prettily, every jot; for said she, *Songes a ma vie Mounsieur;* whereupon I presently snapt this upon her; *Non, non, Madam—Songes vous a mon,* by gad, and nam'd the thing directly to her.

Smi. This is one of the richest Stories, Mr. *Bayes,* that ever I heard of.

Bayes. I, let me alone, I gad, when I get to 'em; I'l nick 'em, I warrant you: But I'm a little nice; for you must know, at this time, I am kept by another woman, in the City.   52

Smi. How kept? for what?

Bayes. Why, for a *Beau Gerson:* I am, ifackins.

Smi. Nay, then we shall never have done.

Bayes. And the Rogue is so fond of me, Mr. *Johnson,* that I vow to gad, I know not what to do with my self.

Johns. Do with thy self! no; I wonder how thou canst make a shift to hold out, at this rate.

Bayes. O Devil, I can toil like a Horse; only, sometimes, it makes me melancholy: and then I vow to gad, for a whole day together, I am not able to say you one good thing if it were to save my life.   62

Smi. That we do verily believe, Mr. *Bayes.*

Bayes. And that's the only thing, I gad, which mads me, in my Amours, for I'l tell you, as a friend, Mr. *Johnson,* my acquaintances, I hear, begin to give it out that I am dull: now I am the farthest from it in the whole World, I gad; but only, forsooth, they think I am so, because I can say nothing.

Johns. Phoo pox. That's ill natur'dly done of 'em.

32 she is my Mistress] An allusion to Mrs. Anne Reeve, an actress endowed with more beauty than talent, who was almost certainly Dryden's mistress.   54 *Beau Gerson*] I.e. *beau garçon,* fine fellow, dandy.

Bayes. Ay gad, there's no trusting o' these Rogues; but—a— Come, let's sit down. Look you, Sirs, the chief hinge of this Play, upon which the whole Plot moves and turns, and that causes the variety of all the several accidents, which, you know, are the things in Nature that make up the grand refinement of a Play, is, that I suppose two Kings to be of the same place: as, for example, at *Brentford*; for I love to write familiarly. Now the people having the same relations to 'em both, the same affections, the same duty, the same obedience, and all that; are divided among themselves in point of devoir and interest, how to behave themselves equally between 'em: these Kings differing sometimes in particular; though, in the main, they agree. (I know not whether I make my self well understood.)   80

Johns. I did not observe you, Sir: pray say that again.

Bayes. Why, look you, Sir, (nay, I beseech you, be a little curious in taking notice of this, or else you'l never understand my notion of the thing) the people being embarrast by their equal tyes to both, and the Soveraigns concern'd in a reciprocal regard, as well to their own interest, as the good of the people; may make a certain kind of a—you understand me—upon which, there does arise several disputes, turmoils, heart-burnings, and all that—In fine, you'l apprehend it better when you see it.

[*Exit, to call the Players.*

Smi. I find the Author will be very much oblig'd to the Players, if they can make any sence out of this.

Enter Bayes.

Bayes. Now, Gentlemen, I would fain ask your opinion of one thing. I have made a Prologue and an Epilogue, which may both serve for either: [that is, the Prologue for the Epilogue, or the Epilogue for the Prologue]: (do you mark?) nay, they may both serve too, I gad, for any other Play as well as this.

Smi. Very well. That's, indeed, Artificial.   94

Bayes. And I would fain ask your judgements, now, which of them would do best for the Prologue? For, you must know there is, in nature, but two ways of making very good Prologues. The one is by civility, by insinuation, good language, and all that, to—a—in a manner, steal your plaudit from the courtesie of the Auditors: the other, by making use of some certain personal things, which may keep a hank upon such censuring persons, as cannot otherways, A gad, in nature, be hindred from being too free with their tongues. To which end, my first Prologue is, that I come out in a long black Veil, and a great Huge Hang-man behind me, with a Furr'd-cap, and his Sword drawn; and there tell 'm plainly, That if, out of good nature, they

---

73-4 two Kings ... at *Brentford*] The two-kings motif probably derives from Henry Howard's unprinted play *The United Kingdoms*, against which Buckingham led a disturbance in 1663.   94 Artificial] Resulting from artifice, well-constructed.

will not like my Play, I gad, I'l e'en kneel down, and he shall cut my head off. Whereupon they all clapping—a— 106

Smi. I, But suppose they don't.

Bayes. Suppose! Sir, you may suppose what you please, I have nothing to do with your suppose, Sir; nor am not at all mortifi'd at it; not at all, Sir; I gad, not one jot, Sir. Suppose quoth a!—ha, ha, ha. [*Walks away.*

Johns. Phoo! pr'ythee, *Bayes*, don't mind what he says: he is a fellow newly come out of the Country, he knows nothing of what's the relish, here, of the Town.

Bayes. If I writ, Sir, to please the Country, I should have follow'd the old plain way; but I write for some persons of Quality, and peculiar friends of mine, that understand what Flame and Power in writing is: and they do me the right, Sir, to approve of what I do. 117

Johns. I, I, they will clap, I warrant you; never fear it.

Bayes. I'm sure the design's good: that cannot be denyd. And then, for language, I gad, I defie 'em all, in nature, to mend it. Besides, Sir, I have printed above a hundred sheets of papyr, to insinuate the Plot into the Boxes: and, withal, have appointed two or three dozen of my friends, to be ready in the Pit, who, I'm sure, will clap, and so the rest, you know, must follow; and then, pray, Sir, what becomes of your suppose? ha, ha, ha.

Johns. Nay, if the business be so well laid, it cannot miss. 125

Bayes. I think so, Sir: and therefore would chuse this to be the Prologue. For, if I could engage 'em to clap, before they see the Play, you know 'twould be so much the better; because then they were engag'd: for let a man write never so well, there are, now-a-days, a sort of persons, they call Critiques, that, I gad, have no more wit in them than so many Hobby-horses; but they'll laugh you, Sir, and find fault, and censure things, that, I gad, I'm sure, they are not able to do themselves. A sort of envious persons, that emulate the glories of persons of parts, and think to build their fame, by calumniating of persons, that, I gad, to my knowledge, of all persons in the world are, in nature, the persons that do as much despise all that as—a— In fine, I'll say no more of 'em. 136

Johns. Nay, you have said enough of 'em, in all conscience: I'm sure more than they'll e're be able to answer.

Bayes. Why, I'll tell you, Sir, sincerely, and *bona fide*; were it not for the sake of some ingenious persons, and choice female spirits, that have a value for me, I would see 'em all hang'd, I gad, before I would e'er more set pen to papyr; but let 'em live in ignorance like ingrates.

Johns. I marry! that were a way to be reveng'd of 'em indeed: and, if I were in your place, now, I would do so. 144

Bayes. No, Sir; there are certain tyes upon me, that I cannot be disingag'd from; otherwise, I would. But pray, Sir, how do you like my hang-man?

Smi. By my troth, Sir, I should like him very well.

Bayes. But how do you like it Sir? (for, I see, you can judge) Would you have it for a Prologue, or the Epilogue?

Johns. Faith, Sir, 'tis so good, let it e'en serve for both.   150

Bayes. No, no; that wont do. Besides I have made another.

Johns. What other, Sir?

Bayes. Why, Sir, my other is *Thunder* and *Lightning*.

Johns. That's greater: I'd rather stick to that.

Bayes. Do you think so? I'l tell you then; tho there have been many witty Prologues written of late, yet, I think, you'l say this is a *non pareillo*: I'm sure no body has hit upon it yet. For here, Sir, I make my Prologue to be Dialogue; and as, in my first, you see I strive to oblige the Auditors by civility, by good nature, good language, and all that; so, in this, by the other way, *in Terrorem*, I chuse for the persons *Thunder* and *Lightning*. Do you apprehend the conceipt?   161

Johns. Phoo, Pox! then you have it cock-sure. They'l be hang'd before they'l dare to affront an Author, that has 'em at that lock.

Bayes. I have made, too, one of the most delicate dainty *Simile's* in the whole world, I gad, if I knew but how to applie it.

Smi. Lets hear it, I pray you.

Bayes. 'Tis an allusion to love.

So Boar and Sow, when any storm is nigh,
Snuff up, and smell it gath'ring in the Sky;
Boar beckons Sow to trot in Chestnut Groves,   170
And there consummate their unfinish'd Loves:
Pensive in mud they wallow all alone,
And snore and gruntle to each others moan.
How do you like it now, ha?

Johns. Faith, 'tis extraordinary fine: and very applicable to *Thunder* and *Lightning*, methinks, because it speaks of a storm.

Bayes. I gad, and so it does, now I think on't Mr. *Johnson*, I thank you; and I'l put it in *profecto*. Come out, *Thunder* and *Lightning*.

Enter Thunder *and* Lightning.

Thun. I am the bold *Thunder*.

Bayes. Mr. *Cartwright*, pr'ythee speak that a little louder, and with a hoarse voice. I am the bold *Thunder*! Pshaw! speak it me in a voice that thunders it out indeed: I am the bold *Thunder*.   182

Thun. I am the bold *Thunder*.

Light. The brisk *Lightning*, I.

Bayes. Nay, you must be quick and nimble.

178 *profecto*] At once, immediately.

The brisk *Lightning*, I. That's my meaning.

   Thun. I am the bravest *Hector* of the Sky.

   Light. And I fair *Helen* that made *Hector* die.

   Thun. I strike men down.

   Light. I fire the Town.   190

   Thun. Let the Critiques take heed how they grumble,

For then begin I for to rumble.

   Light. Let the Ladies allow us their Graces.

Or I'l blast all the paint on their faces,

And dry up their Peter to Soot.

   Thun. Let the Critiques look to't.

   Light. Let the Ladies look to't.

   Thun. For *Thunder* will do't.

   Light. For *Lightning* will shoot.

   Thun. I'l give you dash for dash.   200

   Light. I'l give you flash for flash.

Gallants I'l singe your Feather.

   Thun. I'l *Thunder* you together.

   Both. Look to't, look to't; we'l do't, we'l do't: look to't, we'l do't.

                                           [Twice or thrice repeated.

                                               [Exeunt ambo.

   Bayes. There's no more. 'Tis but a flash of a Prologue: a Droll.

   Smi. Yes, 'Tis short, indeed; but very terrible.

   Bayes. Ay, when the *similes* in, it will do to a Miracle, I gad. Come, come begin the Play.

                      Enter first Player.

   1 Play. Sir, Mr. *Ivory* is not come yet; but hee'l be here presently, he's but two doors off.   210

   Bayes. Come then, Gentlemen, let's go out and take a pipe of Tobacco.

                                             [Exeunt.

   Finis Actus Primi.

ACTUS II. SCÆNA I.

Bayes, Johnson *and* Smith.

Bayes. NOW, Sir, because I'll do nothing here that ever was done before, instead of beginning with a Scene that discovers something of the Plot, I begin this Play with a whisper.

   195 Peter] Cosmetics, particularly rouge.

Smi. Umph! very new, indeed.

Bayes. Come, take your seats. Begin, Sirs.

Enter Gentleman-Usher and Physician.

Phys. Sir, by your habit, I should ghess you to be the Gentleman-Usher of this sumptuous place.

Ush. And, by your gait and fashion, I should almost suspect you rule the healths of both our noble Kings, under the notion of Physician.

Phys. You hit my Function right.   10

Ush. And you, mine.

Phys. Then let's embrace.

Ush. Come.

Phys. Come.

Johns. Pray, Sir, who are those so very civil persons?

Bayes. Why, Sir, the Gentleman-Usher, and Physician of the two Kings of *Brentford*.

Johns. But, pray then, how comes it to pass, that they know one another no better?

Bayes. Phoo! that's for the better carrying on of the Plot.   20

Johns. Very well.

Phys. Sir, to conclude.

Smi. What, before he begins?

Bayes. No, Sir; you must know, they had been talking of this a pretty while without.

Smi. Where? in the Tyring-room?

Bayes. Why ay, Sir. He's so dull! Come, speak again.

Phys. Sir, to conclude, the place you fill, has more than amply exacted the Talents of a wary Pilot, and all these threatning storms, which, like impregnate Clouds, hover o'er our heads, will (when they once are grasp'd but by the eye of reason) melt into fruitful showers of blessings on the people.   31

Bayes. Pray mark that Allegory. Is not that good?

Johns. Yes; that grasping of a storm, with the eye, is admirable.

Phys. But yet some rumours great are stirring; and if *Lorenzo* should prove false (which none but the great Gods can tell) you then perhaps would find that—   [*Whispers.*

Bayes. Now he whispers.

Ush. Alone, do you say?

Phys. No; attended with the noble—   [*Whispers.*

Bayes. Again.   40

Ush. Who, he in gray?

Phys. Yes; and at the head of—   [*Whispers.*

Bayes. Pray mark.

Ush. Then, Sir, most certain, 'twill in time appear. These are the reasons that have mov'd him to't; First, he—   [*Whispers.*

Bayes. Now, the other whispers.

Ush. Secondly, they—   [*Whispers.*

Bayes. At it still.

Ush. Thirdly, and lastly, both he, and they—   [*Whispers.*

Bayes. Now they both whisper.   [*Exeunt Whispering.*

Now, Gentlemen, pray tell me true, and without flattery, is not this a very odd beginning of a Play?   52

Johns. In troth, I think it is, Sir. But why two Kings of the same place?

Bayes. Why? becase it's new; and that's it I aim at. I despise your *Johnson* and *Beaumont,* that borrow'd all they writ from Nature: I am for fetching it purely out of my own fancy, I.

Smi. But what think you, Sir, of Sir *John Suckling*?

Bayes. By gad, I am a better Poet than he.

Smi. Well, Sir, but pray why all this whispering?

Bayes. Why, Sir, (besides that it is new, as I told you before) because they are suppos'd to be Politicians; and matters of State ought not to be divulg'd.

Smi. But then, Sir, why—   62

Bayes. Sir, if you'l but respite your curiosity till the end of the fifth Act, you'l find it a piece of patience not ill recompenc'd.   [*Goes to the door.*

Johns. How dost thou like this, *Frank*? Is it not just as I told thee?

Smi. Why, I did never, before this, see any thing in Nature, and all that, (as Mr. *Bayes* says) so foolish, but I could give some ghess at what mov'd the Fop to do it; but this, I confess, does go beyond my reach.

Johns. It is all a like: Mr. *Wintershul* has inform'd me of this Play already. And I'l tell thee, *Franck*, thou shalt not see one Scene here worth one farthing, or like any thing thou canst imagine has ever been the practice of the World. And then, when he comes to what he calls good language, it is, as I told thee, very fantastical, most abominably dull, and not one word to the purpose.   74

Smi. It does surprise me, I'm sure, very much.

Johns. I, but it won't do so long: by that time thou hast seen a Play or two, that I'l shew thee, thou wilt be pretty well acquainted with this new kind of Foppery.

Smi. Pox on't but there's no Pleasure in him: he's too gross a fool to be laugh'd at.

Enter Bayes.

Johns. I'l swear, Mr. *Bayes* you have done this Scene most admirably; tho, I must tell you, Sir; it is a very difficult matter to pen a Whisper well.

B

Bayes. I, Gentlemen, when you come to write your selves, O' my word, you'l find it so.

Johns. Have a care of what you say, Mr. *Bayes*, for Mr. *Smith* there, I assure you, has written a great many fine things already.

Bayes. Has he, ifackins? Why then Pray, Sir, how do you do, when you write?

Smi. Faith, Sir, for the most part, I am in pretty good health.

Bayes. I but I mean, what do you do, when you write?   90

Smi. I take Pen, Ink, and Paper, and Sit down.

Bayes. Now, I write standing; that's one thing: and then, another thing is, with what do you prepare your self?

Smi. Prepare my self! what, the Devil, does the fool mean?

Bayes. Why, I'l tell you, now, what I do. If I am to write familiar things, as Sonnets to *Armida*, and the like, I make use of Stew'd Prunes only; but, when I have a grand design in hand, I ever take Phisic, and let blood: for, when you would have pure swiftness of thought, and fiery flights of fancy, you must have a care of the pensive part. In fine, you must purge the Belly.

Smi. By my troth, Sir, this is a most admirable Receipt, for writing.

Bayes. Ay, 'tis my Secret; and, in good earnest, I think, one of the best I have.   102

Smi. In good faith, Sir, and that may very well be.

Bayes. May be, Sir? I gad, I'm sure on't: *Experto crede Roberto*. But I must give you this caution by the way, be sure you never take snuff, when you write.

Smi. Why so Sir?

Bayes. Why, it spoil'd me once, I gad, one of the sparkishest Playes in all *England*. But a friend of mine, at *Gresham Colledge*, has promis'd to help me to some spirit of Brains, and, I gad, that shall do my business.

SCÆNA II.

Enter the two Kings, hand in hand.

Bayes. OH, These now are the two Kings of *Brentford*; take notice of their stile: 'twas never yet upon the Stage; but, if you like it, I could make a shift, perhaps, to shew you a whole Play, writ all just so.

1 King. Did you observe their whisper, Brother King?

2 King. I did; and heard, besides, a grave bird sing
That they intend, sweet-heart, to play us pranks.

96 I make use of Stew'd Prunes . . .] A reliance upon stewed prunes, physic, and purgation did, apparently, stimulate Dryden to creative work

Bayes. This is now, familiar, because they are both persons of the same Quality.

Smi. 'Sdeath, this would make a man spew.

1 King. If that design appears,   10
I'l lug 'em by the ears
Until I make 'em crack.

2 King. And so will I, i'fack.

1 King. You must begin, *Mon foy*.

2 King. Sweet, Sir, *Pardonnes moy*.

Bayes. Mark that: I makes 'em both speak *French*, to shew their breeding.

Johns. O, 'tis extraordinary fine:

2 King. Then, spite of Fate, we'll thus combined stand;
And like true brothers, walk stil hand in hand.   *[Exeunt Reges.*

Johns. This is a very Majestic Scene indeed.   20

Bayes. Ay, 'tis a crust, a lasting crust for your Rogue Critiques, I gad: I would fain see the proudest of 'em all but dare to nibble at this; I gad, if they do, this shall rub their gums for 'em, I promise you. It was I, you must know, that have written a whole Play just in this very same stile; but it was never Acted yet.

Johns. How so?

Bayes. I gad, I can hardly tell you, for laughing (ha, ha, ha) it is so pleasant a story: ha, ha, ha.

Smi. What is't?

Bayes. I gad, the Players refus'd to act it, Ha, ha, ha.   30

Smi. That's impossible.

Bayes. I gad they did it, Sir, point blank refus'd it, I gad, Ha, ha, ha.

Johns. Fie, that was rude.

Bayes. Rude! Ay, I gad, they are the rudest, uncivilest persons, and all that, in the whole world, I gad: I gad, there's no living with 'em, I have written, Mr. *Johnson*, I do verily believe, a whole cart-load of things, every whit as good as this, and yet, I vow to gad, these insolent Raskals have turned 'em all back upon my hands again.

Johns. Strange fellows indeed!

Smi. But pray, Mr. *Bayes*, how came these two Kings to know of this whisper? for, as I remember, they were not present at it.   41

Bayes. No, but that's the Actors fault, and not mine; for the two Kings should (a pox take 'em) have pop'd both their heads in at the door, just as the other went off.

Smi. That, indeed, would ha' done it.

Bayes. Done it! Ay, I gad, these fellows are able to spoil the best things in Christendome. I'l tell you, Mr. *Johnson*, I vow to gad I have been so highly disoblig'd by the peremptoriness of these fellows, that I'm resolv'd hereafter, to bend my thoughts wholly for the service of the *Nursery*, and mump your proud Players, I gad. So; now Prince Pretty-man comes in, and falls a sleep, making love to his Mistress, which, you know, was a grand Intrigue in a late Play, written by a very honest Gentleman: a Knight.   52

SCÆNA III.

Enter Prince Pretty-man.

Pret. HOW strange a captive am I grown of late!
　　　 Shall I accuse my Love, or blame my Fate?
My Love, I cannot; that is too Divine:
And, against Fate, what mortal dares repine?

Enter Cloris.

But here she comes.
Sure 'tis some blazing Comet is it not?   [*Lyes down.*
　　Bayes. Blazing Comet! mark that, I gad, very fine!
　　Pret. But I am so surpris'd with sleep, I cannot speak the rest.   [*Sleeps.*
　　Bayes. Does not that, now, surprise you, to fall a sleep in the nick? His spirits exhale with the heat of his passion, and all that, and swop falls a sleep, as you see. Now, here, she must make a *simile*.   11
　　Smi. Where's the necessity of that Mr. *Bayes?*
　　Bayes. Because she's surpris'd. That's a general Rule, you must ever make a *simile*, when you are surpris'd; 'tis the new way of writing.
　　Cloris. As some tall Pine, which we, on *Ætna*, find
T' have stood the rage of many a boist'rous wind,
Feeling without, that flames within do play,
Which would consume his Root and Sap away;
He spreads his woorsted Arms unto the Skies,
Silently grieves, all pale, repines and dies: 20
So, shrowded up, your bright eye disappears.
Break forth, bright scorching Sun, and dry my tears.   [*Exit.*
　　Johns. Mr. *Bayes*, Methinks, this *simile* wants a little application too.
　　Bayes. No, faith; for it alludes to passion, to consuming, to dying, and all that; which, you know, are the natural effects of an Amour. But I'm afraid, this Scene has made you sad; for, I must confess, when I writ it, I wept my self.
　　Smi. No, truly, Sir, my spirits are almost exhal'd to, and I am likelier to fall a sleep.   29

Prince Pretty-man *starts up, and says—*

　　Pret. It is resolv'd.   [*Exit.*

Bayes. That's all.

Smi. Mr. *Bayes,* may one be so bold as to ask you a question, now, and you not be angry?

Bayes. O Lord, Sir, you may ask me any thing; what you please, I vow to gad, you do me a great deal of honour: you do not know me, if you say that, Sir.

Smi. Then, pray, Sir, what is it that this Prince here has resolv'd in his sleep?

38

Bayes. Why, I must confess, that question is well enough ask'd, for one that is not acquainted with this new way of writing. But you must know, Sir, that, to out-do all my fellow-Writers, whereas they keep their *Intrigo* secret, till the very last Scene before the Dance; I now, Sir, (do you mark me)—a—

Smi. Begin the Play, and end it, without ever opening the Plot at all?

Bayes. I do so, that's the very plain troth on't; ha, ha, ha; I do, I gad. If they cannot find it out themselves, e'en let 'em alone for *Bayes,* I warrant you. But here, now, is a Scene of business: pray observe it; for I dare say you'l think it no unwise discourse this, nor ill argu'd. To tell you true, 'tis a Discourse I over-heard once betwixt two grand, sober, governing persons.

SCÆNA IV.

Enter Gentleman-Usher and Physician.

Ush. COME, Sir; let's state the matter of Fact, and lay our heads to-gether.

Phys. Right: lay our heads together. I love to be merry sometimes; but when a knotty point comes I lay my head close to it, with a snuff box in my hand, and then I fegue it away, i'faith.

Bayes. I do just so, I gad, alwayes.

Ush. The grand question is, whether they heard us whisper? which I divide thus.

Phys. Yes, it must be divided so indeed.

Smi. That's very complaisant, I swear, Mr. *Bayes,* to be of another man's opinion, before he knowes what it is.

11

Bayes. Nay, I bring in none, here, but wel-bred persons, I assure you.

Ush. I divided the question into when they heard, what they heard, and whether they heard or no.

Johns. Most admirably divided, I swear!

Ush. As to the when; you say, just now: So that is answer'd. Then, as for what; why, what answers it self: for what could they hear, but what we talk'd

5 fegue it away] Work at full stretch.

of? So that, naturally, and of necessity, we come to the last question, *Vide-licet*, whether they heard or no.

Smi. This is a very wise Scene, Mr. *Bayes*.   20

Bayes. Ay, you have it right: they are both Politicians.

Ush. Pray then to proceed in method, let me ask you that question.

Phys. No, you'l answer better, pray let me ask it you.

Ush. Your will must be a Law.

Phys. Come then, what is it I must ask?

Smi. This Politician, I perceive, Mr. *Bayes*, has somewhat a short memory.

Bayes. Why, Sir, you must know, that t'other is the main Politician, and this is but his pupil.

Ush. You must ask me whether they heard us whisper.

Phys. Well, I do so.   30

Ush. Say it then.

Smi. Hey day! here's the bravest work that ever I saw.

Johns. This is mighty methodical!

Bayes. Ay, Sir; that's the way: 'tis the way of Art; there is no other way, I gad, in business.

Phys. Did they hear us whisper?

Ush. Why, truly, I can't tell; there's much to be said upon the word Whisper: to whisper, in Latin is *Susurrare*, which is as much as to say, to speak softly; now, if they heard us speak softly, they heard us whisper: but then comes in the *Quomodo*, the how; how did they hear us whisper? Why, as to that, there are two wayes; the one, by chance, or accident: the other, on purpose; that is, with design to hear us whisper.   42

Phys. Nay, if they heard us that way, I'll never give 'em Physic more.

Ush. Nor I e'er more will walk abroad before 'em.

Bayes. Pray mark this; for a great deal depend upon it, towards the latter end of the Play.

Smi. I suppose, that's the reason why you brought in this Scene Mr. *Bayes*?

Bayes. Partly, it was, Sir; but, I confess, I was not unwilling, besides, to shew the world a pattern, here, how men should talk of business.   50

Johns. You have done it exceeding well indeed.

Bayes. Yes, I think, this will do.

Phys. Well, if they heard us whisper, they'l turn us out, and no body else will take us.

Smi. Not for Politicians, I dare answer for it.

Phys. Let's then no more our selves in vain bemoan:
We are not safe until we them unthrone.

Ush. 'Tis right:
And, since occasion now seems debonair,

I'l seize on this, and you shall take that Chair.   60

> [*They draw their Swords, and sit down in*
> *the two great Chairs upon the Stage.*

Bayes. There's now an odd surprize; the whole State's turn'd quite topsie-turvy, without any puther or stir in the whole world, I gad.

Johns. A very silent change of a Government, truly, as ever I heard of.

Bayes. It is so. And yet you shall see me bring 'em in again, by and by, in as odd a way every jot.

> [*The Usurpers march out flourishing their Swords.*

Enter Shirly.

Shir. Hey ho, hey ho: what a change is here! Hey day, hey day! I know not what to do, nor what to say.   [*Exit.*

Johns. Mr. *Bayes*, in my opinion, now, that Gentleman might have said a little more, upon this occasion.

Bayes. No, Sir, not at all; for I under writ his Part, on purpose to set off the rest.   71

Johns. Cry you mercy, Sir.

Smi. But, pray, Sir, how came they to depose the Kings so easily?

Bayes. Why, Sir, you must know, they long had a design to do it before; but never could put it in practice till now: and, to tell you true, that's one reason why I made 'em whisper so at first.

Smi. O very well: now I'm fully satisfi'd.

Bayes. And then to shew you, Sir, it was not done so very easily neither; in this next Scene you shall see some fighting.

Smi. O, ho: so then you make the struggle to be after the business is done?

Bayes. Aye.   81

Smi. O, I conceive you: that, I swear, is very natural.

SCÆNA V.

Enter four men at one door, and four at another, with their Swords drawn.

1 Soldier. STAND. Who goes there?
        2 Sol. A Friend.

  1 Sol. What Friend?

  2 Sol. A Friend to the House.

  1 Sol. Fall on.   [*They all kill one another. Music strikes.*

  Bayes. Hold, hold.   [*To the Music. It ceaseth.*

Now here's an odd surprize: all these dead men you shall see rise up presently,

s.d. *at one door . . . at another*] The doors were those at opposite sides of the proscenium arch.

at a certain Note that I have made, in *Effaut flat*, and fall a Dancing. Do you
hear, dead men? remember your note in *Effaut flat*. Play on. 9

> [*To the Music.*

Now, now, now. [*The music play his Note, and the dead men rise,*
O Lord, O Lord! *but cannot get in order.*

Out, out, out! Did ever men spoil a good thing so? no figure, no ear, no
time, nothing? Udzookers, you dance worse than the Angels in *Harry* the
Eight, or the fat Spirits in *The Tempest*, I gad.

1 Sol. Why, Sir, 'tis impossible to do any thing in time, to this Tune.

Bayes. O Lord, O Lord! impossible? why, Gentlemen, if there be any
faith in a person that's a Christian, I sate up two whole nights in composing
this Air, and apting it for the business: for, if you observe, there are two
several Designs in this Tune; it begins swift, and ends slow. You talk of time,
and time; you shall see me do't. Look you now. Here I am dead. 20

> [*Lies down flat on his face.*

Now mark my Note *Effaut flat*. Strike up Music.

Now. [*As he rises up hastily, he falls down again.*
Ah, gadsookers, I have broke my Nose.

Johns. By my troth, Mr. *Bayes*, this is a very unfortunate Note of yours, in
Effaut.

Bayes. A plague of this damn'd Stage, with your nails, and your tenter-
hooks, that a Gentleman cannot come to teach you to Act, but he must
break his nose, and his face, and the devil and all. Pray, Sir, can you help me
to a wet piece of brown paper?

Smi. No indeed, Sir; I don't usually carry any about me. 30

2 Sol. Sir, I'l go get you some within presently.

Bayes. Go, go then; I follow you. Pray dance out the dance and I'l be with
you in a moment. Remember you dance like Horsmen. [*Exit* Bayes.

Smi. Like Horsemen! what, a plague, can that be?

> [*They dance the Dance, but can make nothing of it.*

1 Sol. A Devil! let's try this no longer: play my Dance that Mr. *Bayes*
found fault with so. [*Dance & exeunt.*

Smi. What can this fool be doing all this while about his Nose?

Johns. Pr'ythe lets go see. [*Exeunt.*

Finis Actus secundi.

---

23 I have broke my Nose] A personal hit at Sir William Davenant, whose nose was so
snub as to appear deformed. 26 tenter-hooks] Hooks for securing cloths stretched over a
wooden framework.

ACTUS III. SCÆNA I.

Bayes with a Papyr on his Nose, and the two Gentlemen.

Bayes. NOW, Sirs, this I do, because my Fancy, in this Play, is to end every Act with a Dance.

Smi. Faith, that Fancy is very good, but I should hardly have broke my Nose for it, tho.

Johns. That Fancy, I suppose, is new too.

Bayes. Sir, all my Fancies are so. I tread upon no mans heels: but make my flight upon my own wings, I assure you. Now, here comes in a Scene of sheer Wit, without any mixture in the whole World, I gad, between Prince Pretty-man and his Taylor: it might properly enough be call'd a prize of Wit; for you shall see 'em come in upon one another snip snap, hit for hit, as fast as can be. First one speaks, then presently t'others upon him, slap, with a Repartee; then he at him again, dash with a new conceipt; and so eternally, eternally, I gad, till they go quite off the Stage.   [*Goes to call the Players.*

Smi. What a plague, does this Fop mean by his snip snap, hit for hit, and dash?

Johns. Mean! why, he never meant any thing in's life: what dost talk of meaning for? ^15

Enter Bayes.

Bayes. Why don't you come in?

Enter Prince Pretty-man *and* Tom Thimble.

This Scene will make you dye with laughing, if it be well Acted; for 'tis as full of Drollery as ever it can hold: 'tis like an Orange stuff'd with Cloves, as for conceit. ^21

Pret. But pr'ythee, *Tom Thimble*, why wilt thou needs marry? If nine Taylors make but one man; and one woman cannot be satisfied with nine men: what work art thou cutting out here for thy self, trow?

Bayes. Good.

Thim. Why, an't please your Highness, if I can't make up all the work I cut out, I shan't want Journey-men enough to help me, I warrant you.

Bayes. Good again.

Pret. I am afraid thy Journey-men, tho, *Tom*, wont work by the day, but by the night. ^30

Bayes. Good still.

Thim. However if my wife sits but cross-leg'd, as I do, there will be no great danger: not half so much as when I trusted you, Sir, for your Coronation-suit.

Bayes. Very good, i'faith.

Pret. Why, the times then liv'd upon trust; it was the fashion. You would not be out of time, at such a time as that, sure: a Taylor, you know, must never be out of fashion.

Bayes. Right.

Thim. I'm sure, Sir, I made your Cloaths, in the Court-fashion, for you never paid me yet.   41

Bayes. There's a bob for the Court!

Pret. Why, *Tom*, thou art a sharp rogue when thou art angry, I see: thou pay'st me now, methinks.

Bayes. There's pay, upon pay! as good as ever was written, I gad!

Thim. I, Sir, in your own coyn: you give me nothing but words.

Bayes. Admirable, before gad!

Pret. Well, *Tom*, I hope shortly I shall have another coyn for thee; for now the Wars are coming on, I shall grow to be a man of mettal.

Bayes. O, you did not do that half enough.   50

Johns. Methinks he does it admirably.

Bayes. I, pretty well; but he does not hit me in't: he does not top his part.

Thim. That's the way to be stamp'd your self, Sir. I shall see you come home, like an Angel for the Kings-Evil, with a hole bor'd through you. [*Exeunt.*

Bayes. Ha, there he has hit it up to the hilts, I gad! How do you like it now, Gentlemen? Is not this pure Wit?

Smi. 'Tis snip snap, Sir, as you say; but, methinks, not pleasant, nor to the purpose, for the Play does not go on.

Bayes. Play does not go on? I don't know what you mean: why, is not this part of the Play?   60

Smi. Yes, but the Plot stands still.

Bayes. Plot stand still! why, what a Devil is the Plot good for, but to bring in fine things?

Smi. O, I did not know that before.

Bayes. No, I think you did not: nor many things more, that I am Master of. Now, Sir, I gad, this is the bane of all us Writers: let us soar but never so little above the common pitch, I gad, all's spoil'd; for the vulgar never understand it, they can never conceive you, Sir, the excellency of these things.

Johns. 'Tis a sad fate, I must confess: but you write on still; for all that?

Bayes. Write on? I, I gad, I warrant you. 'Tis not their talk shall stop me: if they catch me at that lock, I'l give 'em leave to hang me. As long as I know my things are good, what care I, what they say? What, are they gone, without singing my last new Song? 'Sbud, would it were in their Bellies. I'l

---

42 bob] A taunt, scoffing remark.   52 top his part] Apparently a favourite expression of Edward Howard's.   54 an Angel . . . with a hole bor'd through you] A reference to the coin hung round the necks of those whom the sovereign 'touched' to cure scrofula.

tell you, Mr. *Johnson*, if I have any skill in these matters, I vow to gad, this Song is peremtorily the very best that ever yet was written: you must know, it was made by *Tom Thimble's* first wife after she was dead. 76

Smi. How, Sir? after she was dead?

Bayes. Ay, Sir, after she was dead. Why, what have you to say to that?

Johns. Say? Why, nothing: he were a Devil that had any thing to say to that?

Bayes. Right.

Smi. How did she come to dye, pray Sir?

Bayes. Phoo! that's no matter; by a fall: but here's the conceit, that upon his knowing she was kill'd by an accident, he supposes, with a Sigh, that she dy'd for love of him. 85

Johns. I, I, that's well enough: let's hear it, Mr. *Bayes.*

Bayes. 'Tis to the Tune of Farewel, fair *Armida*, on Seas, and in battels, in Bullets, and all that.

SONG.

In swords, Pikes, and Bullets, 'tis safer to be,
Than in a Strong Castle, remoted from thee:
My deaths-bruise pray think you gave me, tho a fall
Did give it me more, from the top of a wall;
For then if the Moat on her mud would first lay,
And after before you my body convey:
The blew on my brest when you happen to see,
You'l say, with a Sigh, there's a True blew for me. 96

Ha, Rogues! when I am merry, I write these things as fast as hops, I gad; for, you must know, I am as pleasant a Debauchtee, as ever you saw: I am ifaith.

Smi. But Mr. *Bayes*, how comes this song in here? for, methinks, there is no great occasion for it.

Bayes. Alack, Sir, you know nothing: you must ever interlard your Playes with Songs, Ghosts, and Dances, if you mean to—a—

Johns. Pit, Box, and Gallery, Mr. *Bayes.*

Bayes. I gad, and you have nick'd it. Hark you, Mr. *Johnson*, you know I don't flatter, a gad, you have a great deal of Wit. 106

Johns. O Lord, Sir, you do me too much honour.

Bayes. Nay, nay, come, come, Mr. *Johnson*, I faith this must not be said, amongst us that have it. I know you have wit by the judgment you make of this Play; for that's the measure I go by: my Play is my Touchstone. When a man tells me such a one is a person of parts; is he so, say I? what do I do, but bring him presently to see this Play: If he likes it, I know what to think of him; if not, your most humble Servant, Sir, I'l no more of him upon my word, I thank you. I am *Clara voyant*, I gad. Now here we go on to our business.   115

SCÆNA II.

Enter the two Usurpers, hand in hand.

Ush. BUT what's become of *Volscius* the great?
His presence has not grac'd our Courts of late.
   Phys. I fear some ill, from emulation sprung,
Has from us that Illustrious *Hero* wrung.
   Bayes. Is not that Majestical?
   Smi. Yes, but who a Devil is that *Volscius?*
   Bayes. Why, that's a Prince I make in love with *Parthenope.*
   Smi. I thank you Sir.

Enter Cordelio.

   Cor. My Lieges, news from *Volscius* the Prince.
   Ush. His news is welcome, whatsoe'er it be.   10
   Smi. How, Sir, do you mean whether it be good or bad.
   Bayes. Nay, pray, Sir, have a little patience: Godsookers you'l spoil all my Play. Why, Sir, 'tis impossible to answer every impertinent question you ask.
   Smi. Cry you mercy, Sir.
   Cor. His Highness Sirs, commanded me to tell you,
That the fair person whom you both do know,
Despairing of forgiveness for her fault,
In a deep sorrow, twice she did attemt
Upon her precious life; but by the care
Of standers by prevented was.   20
   Smi. 'Sheart, what stuff's here!
   Cor. At last.
Volscius the great this dire resolve embrac'd:
His servants he into the Countrey sent,
And he himself to *Peccadille* went.
Where he's inform'd, by Letters that she's dead.
   Ush. Dead! is that possible? Dead!
   Phys. O ye Gods!   [*Exeunt.*
   Bayes. There's a smart expression of a passion; O ye Gods! That's one of my bold strokes, I gad.   30
   Smi. Yes; but who is the fair person that's dead?

29 O ye Gods!] Actually, one of the commonest of all tragical exclamations, particularly in the plays of Thomas Killigrew.

Bayes. That you shall know anon Sir.

Smi. Nay; if we know it at all, 'tis well enough.

Bayes. Perhaps you may find too, by and by, for all this that she's not dead neither.

Smi. Marry, that's good news indeed: I am glad of that with all my heart.

Bayes. Now here's the man brought in that is suppos'd to have kill'd her.

[*A great shout within.*

SCÆNA III.

Enter Amarillis *with a Book in her hand, and Attendants.*

Ama. WHAT shout triumphant's that?

Enter a Souldier.

Sol. Shie maid, upon the River brink, near *Twick'nam* Town, the false Assassinate is tane.

Ama. Thanks to the Powers above, for this deliverance. I hope its slow beginning will portend
A forward *Exit* to all future end.

Bayes. Pish, there you are out; to all Future end? No, no; to all future End: you must lay the accent upon end, or else you lose the conceipt.

Smi. I see you are very perfect in these matters.

Bayes. I, Sir; I have been long enough at it, one would think, to know some thing.   11

Enter Souldiers dragging in an old Fisher-man.

Ama. Villain, what Monster did corrupt thy mind.
T'attaque the noblest soul of humane kind?
Tell me who set thee on.

Fish. Prince *Pretty-man.*

Ama. To kill whom?

Fish. Prince *Pretty-man.*

Ama. What, did Prince *Pretty-man* hire you to kill Prince *Pretty-man*?

Fish. No; Prince *Volscius.*

Ama. To kill whom?   20

Fish. Prince *Volscius.*

Ama. What did Prince *Volscius* hire you to kill Prince *Volscius*?

Fish. No; Prince *Pretty-man.*

Ama. So drag him hence,
Till torture of the Rack produce his Sense.   [*Exeunt.*

Bayes. Mark how I make the horrour of his guilt confound his intellects; for he's out at one and t'other: and that's the design of this Scene.

Smi. I see, Sir, you have a several design for every Scene.

Bayes. I, that's my way of writing; and so Sir, I can dispatch you a whole Play, before another man, I gad, can make an end of his Plot.   30

SCÆNA IV.

Bayes. SO now enter Prince *Pretty-man* in a rage. Where the Devil is he? Why *Pretty-man*? why when, I say? O fie, fie, fie, fie! all's marr'd, I vow to gad, quite marr'd.

Enter Pretty-man.

Phoo, pox! you are come to late, Sir, now you may go out again, if you please. I vow to gad, Mr.—a—I would not give a button for my Play, now you have done this.

Pret. What Sir?

Bayes. What Sir! 'Slife, Sir, you should have come out in choler, rous upon the Stage, just as the other went off. Must a man be eternally telling you of these things?   10

Johns. Sure this must be some very notable matter that he's so angry at.

Smi. I am not of your opinion.

Bayes. Pish! come, let's hear your part, Sir.

Pret. Bring in my Father; why d'ye keep him from me?

Altho a Fisherman, he is my Father,

Was ever Son, yet brought to this distress,

To be, for being a Son, made fatherless?

Ah, you just Gods, rob me not of a Father:

The being of a Son take from me rather.   [*Exit.*

Smi. Well, *Ned*, what think you now?   20

Johns. A Devil this is worst of all. Mr. *Bayes*, pray what's the meaning of this Scene?

Bayes. O, cry you mercy, Sir: I purtest I had forgot to tell you. Why, Sir, you must know, that long before the beginning of this Play, this Prince was taken by a Fisherman.

Smi. How, Sir, taken Prisoner?

Bayes. Taken Prisoner! O Lord, what a question's there! did ever any man ask such a question? Godsookers, he has put the Plot quite out of my head, with this damn'd question. What was I going to say?

Johns. Nay, the Lord knows: I cannot imagine.   30

Bayes. Stay, let me see; taken: O 'tis true. Why, Sir, as I was going to say, his Highness here, the Prince, was taken in a Cradle by a Fisherman, and brought up as his Child.

8 rous] With a bounce or bang.

Smi. Indeed?

Bayes. Nay, pr'ythe hold thy peace. And so, Sir, this murder being committed by the River-side, the Fisherman, upon suspition, was seiz'd; and there upon the Prince grew angry.

Smi. So, so; now 'tis very plain.

Johns. But Mr. *Bayes*, is not this some disparagement to a Prince, to pass for a Fishermans Son? Have a care of that I pray.   40

Bayes. No, no; not at all; for 'tis but for a while: I shall fetch him off again, presently, you shall see.

Enter Pretty-man *and* Thimble.

Pret. By all the Gods, I'l set the world on fire
Rather than let 'em ravish hence my Sire.

Thim. Brave *Pretty-man*, it is at length reveal'd,
That he is not thy Sire who thee conceal'd.

Bayes. Lo you now; there he's off again.

Johns. Admirably done i'faith.

Bayes. Ay, now the Plot thickens very much upon us.

Pret. What Oracle this darkness can evince?   50
Sometimes a Fishers Son, sometimes a Prince.
It is a secret, great as is the world;
In which, I like the Soul, am tos'd and hurl'd.
The blackest Ink of Fate, sure, was my Lot,
And, when she writ my Name, she made a blot.   [*Exit.*

Bayes. There's a blust'ring verse for you now.

Smi. Yes, Sir; but why is he so mightily troubled to find he is not a Fishermans Son?

Bayes. Phoo! that is not because he has a mind to be his Son, but for fear he should be thought to be no bodies Son at all.   60

Smi. Nay, that would trouble a man, indeed.

Bayes. So let me see.

SCÆNA V.

Enter Prince Volscius, *going out of Town.*   [*Reads.*

Smi. I THOUGHT he had been gone to *Peccadille*.

Bayes. Yes, he gave it out so; but that was only to cover his design.

Johns. What design?

Bayes. Why, to head the Army, that lies conceal'd for him in *Knightsbridge*.

Johns. I see here's a great deal of Plot, Mr. *Bayes*.

Bayes. Yes, now it begins to break; but we shall have a world of more business anon.

Enter Prince Volscius, Cloris, Amarillis, *and* Harry
with a Riding-Cloak and Boots.

Ama. Sir, you are cruel, thus to leave the Town,   10
And to retire to Country solitude.

Clo. We hop'd this Summer that we should at least
Have held the honour of your Company.

Bayes. Held the honour of your Company! prettily exprest! Held the honour of your Company! Godsookers, these fellows will never take notice of any thing.

Johns. I assure you Sir, I admire it extreamly: I don't know what he does.

Bayes. I, I, he's a little envious; but 'tis no great matter. Come.

Ama. Pray let us two this single boon obtain,
That you will here, with poor us, still remain.   20
Before your Horses come pronounce our fate,
For then, alas! I fear, 'twill be too late.

Bayes. Sad!

Vols. *Harry*, my Boots; for I'l go rage among
My Blades encamp'd, and quit this *Urban* throng.

Smi. But pray, Mr. *Bayes*, is not this a little difficult, that you were saying e'en now, to keep an army thus conceal'd in *Knights-bridge*.

Bayes. In *Knights-bridge*? stay.

Johns. No, not if the Inn-keepers be his friends.

Bayes. His Friends! Ay, Sir, his intimate acquaintance; or else, indeed, I grant it could not be.   31

Smi. Yes, faith, so it might be very easie.

Bayes. Nay, if I do not make all things easie, I gad, I'l give you leave to hang me. Now you would think that he is going out of Town; but you shall see how prettily I have contriv'd to stop him, presently.

Smi. By my troth, Sir, you have so amaz'd me, that I know not what to think.

Enter Parthenope.

Vols. Bless me! how frail are all my best resolves!
How, in a moment, is my purpose chang'd!
Too soon I thought my selfe secure from Love.   40
Fair, Madam, give me leave to ask her name
Who does so gently rob me of my fame?
For I should meet the Army out of town,
And, if I fail, must hazard my renown.

Par. My Mother, Sir, sells Ale by the Town-walls,
And me, her dear *Parthenope* she calls.

Bayes. Now that's the *Parthenope*, I told you of.

Johns. I, I: I gad you are very right.

Vols. Can vulgar vestments high-born beauty shroud?
Thou bring'st the Morning pictur'd in a Cloud.   50

Bayes. The Morning pictur'd in a Cloud! A, Gadsookers, what a conceipt
is there!

Par. Give you good Ev'n, Sir.   [*Exit.*

Vols. O inauspicious Stars! that I was born
To sudden love, and to more sudden scorn!

Ama.⎫
Clor.⎭How! Prince *Volscius* in love? Ha, ha, ha.   [*Exeunt laughing.*

Smi. Sure, Mr. *Bayes*, we have lost some jest here, that they laugh at so.

Bayes. Why, did you not observe? He first resolves to go out of Town, and
then, as he is pulling on his Boots falls in love with her. Ha, ha, ha.

Smi. Well, and where lyes the jest of that?   60

Bayes. Ha?   [*Turns to Johnson.*

Johns. Why; In the Boots: where should the jest lie?

Bayes. I Gad, you are in the right: it does [*Turns to Smith.*] Lie in the
Boots—Your friend, and I know where a good jest lies, tho you don't, Sir.

Smi. Much good do't you, Sir.

Bayes. Here, now, Mr. *Johnson*, you shall see a combat betwixt Love and
Honour. An ancient Author has made a whole Play on't; but I have dispatch'd it all in this Scene.

> Volscius *sits down to pull on his Boots:* Bayes *Stands
> by and over acts the Part as he speaks it.*

Vols. How has my passion Made me *Cupid's* scoff!
This hasty Boot is on, the other off,   70
And sullen lies, with amorous design
To quit loud fame, and make that Beauty mine.

Smi. Pr'ythee mark what pains Mr. *Bayes* takes to Act this speech himselfe!

Johns. Yes, the fool, I see, is mightily transported with it.

Vols. My Legs, the Emblem of my various thought,
Shew to what sad distraction I am brought.
Sometimes with stubborn Honour, like this Boot,
My mind is guarded, and resolv'd: to do't:
Sometimes, again, that very mind, by Love
Disarmed, like this other Leg does prove.   80

66 Love and Honour] Bayes is referring to a play of this title by Sir William Davenant,
which had been revived in 1661.

Shall I to Honour or to Love give way?
Go on, cries Honour; tender Love saies, nay:
Honour, aloud, commands, pluck both Boots on;
But softer Love does whisper put on none.
What shall I do? what conduct shall I find
To lead me through this twy-light of my mind?
For as bright Day with black approach of Night
Contending, makes a doubtful puzling light;
So does my Honour and my Love together
Puzzle me so, I can resolve for neither.   90
        [*Goes out hopping with one Boot on, and the other off.*

Johns. By my troth, Sir, this is as difficult a Combat as ever I saw, and as equal; for 'tis determin'd on neither side.

Bayes. Ay, is't not now I gad, ha? For, to go off hip hop, hip hop, upon this occasion, is a thousand times better than any conclusion in the world, I gad.

Johns. Indeed, Mr. *Bayes*, that hip hop, in this place as you say, does a very great deal.

Bayes. O, all in all Sir; they are these little things that mar, or set you off a Play: as I remember once, in a Play of mine, I set off a Scene I gad, beyond expectation, only with a Petticoat, and the Belly ake.

Smi. Pray, how was that, Sir?   100

Bayes. Why, Sir, I contriv'd a Petticoat to be brought in upon a Chair, (no body knew how) into a Prince's Chamber, whose Father was not to see it, that came in by chance.

Johns. God's my life, that was a notable Contrivance indeed.

Smi. I but, Mr. *Bayes*, how could you contrive the Belly-ake?

Bayes. The easiest i th' World, I Gad: I'l tell you how, I made the Prince sit down upon the Petticoat, no more than so, and pretended to his Father that he had just then got the Belly-ake: whereupon, his Father went out to call a Physician, and his man ran away with the Petticoat.

Smi. Well and what follow'd upon that?   110

Bayes. Nothing, no Earthly thing, I vow to Gad.

Johns. O, my word, Mr. *Bayes*, there you hit it.

Bayes. Yes it gave a world of content. And then I paid 'em away besides, for I made 'em all talk baudy; ha, ha, ha: beastly, downright baudy upon the Stage, I gad; ha, ha, ha; but with an infinite deal of wit, that I must say.

Johns. That, I that, we know well enough, can never fail you.

Bayes. No, I Gad can't it: come bring in the Dance.   [*Exit, to call 'em.*

Smi. Now, the Devil take thee for a silly, confident, unnatural, fulsom Rogue.

---

99 a Petticoat, and the Belly ake] The reference is to Dryden's *Assignation, or Love in a Nunnery*, in which Prince Frederick feigns illness to distract attention from the presence of tell-tale garments in his chamber.

Enter Bayes *and* Players.

Bayes. Pray Dance well, before these Gentlemen: you are commonly so
lazy; but you should be light and easie, tah, tah, tah.   120

> *All the while they Dance*, Bayes *puts 'em out*
> *with teaching 'em.*

Well Gentlemen, you'l see this Dance, if I am not deceiv'd, take very well
upon the Stage, when they are perfect in their motions, and all that.

Smi. I don't know how 'twill take, Sir; but I am sure you sweat hard for't.

Bayes. Ay, Sir, it costs me more pains and trouble, to do these things, than
almost the things are worth.

Smi. By my troth, I think so, Sir.

Bayes. Not for the things themselves, for I could write you, Sir, forty of
'em in a day; but, I gad, these Players are such dull persons, that, if a man
be not by 'em upon every point, and at every turn, I gad, they'l mistake you,
Sir, and spoil all.   130

> *Enter a Player.*

What, is the Funeral ready?

Play. Yes, Sir.

Bayes. And is the Lance fill'd with Wine?

Play. Sir, 'tis just now a doing.

Bayes. Stay then, I'l do it my self.

Smi. Come, let's go with him.

Bayes. A Match. But Mr. *Johnson*, I gad, I am not like other persons; they
care not what becomes of their things, so they can but get mony for 'em;
now, I gad, when I write, if it be not just as it should be in every circumstance, to every particular, I gad; I am no more able to endure it, I am not
my self, I'm out of my wits, and all that, I'm the strangest person in the
whole world. For what care I for mony? I write for Reputation.   [*Exeunt.*

> *Finis Actus tertii.*

ACTUS IV. SCÆNA I.

Bayes, *and the two Gentlemen.*

Bayes. GENTLEMEN, because I would not have any two things alike
in this Play, the last Act beginning with a witty Scene of Mirth,
I make this to begin with a Funeral.

Smi. And is that all your reason for it, Mr. *Bayes?*

Bayes. No, Sir, I have a Precedent for it besides. A person of Honour, and a *Scholar*, brought in his Funeral just so: and he was one (let me tell you) that knew as well what belong'd to a Funeral, as any man in *England*, I gad.

Johns. Nay if that be so, you are safe.

Bayes. I gad, but I have another device, a frolick, which I think yet better than all this; not for the Plot or Characters, (for in my heroic Plays, I make no difference, as to those matters) but for another contrivance.   11

Smi. What is that, I pray?

Bayes. Why, I have design'd a Conquest, that cannot possibly, I gad, be acted in less than a whole week: and I'l speak a bold word, it shall Drum, Trumpet, Shout, and Battle, I gad with any the most warlike Tragœdy we have, either ancient or modern.

Johns. I, marry, Sir, there you say something.

Smi. And pray, Sir, how have you order'd this same frolic of yours?

Bayes. Faith, Sir, by the Rule of Romance. For example: they divided their things into three, four, five, six, seven, eight, or as many Tomes as they please: now, I would very fain know what should hinder me, from doing the same with my things, if I please?   22

Johns. Nay, if you should not be Master of your own works, 'tis very hard.

Bayes. That is my sence. And then, Sir, this contrivance of mine has something of the reason of a Play in it too; for as every one makes you five Acts to one Play, what do me I, but make five Playes to one Plot: by which means the Auditors have every day a new thing.

Johns. Most admirably good, i'faith! and must certainly take, because it is not tedious.

Bayes. I, Sir, I know that, there's the main point. And then, upon *Saturday*, to make a close of all, (for I ever begin upon a *Monday*) I make you, Sir, a sixth Play, that sums up the whole matter to 'em, and all that, for fear they should have forgot it.   33

Johns. That consideration, Mr. *Bayes*, indeed, I think, will be very necessary.

Smi. And when comes in your share, pray Sir?

Bayes. The third week.

Johns. I vow you'l get a world of money.

Bayes. Why, faith, a man must live: and if you don't, thus, pitch upon some new device, I gad, you'l never do it, for this Age (take it o'my word) is somewhat hard to please. But there's one pretty odd passage, in the last

20 as many Tomes as they please] A reference to the several volumes in which the lengthy romances of Mlle de Scudéry and others were wont to appear.   26 five Playes to one Plot] Bayes intends to improve on the contemporary fashion for sequels, and for two-part and even three-part plays.   37 The third week] I.e. instead of the third *night*, which was normally the author's benefit performance.

of these Plays which may be executed two several ways, wherein I'd have
your opinion, Gentlemen.   43
 Johns. What is't, Sir?
 Bayes. Why, Sir, I make a Male person to be in Love with a Female.
 Smi. Do you mean that, Mr. *Bayes*, for a new thing?
 Bayes. Yes, Sir, as I have order'd it. You shall hear. He having passionately
lov'd her through my five whole Playes, finding at last that she consents to
his love, just after that his Mother had appear'd to him like a Ghost, he kills
himself. That's one way. The other is that she coming at last to love him,
with as violent a passion as he lov'd her, she kills her self. Now my question is,
which of these two persons should suffer upon this occasion?   52
 Johns. By my troth, it is a very hard case to decide.
 Bayes. The hardest in the World, I gad, and has puzled this pate very
much. What say you Mr. *Smith*?
 Smi. Why truly Mr. *Bayes*, if it might stand with your justice now, I
would spare 'em both.
 Bayes. I gad, and I think—ha—why then, I'l make him hinder her from
killing her selfe. Ay, it shall be so. Come, come, bring in the Funeral.

Enter a Funeral, with the two Usurpers and Attendants.

Lay it down there: no, no, here, Sir. So now speak.   60
 K. Ush. Set down the Funeral Pile, and let our grief
Receive, from its imbraces, some relief.
 K. Phys. Was't not unjust to ravish hence her breath,
And, in life's stead, to leave us nought but death?
The World discovers now its emptiness,
And, by her loss, demonstrates we have less.
 Bayes. Is not this good language now? is not that elevate? 'Tis my *non
ultra*, I gad. You must know they were both in love with her.
 Smi. With her? with whom?
 Bayes. Why, this is *Lardella's* Funeral.   70
 Smi. Lardella! I, who is she?
 Bayes. Why, Sir, the Sister of *Drawcansir*. A Lady that was drown'd at
Sea, and had a wave for her Winding sheet.
 K. Ush. Lardella, O *Lardella*, from above,
Behold the Tragic issues of our Love.
Pity us, sinking under grief and pain,
For thy being cast away upon the Main.
 Bayes. Look you now, you see I told you true.
 Smi. I, Sir, and I thank you for it, very kindly.
 Bayes. Ay, I gad, but you will not have patience; honest M.—a— you will
not have patience.   81

Johns. Pray, Mr. *Bayes*, who is that *Drawcansir*?

Bayes. Why, Sir, a fierce *Hero*, that frights his Mistress, snubs up Kings, baffles Armies, and does what he will, without regard to numbers, good manners, or justice.

Johns. A very pretty Character.

Smi. But, Mr. *Bayes*, I thought your *Heroes* had ever been men of great humanity and justice.   88

Bayes. Yes, they have been so; but for my part, I prefer that one quality of singly beating of whole Armies above all your moral virtues put together, I gad. You shall see him come in presently. Zookers, why don't you read the paper?   [*To the Players.*

K. Phys. O, cry you mercy.   [*Goes to take the paper.*

Bayes. Pish! nay you are such a fumbler. Come I'l read it my self.
                                        [*Takes a paper from off the Coffin.*
Stay, it's an ill hand, I must use my Spectacles. This, now, is a Copy of Verses, which I make *Lardella* compose, just as she is dying, with design to have it pin'd upon her Coffin, and so read by one of the Usurpers, who is her Cousin.

Smi. A very shrewd design that, upon my word, Mr. *Bayes*.   99

Bayes. And what do you think now I fancy her to make Love like, here, in the paper?

Smi. Like a Woman: what should she make Love like?

Bayes. O'my word you are out tho, Sir; I gad, you are.

Smi. What then? like a man?

Bayes. No, Sir; like a Humble Bee.

Smi. I confess, that I should not have fancy'd.

Bayes. It may be so, Sir. But it is, tho, in order to the opinion of some of your ancient Philosophers, who held the transmigration of the soul.

Smi. Very fine.

Bayes. I'l read the Title. *To my dear Couz, King* Phys.   110

Smi. That's a little too familiar with a King, tho, Sir, by your favor, for a Humble Bee.

Bayes. Mr. *Smith*, in other things, I grant your knowledge may be above me; but, as for Poetry, give me leave to say, I understand that better: it has been longer my practice; it has indeed, Sir.

Smi. Your servant, Sir.

Bayes. Pray mark it.

Since death my earthly part will thus remove   [*Reads.*
I'l come a Humble Bee to your chaste love.
With silent wings I'll follow you, dear Couz;   120
Or else, before you, in the Sun-beams, buz.
And when to Melancholy Groves you come,

An Airy Ghost, you'l know me by my Hum;
For sound, being Air, a Ghost does well become.
   Smi. (*After a pause.*) Admirable!
   Bayes. At night, into your bosom I will creep,
And buz but softly if you chance to sleep;
Yet in your Dreams, I will pass sweeping by,
And then, both Hum and Buz before your eye.
   Johns. By my troth, that's a very great promise.   130
   Smi. Yes, and a most extraordinary comfort to boot.
   Bayes. Your bed of love from dangers I will free;
But most from love of any future Bee.
And when with pity your heart strings shall crack,
With empty arms I'l bear you on my back.
   Smi. A pick-a-pack, a pick-a-pack.
   Bayes. Ay, I gad, but is not that *tuant* now, ha? is it not *tuant*? Here's
the end.
Then at your birth of immortality,
Like any winged Archer, hence I'l fly,   140
And teach you your first flutt'ring in the Sky.
   Johns. O rare! This is the most natural, refin'd fancy that ever I heard, I'l
swear.
   Bayes. Yes, I think, for a dead person, it is a good enough way of making
love: for being divested of her Terrestrial part, and all that, she is only
capable of these little, pretty, amorous designs that are innocent, and yet
passionate. Come, draw you swords.
   K. Phys. Come sword, come sheath thy self within this breast,
Which only in *Lardella's* Tomb can rest.
   K. Ush. Come, dagger, come, and penetrate this heart,   150
Which cannot from *Lardella's* Love depart.

Enter Pallas.

   Pal. Hold, stop your murd'ring hands
At *Pallases* commands:
For the supposed dead, O Kings,
Forbear to act such deadly things.
Lardella lives; I did but try
If Princes for their Loves could dye.
Such Celestial constancy
Shall, by the Gods, rewarded be:
And from these Funeral Obsequies   160
A Nuptial Banquet shall arise.
          [*The Coffin opens, and a Banquet is discover'd.*

Bayes. So, take away the Coffin. Now it's out. This is the very Funeral of the fair person which *Volscius* sent word was dead, and *Pallas*, you see, has turn'd it into a Banquet.

Smi. Well, but where is this Banquet?

Bayes. Nay, look you Sir, we must first have a Dance, for joy that *Lardella* is not dead. Pray, Sir, give me leave to bring in my things properly at least.

Smi. That, indeed, I had forgot: I ask your pardon.

Bayes. O, d'ye so, Sir? I am glad you will confess your selfe once in an error, Mr. *Smith*.   170

Dance.

K. Ush. Resplendent *Pallas*, we in thee do find
The fiercest Beauty, and a fiercer mind:
And since to thee *Lardella's* life we owe,
We'll supple Statues in thy Temple grow.

K. Phys. Well, since alive *Lardella's* found,
Let, in full Boles, her Health go round.
          [*The two Usurpers take each of them a Bole in their hands.*
K. Ush. But where's the Wine?
Pal. That shall be mine.
Lo, from this conquering Lance,
Does flow the purest Wine of *France*:   [*Fills the Boles out of her Lance.*
And, to appease your hunger, I   181
Have, in my Helmet, brought a Pye:
Lastly, to bear a part with these,
Behold a Buckler made of Cheese.   [*Vanish Pallas.*

Bayes. There's the Banquet. Are you satisfi'd now, Sir?

Johns. By my troth, now, that is new, and more than I expected.

Bayes. Yes, I knew this would please you: for the chief Art in Poetry is to elevate your expectation, and then bring you off some extraordinary way.

Enter Drawcansir.

K. Phys. What man is this, that dares disturb our Feast?

Draw. He that dares drink, and for that drink dares dye,   190
And, knowing this, dares yet drink on, am I.

Johns. That is, Mr. *Bayes*, as much as to say, that tho he would rather die than not drink, yet he would fain drink for all that too.

Bayes. Right; that's the conceipt on't.

Johns. 'Tis a marvellous good one, I swear.

Bayes. Now there are some Critics that have advis'd me to put out the Second *Dare*, and print *Must* in the place on't; but, I gad, I think 'tis better thus a great deal.

Johns. Whoo! a thousand times.
Bayes. Go on then.   200
K. Ush. Sir, if you please, we should be glad to know,
How long you here will stay, how soon you'l go?
Bayes. Is not that now like a well bred person, I gad? So modest, so gent!
Smi. O, very like.
Draw. You shall not know how long I here will stay;
But you shall know I'l take your Bowles away.

> *Snatches the Boles out of the Kings
> hands, and drinks 'em off.*

Smi. But, Mr. Bayes, is that (too) modest and gent?
Bayes. No, I gad, Sir, but it's great.
K. Ush. Tho, Brother, this grum stranger be a Clown,
He'l leave us, sure, a little to gulp down.   210
Draw. Who e'er to gulp one drop of this dares think
I'l stare away his very pow'r to drink.

> *The two Kings sneak off the Stage,
> with their Attendants.*

I drink I huff, I strut, look big and stare;
And all this I can do, because I dare.   [*Exit.*
Smi. I suppose, Mr. *Bayes*, this is the fierce *Hero* you spoke of.
Bayes. Yes; but this is nothing: you shall see him, in the last Act, win above
a dozen Battles, one after another, I gad, as fast as they can possible come upon
the Stage.
Johns. That will be a sight worth the seeing indeed.
Smi. But pray, Mr. *Bayes*, why do you make the Kings let him use 'em so
scurvily?   221
Bayes. Phoo! that is to raise the character of *Drawcansir*.
Johns. O' my word, that was well thought on.
Bayes. Now, Sirs I'l shew you a Scene indeed; or rather, indeed, the
Scene of Scenes. 'Tis an Heroic Scene.
Smi. And pray, Sir, what's your design in this Scene?
Bayes. Why, Sir, my design is guilded Truncheons, forc'd conceipt, smooth
Verse, and a Rant: In fine, if this Scene do not take, I gad, I'l write no more.
Come, come in, Mr.—a—nay, come in as many as you can. Gentlemen, I
must desire you to remove a little, for I must fill the Stage.   230
Smi. Why fill the Stage?
Bayes. O, Sir, because your Heroic Verse never sounds well, but when the
Stage is full.

SCÆNA II.

Enter Prince Pretty-man, *and Prince* Volscius.

Bayes. NAY, hold, hold; pray by your leave a little. Look you, Sir, the drift of this Scene is somewhat more than ordinary: for I make 'em both fall out because they are not in love with the same Woman.

Smi. Not in love? you mean, I suppose, because they are in love, Mr. *Bayes?*

Bayes. No, Sir; I say not in love: there's a new conceit for you. Now speak.

Pret. Since fate, Prince *Volscius*, now has found the way
For our so long'd for meeting here this day,
Lend thy attention to my grand concern.

Vols. I gladly would that story from thee learn;   10
But thou to love dost *Pretty-man*, incline:
Yet love in thy breast is not love in mine?

Bayes. Antithesis! Thine and mine.

Pret. Since love it self's the same, why should it be
Diff'ring in you from what it is in me?

Bayes. Reasoning! I gad, I love reasoning in verse.

Vols. Love takes *Cameleon*-like, a various dye
From every Plant on which it self does lye.

Bayes. Simile!

Pret. Let not thy love the course of Nature fright: 20
Nature does most in harmony delight.

Vols. How weak a *Deity* would nature prove
Contending with the pow'rful God of Love?

Bayes. There's a great Verse!

Vols. If Incense thou wilt offer at the Shrine
Of mighty Love, burn it to none but mine.
Her Rosie-lips eternal sweets exhale;
And her bright flames make all flames else look pale.

Bayes. I gad that is right.

Pret. Perhaps dull Incense may thy love suffice;   30
But mine must be ador'd with Sacrifice.
All hearts turn ashes which her eyes controul:
The Body they consume as well as Soul.

Vols. My love has yet a power more Divine;
Victims her Altars burn not, but refine:
Amidst the flames they ne're give up the Ghost,
But, with her looks, revive still as they roast.

In spite of pain and death, they're kept alive:
Her fiery eyes makes 'em in fire survive.
   Bayes. That is as well, I gad, as I can do.   40
   Vols. Let my *Parthenope* at length prevail.
   Bayes. Civil, I gad.
   Pret. I'l sooner have a passion for a Whale:
In whose vast bulk, tho store of Oyl doth lye,
We find more shape, more beauty in a Fly.
   Smi. That's uncivil, I gad.
   Bayes. Yes; but as far a fetch'd fancy, tho, I gad, as e're you saw.
   Vols. Soft, *Pretty-man*, let not thy vain pretence
Of perfect love, defame loves excellence.
Parthenope is sure, as far above   50
All other loves, as above all is Love.
   Bayes. Ah! I gad, that strikes me.
   Pret. To blame my *Cloris*, Gods would not pretend.
   Bayes. Now mark.
   Vols. Were all Gods join'd, they could not hope to mend
My better choice: for fair *Parthenope*,
Gods would, themselves, un-god themselves to see.
   Bayes. Now the Rant's a coming.
   Pret. Durst any of the Gods be so uncivil,
I'ld make that God subscribe himself a Devil.   60
   Bayes. Ah, Godsookers, that's well writ!
                                  [Scratching his head, his Perruke falls off.
   Vols. Could'st thou that God from Heav'n to Earth translate,
He could not fear to want a Heav'nly State.
Parthenope, on Earth, can Heav'n create.
   Pret. *Cloris* does Heav'n it self so far excel,
She can transcend the joys of Heav'n in Hell.
   Bayes. There's a bold flight for you now! 'Sdeath, I have lost my Perruke.
Well, Gentlemen, this is that I never yet saw any one could write, but my
self. Here's true spirit and flame all through, I gad. So, So; pray clear the
Stage.   *[He puts 'em off the Stage.*
   Johns. I wonder how the coxcomb has got the knack of writing smooth
Verse thus.   72
   Smi. Why there's no need of brain for this: 'tis but scanning, the labour's
in the finger; but where's the sence of it?
   Johns. O, for that, he desires to be excus'd: he is too proud a man to creep
servily after Sense, I assure you. But pray, Mr. *Bayes*, why is this Scene all
in Verse?
   Bayes. O, Sir, the subject is too great for Prose.

Smi. Well said, i'faith; I'l give thee a pot of Ale for that answer: 'tis well
worth it.   80

Bayes. Come, with all my heart.
I'll make that God subscribe himself a Devil.
That single line, I gad, is worth all that my brother Poets ever writ. Let down
the Curtain.   [*Exeunt.*

Finis Actus Quarti.

ACTUS V. SCÆNA I.

Bayes, *and the two Gentlemen.*

Bayes. NOW, Gentlemen, I will be bold to say, I'l shew you the greatest
Scene that ever *England* saw: I mean not for words, for those
I do not value; but for state, shew, and magnificence. In fine I'll justifie it to
be as grand to the eye every whit, I gad, as that great Scene in *Harry* the
Eight, and grander too, I gad; for instead of two Bishops, I bring in here four
Cardinals.

> *The Curtain is drawn up, the two usurping Kings
> appear in State, with the four Cardinals, Prince*
> Pretty-man, *Prince* Volscius, Amarillis, Cloris,
> Parthenope, &c. *before them, Heralds and
> Serjeants at Arms with Maces.*

Smi. Mr. *Bayes,* pray what is the reason that two of the Cardinals are in
Hats, and the other in Caps?

Bayes. Why, Sir, because—By gad, I won't tell you. Your Country friend,
Sir, grows so troublesome.   10

K. Ush. Now, Sir, to the business of the day.

K. Phys. Speak *Volscius.*

Vols. Dread Soveraign Lords, my zeal to you, must not invade my duty
to your Son; let me intreat that great Prince *Pretty-man* first do speak:
whose high preheminence, in all things that do bear the name of good, may
justly claim that priviledge.

Bayes. Here it begins to unfold: you may perceive, now, that he is his Son.

Johns. Yes, Sir; and we are very much beholding to you for that discovery.

Pret. Royal Father, upon my knees I beg,
That the Illustrious *Volscius* first be heard.   20

Vols. That preference is only due to *Amarillis,* Sir.

---

83 Let down the Curtain] This would have been customary at the end of the performance,
but not normal between the acts. Act V thus opens on the apron stage, and the curtain rises
after Bayes's opening speech.

Bayes. I'l make her speak very well, by and by, you shall see.

Ama. Invincible Soveraigns—   [*Soft Music.*

K. Ush. But stay, what sound is this invades our ears?

K. Phys. Sure 'tis the Musick of the moving Spheres.

Pret. Behold, with wonder, yonder comes from far
A God-like Cloud, and a triumphant Carr:
In which, our two right Kings sit one by one,
With Virgins Vests, and Laurel Garlands on.

K. Ush. Then, Brother *Phys* 'tis time we should begon.   30
{ *The two Usurpers steal out of the Throne,*
{   *and go away.*

Bayes. Look you now, did not I tell you that this would be as easie a change as the other?

Smi. Yes, faith, you did so; tho I confess, I could not believe you; but you have brought it about, I see.
{ *The two right Kings of* Brentford *descend in the*
{   *Clouds, singing in white garments; and three*
{   *Fidlers sitting before them, in green.*

Bayes. Now, because the two right Kings descend from above, I make 'em sing to the Tune and Stile of our modern Spirits.

1 King. Haste, Brother King, we are sent from above.

2 King.   Let us move, let us move:
                   Move to remove the Fate
                   Of *Brentfords* long united State.   40

1 King. Tarra, tan tara, full East and by South,

2 King. We sail with Thunder in our mouth,
In scorching noon day, whil'st the traveller stayes,
                   Busie, busie, busie, busie, we bustle a long.
                   Mounted upon warm *Phœbus* his Rayes,
                   Through the Heavenly throng,
                   Hasting to those
Who will feast us, at night, with a Pigs Petty-toes.

1 King.   And we'l fall with our pate
                   In an *Ollio* of hate.   50

2 King. But now supper's done, the Servitors try,
Like Souldiers, to storm a whole half-moon-pye.

1 King. They gather, they gather hot Custard in spoons,
But Alas, I must, leave these half-moons,
And repair to my trusty Dragoons.

2 King. O stay, for you need not as yet go astray;
The Tyde, like a friend, has brought ships in our way,

50 *Ollio*] Hotchpotch, mix up.

         And on their high ropes we will play.
           Like Maggots in Filberds, we'l snug in our shell,
             We'l frisk in our shell   60
             We'l firk in our shell,
                And farewel.

  1 King. But the Ladies have all inclination to dance,
And the green Frogs croak out a Coranto of *France*.

  Bayes. Is not that pretty, now? The Fiddlers are all in green.

  Smi. I, but they play no Coranto.

  Johns. No, but they play a Tune, that's a great deal better.

  Bayes. No Coranto, quoth a! that's a good one, with all my heart. Come,
sing on.

  2 King.   Now Mortals that hear   70
                  How we Tilt and Carreer,
                  With wonder will fear
The event of such things as shall never appear.

  1 King. Stay you to fulfil what the Gods have decreed.

  2 King. Then call me to help you, if there shall be need.

  1 King. So firmly resolv'd is a true *Brentford* King
To save the distressed, and help to 'em bring,
That ere a Full-pot of good Ale you can swallow,
He's here with a whoop, and gone with a holla.

                [Bayes *phillips his finger, and sings after 'em.*

  Bayes. He's here with a whoop, and gone with a holla. This, Sir, you must
know, I thought once to have brought in with a Conjurer.   81

  Johns. I, that would have been better.

  Bayes. No, faith, not when you consider it: for thus 'tis more compendious,
and does the thing every whit as well.

  Smi. Thing! what thing?

  Bayes. Why, bring 'em down again into the Throne, Sir; what thing would
you have?

  Smi. Well; but, methinks the Sence of this Song is not very plain.

  Bayes. Plain? why did you ever hear any people in Clouds speak plain?
They must be all for flight of fancie, at its full range, without the least check,
or controul upon it. When once you tye up spirits, and people in Clouds to
speak plain, you spoil all.   92

  Smi. Bless me, what a Monster's this!

                         { *The two Kings light out of the Clouds, and*
                             step into the Throne.

  1 King. Come, now to serious counsel we'l advance.

    61 We'l firk] We'll be frisky, lively.   64 a Coranto of *France*] A 'quick lively dance
of French origin' (Montague Summers).

2 King. I do agree; but first, let's have a Dance.

Bayes. Right. You did that very well, Mr. *Cartwright.* But first, let's have a Dance. Pray remember that; be sure you do it always just so: for it must be done as if it were the effect of thought, and premeditation. But first, let's have a Dance. Pray remember that.

Smi. Well, I can hold no longer, I must gag this rogue; there's no induring of him. 101

Johns. No, pr'thee make use of thy patience a little longer: let's see the end of him now. [*Dance a grand Dance.*

Bayes. This, now, is an ancient Dance, of right belonging to the Kings of *Brentford*; but since deriv'd, with a little alteration, to the Inns of Court.

An Alarm. Enter two Heralds.

1 King. What sawcie Groom molests our privacies?

1 Her. The Army's at the door, and in disguise,
Desires a word with both your Majesties:

2 Her. Having from *Knights Bridge* hither march'd by stealth.

2 King. Bid 'em attend a while, and drink our health. 110

Smi. How, Mr. *Bayes*? the Army in disguise?

Bayes. Ay, Sir, for fear the Usurpers might discover them that went out but just now.

Smi. Why, what if they had discover'd them?

Bayes. Why, then they had broke the design.

1 King. Here, take five Guineys for those warlike men.

2 King. And here's five more; that makes the sum just ten.

1 Her. We have not seen so much the Lord knowes when.

[*Exeunt Heralds.*

1 King. Speak on, brave *Amarillis.*

Ama. Invincible Soveraigns, blame not my modesty, 120
If at this grand conjuncture— [*Drum beat behind the Stage.*

1 King. What dreadful noise is this that comes and goes?

Enter a Souldier with his Sword drawn.

Sould. Haste hence, great Sirs, your Royal persons save,
For the event of war no mortal knowes:
The Army, wrangling for the gold you gave,
First fell to words and then to handy-blows. [*Exit.*

Bayes. Is not that now a pretty kind of a Stanza, and a handsome come off?

2 King. O dangerous estate of Soveraign pow'r!
Obnoxious to the change of every hour.

1 King. Let us for shelter in our Cabinet stay: 130
Perhaps these threat'ning storms may pass away. [*Exeunt.*

Johns. But Mr. *Bayes*, did not you promise us, just now, to make *Amarillis* speak very well.

Bayes. Ay, and so she would have done, but that they hinder'd her.

Smi. How, Sir, whether you would or no?

Bayes. Ay, Sir, the Plot lay so that, I vow to gad, it was not to be avoided.

Smi. Marry, that was hard.

Johns. But, pray, who hindr'd her?

Bayes. Why, the battel, Sir, that's just coming in at door: And I'll tell you now a strange thing, tho I don't pretend to do more than other men, I gad, I'l give you both a whole week to ghess how I'l represent this Battel.   141

Smi. I had rather be bound to fight your Battle, I assure you, Sir.

Bayes. Whoo! there's it now: fight a Battle? there's the common error. I knew presently where I should have you. Why pray, Sir, do but tell me this one thing, Can you think it a decent thing, in a Battle before Ladies, to have men run their Swords through one another, and all that?

Johns. No, faith, 'tis not civil.

Bayes. Right on the other side; to have a long relation of Squadrons here, and Squadrons there: what is it but dull prolixity?

Johns. Excellently reason'd by my troth!   150

Bayes. Wherefore, Sir, to avoid both those Indicorums, I sum up my whole Battle in the representation of two persons only, no more: and yet so lively, that, I vow to gad, you would swear ten thousand men were at it really engag'd. Do you mark me?

Smi. Yes, Sir; but I think I should hardly swear tho, for all that.

Bayes. By my troth, Sir, but you would, tho, when you see it: for I make 'em both come out in Armor *Cap-a-pea*, with their Swords drawn, and hung, with a scarlet Ribbon at their wrists, (which you know, represents fighting enough.)

Johns. I, I; so much, that, if I were in your place I would make 'em go out again without ever speaking one word.   161

Bayes. No; there you are out; for I make each of 'em hold a Lute in his hand.

Smi. How Sir? instead of a Buckler?

Bayes. O Lord, O Lord! instead of a Buckler? Pray Sir do you ask no more questions. I make 'em, Sir, play the battel in *Recitativo*. And here's the conceipt. Just at the very same instant that one sings, the other, Sir, recovers you his Sword, and puts himself in a warlike posture: so that you have at once your ear entertained with Music and good Language; and your eye satisfied with the garb, and accoutrements of war.   170

Smi. I confess Sir, you stupifie me.

Bayes. You shall see.

157 Armor *Cap-a-pea*] In armour from head to foot.

Johns. But Mr. *Bayes,* might not we have a little fighting? for I love those playes, where they cut and slash one another upon the Stage, for a whole hour together.

Bayes. Why, then, to tell you true I have contriv'd it both wayes. But you shall have my *Recitativo* first.

Johns. I, now you are right: there is nothing then can be objected against it.

Bayes. True: and so, I gad, I'l make it, too, a Tragedy, in a trice.

> *Enter, at several doors, the General, and*
> *Lieutenant General, arm'd Cap-a-pe,*
> *with each of them a Lute in his hand,*
> *and his sword drawn, and hung with a*
> *scarlet Ribbon at his wrist.*

Lieut. Gen. Villain, thou lyest.   180

Gen. Arm, arm, *Gonsalvo,* arm; what ho?
The lye no flesh can brook I trow.

Lieut. Gen. Advance, from *Acton,* with the Musquetiers.

Gen. Draw down the *Chelsey* Curiasiers.

Lieut. Gen. The Band you boast of, *Chelsey* Curiasiers,
Shall, in my *Putney* Pikes, now meet their Peers.

Gen. Chiswickians, aged, and renown'd in fight,
Join with the *Hammersmith* Brigade.

Lieut. Gen. You'l find my *Mortlake* Boys will do them right,
Unless by *Fulham* numbers over-laid.   190

Gen. Let the left-wing of *Twick'nam* Foot advance,
And line that Eastern hedge.

Lieut. Gen. The Horse I rais'd in *Petty-France*
Shall try their chance.
And scour the Meadows, over grown with Sedge.

Gen. Stand: give the word.

Lieut. Gen. Bright Sword.

Gen. That may be thine.
But 'tis not mine.

Lieut. Gen. Give fire, give fire, at once give fire,   200
And let those recreant Troops perceive mine ire.

Gen. Pursue, pursue; they fly
That first did give the lie.   [*Exeunt.*

Bayes. This, now, is not improper, I think, because the Spectators know all these Towns, and may easily conceive them to be within the Dominions of the two Kings of *Brentford.*

Johns. Most exceeding well design'd!

Bayes. How do you think I have contriv'd to give a stop to this battle?

Smi. How?

C

Bayes. By an Eclipse: Which, let me tell you, is a kind of fancy that was yet never so much as thought of, but by my self, and one person more, that shall be nameless.   212

Enter Lieutenant General.

Lieut. Gen. What mid-night darkness does invade the day
And snatch the Victor from his conquer'd prey?
Is the Sun weary of this bloody sight,
And winks upon us with the eye of light?
'Tis an Eclipse. This was unkind, O Moon,
To clap between me, and the Sun so soon.
Foolish Eclipse: thou this in vain hast done;
My brighter honour had Eclips'd the Sun: 220
But now behold Eclipses two in one.   [*Exit.*

Johns. This is an admirable representation of a Battel, as ever I saw.

Bayes. I, Sir. But how would you fancy now to represent an Eclipse?

Smi. Why, that's to be suppos'd.

Bayes. Suppos'd! Ay, you are ever at your suppose: ha, ha, ha. Why you may as well suppose the whole Play. No, it must come in upon the Stage, that's certain; but in some odd way, that may delight, amuse, and all that. I have a conceipt for't, that I am sure is new, and, I believe to the purpose.

Johns. How's that?

Bayes. Why, the truth is, I took the first hint of this out of a Dialogue, between *Phœbus* and *Aurora* in the *Slighted Maid*: which by my troth, was very pretty; but I think, you'l confess this is a little better.   232

Johns. No doubt on't, Mr. *Bayes.* A great deal better.

            [Bayes *hugs* Johnson, *then turns to* Smith.

Bayes. Ah dear Rogue: but—a—Sir, you have heard I suppose, that your Eclipse of the Moon, is no thing else, but an interposition of the Earth, between the Sun and Moon: as likewise your Eclipse of the Sun is caus'd by an interlocation of the Moon, betwixt the Earth and Sun?

Smi. I have heard some such thing indeed.

Bayes. Well, Sir, then what do me I, but make the Earth, Sun, and Moon, come out upon the Stage, and dance the Hey: hum; And, of necessity, by the very nature of this Dance, the Earth must be sometimes between the Sun and the Moon, and the Moon between the Earth and Sun; and there you have both your Eclipses, by demonstration.   243

Johns. That must needs be very fine truly.

Bayes. Yes, it has fancy in't. And then, Sir, that there may be something

220 a Dialogue ... in the *Slighted Maid*] The reference is to a comedy by Sir Robert Stapylton, first staged in 1663.   240 the Hey] It 'seems to have been a kind of reel' (Montague Summers).

in't too of a Joque, I bring 'em in all singing, and make the Moon sell the
Earth a bargain. Come, come out Eclipse to the Tune of *Tom Tyler*.

Enter Luna.

Luna. Orbis, O *Orbis*.
Come to me thou little rogue *Orbis*.

Enter the Earth.

Orb. Who calls *Terra firma*, pray?   250
Luna. Luna that ne'r shines by day.
Orb. What means *Luna* in a veil?
Luna. Luna means to shew her tail.
Bayes. There's the bargain.

Enter Sol, *to the Tune of* Robin Hood.

Sol. Fie, Sister, fie; thou mak'st me muse,
              Derry, derry down.
To see the *Orb* abuse.
Luna. I hope his anger 'twill not move;
Since I shew'd it out of love.
              Hey down derry down.   260
Orb. Where shall I thy true love know,
Thou pretty, pretty Moon?
Luna. To morrow soon, ere it be noon,
On Mount *Vesuvio*.   [*Bis.*
Sol. Then I will shine.   [*To the Tune of* Trenchmore.
Orb. And I will be fine.
Luna. And I will drink nothing but Lippary wine.
Omnes. And we, &c.

                              [*As they Dance the Hey*, Bayes *speaks.*
Bayes. Now the earth's before the Moon; now the Moon's before the
Sun: there's the Eclipse again.   270
Smi. He's mightily taken with this I see.
Johns. I, 'tis so extraordinary, how can he chuse?
Bayes. So, now, vanish Eclipse, and enter t'other Battle, and fight. Here
now, if I am not mistaken, you will see fighting enough.

> *A battel is fought between foot and great Hobby*
> *horses. At last,* Drawcansir *comes in and kills*
> *'em all on both sides. All this while the Battel*
> *is fighting* Bayes *is telling them when to shout,*
> *and shouts with 'em.*

246 sell . . . a bargain] Give ribald replies to serious questions.

Draw. Others may boast a single man to kill;
But I, the blood of thousands daily spill.
Let petty Kings the names of Parties know:
Where e'er I come, I slay both friend and foe.
The swiftest Horsemen my swift rage controuls,
And from their Bodies drives their trembling souls.   280
If they had wings, and to the Gods could flie,
I would pursue and beat 'em through the skie:
And make proud *Jove*, with all his Thunder, see
This single Arm more dreadful is, than he.   [*Exit.*

Bayes. There's a brave fellow for you now, Sirs. You may talk of your
Hector, and *Achilles*, and I know not who; but I defie all your Histories, and
your Romances too, to shew me one such Conqueror, as this *Drawcansir*.

Johns. I swear, I think you may.

Smi. But Mr. *Bayes*, how shall all these dead men go off? for I see none
alive to help 'em.   290

Bayes. Go off! why, as they came on; upon their legs: how should they go
off? Why do you think the people here don't know they are not dead? He
is mighty ignorant, poor man; your friend here is very silly, Mr. *Johnson*, I
gad, he is, ha, ha, ha. Come, Sir, I'l show you how they shall go off. Rise,
rise, Sirs, and go about your business. There's go off for you now. Ha, ha, ha.
Mr. *Ivory*, a word. Gentlemen, I'l be with you presently.   [*Exit.*

Johns. Will you so? then we'l be gone.

Smi. I, pr'ythee let's go, that we may preserve our hearing. One Battel
more will take mine quite away.   [*Exeunt.*

Enter Bayes *and Players.*

Bayes. Where are the Gentlemen?   300

1 Play. They are gone, Sir.

Bayes. Gone! 'Sdeath, this last Act is best of all. I'l go fetch 'em again.
          [*Exit.*

1 Play. What shall we do, now he is gone away?

2 Play. Why, so much the better; then let's go to dinner.

3 Play. Stay, here's a foul piece of papyr of his. Let's see what 'tis.

3 or 4 Play. I, I; come let's hear it.
          [*Reads. The Argument of the Fifth Act.*

3 Play. Cloris at length, being sensible of Prince *Pretty-man's* passion,
consents to marry him; but, just as they are going to Church, Prince *Pretty-
man* meeting, by chance, with old *Joan* the Chandlers widdow, and remem-
bring it was she that first brought him acquainted with *Cloris*: out of a high
point of honour, brake off his match with *Cloris*, and marries old *Joan.*
Upon which, *Cloris*, in despair, drowns her self: and Prince *Pretty-man*,

discontentedly, walkes by the River side. This will never do: 'tis just like the rest. Come, let's begone.   314

Most of the Play. Ay, pox on't, let's go away.   [*Exeunt.*

Enter Bayes.

Bayes. A plague on 'em both for me, they have made me sweat, to run after 'em. A couple of senceless raskals, that had rather go to dinner then see this play out, with a pox to 'em. What comfort has a man to write for such dull rogues? Come Mr.—a—Where are you, Sir? come away quick, quick.

Enter Stage-keeper.

Stage. Sir, they are gone to dinner.   320

Bayes. Yes, I know the Gentlemen are gone; but I ask for the Players.

Stage. Why, an't please your worship, Sir, the Players are gone to dinner too.

Bayes. How! are the Players gone to Dinner? 'Tis impossible: the Players gone to dinner! I gad, if they are, I'l make 'em know what it is to injure a person that does 'em the honour to write for 'em, and all that. A company of proud, conceited, humorous, cross-grain'd persons, and all that. I gad, I'l make 'em the most contemptible, despicable, inconsiderable persons, and all that, in the whole world for this trick. I gad I'l be reveng'd on 'em; I'l sell this play to the other House.   330

Stage. Nay, good Sir, don't take away the Book; you'l disappoint the company that comes to see it acted here, this afternoon.

Bayes. That's all one. I must reserve this comfort to my self, my Play and I shall go together, we will not part indeed, Sir.

Stage. But what will the Town say, Sir?

Bayes. The Town! why, what care I for the Town? I gad, the Town has us'd me as scurvily, as the Players have done: but I'l be reveng'd on them too; for I'l Lampoon 'em all. And since they will not admit of my Plays, they shall know what a Satyrist I am. And so farewel to this Stage, I gad, for ever.   [*Exit Bayes.*

Enter Players.

1 Play. Come then, let's set up Bills for another Play.   341

2 Play. I, I; we shall lose nothing by this I warrant you.

1 Play. I am of your opinion. But before we go, let's see *Haynes* and *Shirley* practise the last dance; for that may serve us another time.

2 Play. I'l call 'em in. I think they are but in the Tiring-room.

The Dance done.

1 Play. Come, come; let's go away to dinner.   [*Exeunt Omnes.*

EPILOGUE.

THE Play is at an end, but where's the Plot?
    That circumstance our Poet Bayes *forgot.*
And we can boast, tho 'tis a plotting Age,
No place is freer from it than the Stage.
The Ancients plotted, tho, and strove to please
With sence that might be understood with ease;
They every Scene with so much wit did store,
That who brought any in, went out with more:
But this new way of wit does so surprise,
Men lose their wits in wondring where it lyes.   10
If it be true, that Monstrous births presage
The following mischiefs that afflict the Age,
And sad disasters to the State proclaim;
Plays without head or tail, may do the same.
Wherefore, for ours, and for the Kingdomes peace,
May this prodigious way of writing cease.
Let's have, at least, once in our lives, a time
When we may hear some reason, not all Rhyme:
We have these ten years felt it's Influence;
Pray let this prove a year of Prose and Scence.   20

FINIS.

THE
WHAT D'YE CALL IT

John Gay
1685–1732

The What d'ye Call it has its descent not so much from *The Rehearsal* as from a little-known play by Thomas Duffett dubbed *The Mock-Tempest*. Duffett's bawdy-house version of Shakespeare's romance was written in 1674, and virtually marked the eclipse of that false dawn of burlesque which brightened the early Restoration theatre. Forty years were to elapse before Gay's *What d'ye Call it* revived the tradition—a tradition, in this case, of travesty rather than of close textual parody. For Gay set out not to echo particular pomposities of tragic diction, as had Buckingham, but to expose the moral and emotional falsity of heroic assumptions—which, with or without the assistance of rhyme, now infused not only tragedy, but also the rapidly developing comedy of sentiment.

The What d'ye Call it is thus mock-heroic in rather the same sense as *The Rape of the Lock*—its ridicule embodied less in the rhyming couplets it adopts than in the lowness of its setting and its subject. Such a confusion between the heroic and the vulgar is, of course, one of the characteristic techniques of burlesque, distinguishing works in the genre from *The Mock-Tempest* to *The Covent-Garden Tragedy* to the punning pantomimes of J. R. Planché. It is notable too that, although the burlesque elements of *The What d'ye Call it* are chiefly contained in its play-within-a-play, the action is not a rehearsal of itself, but a finished performance. This was also to be a feature of many later burlesques—as distinct from the primarily *political* satires, such as Fielding's *Pasquin* and *Historical Register*, which exploited the rehearsal-formula not for purposes of formal parody, as did *The Rehearsal* itself, but as a convenient vehicle for discursive social comment.

It is possible that Pope—already collecting the gems of absurdity which were later to embellish his *Peri Bathous*—contributed certain ideas to the play, but of Gay's virtually sole authorship there can be no doubt. The dramatist's name was, however, inevitably linked with those of his fellow-members in the Scriblerus Club, and his play therefore became a target for the abuse of Pope's enemies. Partisans of Ambrose Philips were probably responsible for a *Complete Key* appended to some editions of the play, which is a model of perverse misreading—attacking Gay, for instance, for daring to burlesque *Othello*, in Sir Roger's awed recollection of Betterton putting 'the light out so cleverly'. Thus, not only did Gay's critics fail to 'consider that there is such a Figure as the Irony', as the author claimed in his tongue-in-cheek Preface, but to distinguish between parody and a nice touch of rustic characterization. However, the *Key* is curiously accurate in noting that *The What d'ye Call it* 'seems rather to be a Banter on the solemn stile of Tragedy in general, than a Satyr upon faulty Passages'. For this reason, it has been regarded by some critics as itself an ironical product of the Scriblerus association. It is, at least, a testimony to the interest and the controversy aroused by the play.

Gay's Preface, full of almost serious defences of his hybrid piece, was probably intended in part as a slight to the pedantic Dennis, and parodies of passages by Young, Addison, Philips, and Rowe—not to mention Shakespeare—can be tracked down in the play itself. Much more important, however, are the general satirical points—the sustained criticism of the idealization of rusticity by pastoral writers, for instance. Gay's country folk are of flesh and blood—particularly flesh—and as likely to filch sheep as act the shepherd. In his countryside, the squirarchy is tyrannical rather than benevolent, and the temptations of military life are regarded with a healthy scepticism reminiscent of Farquhar's *Recruiting Officer*. That *The What d'ye Call it* remained popular in revival only till the middle of the eighteenth century is difficult to explain: its freshness and vigour, and more particularly its apt combination of formal originality and critical purpose, might seek as successfully as Gay's later *Beggar's Opera* the applause of a modern audience.

THE

WHAT D'YE CALL IT:

A

Tragi-Comi-Paſtoral

FARCE.

By Mr. *GAY.*

—*Spirat Tragicum ſatis, & feliciter audet.*

Hor.

——*Locus eſt & pluribus Umbris.*

Hor.

LONDON:

Printed for BERNARD LINTOTT between the
two *Temple* Gates in *Fleet-ſtreet.*

THE
PREFACE.

AS I am the first who have introduced this kind of Dramatick entertainment upon the stage, I think it absolutely necessary to say something by way of Preface, not only to shew the nature of it, but to answer some objections that have been already rais'd against it by the graver sort of Wits, and other interested people.

We have often had Tragi-Comedies upon the English Theatre with success: but in that sort of composition the Tragedy and Comedy are in distinct Scenes, and may be easily separated from each other. But the whole Art of the Tragi-Comi-Pastoral Farce lies in interweaving the several kinds of the Drama with each other, so that they cannot be distinguish'd or separated.

The objections that are rais'd against it as a Tragedy, are as follow.   10

First, As to the Plot, they deny it to be Tragical, because its Catastrophe is a wedding, which hath ever been accounted Comical.

Secondly, As to the Characters; that those of a Justice of Peace, a Parish-Clark, and an Embryo's Ghost, are very improper to the dignity of Tragedy, and were never introduc'd by the Antients.

Thirdly, They say the Sentiments are not Tragical, because they are those of the lowest country people.

Lastly, They will not allow the Moral to be proper for Tragedy, because the end of Tragedy being to shew human life in its distresses, imperfections and infirmities, thereby to soften the mind of man from its natural obduracy and haughtiness, the Moral ought to have the same tendency; but this Moral, they say, seems entirely calculated to flatter the Audience in their vanity and self-conceitedness.   23

You all have sense enough to find it out.

To the first objection I answer, that it is still a disputable point, even among the best Criticks, whether a Tragedy may not have a happy Catastrophe; that the French Authors are of this opinion, appears from most of their Modern Tragedies.

In answer to the second objection, I cannot affirm, that any of the Antients have either a Justice of Peace, a Parish Clark, or an Embryo Ghost in their Tragedies; yet whoever will look into Sophocles, Euripides, or Seneca, will find that they greatly affected to introduce Nurses in all their pieces, which every

7 the Tragi-Comi-Pastoral Farce] No doubt in part a conscious echo of Polonius's generic confusion in Hamlet, II. ii.

one must grant to be an inferior Character to a Justice of Peace; in imitation of
which also, I have introduced a Grandmother and an Aunt.   33

To the third objection, which is the meanness of the sentiments, I answer that
the sentiments of Princes and clowns have not in reality that difference which
they seem to have: their thoughts are almost the same, and they only differ as
the same thought is attended with a meanness or pomp of diction, or receive
a different light from the circumstances each Character is conversant with. But
these Criticks have forgot the precept of their Master Horace, *who tells them,*

Tragicus plerumque dolet sermone pedestri.

In answer to the objection against the Moral, I have only this to alledge, That
the Moral of this piece is conceal'd; and Morals that are couch'd so as to exercise
the judgments of the audience, have not been disapprov'd by the best Criticks*.
And I would have those that object against it as a piece of Flattery, consider, that
there is such a Figure as the Irony.   45

The Objections against it as a Comedy *are,*

First, They object to the Plot, that it throws the Characters into the deepest
circumstances of distress: Inferiors trampled upon by the Tyranny of Power,
a soldier to be shot for desertion, and an innocent maid in the utmost despair.

Secondly, That Ghosts are introduced, which move terror, a Passion not proper
to be moved in Comedy.

Thirdly, They will not allow the Sentiments to be comical, because they are
such as naturally flow from the deep distresses abovementioned. The Speech
of a dying man, and his last advice to his child, are what one could not reasonably
expect should raise the mirth of an audience.   55

First, That the Plot is comical, I argue from the Peripaetia *and the* Catastrophe. Peascod's *change of fortune upon the reprieves being produced,* Kitty's
distress ending in the discharge of her sweetheart, and the wedding, are all
incidents that are truly comical.

To the second objection I answer, That Ghosts have not been omitted in the
antient Comedy; Aristophanes *having laid the Scene of his* Βάτραχοι *among the*
shades; and Plautus *has introduc'd a* Lar familiaris *in his Prologue to the*
Aulularia, *which tho' not actually a Ghost, is very little better.*   63

As to the third objection, That the Sentiments are not Comical, I answer, That
the Ghosts are the only characters which are objected to as improper for Comedy,
which I have already proved to be justly introduced, as following the manner of
the old Comedy; but as they allow that the Sentiments naturally flow from the
characters, those of the Justice, Clowns, &c. *which are indisputably Comical*

* *See* Bossu's *Chapter* of concealed Sentences.

characters, must be Comical. *For the Sentiments being convey'd in number and rhime, I have the authority of the best Modern* French *Comedies.* 70

The only objection against it as a Pastoral *falls upon the characters, which they say are partly* Pastoral, *and partly not so. They insist particularly, that a Sergeant of Granadiers is not a Pastoral character, and that the others are so far from being in the state of innocence, that the clowns are whoremasters, and the damsels with child.*

To this I reply, that Virgil *talks of Soldiers among his Shepherds.*

Impius haec tam culta Novalia miles habebit.

And the character of the Sergeant is drawn according to the Epithet of Virgil, Impius Miles, *which may be seen in that speech of his,*

You Dog, die like a Soldier——and be damn'd. 80

For, in short, a Soldier *to a Swain is but just the same thing that a* Wolf *is to his Flocks, and is as naturally talk'd of or introduc'd. As for the rest of the characters, I can only say I have copied nature, making the youths amorous before wedlock, and the damsels complying and fruitful. Those that are the most conversant in the country are the best judges of this sort of nature.*

Lastly, They object against it as a Farce,

First, Because the irregularity of the Plot should answer to the Extravagance of the characters, which they say this piece wants, and therefore is no Farce.
Secondly, They deny the characters to be Farcial, because they are actually in nature. 90
Thirdly, If it was a true Farce, *the Sentiments ought to be strain'd, to bear a proportional irregularity with the plot and characters.*

To the First I answer, That the Farcical Scene of the Ghosts is introduced without any coherence with the rest of the piece, might be entirely left out, and would not be allowed in a regular Comedy. There are indeed a great number of Dramatick entertainments, where are Scenes of this kind; but those pieces in reality are not Comedies, *but five Act Farces.*
Secondly, Let the Criticks consider only the nature of Farce, that it is made up of absurdities and incongruities, and that those pieces which have these Qualities in the greatest degree are the most Farces; and they will allow this to be so from the characters, and particularly from that of the speaking Ghost of an Embryo, *in the conclusion of the first Act. I have, 'tis true,* Aristophanes' *Authority*

for things of this sort in Comedy, who hath introduced a Chorus of Frogs, *and made them talk in the following manner:*   104

Βρεκεκεκὲξ, κοὰξ, κοὰξ,
Βρεκεκεκὲξ, κοὰξ, κοὰξ,
Λιμναῖα κρηυῶυ τέκνα, &c.

Mr. D'Urfey *of our own nation has given all the fowls of the air the faculty of speech equal with the parrot. Swans and elbow-chairs in the Opera of* Dioclesian *have danc'd upon the* English *Stage with good success.* Shakespear *hath some characters of this sort, as a* speaking wall, *and* Moonshine*. *The former he designed to introduce (as he tells us himself) with* something rough cast about him, *and the latter comes in with a lanthorn and candle; which in my opinion are characters that make a good figure in the modern Farce.*   114

Thirdly, The sentiments are truly of the Farce kind, as they are the sentiments of the meanest Clowns convey'd in the pomp of numbers and rhyme; which is certainly forc'd and out of nature, and therefore Farcical.

After all I have said, I would have these Criticks only consider, when they object against it as a Tragedy, that I design'd it something of a Comedy; when they cavil at it as a Comedy, that I had partly a view to Pastoral; when they attack it as a Pastoral, that my endeavours were in some degree to write a Farce; and when they would destroy its character as a Farce, that my design was a Tragi-Comi-Pastoral: I believe when they consider this, they will all agree, that I have happily enough executed what I purpos'd, which is all I contend for. Yet that I might avoid the cavils and misinterpretations of severe Criticks, I have not call'd it a Tragedy, Comedy, Pastoral, or Farce, but left the name entirely undetermin'd in the doubtful appellation of the What d'ye call it, *which name I thought unexceptionable; but I added to it a* Tragi-Comi-Pastoral Farce, *as it comprized all those several kinds of the* Drama.   129

The Judicious Reader will easily perceive, that the unities are kept as in the most perfect pieces, that the Scenes are unbroken, and Poetical Justice strictly observ'd; the Ghost of the Embryo *and the* Parish-Girle *are entire new charac-*

* *See his* Midsummer Night's Dream.

---

108 *Mr.* D'Urfey . . . *the parrot*] The reference is to D'Urfey's comic opera *Wonders in the Sun; or, the Kingdom of the Birds* (1706), in which the actors were dressed as various kinds of birds.   127 *the What d'ye call it*] The phrase was already familiar as a substitute for a forgotten name or place. 'His Father was Squire what d'you call him, of what d'you call 'em Shire' (Dryden, *The Kind Keeper*, 1678).   131 *Poetical Justice*] A morally appropriate (rather than psychologically or dramatically probable) conclusion.

ters. I might enlarge further upon the conduct of the particular Scenes, and of the piece in general, but shall only say, that the Success this piece has met with upon the Stage, gives encouragement to our Dramatick Writers to follow its Model; and evidently demonstrates that this sort of Drama *is no less fit for the Theatre than those they have succeeded in.*

Dramatis Personæ.

MEN.

Sir *Roger*   Mr. *Miller*.
Sir *Humphry*   Mr. *Cross*.
Justice *Statute*   Mr. *Shepherd*.
Squire *Thomas*, Sir *Roger*'s Son, }Mr. *Johnson*.
    alias, *Thomas Filbert*
Jonas Dock, alias *Timothy Peascod*   Mr. *Penkethman*.
Peter Nettle, the Sergeant   Mr. *Norris*.
Steward to Sir *Roger*   Mr. *Quin*.
Constable   Mr. *Penroy*.
Corporal   Mr. *Weller*.
Stave, a Parish-Clark.
The Ghost of a Child unborn   Mr. *Norris* Junior.
Countrymen, Ghosts, and Soldiers.

WOMEN.

Kitty, the Steward's Daughter, alias }Mrs. *Bicknell*.
    Kitty Carrot
Dorcas, *Peascod*'s Sister   Mrs. *Willis* Senior.
Joyce, *Peascod*'s Daughter left upon }Miss *Younger*.
    the Parish
Aunt   Mrs. *Baker*.
Grandmother.

THE
WHAT D'YE CALL IT:
A
TRAGI-COMI-PASTORAL
FARCE.

SCENE, *A Country Justice's Hall, adorn'd with Scutcheons and Stag's Horns.*

Enter Steward, Squire, Kitty, Dock, *and others in Country Habits.*

Steward. SO, you are ready in your parts, and in your dress too, I see; your own best cloaths do the business. Sure never was Play and actors so suited. Come, range your selves before me, women on the right, and men on the left. Squire *Thomas*, you make a good figure.

[*The Actors range themselves.*

Squire. Ay, thanks to *Barnaby*'s Sunday cloaths; but call me *Thomas Filbert*, as I am in the Play.

Steward. Chear up, daughter, and make *Kitty Carrot* the shining part: Squire *Thomas* is to be in love with you to night, girle.

Kitty. Ay, I have felt Squire *Thomas*'s love to my cost. I have little stomach to play, in the condition he hath put me into.   [*Aside.*

Steward. Jonas Dock, dost thou remember thy name?   11

Dock. My name? *Jo—Jo—Jonas*. No—that was the name my Godfathers gave me. My play name is *Timothy Pea—Pea—Peascod;* ay, *Peascod*—and am to be shot for a deserter.—

Steward. And you, *Dolly?*

Dolly. An't please ye, I am *Dorcas, Peascod*'s sister, and am to be with child, as it were.

1 Countryman. And I am to take her up, as it were—I am the Constable.

2 Countryman. And I am to see *Tim* shot, as it were—I am the Corporal.

Steward. But what is become of our sergeant?   20

Dorcas. Why *Peter Nettle*, Peter, Peter.

Enter Nettle.

Nettle. These stockings of *Susan*'s cost a woundy deal of pains the pulling on: But what's a sergeant without red stockings?

Dock. I'll dress thee, *Peter*, I'll dress thee. Here, stand still, I must twist thy neckcloth; I would make thee hold up thy head, and have a ruddy complexion; but prithee don't look black in the face, man. [*Rolling his neckcloth.*] Thou must look fierce and dreadful. [*Making whiskers with a burnt cork.*] But what shall we do for a grenadier's cap?

Steward. Fetch the leathern bucket that hangs in the belfry; that is curiously painted before, and will make a figure.   30

Nettle. No, no, I have what's worth twenty on't: the Pope's mitre, that my master Sir *Roger* seiz'd, when they would have burnt him at our market town.

Steward. So, now let ev'ry body withdraw, and prepare to begin the play. [*Exeunt Actors.*] My daughter debauched! and by that booby Squire! well, perhaps the conduct of this play may retrieve her folly, and preserve her reputation. Poor girle! I cannot forget thy tears.

Enter Sir Roger.

Sir Roger. Look ye, Steward, don't tell me you can't bring them in. I will have a ghost; nay, I will have a competence of ghosts. What, shall our neighbours think we are not able to make a ghost? A play without a ghost is like, is like,—i'gad it is like nothing.   41

Steward. Sir, be satisfied; you shall have ghosts.

Sir Roger. And is the play as I order'd it, both a Tragedy and a Comedy? I would have it a Pastoral too: and if you could make it a Farce, so much the better—and what if you crown'd all with a spice of your Opera? You know my neighbours never saw a Play before; and d'ye see, I would shew them all sorts of Plays under one.

Steward. Sir *Roger*, it is contrived for that very purpose.

Enter two Justices.

Sir Roger. Neighbours, you are welcome. Is not this Steward of mine a pure ingenious fellow now, to make such a Play for us these *Christmas* holidays. [*Exit Steward bowing.*]—A rare headpiece! he has it here, i'faith. [*Pointing to his own head.*] But indeed, I gave him the hint—To see now what contrivance some folks have! We have so fitted the parts to my tenants, that ev'ry man talks in his own way!—and then we have made just three justices in the play, to be play'd by us three justices of the *Quorum*.   55

22 a woundy deal of] A very great number of.   55 *Quorum*] The number necessary to constitute the bench.

1 Justice. Zooks!—so it is;—main ingenious.—and can we sit and smoke at the same time we act?

Sir Roger. Ay, ay,—we have but three or four words to say,—and may drink and be good company in peace and silence all the while after.

2 Justice. But how shall we know when we are to say these same words?

Sir Roger. This shall be the signal—when I set down the tankard, then speak you, Sir *Humphry,*—and when Sir *Humphry* sets down the tankard, speak you, Squire *Statute.* 63

1 Justice. Ah, Sir *Roger,* you are old dog at these things.

2 Justice. To be sure.

Sir Roger. Why neighbours, you know, experience, experience—I remember your *Harts* and your *Bettertons*—But to see your *Othello,* neighbours,—how he would rave and roar, about a foolish flower'd handkerchief!—and then he would groul so manfully,—and he would put out the light, and put the light out so cleverly! but hush—the Prologue, the Prologue. 70

> [*They seat themselves with much ceremony at the table, on which are pipes and tobacco, and a large silver tankard.*

THE

PROLOGUE,

Spoken by Mr. *Pinkethman.*

THE entertainment of this night—or day,
This something, or this nothing of a Play,
Which strives to please all palates at a time,
With ghosts and men, songs, dances, prose and rhime,
This comic story, or this tragic jest,
May make you laugh, or cry, as you like best;
May exercise your good, or your ill-nature,
Move with distress, or tickle you with satyr.
All must be be pleas'd too with their Parts, we think:
Our maids have sweethearts, and their Worships drink. 80
Criticks, we know, by antient rules may maul it;
But sure Gallants must like—the What d'ye call it.

ACT I. SCENE I.

Sir ROGER, *Sir* HUMPHRY, *Justice* STATUTE, CONSTABLE, FILBERT,
SERGEANT, KITTY, DORCAS, GRANDMOTHER, AUNT.

Sir ROGER.

HERE, *Thomas Filbert*, answer to your name,
    Dorcas hath sworn to you she owes her shame:
Or wed her strait, or else you're sent afar,
To serve his gracious Majesty in war.

FILBERT.

'Tis false, 'tis false—I scorn thy odious touch,
                [*Pushing* Dorcas *from him.*

DORCAS.

When their turn's serv'd, all men will do as much.

KITTY.

Ah, good your Worships, ease a wretched maid.
To the right father let the child be laid.
Art thou not perjur'd?—mark his harmless look.
How canst thou, *Dorcas*, kiss the Bible book?   10
Hast thou no conscience, dost not fear *Old Nick?*
Sure sure the ground will ope, and take thee quick.

SERGEANT.

Zooks! never wed, 'tis safer much to roam;
For what is war abroad to war at home?
Who wou'd not sooner bravely risque his life;
For what's a cannon to a scolding wife?

FILBERT.

Well, if I must, I must—I hate the wench,
I'll bear a musquet then against the *French.*
From door to door I'd sooner whine and beg,
Both arms shot off, and on a wooden leg,   20
Than marry such a trapes—No, no, I'll not:
—Thou wilt too late repent, when I am shot.
But, *Kitty*, why dost cry?—

GRANDMOTHER.

————Stay, Justice, stay:
Ah, little did I think to see this day!
Must Grandson *Filbert* to the wars be prest?
Alack! I knew him when he suck'd the breast,
Taught him his catechism, the fescue held,
And join'd his letters, when the bantling spell'd.
His loving mother left him to my care.   30
Fine child, as like his Dad as he could stare!
Come *Candlemas*, nine years ago she dy'd,
And now lies buried by the yew-tree's side.

AUNT.

O tyrant Justices! have you forgot
How my poor brother was in *Flanders* shot?
You press'd my brother—he shall walk in white,
He shall—and shake your curtains ev'ry night.
What though a paultry hare he rashly kill'd,
That cross'd the furrows while he plough'd the Field?
You sent him o'er the hills and far away;
Left his old mother to the parish pay,
With whom he shar'd his ten pence ev'ry day.
Wat kill'd a bird, was from his farm turn'd out;   43
You took the law of *Thomas* for a trout:
You ruin'd my poor uncle at the sizes,
And made him pay nine pound for *Nisiprises*.
Now will you press my harmless nephew too?
Ah, what has conscience with the rich to do!
                              [*Sir* Roger *takes up the Tankard.*
Though in my hand no silver tankard shine,
Nor my dry lip be dy'd with claret wine,   50
Yet I can sleep in peace—

Sir ROGER.   [*After having drunk.*

————————————Woman, forbear.

Sir HUMPHRY.   [*Drinking.*

The man's within the act————

---

28 fescue] The small stick used for pointing out letters to those learning to read.
46 *Nisiprises*] Actions tried under the authority conferred on justices of assize.

Justice STATUTE.   [*Drinking also.*

——————The law is clear.

SERGEANT.

Haste, let their Worships orders be obey'd.

KITTY.   [*Kneeling.*

Behold how low you have reduc'd a maid.
Thus to your Worships on my knees I sue,
(A posture never known but in the pew)
If we can money for our taxes find,
Take that—but ah! our sweethearts leave behind.
To trade so barb'rous he was never bred,
The blood of vermine all the blood he shed: 60
How should he, harmless youth, how should he then
Who kill'd but poulcats, learn to murder men?

DORCAS.

O *Thomas*, *Thomas!* hazard not thy life;
By all that's good, I'll make a loving wife:
I'll prove a true pains-taker day and night,
I'll spin and card, and keep our children tight.
I can knit stockings, you can thatch a barn;
If you earn ten-pence, I my groat can earn.
How shall I weep to hear this infant cry?
                                    [*Her hand on her belly.*
He'll have no father——and no husband I.   70

KITTY.

Hold, *Thomas*, hold, nor hear that shameless witch:
I can sow plain-work, I can darn and stitch;
I can bear sultry days and frosty weather;
Yes, yes, my *Thomas*, we will go together;
Beyond the seas together will we go,
In camps together, as at harvest, glow.
This arm shall be a bolster for thy head,
I'll fetch clean straw to make my soldier's bed;
There, while thou sleep'st, my apron o'er thee hold,
Or with it patch thy tent against the cold.   80
Pigs in hard rains I've watch'd and shall I do
That for the pigs, I would not bear for you?

FILBERT.

Oh, *Kitty*, *Kitty*, canst thou quit the rake,
And leave these meadows for thy sweetheart's sake?
Canst thou so many gallant soldiers see,
And captains and lieutenants slight for me?
Say, canst thou hear the guns, and never shake,
Nor start at oaths that make a christian quake?
Canst thou bear hunger, canst thou march and toil
A long long way, a thousand thousand mile?   90
And when thy *Tom*'s blown up, or shot away,
Then canst thou starve?—they'll cheat thee of my pay.

Sir *ROGER*.   [*Drinking.*

Take out that wench——

Sir *HUMPHRY*.   [*Drinking.*

——————————But give her pennance meet.

Justice STATUTE.   [*Drinking also.*

I'll see her stand—next Sunday—in a sheet.

DORCAS.

Ah! why does nature give us so much cause
To make kind-hearted lasses break the laws?
Why should hard laws kind-hearted lasses bind,
When too soft nature draws us after kind?

SCENE II.

Sir ROGER, *Sir* HUMPHRY, *Justice* STATUTE, FILBERT, SERGEANT,
KITTY, GRANDMOTHER, AUNT, SOLDIER.

SOLDIER.

Sergeant, the captain to your quarters sent;
To ev'ry ale-house in the town I went.
Our Corp'ral now has the deserter found;
The men are all drawn out, the pris'ner bound.

SERGEANT.   [*To* Filbert.

Come, soldier, come——

KITTY.

——————————Ah! take me, take me too.

GRANDMOTHER.

Stay, forward wench;——

AUNT.

——————————What would the creature do?
This week thy mother means to wash and brew.

KITTY.

Brew then she may her self, or wash or bake;
I'd leave ten mothers for one sweetheart's sake.
O justice most unjust!——

FILBERT.

——————————O tyranny!   10

KITTY.

How can I part?——

FILBERT.

——————————Alas! and how can I?

KITTY.

O rueful day!——

FILBERT.

——————————Rueful indeed, I trow.

KITTY.

O woeful day!——

FILBERT.

——————————A day indeed of woe!

KITTY.

When gentlefolks their sweethearts leave behind,
They can write letters, and say something kind;
But how shall *Filbert* unto me endite,
When neither I can read, nor he can write?
    Yet, Justices, permit us e'er we part
To break this ninepence, as you've broke our heart.

> *FILBERT.*   *[Breaking the Ninepence.*

As this divides, thus are we torn in twain.   20

> *KITTY.*   *[Joining the Pieces.*

And as this meets, thus may we meet again.

> *[She is drawn away on one side of the Stage, by*
> Aunt *and* Grandmother.

Yet one look more———

> *FILBERT.*
>
> *[Haul'd off on the other side by the Sergeant.*

——————————One more e'er yet we go.

> *KITTY.*

To part is death.——

> *FILBERT.*

———————————'Tis death to part.

> *KITTY.*

——————————————Ah!

> *FILBERT.*

———————————————Oh!

SCENE III.

Sir ROGER, *Sir* HUMPHRY, *Justice* STATUTE, *and* CONSTABLE.

> *Sir ROGER.*   *[Drinking.*

See, constable, that ev'ry one withdraw.

> *Sir HUMPHRY.*   *[Drinking.*

We've business———

> *Justice STATUTE.*   *[Drinking also.*

———————To discuss a point of law.

SCENE IV.

Sir ROGER, *Sir* HUMPHRY, *Justice* STATUTE.
They seem in earnest discourse.

Sir ROGER.

I say the Press-act plainly makes it out.

Sir HUMPHRY.

Doubtless, Sir *Roger*.————

Justice STATUTE.

————————Brother, without doubt.

A Ghost rises.

1 *GHOST.*

I'm *Jeffry Cackle*.——You my death shall rue;
For I was press'd by you, by you, by you.
[*Pointing to the Justices.*

Another Ghost rises.

2 *GHOST.*

I'm *Smut* the farrier.—You my death shall rue;
For I was press'd by you, by you, by you.

A Woman's Ghost rises.

3 *GHOST.*

I'm *Bess* that hang'd my self for *Smut* so true;
So owe my death to you, to you, to you.

A Ghost of an Embryo rises.

4 *GHOST*

I was begot before my mother married,
Who whipt by you, of me poor child miscarried.   10

Another Woman's Ghost rises.

5 *GHOST.*

Its mother I, whom you whipt black and blue;
Both owe our deaths to you, to you, to you.
                          [All Ghosts shake their heads.

Sir *ROGER.*

Why do you shake your mealy heads at me?
You cannot say I did it———

BOTH JUSTICES.

———————————No—nor we.

1 *GHOST.*

All three———

2 *GHOST.*

———All three———

3 *GHOST.*

———All three———

4 *GHOST.*

———All three———

5 *GHOST.*

———————————All three.

A SONG sung dismally by a GHOST.

Y E *goblins, and fairys,*
   With frisks and vagarys,
Ye fairys and goblins,
With hoppings and hobblings,
   Come all, come all
To Sir Roger's *great hall.*

                                20

All fairys and goblins,
All goblins and fairys,
With hoppings and hobblings,
With frisks and vagarys.

13 mealy heads]. As if covered with powder or flour.   17 *vagarys*] Pranks.

CHORUS.

Sing, goblins and fairys,
Sing, fairys and goblins,
With frisks and vagarys,
And hoppings and hobblings.

> [*The ghosts dance round the Justices, who go*
> *off in a fright, and the ghosts vanish.*

ACT II. SCENE I.

A Field.

TIMOTHY PEASCOD *bound*; CORPORAL, SOLDIERS, *and*
COUNTRYMEN.

CORPORAL.

STAND off there, countrymen; and you, the guard,
Keep close your pris'ner——see that all's prepar'd.
Prime all your firelocks——fasten well the stake.

PEASCOD.

'Tis too much, too much trouble for my sake.
O fellow-soldiers, countrymen and friends,
Be warn'd by me to shun untimely ends:
For evil courses am I brought to shame,
And from my soul I do repent the same.
Oft my kind *Grannam* told me——*Tim*, take warning,
Be good—and say thy pray'rs—and mind thy learning.   10
But I, sad wretch, went on from crime to crime;
I play'd at nine-pins first in sermon time:
I rob'd the Parson's orchard next; and then
(For which I pray forgiveness) stole—a hen.
When I was press'd, I told them the first day
I wanted heart to fight, so ran away;
> [*Attempts to run off, but is prevented.*
For which behold I die. 'Tis a plain case,
'Twas all a judgment for my want of grace.
> [*The soldiers prime, with their muskets towards him.*
Hold, hold, my friends; nay, hold, hold, hold, I pray;
They may go off——and I have more to say.   20

1 *COUNTRYMAN.*

Come, 'tis no time to talk———

2 *COUNTRYMAN.*

——————————Repent thine ill,
And pray in this good book.——   [*Gives him a book.*

PEASCOD.

————————————————I will, I will.
Lend me thy handkercher—*The Pilgrim's pro*————
                                        [*Reads and weeps.*
(I cannot see for tears) *Pro—Progress—Oh!*
The Pilgrim's Progress—eighth—edi—ti—on
Lon-don-prin-ted—for—Ni-cho-las Bod-ding-ton:
With new ad-di-tions never made before.
Oh! 'tis so moving, I can read no more.   [*Drops the book.*

SCENE II.

PEASCOD, CORPORAL, SOLDIERS, COUNTRYMEN, SERGEANT,
FILBERT.

SERGEANT.

What whining's this?—boys, see your guns well ramm'd.
You dog, die like a soldier—and be damn'd.

FILBERT.

My friend in ropes!————

PEASCOD.

——————————————I should not thus be bound,
If I had Means, and could but raise five pound.
The cruel Corp'ral whisper'd in my ear,
Five pounds, if rightly tipt, would set me clear.

25 *eighth—edi—ti—on*] The *Complete Key* suggests, with typical obtuseness, that this
passage was intended as a hit at Addison's *Cato*, which happened also to be in its eighth
edition.

FILBERT.

Here——*Peascod*, take my pouch—'tis all I own.
(For what is Means and life when *Kitty*'s gone!)
'Tis my press-money——can this silver fail?
'Tis all, except one sixpence spent in ale.   10
This had a ring for *Kitty*'s finger bought,
Kitty on me had by that token thought.
But for thy life, poor *Tim*, if this can do't;
Take it, with all my soul——thou'rt welcome to't.

                                [*Offers him his purse.*

1 COUNTRYMAN.

And take my fourteen pence——

2 COUNTRYMAN.

————————————————And my cramp-ring.
Would, for thy sake, it were a better thing.

3 COUNTRYMAN.

And master Sergeant, take my box of copper

4 COUNTRYMAN.

And my wife's thimble————

5 COUNTRYMAN.

——————————————And this 'bacco-stopper.

SERGEANT.

No bribes. Take back your things—I'll have them not.

PEASCOD.

Oh! must I die?————

CHORUS of COUNTRYMEN.

——————————Oh! must poor *Tim* be shot!   20

PEASCOD.

But let me kiss thee first——   [*Embracing* Filbert.

---

15 cramp-ring] A ring superstitiously believed to ward off the cramp.

SCENE III.

PEASCOD, CORPORAL, SOLDIERS, COUNTRYMEN, SERGEANT,
FILBERT, DORCAS.

DORCAS.

——————————————————Ah, brother *Tim*.
Why these close hugs? I owe my shame to him.
He scorns me now, he leaves me in the lurch;
In a white sheet poor I must stand at church.
O marry me—[*To* Filbert.] Thy sister is with child.   [*To* Tim.
And he, 'twas he my tender heart beguil'd.

PEASCOD.

Could'st thou do this? could'st thou—   [*In anger to* Filbert.

SERGEANT.

——————————————————Draw out the men:
Quick to the stake; you must be dead by ten.

DORCAS.

Be dead! must *Tim* be dead!——

PEASCOD.

——————————————————He must—he must.

DORCAS.

Ah! I shall sink downright; my heart will burst.   10
—Hold, Sergeant, hold—yet e'er you sing the Psalms,
Ah! let me ease my conscience of its qualms.
O brother, brother! *Filbert* still is true.
I fouly wrong'd him——do, forgive me, do.   [*To* Filb.
The Squire betray'd me; nay,—and what is worse,
Brib'd me with two gold guineas in this purse,
To swear the child to *Filbert*.————

PEASCOD.

——————————————————What a *Jew*
My sister is!——Do, *Tom*, forgive her, do.   [*To* Filb.

FILBERT.   [*Kisses* Dorcas.

But see thy base-born child, thy babe of shame,
Who left by thee, upon our parish came;
Comes for thy blessing.————   20

SCENE IV.

PEASCOD, CORPORAL, SOLDIERS, COUNTRYMEN, SERGEANT,
FILBERT, DORCAS, JOYCE.

PEASCOD.

————————————Oh! my sins of youth!
Why on the haycock didst thou tempt me, *Ruth*?
O save me, Sergeant;——how shall I comply?
I love my daughter so——I cannot die.

JOYCE.

Must father die! and I be left forlorn?
A lack a day! that ever *Joyce* was born!
No grandsire in his arms e'er dandled me,
And no fond mother danc'd me on her knee.
They said, if ever father got his pay,
I should have two-pence ev'ry market day.   10

PEASCOD.

Poor child; hang sorrow, and cast care behind thee,
The parish by this badge is bound to find thee.
                     [*Pointing to the badge on her arm.*

JOYCE.

The parish finds indeed——but our church-wardens
Feast on the silver, and give us the farthings.
Then my school-mistress, like a vixen *Turk*,
Maintains her lazy husband by our work:
Many long tedious days I've worsted spun;
She grudg'd me victuals when my task was done.
Heav'n send me a good service! for I now
Am big enough to wash, or milk a cow.   20

PEASCOD.

O that I had by charity been bred!
I then had been much better—taught than fed.
Instead of keeping nets against the law,
I might have learnt accounts, and sung *Sol-fa*.
Farewel, my child; spin on, and mind thy book,
And send thee store of grace therein to look.
Take warning by thy shameless Aunt; lest thou
Should'st o'er thy bastard weep——as I do now.
Mark my last words——an honest living get;
Beware of Papishes, and learn to knit.   30

> [*Dorcas leads out* Joyce *sobbing and crying.*

SCENE V.

PEASCOD, CORPORAL, SOLDIERS, COUNTRYMEN, SERGEANT,
FILBERT.

FILBERT.

Let's drink before we part——for sorrow's dry.
To *Tim's* safe passage——

> [*Takes out a brandy-bottle, and drinks.*

1 COUNTRYMAN.

————————————I'll drink too.

2 COUNTRYMAN.

————————————And I.

PEASCOD.

Stay, let me pledge—'tis my last earthly liquor.   [*Drinks.*
——When I am dead you'll bind my grave with wicker.

> [*They lead him to the stake.*

1 COUNTRYMAN.

He was a special ploughman————   [*Sighing.*

2 COUNTRYMAN.

————————————Harrow'd well!

D

3 *COUNTRYMAN.*

And at our maypole ever bore the bell!

PEASCOD.

Say, is it fitting in this very field,
Where I so oft have reap'd, so oft have till'd;
This field, where from my youth I've been a carter,   10
I, in this field, should die for a deserter?

FILBERT.

'Tis hard, 'tis wondrous hard!——

SERGEANT.

————————————Zooks, here's a pother.
Strip him; I'd stay no longer for my brother.

PEASCOD.

                    [*Distributing his things among his friends.*
Take you my 'bacco-box—my neckcloth, you.
To our kind Vicar send this bottle-skrew.
But wear these breeches, *Tom*; they're quite bran-new.

FILBERT.

Farewell————

1 *COUNTRYMAN.*

————B'ye, *Tim.*————

2 *COUNTRYMAN.*

————B'ye, *Tim.*

3 *COUNTRYMAN.*

————————————Adieu.

4 *COUNTRYMAN.*

————————————————Adieu.
[*They all take their leave of* Peascod *by shaking hands with him.*

SCENE VI.

PEASCOD, CORPORAL, SOLDIERS, COUNTRYMEN, SERGEANT,
FILBERT, *to them a* SOLDIER *in great haste.*

SOLDIER.

Hold——why so furious, Sergeant? by your leave,
Untye the pris'ner—see, here's a reprieve.

> [*Shows a paper.*

CHORUS of *COUNTRYMEN.*   [*Huzzaing.*

A reprieve, a reprieve, a reprieve!

> [Peascod *is unty'd, and embraces his friends.*

SCENE VII.

PEASCOD, CORPORAL, SOLDIERS, COUNTRYMEN, SERGEANT,
FILBERT, CONSTABLE.

CONSTABLE.

Friends, reprehend him, reprehend him there.

SERGEANT.

For what?——

CONSTABLE.

————For stealing gaffer *Gap*'s gray mare.

> [*They seize the* Sergeant.

PEASCOD.

Why, heark ye, heark, ye, friend; you'll go to pot.
Would you be rather hang'd—hah!——hang'd or shot?

SERGEANT.

Nay, hold, hold, hold——

PEASCOD.

————————————Not if you were my brother.
Why, friend, should you not hang as well's another?

CONSTABLE.

Thus said Sir *John*—the law must take its course;
'Tis law that he may 'scape who steals a horse.
But (said Sir *John*) the statutes all declare,
The man shall sure be hang'd—that steals a mare.   10

PEASCOD.   [*To the* Sergeant.

Ay—right—he shall be hang'd that steals a mare.
He shall be hang'd—that's certain; and good cause.
A rare good sentence this—how is't?—the laws
No—not the laws—the statutes all declare,
The man that steals a mare shall sure—be—hang'd,
No, no—he shall be hang'd that steals a mare.
   [*Exit* Sergeant *guarded*, Countrymen, &c. *huzzaing after him.*

SCENE VIII.

KITTY, *with her hair loose*, GRANDMOTHER, AUNT, HAYMAKERS,
CHORUS *of* SIGHS *and* GROANS.

KITTY.

Dear happy fields, farewell; ye flocks, and you
Sweet meadows, glitt'ring with the pearly dew:
And thou, my rake, companion of my cares,
Giv'n by my mother in my younger years:
With thee the toils of full eight springs I've known,
'Tis to thy help I owe this hat and gown;
On thee I lean'd, forgetful of my work,
While *Tom* gaz'd on me, propt upon his fork:
Farewell, farewell; for all thy task is o'er,
Kitty shall want thy service now no more.
                              [*Flings away the rake.*

CHORUS *of* SIGHS *and* GROANS.

Ah———O!——Sure never was the like before!

KITTY.

Happy the maid, whose sweetheart never hears   12
The soldier's drum, nor writ of Justice fears.

Our bans thrice bid! and for our wedding day
My kerchief bought! then press'd, then forc'd away!

CHORUS of SIGHS and GROANS.

Ah! O! poor soul! alack! and well a day!

KITTY.

You, *Bess*, still reap with *Harry* by your side;
You, *Jenny*, shall next *Sunday* be a bride:
But I forlorn!——This ballad shews my care;
                                    [*Gives Susan a ballad.*
Take this sad ballad, which I bought at fair:
Susan can sing——do you the burthen bear.

A BALLAD.

I.

'*TWAS* when the seas were roaring   22
  With hollow blasts of wind;
A damsel lay deploring,
  All on a rock reclin'd.
Wide o'er the rolling billows
  She cast a wistful look;
Her head was crown'd with willows
  That tremble o'er the brook.

II.

Twelve months are gone and over,   30
  And nine long tedious days.
Why didst thou, ven'trous lover,
  Why didst thou trust the seas?
Cease, cease, thou cruel ocean,
  And let my lover rest:
Ah! what's thy troubled motion
  To that within my breast?

III.

The merchant, rob'd of pleasure,
  Sees tempests in despair;
But what's the loss of treasure   40
  To losing of my dear?

Should you some coast be laid on
    Where gold and di'monds grow,
You'd find a richer maiden,
    But none that loves you so.

IV.

How can they say that nature
    Has nothing made in vain;
Why then beneath the water
    Should hideous rocks remain?
No eyes the rocks discover,   50
    That lurk beneath the deep,
To wreck the wand'ring lover,
    And leave the maid to weep.

V.

All melancholy lying,
    Thus wail'd she for her dear;
Repay'd each blast with sighing,
    Each billow with a tear;
When' o'er the white wave stooping,
    His floating corpse she spy'd;
Then like a lilly drooping,   60
    She bow'd her head, and dy'd.

KITTY.

Why in this world should wretched *Kitty* stay?
What if these hands should make my self away?
I could not sure do otherways than well.
A maid so true's too innocent for hell.
But hearkye, *Cis*———   [*Whispers and gives her a penknife.*

AUNT.

————————I'll do't——'tis but to try
If the poor soul can have the heart to die.
                                        [*Aside to the* Haymakers.
Thus then I strike——but turn thy head aside.

KITTY.

'Tis shameless sure to fall as pigs have dy'd.
No—take this cord—   [*Gives her a cord.*

AUNT.

——————————————With this thou shalt be sped.   70
                    [*Putting the noose round her neck.*

KITTY.

But curs are hang'd.——

AUNT.

——————————————Christians should die in bed.

KITTY.

Then lead me thither; there I'll moan and weep,
And close these weary eyes in death.

AUNT.

————————————————————or sleep.   [*Aside.*

KITTY.

When I am cold, and stretch'd upon my bier,
My restless sprite shall walk at midnight here:
Here shall I walk——for 'twas beneath yon tree
Filbert first said he lov'd——lov'd only me.   [*Kitty faints.*

GRANDMOTHER.

She swoons, poor Soul—help, *Dolly*.

AUNT.

————————————————She's in fits.
Bring water, water, water.——   [*Screaming.*

GRANDMOTHER.

——————————————————Fetch her wits.
                    [*They throw water upon her.*

KITTY.

Hah!—I am turn'd a stream—look all below;   80
It flows, and flows, and will for ever flow.
The meads are all afloat—the haycocks swim.
Hah! who comes here!—my *Filbert!* drown not him.
Bagpipes in butter, flocks in fleecy fountains,
Churns, sheep-hooks, seas of milk, and honey mountains.

SCENE IX.

Kitty, Grandmother, Aunt, Haymakers, Filbert.

KITTY.

It is his ghost——or is it he indeed?
Wert thou not sent to war? hah, dost thou bleed?
No——'tis my *Filbert*.

        FILBERT.   [*Embracing her.*

————————————Yes, 'tis he, 'tis he.
Dorcas confess'd; the Justice set me free.
I'm thine again.————

        KITTY.

————————I thine————

        FILBERT.

————————————Our fears are fled.
Come, let's to Church, to Church.————

        KITTY.

————————————To wed.

        FILBERT.

————————————————To bed.

CHORUS of *HAYMAKERS.*

A wedding, a bedding; a wedding, a bedding.
        [*Exeunt all the Actors.*

Sir Roger. Ay, now for the wedding. Where's he that plays the Parson. Now, neighbours, you shall see what was never shewn upon the *London* stage. ——Why, heigh day! what's our Play at a stand?   10

Enter a Countryman.

Countryman. So, please your worship, I should have play'd the Parson, but our Curate would not lend his gown, for he says it is a profanation.

Sir Roger. What a scrupulous whim is this? an innocent thing! believe me, an innocent thing.
        [*The Justices assent by nods and signs.*

Enter Stave *the Parish-Clark.*

Stave. Master Doctor saith he hath two and twenty good reasons against it from the Fathers, and he is come himself to utter them unto your Worship.

Sir Roger. What, shall our Play be spoil'd? I'll have none of his reasons—call in Mr. *Inference.*

Stave *goes out, and re-enters.*

Stave. Sir, he saith he never greatly affected stage Plays.
Within. Stave, Stave, Stave.   20
Sir Roger. Tell him that I say——
Within. Stave, Stave.
Sir Roger. What, shall the Curate controul me? have not I the presentation? tell him that I will not have my Play spoil'd; nay, that he shall marry the couple himself—I say, he shall.

Stave *goes out, and re-enters.*

Stave. The steward hath perswaded him to join their hands in the parlour within—but he saith he will not, and cannot in conscience consent to expose his character before neighbouring gentlemen; neither will he enter into your worship's hall; for he calleth it a stage *pro tempore.*

Sir Humphry. Very likely: The good man may have reason.   30
Justice Statute. In troth, we must in some sort comply with the scrupulous tender conscienc'd doctor.
Sir Roger. Why, what's a Play without a marriage? and what is a marriage, if one sees nothing of it? Let him have his humour—but set the doors wide open, that we may see how all goes on.   [*Exit* Stave.
                                                     [*Sir* Roger *at the door pointing.*
So natural! d'ye see now, neighbours? the ring i-faith. To have and to hold! right again—well play'd, doctor; well play'd, Son *Thomas.* Come, come, I'm satisfy'd—now for the fiddles and dances.

Enter Steward, *Squire* Thomas, Kitty, Stave, *&c.*

Steward. Sir *Roger,* you are very merry.

> So comes a reck'ning when the banquet's o'er,   40
> The dreadful reck'ning, and men smile no more.

I wish you joy of your Play, and of your daughter. I had no way but this to repair the injury your son had done my child—she shall study to deserve your favour.   [*Presenting* Kitty *to Sir* Roger.
Sir Roger. Married! how married! can the marriage of *Filbert* and *Carrot* have any thing to do with my son?

Steward. But the marriage of *Thomas* and *Katherine* may, Sir *Roger.*

Sir Roger. What a plague, am I trick'd then? I must have a stage Play, with a pox!

Sir Humphry. If this speech be in the play, remember the tankard, Sir *Roger.*   51

Squire Thomas. Zooks, these stage plays are plaguy dangerous things—but I am no such fool neither, but I know this was all your contrivance.

Justice Statute. Ay, Sir *Roger*, you told us it was you that gave him the hint.

Sir Roger. Why blockhead! puppy! had you no more wit than to say the ceremony? he should only have married you in rhime, fool.

Squire Thomas. Why, what did I know, ha? but so it is—and since murder will out, as the saying is; look ye father, I was under some sort of a promise too, d'ye see—so much for that—If I be a husband, I be a husband, there's an end on't.—sure I must have been married some time or other.   60

        [*Sir* Roger *walks up and down fretting, and goes out in a passion.*

Sir Humphry. In troth, it was in some sort my opinion before; it is good in law.

Justice Statute. Good in law, good in law—but hold, we must not lose the dance.

A DANCE.

EPILOGUE.

STAVE.

Our stage Play has a moral—and no doubt
You all have sense enough to find it out.

THREE HOURS
AFTER MARRIAGE

John Gay
1685–1732

Alexander Pope
1688–1744

John Arbuthnot
1667–1735

It might well be argued that *Three Hours after Marriage* is properly a dramatic satire rather than a burlesque: but the play's claim to the long-overdue dignity of a modern reprint, and the theatrical interest of much of its satire, have been considered sufficient reasons for its inclusion in the present collection. Those lapses of taste for which it has been condemned and effectively censored by generations of literary historians have at least the virtue of directness, and a similar feeling of frankness distinguishes even the passages of *double-entendre*. Certainly, those who are misled by the title into expecting intimate wedding-night revelations will be sadly disappointed: for at the level of its main action, *Three Hours* is simply an efficient and actable farce, its interest deriving from an ingenious plot, and from characters whose obsession with sex is humorous, in the Jonsonian sense, rather than lascivious.

Three Hours was first staged for seven consecutive nights in January 1717— no mean run in those days. Then—possibly owing to Colley Cibber's belated recognition that his own role of Plotwell was a self-caricature—it went unperformed for twenty years, eventually to be forgotten altogether. It was a product of that collaboration between Pope, Gay, and Arbuthnot which later fathered *The Memoirs of Martin Scriblerus*, and which directly inspired Gay's *Beggar's Opera*, Swift's *Gulliver's Travels*, and Pope's *Dunciad*. Not unexpectedly, therefore, its ostensible horseplay concealed—though not too carefully—barbed attacks on various literary and personal enemies of its authors. Fossile himself caricatured one Doctor Woodward, Townley was the wayward wife of Pope's own physician, and the peripheral Lady Hippokekoana—whose non-appearance is as resounding as that of Mrs. Grundy herself—was the Duchess of Monmouth. These identifications are of no more than historical interest—but the originals of Miss Phoebe Clinket and of Sir Tremendous throw necessary light on the nature of the play's theatrical satire. Miss Clinket (in spite of George Sherburn's arguments in favour of her identification with Susanna Centlivre) was almost certainly intended to make gentle mock of that 'well-bred poetess', the Countess of Winchelsea, who was as obsessive a scribbler as Phoebe herself. And Sir Tremendous was undoubtedly a caricature of John Dennis, whose *Remarks Upon Mr. Pope's Translation of Homer*, made one month after the performances of *Three Hours*, were embittered by the portrayal. Breval's play *The Confederates*—a 'farce in rime' and a cruel but competent burlesque—also attacked the three friends, but much more directly, by showing them awaiting and discussing the reception of their brainchild in a tavern adjoining the theatre. And Cibber himself hit back a month later, by interpolating some adverse references to the crocodile-and-mummy episodes in a revival of *The Rehearsal*.

It was, then, as much its real scurrility as its supposed obscenity which first held back revivals of the piece. Judged as a mannered comedy the play is admittedly coarse-grained. But it is as a comedy of humours—of literary dilettantism, of obsessive antiquarianism and of sexual possessiveness—that *Three Hours after Marriage* really works: its irreverence becomes central to its moral purpose, and its convolutions of plot fully justified. And as burlesque, the Clinket-Tremendous episodes make their unexceptionable points about pretentious tragedizing, and about the critic's wielding of scissors according to his own book of arbitrary rules. It is also significant that contemporary attacks on the piece suggested that it plagiarized Gherardi's collection, *Théâtre Italien*—for this claim, though it could scarcely be substantiated in detail, does suggest validly enough the play's similar freedom from the conventions which usually inhibited overlappings between the comic genres. Thus, an attempt in production to recognize and then to synthesize the elements of humours comedy, of farce, and of burlesque might best bring out the distinctive and surely enduring theatrical qualities of *Three Hours after Marriage*.

Three Hours after Marriage.

A
COMEDY,

As it is Acted at the
Theatre Royal.

Rumpatur, quisquis rumpitur invidia.
MART.

LONDON:
Printed for BERNARD LINTOT between the
Temple Gates, *Fleetstreet.* 1717.

ADVERTISEMENT.

IT may be necessary to acquaint the reader, that this play is printed exactly as it is acted.

I must farther own the assistance I have receiv'd in this piece from two of my friends; who, tho' they will not allow me the honour of having their names join'd with mine, cannot deprive me of the pleasure of making this acknowledgment.

JOHN GAY.

two of my friends] That these friends were, in fact, Pope and Arbuthnot was generally known, in spite of the reticence of Gay's acknowledgement.

PROLOGUE.

Spoke by Mr. WILKS.

*A*UTHORS *are judg'd by strange capricious rules,*
   The great ones are thought mad, the small ones fools.
Yet sure the best are most severely fated,
For fools are only laugh'd at, wits are hated.
Blockheads with reason, men of sense abhor;
But fool 'gainst fool is barb'rous civil war.
Why on all authors then should critics fall?
Since some have writ, and shewn no wit at all.
Condemn a play of theirs, and they evade it,
Cry, damn not us, but damn the French that made it;   10
By running goods, these graceless owlers gain,
Theirs are the rules of France, the plots of Spain:
But wit, like wine, from happier climates brought,
Dash'd by these rogues, turns English common draught:
They pall Moliere's and Lopez sprightly strain,
And teach dull Harlequins to grin in vain.
How shall our author hope a gentle fate,
Who dares most impudently—not translate.
It had been civil in these ticklish times,
To fetch his fools and knaves from foreign climes;   20
Spaniards and French abuse to the world's end
But spare old England, lest you hurt a friend.
If any fool is by your satire bit,
Let him hiss loud, to show you all—he's hit.
Poets make characters as salesmen cloaths,
We take no measure of your fops and beaus.
But here all sizes and all shapes ye meet,
And fit yourselves—like chaps in Monmouth-street.

11 *running goods*] Dealing in contraband.   11 *owlers*] Smugglers, particularly those trafficking between England and France.   15 *Lopez*] Lope de Vega, the prolific Spanish playwright.   28 *chaps*] Chapmen, dealers in cheap goods.   28 *Monmouth-street*] Famous for its market in second-hand clothing.

Gallants look here, this* fool's cap has an air—
Goodly and smart,—with ears of Issachar.   30
Let no one fool engross it, or confine:
A common blessing! now 'tis your's, now mine.
But poets in all ages, had the Care
To keep this cap, for such as will, to wear;
Our author has it now, for ev'ry wit
Of course resign'd it to the next that writ:
And thus upon the stage 'tis fairly† thrown,
Let him that takes it, wear it for his own.

* Shews a cap with ears.
† Flings down the cap and   *Exit.*

30 *Issachar*] Jacob's ninth son, conventionally progenitor of a long-eared race.

Dramatis Personæ.

M E N.

FOSSILE,	} Doctors.	Mr. *Johnson.*
POSSUM,		Mr. *Corey.*
NAUTILUS,		Mr. *Cross.*
PTISAN, Apothecary.		Mr. *Wright.*
PLOTWELL,		Mr. *Cibber.*
UNDERPLOT,		Mr. *Penkethman.*
Sir TREMENDOUS,		Mr. *Bowman.*
First PLAYER,		Mr. *Diggs.*
Second PLAYER,		Mr. *Watson.*
SAILOR,		Mr. *Bickerstaff.*

Footmen, Servants, &c.

W O M E N.

Mrs. TOWNLEY,	Mrs. *Oldfield.*
Mrs. PHOEBE CLINKET,	Mrs. *Bicknell.*
SARSNET,	Mrs. *Garnet.*
PRUE,	Miss *Willis.*

Three Hours after
MARRIAGE:
A
COMEDY.

ACT I.

Enter Fossile, *leading* Townley.

Foss. WELCOME, my bride, into the habitation of thy husband. The scruples of the parson—

Town. And the fatigue of the ceremony—

Foss. Are at last well over.

Town. These blank licences are wonderful commodious.—The clergy have a noble command, in being rangers of the park of matrimony; produce but a warrant, and they deliver a lady into your possession: but I have no quarrel with them, since they have put me into so good hands.

Foss. I now proclaim a solemn suspension of arms between medicine and diseases. Let distempers suspend their malignant influence, and powders, pills, and potions their operations. Be this day sacred to my love. I had rather hold this hand of thine, than a dutchess by the pulse.   12

Town. And I this, than a hand of matadores.

Foss. Who knows but your relations may dispute my title to your person? Come, my dear, the seal of the matrimonial bond is consummation.

Town. Alas! what will become of me!

Foss. Why are thy eyes fix'd on the ground? why so slow? and why this trembling?

Town. Ah! heedless creature that I was, to quit all my relations, and trust myself alone in the hands of a strange man.   20

Foss. Courage, thou best of my curiosities. Know that in husband, is comprehended all relations; in me thou seest a fond father.

Town. Old enough o' my conscience.   [*Aside.*

13 matadores] The most valuable cards in quadrille and ombre.

Foss. You may, you must trust yourself with me.

Town. Do with me as you please: Yet sure you cannot so soon forget the office of the church. Marriage is not to be undertaken wantonly, like brute beasts. If you will transgress, the sin be upon your own head.

Foss. Great indeed is thy virtue, and laudable is thy modesty. Thou art a virgin, and I a philosopher; but learn, that no animal action, *quatenus animal*, is unbecoming of either of us. But hold! where am I going? Prithee, my dear, of what age art thou?   31

Town. Almost three and twenty.

Foss. And I almost at my grand climacterick. What occasion have I for a double-night at these years? She may be an Alcmena, but alas! I am no thunderer.   [*Aside.*

Town. You seem somewhat disturb'd; I hope you are well, Mr. Fossile.

Foss. What business have I in the bed-chamber, when the symptoms of age are upon me? Yet hold, this is the famous corroborative of Crollius; in this vial are included sons and daughters. Oh, for a draught of the *aqua magna-nimitatis* for a vehicle! fifty drops of *liquid laudanum* for her dose would but just put us upon a *par. Laudanum* would settle the present ataxy of her animal spirits, and prevent her being too watchful.   [*Aside.*

Enter a Servant.

Serv. Sir, your pistachoe-porridge is ready.   [*Exit.*

Foss. Now I think of it, my dear; Venus, which is in the first degree of Capricorn, does not culminate till ten; an hour if astrology is not fallible, successful in generation.   46

Town. I am all obedience, Sir.

Foss. How shall I reward thee for so much Goodness? let our wedding as yet be a secret in the family. In the mean time I'll introduce my niece Phoebe Clinket to your acquaintance: but alas, the poor girl has a procidence of the pineal gland, which has occasioned a rupture in her understanding. I took her into my house to regulate my oeconomy; but instead of puddings, she makes pastorals; or when she should be raising paste, is raising some ghost in a new tragedy. In short, my house is haunted by all the underling players, broken booksellers, half-voic'd singing-masters, and disabled dancing-masters in town. In a former will I had left her my estate; but I now resolve that heirs of my own begetting shall inherit. Yonder she comes in her usual occupation. Let us mark her a while.   58

Enter Clinket *and her* Maid *bearing a writing-desk on her back.* Clinket *writing, her head dress stain'd with ink, and pens stuck in her hair.*

34 She may be an Alcmena . . .] The reference is to the wife of Amphitryon, who, during the latter's absence, was seduced by Jove in her husband's shape: conventionally, any faithful wife who deceives her husband unknowingly.

Maid. I had as good carry a raree-show about the streets. Oh! how my back akes! 60

Clink. What are the labours of the back to those of the brain? thou scandal to the muses. I have now lost a thought worth a folio, by thy impertinance.

Maid. Have not I got a crick in my back already, that will make me good for nothing, with lifting your great books?

Clink. Folio's, call them, and not great books, thou monster of impropriety: But have patience, and I will remember the three gallery-tickets I promis'd thee at my new tragedy.

Maid. I shall never get my head-cloaths clear-starch'd at this rate.

Clink. Thou destroyer of learning, thou worse than a book-worm; thou hast put me beyond all patience. Remember how my lyrick ode bound about a tallow-candle; thy wrapping up snuff in an epigram; nay, the unworthy usage of my hymn to Apollo, filthy creature! Read me the last lines I writ upon the deluge, and take care to pronounce them as I taught you. 73

Maid. Swell'd with a dropsy, sickly nature lies,
And melting in a diabetes, dies. [*Reads with an affected tone.*

Clink. Still without cadence!

Maid. Swell'd with a dropsy—

Clink. Hold. I conceive—
The roaring seas o'er the tall woods have broke,
And whales now perch upon the sturdy oak. 80
Roaring? stay. Rumbling, roaring, rustling, no; raging seas. [*Writing.*
The raging seas o'er the tall woods have broke,
Now perch, thou whale, upon the sturdy oak.
Sturdy oak? no; steady, strong, strapping, stiff.
Stiff? no, stiff is too short.

Fossile *and* Townley *come forward.*

What feast for fish! Oh too luxurious treat!
When hungry dolphins feed on butchers meat.

Foss. Niece, why niece, niece! oh, Melpomene, thou goddess of tragedy, suspend thy influence for a moment, and suffer my niece to give me a rational answer. This lady is a friend of mine; her present circumstances oblige her to take sanctuary in my house; treat her with the utmost civility. Let the tea-table be made ready. 92

Clink. Madam, excuse this absence of mind; my animal spirits had deserted the avenues of my senses, and retired to the recesses of the brain, to contemplate a beautiful idea. I could not force the vagrant creatures back again into their posts, to move those parts of the body that express civility.

59 raree-show] A peep-show set up in a portable box.

Town. A rare affected creature this! If I mistake not, flattery will make her an useful tool for my purpose.   [*Aside.*
                    [*Exeunt* Townley, Clinket, *and* Maid.

Foss. Her jewels, her strong box, and all her things left behind! If her uncle should discover her marriage, he may lay an embargo upon her goods. —I'll send for them.   101

Enter a Boy *with a letter.*

Boy. This is the ho-ho-house.
Foss. Child, whom dost thou want?
Boy. Mistress Townley's ma-ma-maid.
Foss. What is your business?
Boy. A l-l-letter.
Foss. Who sent this letter?
Boy. O-o-one.
Foss. Give it me, child. An honest boy. Give it me, and I'll deliver it my-self. A very honest boy.   110
Boy. So.   [*Exit* Boy.
Foss. There are now no more secrets between us. Man and wife are one.

'Madam, either I mistake the encouragement I have had, or I am to be 'happy to-night. I hope the same person will compleat her good offices: I 'stand to articles. The ring is a fine one; and I shall have the pleasure of 'putting it on the first time.
                    'This from your impatient, R.P.'

In the name of Beelzebub, what is this? encouragement! happy to-night! same person! good offices! whom hast thou married, poor Fossile? couldst thou not still divert thyself with the spoils of quarries and coal-pits, thy serpents and thy salamanders, but thou must have a living monster too! 'sdeath! what a jest shall I be to our club! is there no rope among my curiosities? shall I turn her out of doors, and proclaim my infamy; or lock her up and bear my misfortunes? lock her up! impossible. One may shut up volatile spirits, pen up the air, confine bears, lyons and tygers, nay, keep even your gold: but a wanton wife, who can keep?   126

Enter Townley.

Town. Mrs. Clinket's play is to be read this morning at the tea-table: will you come and divert yourself, Sir?
Foss. No: I want to be alone.
Town. I hope my company is not troublesome already. I am as yet a bride; not a wife. [*Sighs.*] What means this sudden change? [*Aside.*] Consider, Mr

Fossile, you want your natural rest: the bed would refresh you. Let me sit by
you.   133

Foss. My head akes, and the bed always makes it worse.

Town. Is it hereabouts?   [*Rubbing his temples.*

Foss. Too sure.   [*Turns from her.*

Town. Why so fretful, Mr. Fossile?

Foss. No, I'll dissemble my passion, and pump her. [*Aside.*] Excess of joy,
my dear, for my good fortune overcomes me. I am somewhat vertiginous, I
can hardly stand.   140

Town. I hope I was ordain'd for thy support.

Foss. My disorder now begins to dissipate: it was only a little flatulency,
occasion'd by something hard of digestion. But pray, my dear, did your uncle
shut you up so close from the conversation of mankind?

Town. Sarsnet and Shock were my only company.

Foss. A very prudent young woman this Sarsnet; she was undoubtedly a
good and faithful friend in your solitude.

Town. When it was her interest; but I made no intimacies with my
chamber-maid.

Foss. But was there no lover offer'd his service to a lady in distress.   150

Town. Tongue, be upon thy guard: these questions must be design'd to
trap me. [*Aside.*] A woman of my condition can't well escape importunity.

Foss. What was the name of that disagreeable fellow, who, you told me,
teaz'd you so?

Town. His name? I think he had a thousand names. In one letter he was
Myrtillo, in another Corydon, Alexis, and I don't know what.

Enter Sarsnet *in haste to her mistress. He runs and embraces her with
great earnestness.*

Foss. Dear Mrs. Sarsnet, how am I oblig'd to thee for thy services: thou
hast made me happy beyond expression.—I shall find another letter upon
her.   [*Aside.*

He gets his hand into Sarsnet's *pocket, as searching for a letter. Whenever*
Sarsnet *goes to whisper her mistress, he gets between them.*

Enter Ptisan.

Ptis. Mrs. Colloquintida complains still of a dejection of appetite; she says
that the genevre is too cold for her stomach.   161

Foss. Give her a quieting draught; but let us not interrupt one another.
Good Mr. Ptisan, we are upon business.

[Fossile *gets between* Sarsnet *and* Townley.

145 Shock] Presumably the lap-dog to which Townley refers later in the act. Also the name
of Belinda's lap-dog in Pope's *Rape of the Lock*.   161 genevre] Obs. form of 'gin'.

Ptis. The colonel's spitting is quite suppress'd.

Foss. Give him a quieting draught. Come tomorrow, Mr. Ptisan; I can see no body till then.

Ptis. Lady Varnish finds no benefit of the waters; for the pimple on the tip of her nose still continues.

Foss. Give her a quieting draught.

Ptis. Mrs. Prudentia's tympany grows bigger and bigger. What, no pearl cordial! must I quiet them all?   171

Foss. Give them all quieting draughts, I say, or blister them all, as you please. Your servant Mr. Ptisan.

Ptis. But then lady Giddy's vapours. She calls her chamber-maids nymphs; for she fancies herself Diana, and her husband Acteon.

Foss. I can attend no patient til to morrow. Give her a quieting draught, I say.

Whenever Fossile *goes to conduct* Ptisan *to the door,* Sarsnet *and* Townley
attempt to whisper; Fossile *gets between them, and* Ptisan *takes that*
opportunity of coming back.

Ptis. Then, sir, there is miss Chitty of the boarding-school has taken in no natural sustenance for this week, but a halfpenny worth of charcoal, and one of her mittens.

Foss. Sarsnet, do you wait on Mr. Ptisan to the door. To morrow let my patients know I'll visit round.   [*A knocking at the door.*

Ptis. Oh, sir; here is a servant of the countess of Hippokekoana. The emetick has over-wrought and she is in convulsions.   183

Foss. This is unfortunate. Then I must go. Mr. Ptisan, my dear, has some business with me in private. Retire into my closet a moment, and divert yourself with the pictures. There lies your way, madam.   [*To* Sarsnet.

                    [*Exit* Townley *at one door and* Sarsnet *at the other.*
Mr. Ptisan, pray, do you run before, and tell them I am just coming.

                                                                [*Exit Ptisan.*

All my distresses come on the neck of one another. Should this fellow get to my bride before I have bedded her, in a collection of cuckolds, what a rarity should I make! What shall I do? I'll lock her up. Lock up my bride? my peace and my honour demand it, and it shall be so. [*Locks the door.*] Thomas, Thomas!   192

Enter Footman.

I dream't last night I was robb'd. The town is over-run with rogues. Who knows but the rascal that sent the letter may be now in the house? [*Aside.*] Look up the chimney, search all the dark closets, the coal hole, the flower-pots, and forget not the empty butt in the cellar. Keep a strict watch at the door, and let no body in till my return.

                              [*Exit* Footman. *A noise at the closet-door.*

Town. [*Within.*] Who's there?—I'm lock'd in. Murder! fire!

Foss. Dear madam, I beg your pardon.   [*Unlocks the door.*

Enter Townley.

'Tis well you call'd. I am so apt to lock this door; an action meerly mechanical, not spontaneous.   201

Town. Your conduct, Mr. Fossile, for this quarter of an hour has been
somewhat mysterious. It has suggested to me what I almost blush to name;
your locking me up, confirms this suspicion. Pray speak plainly, what has
caused this alteration?   [*Fossile shews her the letter.*
Is this all?   [*Gives him the letter back.*

Foss. [*Reads.*] Either I mistake the encouragement I have had. What
encouragement?

Town. From my uncle,—if I must be your interpreter.

Foss. Or I am to be happy to night.   210

Town. To be married.—If there can be happiness in that state.

Foss. I hope the same person.

Town. Parson. Only a word mis-spell'd.—Here's jealousy for you!

Foss. Will compleat her good offices. A she-parson, I find!

Town. He is a Welshman. And the Welsh always say her instead of his.

Foss. I stand to articles.

Town. Of jointure.

Foss. The ring is a fine one, and I shall have the pleasure of putting it on
my self.

Town. Who should put on the wedding-ring but the bridegroom.   220

Foss. I beseech thee, pardon thy dear husband. Love and jealousy are
often companions, and excess of both had quite obnubilated the eyes of my
understanding.

Town. Barbarous man! I could forgive thee, if thou hadst poison'd my
father, debauch'd my sister, kill'd my lap dog; but to murder my reputation!
                                                       [*Weeps.*

Foss. Nay, I beseech thee, forgive me.   [*Kneels.*

Town. I do: but upon condition your jealous fit never returns. To a jealous
man a whisper is evidence, and a dream demonstration. A civil letter makes
him thoughtful, an innocent visit mad. I shall try you, Mr. Fossile; for don't
think I'll be deny'd company.   230

Foss. Nay, prithee, my dear; I own I have abused thee. But lest my
marriage, and this simple story should take air in the neighbourhood, to
morrow we will retire into the country together, till the secret is blown over.
I am call'd to a patient. In less than half an hour I'll be with you again, my
dear.   [*Exit Fossile.*

222 obnubilated] Obscured, clouded over.

Town. Plotwell's letter had like to have ruin'd me. 'Twas a neglect in me, not to intrust him with the secret of my marriage. A jealous bridegroom! every poison has its antidote; as credulity is the cause, so it shall be the cure of his jealousy. To morrow I must be spirited away into the country; I'll immediately let Plotwell know of my distress: and this little time with opportunity, even on his wedding-day, shall finish him a compleat husband. Intrigue assist me! and I'll act a revenge that might have been worthy the most celebrated wife in Boccace.   243

Enter Plotwell *and* Clinket.

Hah! Plotwell! which way got he hither? I must caution him to be upon his guard.

Plot. Madam, I am agreeably surpriz'd to find you here.

Town. Me, Sir? you are certainly mistaken, for I don't remember I ever saw you before.

Plot. Madam, I beg your pardon. How like a truth sounds a lye from the tongue of a fine woman.   [*Aside.*

Clink. This, Madam, is Mr. Plotwell; a Gentleman who is so infinitely obliging, as to introduce my play on the theatre, by fathering the unworthy issue of my muse, at the reading it this morning.   253

Plot. I should be proud, madam, to be a real father to any of your productions.

Clink. Mighty just. Ha, ha, ha. You know, Mr. Plotwell, that both a parrot and a player can utter human sounds, but we allow neither of them to be a judge of wit. Yet some of those people have had the assurance to deny almost all my performances the privilege of being acted. Ah! what a *Goût de travers* rules the understanding of the illiterate!   260

Plot. There are some, madam, that nauseate the smell of a rose.

Whenever Plotwell *and* Townley *endeavour to talk, she interrupts them.*

Clink. If this piece be not rais'd to the sublime, let me henceforth be stigmatiz'd as a reptile in the dust of mediocrity. I am persuaded, Sir, your adopted child will do you no dishonour.

Town. Pray, madam, what is the subject?

Clink. Oh! beyond every thing. So adapted for tragical machines! so proper to excite the passions! not in the least encumber'd with episodes! the vraysemblance and the miraculous are linkt together with such propriety.

Town. But the subject, madam?

Clink. The universal Deluge. I chose that of Deucalion and Pyrrha, because neither our stage nor actors are hallow'd enough for sacred story.   272

Plot. But, madam—   [*To* Townley.

Clink. What just occasion for noble description! these players are exceeding dilatory.—In the mean time, Sir, shall I be oblig'd to you and this lady for the rehearsal of a scene that I have been just touching up with some lively strokes.

Town. I dare assure you, madam, it will be a pleasure to us both. I'll take this occasion to inform you of my present circumstances.

[*To* Plotwell.

Clink. Imagine Deucalion and Pyrrha in their boat. They pass by a promontory, where stands prince Hæmon, a former lover of Pyrrha's, ready to be swallowed up by the devouring flood. She presses her husband to take him into the boat. Your part, Sir, is Hæmon; the lady personates Pyrrha; and I represent Deucalion. To you, Sir.   [*Gives* Plotwell *the manuscript.*

Plot. What ho there, sculler!   [*Reads.*

Town.   —Hæmon!

Plot.   —Yes, 'tis Hæmon!

Town. Thou seest me now sail'd from my former lodgings,
Beneath a husband's ark; yet fain I would reward
Thy proffer'd love. But Hæmon, ah, I fear   290
To morrow's eve will hide me in the country.

Clink. Not a syllable in the part! wrong, all wrong!

Plot. Through all the town, with diligent enquiries,
I sought my Pyrrha—

Clink. Beyond all patience! the part, Sir, lies before you; you are never to perplex the drama with speeches extempore.

Plot. Madam, 'tis what the top players often do.

Town. Though love denies, compassion bids me save thee.

[Plotwell *kisses her.*

Clink. Fye, Mr. Plotwell; this is against all the decorum of the stage; I will no more allow the libertinism of lip-embraces than the barbarity of killing on the stage; your best tragedians, like the ladies of quality in a visit, never turn beyond the back-part of the cheek to a salute, as thus Mr. Plotwell.   [*Kisses* Plotwell.

Plot. I don't find in Aristotle any precept against kissing.   304

Clink. Yet I would not stand upon the brink of an indecorum.

Plot. True, madam, the finishing stroke of love and revenge should never shock the eyes of an audience. But I look upon a kiss in a comedy to be upon a par with a box on the ear in a tragedy, which is frequently given and taken by your best authors.

Clink. Mighty just! for a lady can no more put up a kiss than a gentleman a box on the ear. Take my muse, Sir, into your protection. [*Gives him her play.*] The players I see are here. Your personating the author will infallibly

introduce my play on the stage, and spite of their prejudice, make the theatre
ring with applause, and teach even that injudicious Canaille to know their
own interest.   [*Exit.*

ACT II.

Plotwell, Townley, Clinket, Prue, *with Sir* Tremendous *and two* Players,
discovered seated round a Table.

Plot. GENTLEMEN, this lady who smiles on my performances, has
permitted me to introduce you and my tragedy to her tea-table.
Clink. Gentlemen, you do me honour.
1st Play. Suffer us, Sir, to recommend to your acquaintance, the famous
Sir Tremendous, the greatest critick of our age.
Plot. Sir Tremendous, I rejoice at your presence; though no lady that has
an antipathy, so sweats at a cat as some authors at a critick. Sir Tremendous,
madam, is a Gentleman who can instruct the town to dislike what has
pleased them, and to be pleased with what they disliked.
Sir Trem. Alas! what signifies one good palate when the taste of the whole
town is viciated. There is not in all this Sodom of ignorance ten righteous
cricks, who do not judge things backward.   12
Clink. I perfectly agree with Sir Tremendous: your modern tragedies are
such egregious stuff, they neither move terror nor pity.
Plot. Yes, madam, the pity of the audience on the first night, and the terror
of the author for the third. Sir Tremendous's plays indeed have rais'd a
sublimer passion, astonishment.
Clink. I perceive here will be a wit-combat between these beaux-esprits.
Prue, be sure you set down all the similes.

Prue *retires to the back part of the stage with pen and ink.*

Sir Trem. The subjects of most modern plays are as ill chosen as—
Plot. The patrons of their dedications.   [Clink. *makes signs to* Prue.
Sir Trem. Their plots as shallow—   22
Plot. As those of bad poets against new plays.
Sir Trem. Their episodes as little of a piece to the main action, as—
Clink. A black gown with a pink-colour'd petticoat. Mark that, Prue.
                                                                  [*Aside.*
Sir Trem. Their sentiments are so very delicate—
Plot. That like whipt syllabub they are lost before they are tasted.

314 Canaille] Literally, a pack of hounds, thus a rabble or mob.

Sir Trem. Their diction so low, that—that—

Plot. Why, that their friends are forced to call it simplicity.

1st Play. Sir, to the play if you please.   30

2d Play. We have a rehearsal this morning.

Sir Trem. And then their thefts are so open—

Plot. That the very French taylors can discover them.

Sir Trem. O what felony from the ancients! what petty larceny from the moderns! there is the famous Ephigenia of Racine, he stole his Agamemnon from Seneca, who stole it from Euripides, who stole it from Homer, who stole it from all the ancients before him. In short there is nothing so execrable as our most taking tragedies.

1st Play. O! but the immortal Shakespeare, Sir.

Sir Trem. He had no judgment.   40

2d Play. The famous Ben Johnson!

Clink. Dry.

1st Play. The tender Otway!

Sir Trem. Incorrect.

2d Play. Etheridge!

Clink. Mere chit-chat.

1st Play. Dryden!

Sir Trem. Nothing but a knack of versifying.

Clink. Ah! dear Sir Tremendous, there is that delicatesse in your sentiments!   50

Sir Trem. Ah madam! there is that justness in your notions!

Clink. I am so much charm'd with your manly penetration!

Sir Trem. I with your profound capacity!

Clink. That I am not able—

Sir Trem. That it is impossible—

Clink. To conceive—

Sir Trem. To express—

Clink. With what delight I embrace—

Sir Trem. With what pleasure I enter into—

Clink. Your ideas, most learned Sir Tremendous!   60

Sir Trem. Your sentiments, most divine Mrs. Clinket.

2d Play. The play, for heaven's sake, the play.

A tea-table brought in.

Clink. This finish'd drama is too good for an age like this.

Plot. The Universal Deluge, or the tragedy of Deucalion and Pyrrha.

[Reads.

Clink. Mr. Plotwell, I will not be deny'd the pleasure of reading it, you will pardon me.

1st Play. The deluge! the subject seems to be too recherche.

Clink. A subject untouch'd either by ancients or moderns, in which are terror and pity in perfection.

1st Play. The stage will never bear it. Can you suppose, Sir, that a box of ladies will sit three hours to see a rainy day, and a sculler in a storm; make your best of it, I know it can be nothing else.　　　　72

2d Play. If you please, madam, let us hear how it opens.

Clink. [*Reads*.] The scene opens and discovers the heavens cloudy. A prodigious shower of rain. At a distance appears the top of the mountain Parnassus; all the fields beneath are over-flowed; there are seen cattle and men swimming. The tops of steeples rise above the flood, with men and women perching on their weathercocks—

Sir Trem. Begging your pardon, Sir, I believe it can be proved, that weather-cocks are of a modern invention. Besides, if stones were dissolved, as a late philosopher hath proved, how could steeples stand?　　　81

Plot. I don't insist upon trifles. Strike it out.

Clink. Strike it out! consider what you do. In this they strike at the very foundation of the drama. Don't almost all the persons of your second act start out of stones that Deucalion and Pyrrha threw behind them? This cavil is levell'd at the whole system of the reparation of human race.

1st Play. Then the shower is absurd.

Clink. Why should not this gentleman rain, as well as other authors snow and thunder?—[*Reads*.] Enter Deucalion in a sort of waterman's habit, leading his wife Pyrrha to a boat.—Her first distress is about her going back to fetch a casket of jewels. Mind, how he imitates your great authors. The first speech has all the fire of Lee.　　　93

　　　　　Tho' heav'n wrings all the sponges of the sky,
　　　　　And pours down clouds, at once each cloud a sea.
　　　　　Not the spring tides—

Sir Trem. There were no spring tides in the Mediterranean, and consequently Deucalion could not make that simile.

Clink. A man of Deucalion's quality might have travelled beyond the Mediterranean, and so your objection is answered. Observe, Sir Tremendous, the tenderness of Otway, in this answer of Pyrrha:　　　101

　　　　　—Why do the stays
　　　　　Taper my waist, but for thy circling arms?

Sir Trem. Ah! Anachronisms! Stays are a modern habit, and the whole scene is monstrous, and against the rules of tragedy.

Plot. I submit Sir,—out with it.

80 if stones were dissolved . . .] An occurrence actually coincidental with the flood, according to Dr. Woodward's *Natural History of the Earth* (1695).

Clink. Were the play mine, you should gash my flesh, mangle my face, any thing sooner than scratch my play.

Plot. Blot and insert wherever you please—I submit myself to your judgment.   110

> Plotwell *rises and discourses apart with* Townley.

Sir Trem. Madam, nonsense and I have been at variance from my cradle, it sets my understanding on edge.

2d Play. Indeed, madam, with submission, and I think I have some experience of the stage, this play will hardly take.

Clink. The worst lines of it would be sufficiently clapt, if it had been writ by a known author, or recommended by one.

Sir Trem. Between you and I, madam, who understand better things, this gentleman knows nothing of poetry.

1st Play. The gentleman may be an honest man, but he is a damn'd writer, and it neither can take, nor ought to take.   120

Sir Trem. If you are the gentleman's friend, and value his reputation, advise him to burn it.

Clink. What struggles has an unknown author to vanquish prejudice! Suppose this play acts but six nights, his next may play twenty. Encourage a young author, I know it will be your interest.

2d Play. I would sooner give five hundred pounds than bring some plays on the stage; an audience little considers whether 'tis the author or the actor that is hiss'd, our character suffers.

1st Play. Damn our character.—We shall lose money by it.

Clink. I'll deposit a sum myself upon the success of it. Well, since it is to be play'd—I will prevail upon him to strike out some few things.—Take the play, Sir Tremendous.   132

> Sir Tremendous *reads in a muttering tone.*

Sir. Trem. Absurd to the last degree! [*Strikes out.*] palpable nonsense! [*Strikes out.*]

Clink. What all those lines! spare those for a lady's sake, for those indeed, I gave him.

Sir Trem. Such stuff! [*Strikes out.*] abominable! [*Strikes out.*] most execrable!

1st Play. This thought must out.

2d Play. Madam, with submission, this metaphor.   140

1st Play. This whole speech.

Sir Trem. The Fable!

Clink. To you I answer,—

1st Play. The characters!

Clink. To you I answer—

Sir Trem. The diction!

Clink. And to you—Ah, hold, hold,—I'm butcher'd, I'm massacred. For mercy's sake! murder, murder! ah!   [*Faints.*

Enter Fossile *peeping at the door.*

Foss. My house turn'd to a stage! and my bride playing her part too! What will become of me? but I'll know the bottom of all this. [*Aside.*] I am surprized to see so many patients here so early. What is your distemper, Sir?

1st Play. The cholic, Sir, by a surfeit of green tea and damn'd verses.

Foss. Your pulse is very high, madam. [*To* Townley.] You sympathize, I perceive, for yours is somewhat feverish. [*To* Plotwell.] But I believe I shall be able to put off the fit for this time. And as for you, niece, you have got the poetical itch, and are possess'd with nine devils, your nine muses; and thus I commit them and their works to the flames.

                    [*Takes up a heap of papers and flings them into the fire.*

Clink. Ah! I am an undone woman.

Plot. Has he burnt any bank-bills, or a new Mechlin head-dress?

Clink. My works! my works!   160

1st Play. Has he destroyed the writings of an estate, or your billet doux?

Clink. A Pindarick ode! five similes! and half an epilogue!

2d Play. Has he thrown a new fan or your pearl necklace into the flames?

Clink. Worse, worse! The tag of the acts of a new comedy! a prologue sent by a person of quality! three copies of recommendatory verses! and two Greek mottos!

Foss. Gentlemen, if you please to walk out.

2d Play. You shall have our positive answer concerning your tragedy, madam, in an hour or two.

                    [*Exit Sir* Tremendous, Plotwell *and* Players.

Foss. Though this affair looks but ill; yet I will not be over-rash. What says Lybanius? 'A false accusation often recoils upon the accuser;' and I have suffered already by too great precipitation.   [*Exit* Fossile.

Enter Sarsnet.

Town. A narrow escape, Sarsnet! Plotwells letter was intercepted and read by my husband.   174

Sars. I tremble every joint of me. How came you off?

Town. Invention flow'd, I ly'd, he believ'd. True wife, true husband!

Sars. I have often warn'd you, madam, against this superfluity of gallants; you ought at least to have clear'd all mortgages upon your person before you

164 tag of the acts] The 'fitting-together' or synopsis of the acts. Alternatively, the rhymed couplets with which each act concluded.

leas'd it out for life. Then, besides Plotwell, you are every moment in danger of Underplot, who attends on Plotwell like his shadow; he is unlucky enough to stumble upon your husband, and then I'm sure his shatterbrains would undo us at once.   182

Town. Thy wit and industry, Sarsnet, must help me out. To day is mine, to morrow is my husband's.

Sars. But some speedy method must be thought of, to prevent your letters from falling into his hands.

Town. I can put no confidence in my landlady Mrs. Chambers, since our quarrel at parting. So I have given orders to her maid to direct all letters and messages hither, and I have plac'd my own trusty servant Hugh at the door to receive them—but see, yonder comes my husband, I'll retire to my closet.   [*Exit* Townley *and* Sarsnet.

Enter Fossile.

Foss. O marriage, thou bitterest of potions, and thou strongest of astringents. This Plotwell that I found talking with her must certainly be the person that sent the letter. But if I have a Bristol stone put upon me instead of a diamond, why should I by experiments spoil its lustre? she is handsome, that is certain. Could I but keep her to myself for the future! Cuckoldom is an accute case, it is quickly over; when it takes place, it admits of no remedy but palliatives.—Be it how it will, while my marriage is a secret—

Within. Bless the noble doctor Fossile and his honourable lady. The city musick are come to wish him much joy of his marriage.   200
                                                                [*A flourish of Fiddles.*

Foss. Joy and marriage; never were two words so coupled.

Within. Much happiness attend the learned doctor Fossile and his worthy and virtuous lady. The drums and trumpets of his majesty's guards are come to salute him—   [*A flourish of Drums and Trumpets.*

Foss. Ah, Fossile! wretched Fossile! into what state hast thou brought thy self! thy disgrace proclaim'd by beat of drum! New married men are treated like those bit by a Tarantula, both must have musick: But where are the notes that can expell a wife!   [*Exit.*

---

194 Bristol stone] A transparent crystal resembling a diamond in brilliance.

E

ACT III.

Enter Fossile *in a footman's cloaths.*

Foss. A SPECIAL dog; this footman of my wife's! as mercenary as the
porter of a first minister! Why should she place him as a centinal
at my door? unquestionably, to carry on her intrigues. Why did I bribe him
to lend me his livery? to discover those intrigues. And now, O wretched
Fossile, thou hast debas'd thyself into the low character of a footman. What
then? gods and demi gods have assum'd viler shapes: they, to make a
cuckold; I, to prove myself one. Why then should my metamorphosis be
more shameful, when my purpose is more honest?

Knocking at the door. Enter Footman.

Foot. Ay, this is her livery. Friend, give this to your mistress.   9
[*Gives a letter to* Fossile *and exit.*
Foss. [*Reads.*] 'Madam, you have jilted me. What I gave you cost me dear;
'what you might have given me, would have cost you nothing. You shall
'use my next present with more respect. I presented you a fine snuff-box;
'you gave it to that coxcomb Underplot, and Underplot gave it to my wife.
'Judge of my surprise.

'Freeman.'

A fine circulation of a snuff-box! in time I shall have the rarest of my
shells set off with gold hinges, to make presents to all the fops about town.
My *Conchae Veneris*; and perhaps, even my *Nautilus.*

A knocking at the door. Enter an Old Woman.

Old Wom. Can I speak with your good mistress, honest friend?
Foss. No, she's busy.   20
Old Wom. Madam Wyburn presents her service and has sent this letter.
[*Exit.*
Foss. [*Reads.*] 'Being taken up with waiting upon merchants ladies this
'morning, I have sent to acquaint you, my dear sweet Mrs. Townley, that
'the alderman agrees to every thing but putting away his wife, which he
'says is not decent at that end of the town. He desires a meeting this evening.'
Postscript.
'He does not like the grocer's wife at all.'

1 the porter of a first minister] Who would demand bribes before admitting a petitioner to
his master's presence.

Bless me! what a libidinous age we live in! neither his own wife! nor the grocer's wife! Will people like nobody's wife but mine!

Knocking at the door. Enter Footman, *gives a letter, and exit.*

Enter another Footman, *gives a letter, and exit.*

Foss. [*Reads.*] 'Sincerely, madam, I cannot spare that sum; especially in 'monthly payments. My good friend and neighbour Pinch, a quiet sober man, 'is content to go a third part, only for leave to visit upon sabbath days.

'Habakkuk Plumb.'

Well, frugallity is laudable even in iniquity! Now for this other.   34

[*Opens the second letter.*

Foss. [*Reads.*] 'Madam, I can't make you rich, but I can make you 'immortal.

'Verses on Mrs. Susanna Townley, in the front box dress'd in green.

'In you the beauties of the spring are seen,
'Your cheeks are roses, and your dress is green.'

A poor dog of a poet! I fear him not.   40

Enter a Ragged Fellow *with a letter.*

Foot. My master is at present under a cloud—He begs you will deliver this letter to your lady.   [*Exit.*

Foss. [*Reads.*] 'I am reduced by your favours to ask the thing I formerly 'deny'd; that you would entertain me as a husband, who can no longer keep 'you as a mistress.

'Charles Bat.'

Why did I part with this fellow? This was a proposal indeed, to make both me and himself happy at once! He shall have her, and a twelve-month's fees into the bargain. Where shall I find him?—Why was the mistress of all mankind unknown to thee alone? Why is nature so dark in our greatest concerns? Why are there no external symptoms of defloration, nor any pathognomick of the loss of virginity but a big belly? Why has not lewdness its tokens like the plague? Why must a man know rain by the aking of his corns, and have no prognostick of what is of infinitely greater moment, cuckoldom? Or if there are any marks of chastity, why is the enquiry allowed only to Turks and Jews, and denyed to Christians? O Townley, Townley! once to me the fragrant rose; now aloes, wormwood and snake-root! but I must not be seen.   58

As Townley *and* Sarsnet *enter,* Fossile *sneaks off.*

Town. Sarsnet, we are betray'd. I have discovered my husband posted at the door in Hugh's livery, he has intercepted all my letters. I immediately

writ this, which is the only thing that can bring us off. Run this moment to
Plotwell, get him to copy it, and send it directed to me by his own servant
with the utmost expedition. He is now at the chocolate-house in the next
street.

Sars. I fly, madam; but how will you disengage yourself from the affair
with Underplot?

Town. Leave it to me. Though he wants sense, he's handsome, and I like
the fellow; and if he is lucky enough to come in my husband's absence.—
But prithee Sarsnet make haste.

Exit Townley *and* Sarsnet, *upon which* Fossile *re-enters, to him* Underplot.

Underp. Harke'e, friend. I never talk with one of your coat, but I first tip
him.   71

Foss. Behold the lucre of a pimp! Between the pox abroad, and my plague
at home, I find a man may never want fees. [*Aside.*] Your honour's commands,
I pray. I long to serve you.

Underp. Ah, boy! thou hast a rare mistress for vails. Come I know thou
art a sly dog; can'st thou introduce me to her for a moment's conversation?

Foss. Impossible.

Underp. What, still impossible?   [*Gives more money.*

Foss. Still impossible.

Underp. Poh, pox. But prithee, friend, by the by, is there any thing in this
report that she is marry'd to the doctor here?   81

Foss. I am afraid there is something in it.

Underp. What a spirit does a jealous husband give to an intrigue! Pray, is
he not a most egregious silly animal?

Foss. Not exceeding wise indeed.

Underp. Rich?

Foss. He has money.

Underp. That will save the expence of her gallants. Old?

Foss. Ay, too old, heaven knows.

Underp. How came it in to the puppy's head to marry?   90

Foss. By the instigation of Satan.

Underp. I'll help the old fool to an heir.

Foss. No doubt on't. If the whole town can do it, he will not want one.
                                                                                    [*Aside.*

Underp. Come, prithee deal freely with me, has Plotwell been here since
the wedding?

Foss. He has! too sure. [*Aside.*] He's a dangerous rival to you; if you have

75 a rare mistress for vails] A mistress in whose service you will secure many bribes.

a mind to succeed, keep a strict watch upon him, that he may not get admittance before you.

Underp. Well since thou hast shown thyself so much my friend, I'll let thee into a secret. Plotwell and I no sooner heard of the wedding, but we made a bett of a hundred guineas, who should dub the doctor first. Remember you go twenty pieces with me.   102

Foss. But here is some body coming. Away, you are sure of my interest.

[*Exit* Underplot.

Foss. This was well judg'd. I have a small territory coveted by two rival potentates. It is profound policy to make them watch one the other, and so keep the ballance of power in my own hands. Certainly nothing so improves one's politicks, as to have a coquet to one's wife.

Enter a Footman *with a letter.*

Foot. This is for your lady. Deliver it safe into her own hands.

[*Exit* Footman.

Foss. [*Reads.*] 'Know, cruel woman, I have discovered the secret of your marriage; you shall have all the plague of a jealous husband, without the 'pleasure of giving him cause. I have this morning counterfeited billetdoux 'and letters from bawds; nay, I have sent pimps; some of which, I hope, are 'fallen into your old coxcomb's hands. If you deny me the pleasure of tipping 'him a real cuckold, at least, I'll have the resentment to make him an 'imaginary one. Know that this is not the hundredth part of the revenge 'that shall be executed upon thee, by   R.P.'

Town. [*Peeping.*] So. The letter works as I would have it.   [*Aside.*

Foss. How true is that saying of the philosopher! 'We only know, that we know nothing.' The eruption of those horns which seem'd to make so strong a push is now suppress'd. Is the mystery of all these letters nothing but the revenge of a disappointed lover? The hand and seal are just the same with the Welchman's that I intercepted a while ago. Truly, these Welch are a hot revengeful people. My wife may be virtuous; she may not. Prevention is the safest method with diseases and intrigues. Women are wanton, husbands weak, bawds busy, opportunities dangerous, gallants eager; therefore it behoves honest men to be watchful. But here comes my Wife, I must hide myself; for should I be detected, she might have a just cause of complaint for my impertinent curiosity.   [*Exit* Fossile.

Enter Townley; *and to her* Sarsnet *at the other door.*

Sars. Your orders, madam, have been executed to a tittle, and I hope with success.   130

Town. Extremely well. Just as we could have wish'd. But I can't forgive that rascal Hugh. To turn him away would be dangerous. We will rather

take the advantage of the confidence my husband has in him. Leave the husband to me, and do you discipline the footman. Such early curiosity must be crush'd in the bud. Hugh, Hugh, Hugh. [*Calls aloud, and rings.*] What is become of the rogue? [Townley *runs in, and drags out* Fossile *changing his cloaths with* Hugh.] Why sirrah! must one call all day for you?
[*Cuffs him.*

Sars. This is not Hugh, madam; a rogue in disguise, got in to rob the house! thieves, thieves!

Enter Clinket, Prue *with the writing-desk, and Servants.*

Foss. St. St—no noise. Prithee, dearee, look upon me. See, see, thy own dear husband. It is I.   141

Town. What an unfortunate woman am I! Could not you pass one day without an intrigue? and with a cookwench too! for you could put on a livery for no other end. You wicked man.

Sars. His coldness, madam, is now no longer a mystery. Filthy monster! wer't not thou provided with my mistress as a remedy for thy rampant unchastity?

Town. Was all your indifference to me for this! you brute you.   [*Weeps.*

Foss. Nay, prithee, dearee, judge not rashly. My character is establish'd in the world. There lives not a more sober, chaste, and virtuous person than doctor Fossile.   151

Town. Then why this disguise?

Foss. Since it must come out; ha, ha, ha, only a frolick on my wedding day between Hugh and I. We had a mind to exhibit a little mummery.

Clink. What joy arises in my soul to see my uncle in a dramatick character! Since your humour lead you to the drama, uncle, why would you not consult a relative muse in your own family? I have always used you as my physician; and why should not you use me as your poet?

Foss. Prithee, dear, leave me a moment. This is a scandal to my gravity. I'll be with you, as my self, immediately.   160

Exeunt omnes, except Fossile *and* Hugh.
As they are changing habits, Fossile *says,*

As a mark of my confidence in thee, I leave thee guardian of my house while I go my rounds. Let none in but patients; wan sickly fellows, no person in the least degree of bodily strength.

Hugh. Worthy doctor, you may rely upon my honour.   [*Exit* Fossile. I have betray'd my mistress. My conscience flies in my face, and I can ease it no way but by betraying my master.

Knocking at the door.

This is not the doctor; but he is dress'd like him, and that shall be my excuse.

He lets Plotwell *in*, Townley *meets him, they embrace.*

Town. Hugh, go, wait at the door.   [*Exit* Hugh.

Plot. This disguise gives spirit to my intrigue. Certainly I am the first person that ever enjoy'd a bride without the scandal of matrimony.   171

Town. I have a different relish, Mr. Plotwell, for now I can't abide you, you are so like my husband.

Plot. Underplot, I defy thee. I have laid the wager, and now I hold the stakes.

Town. Opportunity Mr. Plotwell, has been the downfall of much virtue.

As he is leading her off, enter Hugh.

Hugh. Ah, madam! the doctor! the doctor!   [*Exit* Hugh.

Plot. Fear nothing. I'll stand it. I have my part ready.   [*Exit* Townley.

Enter Fossile.

Foss. I promis'd lady *Langfort* my eagle-stone. The poor lady is like to miscarry, and 'tis well I thought on't. Ha! who is here! I do not like the aspect of the fellow. But I will not be over censorious.   181

They make many bows and cringes in advancing to each other.

Plot. Illustrissime domine, huc adveni—

Foss. Illustrissime domine—non usus sum loquere Latinum—If you cannot speak English, we can have no lingual conversation.

Plot. I can speak but a little Englise. Me ave great deal heard of de fame of de great luminary of all arts and sciences, de illustrious doctor Fossile. I would make commutation (what do you call it) I would exchange some of my tings for some of his tings.

Foss. Pray, Sir, what university are you of?

Plot. De famous university of Cracow in Polonia minor. I have cured de king of Sweden of de wound. My name be doctor Cornelius Lubomirski.

Foss. Your Lubomirskis are a great family. But what Arcana are you master of, Sir?   193

Plot. [*Shows a large snuff-box.*] See dere, Sir, dat box de snuff.

Foss. Snuff-box.

Plot. Right. Snuff-box. Dat be de very true gold.

Foss. What of that?

Plot. Vat of dat? me make dat gold my own self, of de lead of de great church of Cracow.

Foss. By what operations?   200

Plot. By calcination; reverberation; purification; sublimation; amalgamation; precipitation; volitilization.

Foss. Have a care what you assert. The volitilization of gold is not an obvious process. It is by great elegance of speech called, *fortitudo fortitudinis fortissima.*

Plot. I need not acquaint de illustrious doctor Fossile, dat all de metals be but unripe gold.

Foss. Spoken like a philosopher. And therefore there should be an act of parliament against digging of lead mines, as against felling young timber. But inform me, Sir, what might be your menstruum, snow-water, or May-dew?   211

Plot. Snow-vater.

Foss. Right. Snow is the universal pickle of nature for the preservation of her productions in the hyemal season.

Plot. If you will go your self, and not trust de servant, to fetch some of de right Thames sand dat be below de bridge, I will show you de naked Diana in your study before I go hence.

Foss. Perhaps you might. I am not at present dispos'd for experiments.

Plot. This bite wont take to send him out of the way, I'll change my subject. [*Aside.*] Do you deal in longitudes, Sir?   220

Foss. I deal not in impossibilities. I search only for the grand elixir.

Plot. Vat do you tink of de new metode of fluxion?

Foss. I know no other but by mercury.

Plot. Ha, ha. Me mean de fluxion of de quantity.

Foss. The greatest quantity I ever knew, was three quarts a day.

Plot. Be dere any secret in the hydrology, zoology, minerology, hydraulicks, acausticks, pneumaticks, logarithmatechny, dat you do want de explanation of?

Foss. This is all out of my way. Do you know of any hermaphrodites, monstrous twins, antediluvian shells, bones, and vegetables?   230

Plot. Vat tink you of an antediluvian knife, spoon, and fork, with the mark of Tubal Cain in Hebrew, dug out of the mine of Babylon?

Foss. Of what dimensions, I pray, Sir?

Plot. De spoon be bigger dan de modern ladle; de fork, like de great fire-fork; and de knife, like de cleaver.

Foss. Bless me! this shows the stature and magnitude of those anti-diluvians!

Plot. To make you convinc'd that I tell not de lie, dey are in de Turkey ship at Vapping, just going to be disposed of. Me would go there vid you, but de business vil not let me.   240

Foss. An extraordinary man this! I'll examine him further. [*Aside.*] How could your country lose so great a man as you?

Plot. Dat be de secret. But because me vil have de fair correspondence with de illustrious doctor Fossile, me vil not deny dat Orpheus and me had near run de same fate for different reason. I was hunted out of my country by de general insurrection of de women.

Foss. How so pray?

Plot. Because me have prepare a certain liquor which discover whether a woman be a virgin or no.

Foss. A curious discovery! have you any of it still?   250

Plot. Dere it is, Sir. It be commonly called de *Lapis Lydius Virginitatis*, or touch-stone of virginity.   [*Gives him a vial.*

Foss. It has the smell of your common hart's-horn. But all your volatile spirits have a near resemblance.

Plot. Right, Sir. De distillation be made from the *Hippomanes* of a young mare. When a deflower'd virgin take ten drops, she will faint and sneeze, and de large red spot appear on the cheek; which we call de spot of infamy. All de young bridegroom make de experiment. De archbishop did make obligation to de nun to take it every ninth month. And I fly for the hurlyburly it make.   260

Enter Hugh.

Hugh. Sir, here is a patient in a chair.

Foss. Doctor Lubomirski, let me conduct you into my study, where we will farther discuss the wonderful virtues of this liquor. Tell the patient I will attend him this instant.   [*Exeunt* Plotwell *and* Fossile.

Enter Underplot *in a chair like a sick man.*

Hugh. The doctor will wait upon you immediately.   [*Exit* Hugh.

Underp. I dogg'd Plotwell to this door in a doctor's habit. If he has admittance as a doctor, why not I as a patient? Now for a lucky decision of our wager! If I can't succeed myself, I will at least spoil his intrigue.

Enter Fossile.

Underp. Ah! ah! have you no place? Ah! where can I repose a little? I was taken suddenly. Ah! ah! 'tis happy I was so near the house of an eminent physician.   271

Foss. Rest yourself upon that couch.

Underp. If I lay a few minutes cover'd up warm in a bed, I believe I might recover.   [*Fossile feels his pulse.* Plotwell *peeps.*

Plot. Underplot in disguise! I'll be his doctor, and cure him of these frolicks.   [*Aside.*

Foss. What are your symptoms, Sir? a very tempestuous pulse, I profess!

Underp. Violent head-ach, ah! ah!

Foss. All this proceeds from the fumes of the kitchen, the stomachic digester wants reparation for the better concoction of your aliment. But, Sir, is your pain pungitive, tensive, gravitive, or pulsatory?   281

Plot. All together, ah!

Foss. Impossible Sir; but I have an eminent physician now in the house, he shall consult. Doctor Lubomirski, here is a person in a most violent cephalalgy, a terrible case!

Enter Plotwell.

Foss. Feel his pulse. [Plotwell *feels it.*] You feel it, Sir, strong, hard and labouring.

Plot. Great plenitude, Sir.

Foss. Feel his belly, Sir; a great tension and heat of the abdomen.—A hearty man, his muscles are torose; how soon are the strongest humbled by diseases! let us retire, and consult.   291

Enter Sarsnet *in haste.*

Sars. My mistress approves your design, bear it out bravely, perhaps I shall have a sudden opportunity of conveying you into her bed-chamber, counterfeit a fainting fit and rely upon me.   [*Exit.*

Underp. As yet I find I am undiscover'd by Plotwell; neither is his intrigue in such forwardness as mine, though he made a fair push for it before me.
                                                                    [*Aside.*

Fossile *and* Plotwell *come forward.*

Foss. I am entirely for a glister.

Plot. My opinion is for de strong vomit.

Foss. Bleed him.

Plot. Make de scarrification, give me de lancet, me will do it myself, and after dat will put de blister to de sole of de feet.   301

Foss. Your dolor proceeds from a frigid *intemperies* of the brain, a strong disease! the enemy has invaded the very citadel of your microcosm, the magazine of your vital functions; he has set down before it; yet there seems to be a good garrison of vital spirits, and we don't question to be able to defend it.

Plot. Ve will cannonade de enemy with pills, bombard him wid de bolus, blow him up with volatiles, fill up the trenches wid de large innundation of apozems, and dislodge him wid de stink-pot; let de apotecary bring up de artillery of medicine immediately.   310

Foss. True, we might unload the stomach by gentle emeticks, and the intestines by clysters stimulative, carminative, and emollient, with strong

290 torose] Swollen.

hydroticks, quiet the spasms of the viscera by paregoricks, draw off the stagnant blood by deep scarrifications, and depurate its fæculencies by volatiles; after this, let there be numerous blisters and potential cauteries—I consult my patient's ease; I am against much physick.—He faints, he is apoplectic, bleed him this moment.

Plot. Hoy de servant dere, make haste, bring de pan of hot coals; or de red hot iron to make application to de temples.

Enter Hugh.

Hugh. Here's the poker red hot from the fire.   320
Plot. Very well, make de burn dere, exactly dere.
                            [*Putting the poker near his head.*
Underp. Hold, hold, am I to be murder'd? [*Starts up.*] I know you, Plotwell, and was I not oblig'd by honour and friendship, I'd expose you to the doctor.
                                              [*Aside to* Plotwell.
Plot. Very lunatick, mad, fetch me de cord to make de tie upon de leg and de arm, take off thirty ounces of blood, and den plunge him into de cold bath.

Foss. Your judgment, doctor Lubomirski, is excellent, I will call my servants to assist us.

Underp. Hearke'e, old put; I came to take your advice, and not that French son of a whore's scarrifications; and so plague take you both.   330
                                              [*Exit* Underplot *and* Hugh.

ACT IV.

Enter Dr. Fossile, *and* Plotwell.

Foss. **D**OCTOR Lubomirski, this vial that you have intrusted into my custody, shall be with acknowledgment return'd after a few experiments; I must crave your indulgence; diseases, you know, Sir, are impertinent, and will tie themselves to no hours, poor lady Hippokekoana!

Plot. Ah Sir! I beg your pardon, if you make visit to de patient, me will divert myself in your study till you make return.

Foss. That cannot be, I have a lady just coming to consult me in a case of secrecy.

Plot. Have you not de wife? me will make conversation wid de ladies till you come.   10

Foss. They see no company in the morning, they are all in *deshabillee* most learned doctor Lubomirski, your humble servant.

Plot. Most illustrious doctor Fossile, me be, with de profoundest adoration
Foss. With the greatest admiration
Plot. Your most humble
Foss. Most obedient servant.
Plot. Ah, Monsieur, point de ceremonie.   [*Exit* Plotwell.

Enter Hugh.

Foss. Hugh, bring me a pint of sack; let your mistress know I want to see her. Take care that her orders be obey'd, and that her trunks and boxes be immediately brought hither. Sarsnet will give you directions.   20
                    [*Exit* Hugh. Fossile *sits down on a couch.*
Ah Fossile! if the cares of two hours of a married life have so reduc'd thee, how long can'st thou hold out! to watch a wife all day, and have her wake thee all night! 'twill never do. The fatigue of three fevers, six small poxes, and five great ones, is nothing to that of one wife. Now for my touch-stone; I will try it upon her presently. If she bear it to day—I am afraid she will bear it to morrow too.

Enter Hugh *with a bottle of sack, and after him* Townley.
Hugh *gives the bottle and glass to* Fossile *and exit.*
Sit down by me, my dear, I was going to refresh myself with a glass of canary. You look pale. It will do you good.
Town. Faugh. Wine in the morning!

Fossile *drinks and fills again, and drops some of the liquor into the glass.*

What is the meaning of this? am I to be poison'd.   [*Aside.*
Foss. You must drink it. Sack is sacred to Hymen; of it is made the nuptial posset.   32
Town. Don't press me, Mr. Fossile, I nauseate it. It smells strangely. There is something in it.
Foss. An ill symptom! she can't bear the smell. [*Aside.*] Pray, my dear, oblige me.
Town. I'm for none of your slops. I'll fill myself.
Foss. I must own, I have put some restorative drops in it, which are excellent. I may drink it safely. [*Aside. Drinks.*] The next glass I prepare for you.   [*Fills, and pours some drops in.*

Townley *drinks.* Fossile *runs behind to support her; then pores upon her cheek, and touches it with his finger.*

Town. Your insolence is insupportable. 'Twas but this moment you suspected my virtue; and now my complexion. Put on your spectacles. No red

32 posset] A drink composed of milk curdled with liquor.

was ever laid upon these cheeks. I'll fly thee, and die a maid, rather than live under the same roof with jealousy and caprice.   44

Foss. O thou spotless innocence! I cannot refrain tears of joy. Forgive me, and I'll tell thee all. These drops have been a secret in our family for many years. They are call'd the touch-stone of virginity. The males administer it to the brides on their wedding-day; and by its virtue have ascertain'd the honour of the Fossiles from generation to generation. There are family customs, which it is almost impious to neglect.   50

Town. Had you married a person of doubtful reputation—But me, Mr. Fossile!

Foss. I did not indeed suspect thee. But my mother obliged me to this experiment with her dying words.—My wife is chaste: And to preserve her so, 'tis necessary that I have none but chaste servants about her. I'll make the experiment on all my female domesticks. [*Aside.*] I will now, my dear, in thy presence, put all my family to the trial. Here! bid my niece, and all the maid-servants come before me.   [*Calling out.*

Enter Clinket, Prue, *and Servants.*

Give ear, all ye virgins: We make proclamation in the name of the chaste Diana, being resolv'd to make a solemn essay of the virtue, virginity, and chastitity of all within our walls. We therefore advise, warn and precaution all spinsters, who know themselves blemish'd, not on any pretence whatsoever to taste these our drops, which will manifest their shame to the world by visible tokens.   64

Clink. I abominate all kind of drops. They interrupt the series of ideas. But have they any power over the virgin's dreams, thoughts, and private meditations?

Foss. No. They do not affect the *motus Primo-primi*, or intentions; only actualities, niece.

Clink. Then give it me. I can drink as freely of it as of the waters of Helicon. My love was always Platonick.   [*Drinks.*

Foss. Yet I have known a Platonick lady lodge at a mid wife's.   72
                                                        [Fossile *offers it round.*

1st Wom. I never take physick.

Foss. That's one. Stand there. My niece professes herself a Platonick. You are rather a Cartesian.

Clink. Ah dear uncle! how do the Platonicks and Cartesians differ.

Foss. The Platonicks are for ideas, the Cartesians for matter and motion.

Town. Mr. Fossile, you are too severe.

2d Wom. I am not a-dry.   [*Curtsies.*

Foss. There's two. Stand there.   80

Prue. My mistress can answer for me. She has taken it.

Foss. She has. But however stand there, among the Cartesians.

3d Wom. My innocence would protect me, though I trod over red-hot iron. Give me a brimmer.

She takes a mouthful and spits it out again.

Foss. 'Twas a presumptuous thing to gargle with it: but however, madam, if you please—walk among the Cartesians.   [*Two young wenches run away.*

Clink. Prue, follow me. I have just found a rhime for my Pindarick.
                                          [*They all sneak off.*

Foss. All gone! what no more ladies here? no more ladies! [*Looking to the audience.*] O that I had but a boarding-school, or a middle gallery!

Enter Sarsnet, *follow'd by two* Porters *bearing a chest.*

Set down the things here: there is no occasion for carrying them up stairs, since they are to be sent into the country to morrow.   [*Exit Porters.*

What have I done? My marriage, these confounded whimsies, and doctor Lubomirski, have made me quite forget poor lady Hippokekoana. She was in convulsions, and I am afraid dead by this time.   [*Exit Fossile.*

Sars. I have brought you a present, madam, make good use of it. So I leave you together.   [*Exit Sarsnet.*

Townley *opens the chest:* Plotwell, *who was cover'd with a gown and petticoat, gets out.*

Town. Never was any thing so lucky. The doctor is just this minute gone to a patient.   98

Plot. I tempt dangers enough in your service. I am almost crippled in this chest-adventure. Oh my knees! Prithee, my dear, lead me to a bed where I may stretch myself out.   [*Leading her off.*

Enter Sarsnet.

Sars. Oh madam! yonder is the doctor in deep discourse with Underplot: I fear he has dogg'd me, and betray'd us. They are both coming back together.   [*Exit Sarsnet.*

Plot. I'll shrink snug into my shell again.

Town. That he may directly pop upon you. The trunk will be the first place he will examine. Have you no presence of mind? You fit for an intrigue!

Plot. What shall I do?

Town. Fear not, you shall be invisible in this very spot.   109

Plot. What do you mean? he's just at the door. You intend to discover me.

Town. Mistrust me not: You shall walk out before his face at that very door, though he bring in a hundred spies, and not one of them shall perceive you.

Plot. Don't trifle. Are you mad? [*Knocking at the door.*] Nay, now 'tis too late.

Town. Arm thyself with flounces, and fortify thyself with whalebone; enter beneath the cupulo of this petticoat.

Plot. The best security in the world! an old fellow has seldom any thing to do beneath that circumferance.

Town. No more, but under it immediately.   [Plotwell *goes under it.*

        Thus Venus, when approaching foes assail,   120
        Shields her Æneas with a silken veil.

Enter Fossile.

Town. O my dear you come opportunely. How do you like my fancy in this new petticoat? there is something in it so odd!

Foss. You have another in your chest much odder. I want to see that.

Town. How jaunty the flounces!

Foss. Ay, 'tis plain she would lure me from the chest; there I shall find him.   [*Aside.*

Town. The lace! the fringe!

Foss. All this is nothing to the embroider'd sattin. Prithee, my dear, give me the key.   130

Town. Sure never was any thing so prettily disposed. Observe but the air of it: So *degagee!* But the lining is so charming.

She walks to the door, and Fossile *to the trunk.*
Plotwell *kisses her out of the top of the petticoat, and then goes off.*

As Fossile *is cautiously opening the trunk with his sword drawn,*
Townley *comes up to him.*

What, more of your frolicks, Mr. Fossile. What time of the moon is this?

Foss. This Underplot is a confounded villain, he would make me jealous of an honest civil gentleman, only for an opportunity to cuckold me himself. [*Aside.*] Come, my dear, forget all that is past. I know—I have proved thee virtuous. But prithee, love, leave me a moment; I expect some Egyptian rarities.   [*Exeunt severally.*

ACT V.

Enter Fossile *with a vial in his hand.*

Foss. THIS is all we have for the flying dragon so celebrated by antiquity. A cheap purchase! It cost me but fifteen guineas. But the Jew made it up in the butterfly and the spider.

Enter two Porters *bearing a Mummy*.

Oh! here's my mummy. Set him down. I am in haste. Tell captain Bantam, I'll talk with him at the coffee-house.   [*Exit* Porters.

Enter two Porters *bearing an Alligator*.

A most stupendous animal! set him down.   [*Exit* Porters.
Poor lady Hippokekoana's convulsions! I believe there is fatality in it, that I can never get to her. Who can I trust my house to in my absence? Were my wife as chaste as Lucretia, who knows what an unlucky minute may bring forth! In cuckoldom, the art of attack is prodigiously improved beyond the art of defence. So far it is manifest, Underplot has a design upon my honour. For the ease of my mind, I will lock up my wife in this my musæum, 'till my return.   13

Enter Townley, *and* Sarsnet.

You will find something here, my dear, to divert yourself.
   Town. I hate the sight of these strange creatures; but since I am Mr. Fossiles wife, I shall endeavour to conquer my aversion.
   Foss. Thou may'st safely be here to day, my dear; to-morrow thou shouldst no more enter this room than a pest-house. 'Tis dangerous for women that are impregnated. But poor lady Hippokekoana suffers all this while.
                            [*Exit* Fossile *with a key in his hand*.
   Town. Since he has lock'd me in, to be even with him, I'll bolt him out.
                  [Plotwell *dress'd like a Mummy, comes forward*.
   Plot. Thus trav'ling far from his Egyptian tomb,   21
Thy Anthony salutes his Cleopatra.
   Town. Thus Cleopatra, in desiring arms,
Receives her Anthony—But prithee dear pickled Hieroglyphic, who so suddenly could assist thee with this shape.
   Plot. The play-house can dress mummies, bears, lions, crocodiles, and all the monsters of Lybia. My arms madam are ready to break their past-board prison to embrace you.
   Town. Not so hasty. Stay till the jealous fool is out of sight.
   Plot. Our ill stars, and the devil, have brought him back so often.   30
   Town. He can never parry this blow, nor grow jealous of his mummy. A mummy is his intimate friend.
   Plot. And a man cannot easily be cuckolded by any body else.
   Town. Here may'st thou remain the ornament of his study, and the support of his old age. Thou shalt divert his company and be a father to his children. I will bring thee legs of pullets, remnants of tarts, and fragments of desarts. Thou shalt be fed like Bell and the Dragon.

Plot. But madam; before you entertain me as your mummy in ordinary, you ought to be acquainted with my abilities to discharge that office. Let me slip off this habit of death, you shall find I have some symptoms of life.—Thus Jove within the milk-white swan compress'd his Leda. 41

[Underplot *in the Alligator crawls forward, then rises up and embraces her.*

Underp. Thus Jove within the serpents scaly folds,
Twin'd round the Macedonian queen.

Town. Ah! [*Shrieks.*

Plot. Fear not, madam. This is my evil genius Underplot that still haunts me. How the devil got you here?

Underp. Why should not the play-house lend me a crocodile as well as you a mummy?

Town. How unlucky is this! [*Aside.*] Nay, I don't know but I may have twenty lovers in this collection. You snakes, sharks, monkeys, and mantygers, speak, and put in your claim before it is too late. 51

Underp. Mr. Mummy, your humble servant; the lady is pre-engag'd.

Plot. Pray, Mr. Crocodile, let the lady make her own choice.

Underp. Crocodile as I am, I must be treated with common humanity. You can't, madam, disown the message you sent me.

Town. Well! ye pair of Egyptian lovers, agree this matter between you, and I will acquit myself like a person of honour to you both.

Plot. Madam! If I don't love you above all your sex, may I be banish'd the studies of virtuoso's; and smoak'd like dutch beef in a chimney—

Underp. If I don't love you more than that stale mummy, may I never more be proclaim'd at a show of monsters, by the sound of a glass-trumpet.

Plot. May I be sent to 'Pothecary's-hall, and beat up into venice treacle for the fleet and the army, if this heart— 63

Underp. May I be stuff'd with straw, and given to a mountebank, if this soul—

Plot. Madam I am a human creature. Taste my balsamick kiss.

Underp. A lover in swadling-clouts! What is his kiss, to my embrace?

Plot. Look upon me, madam. See how I am embroider'd with hieroglyphicks.

Underp. Consider my beautiful row of teeth. 70

Plot. My balmy breath.

Underp. The strong joints of my back.

Plot. My erect stature.

Underp. My long tail.

Town. Such a contest of beauty! How shall I decide it?

Plot. Take me out of my shell, madam, and I'll make you a present of the kernel.

50 mantygers] A kind of baboon.

Underp. Then I must be upon a level with him, and be uncrocodil'd.

Town. Keep both of you your shapes, and we are in no fear of a surprize from the doctor: If you uncase, his presence would undo us. Sure never was any thing so unlucky—I hear his foot-steps; quick to your posts.   81

[*Mummy and Crocodile run to their places.*

Enter Fossile, *Dr.* Nautilus, *and Dr.* Possum.

Naut. Much joy to the learned Dr. Fossile. To have a mummy, an alligator, and a wife, all in one day, is too great happiness for mortal man!

Poss. This an alligator! Alack a day, brother Nautilus, this is a mere lizard, an eft, a shrimp to mine.

Naut. How improving would it be to the female understanding, if the closets of the ladies were furnish'd, or, as I may say, ornamented and embellish'd with preserv'd butterflies, and beautiful shells, instead of China jars, and absurd Indian pictures.

Town. Now for a stratagem to bring off my unsuccessful pair of gallants.

[*Aside.*

[*Exit* Townley.

Foss. Ah, Dr. Nautilus, how have I languish'd for your feather of the bird Porphyrion!   92

Naut. But your dart of the Mantichora!

Foss. Your haft of the antediluvian trowel, unquestionably the tool of one of the Babel masons!

Naut. What's that to your fragment of Seth's pillar?

Poss. Gentlemen, I affirm I have a greater curiosity than all of them. I have an entire leaf of Noah's journal aboard the ark, that was hewen out of a porphyry pillar in Palmyra.

[Fossile *opens the case of the Mummy.*

Naut. By the formation of the muscular parts of the visage, I conjecture that this mummy is male.   101

Poss. Male, brother! I am sorry to observe your ignorance of the symetry of a human body. Do but observe the projection of the hip; besides, the bloom upon the face; 'tis a female beyond all contradiction.

Foss. Let us have no rash dispute, brothers; but proceed methodically— Behold the vanity of mankind! [*Pointing to the Mummy.*] Some Ptolemy perhaps!—

Naut. Who by his pyramid and pickle thought to secure to himself death immortal.

Foss. His pyramid, alas! is now but a wainscot case.   110

Poss. And his pickle can scarce raise him to the dignity of a collar of brawn.

Foss. Pardon me, Dr. Possum: The musæum of the curious is a lasting monument. And I think it no degradation to a dead person of quality, to bear the rank of an anatomy in the learned world.

Naut. By your favour, Dr. Possum, a collar of brawn! I affirm, he is better to be taken inwardly than a collar of brawn.

Foss. An excellent medicine! he is hot in the first degree, and exceeding powerful in some diseases of women.

Naut. Right, Dr. Fossile; for your Asphaltion.   120

Poss. Pice-Asphaltus, by your leave.

Naut. By your leave, doctor Possum, I say, Asphaltion.

Poss. And I positively say, Pice-Asphaltus.

Naut. If you had read Dioscorides or Pliny—

Poss. I have read Dioscorides. And I do affirm Pice-Asphaltus.

Foss. Be calm, Gentlemen. Both of you handle this argument with great learning, judgment, and perspicuity. For the present, I beseech you to concord, and turn your speculations on my alligator.

Poss. The skin is impenetrable even to a sword.

Naut. Dr. Possum I will show you the contrary.   [*Draws his sword.*

Poss. In the mean time I will try the mummy with this knife, on the point of which you shall smell the pitch, and be convinc'd that it is the Pice-Asphaltus.   [*Takes up a rusty knife.*

Foss. Hold, Sir: You will not only deface my mummy, but spoil my Roman sacrificing-knife.   135

Enter Townley.

Town. I must lure them from this experiment, or we are discover'd. [*Aside.*
                          [*She looks through a telescope.*
What do I see! most prodigious! a star as broad as the moon in the day-time!
                          [*The doctors go to her.*

Poss. Only a halo about the sun, I suppose.

Naut. Your suppositions, doctor, seem to be groundless. Let me make my observation.   [Nautilus *and* Possum *struggle to look first.*

Town. Now for your escape.   [*To* Plotwell *and* Underplot.
                          [*They run to the door, but find it lock'd.*

Underp. What an unlucky dog I am!

Town. Quick. Back to your posts. Don't move, and rely upon me. I have still another artifice.   [*They run back to their places.*
                          [*Exit* Townley.

Naut. I can espy no celestial body but the sun.   145

Poss. Brother Nautilus, your eyes are somewhat dim; your sight is not fit for astronomical observations.

Foss. Is the focus of the glass right? hold gentlemen, I see it; about the bigness of Jupiter.

Naut. No phenomenon offers itself to my speculation.   150

Poss. Point over yonder chimney. Directly south.

Naut. Thitherward, begging your pardon, Dr. Possum, I affirm to be the north.

Foss. East.

Poss. South.

Naut. North. Alas! what an ignorant thing is vanity! I was just making a reflection on the ignorance of my brother Possum, in the nature of the crocodile.

Poss. First, brother Nautilus, convince yourself of the composition of the mummy.   160

Naut. I will insure your alligator from any damage. His skin I affirm once more to be impenetrable.   [*Draws his sword.*

Poss. I will not deface any hieroglyphick.

[*Goes to the Mummy with the knife.*

Foss. I never oppose a luciferous experiment. It is the beaten highway to truth.

Plotwell *and* Underplot *leap from their places; the doctors are frighted.*

Foss. Speak, I conjure thee. Art thou the ghost of some murder'd Egyptian monarch?

Naut. A rational question to a mummy! But this monster can be no less than the devil himself, for crocodiles don't walk.

Enter Townley *and* Clinket. Townley *whispers* Clinket.

Foss. Gentlemen, wonder at nothing within these walls; for ever since I was married, nothing has happen'd to me in the common course of human life.   172

Clink. Madam, without a compliment, you have a fine imagination. The masquerade of the mummy and crocodile is extremely just; I would not rob you of the merit of the invention, yet since you make me the compliment, I shall be proud to take the whole contrivance of this masquerade upon myself.

[*To* Townley.

Sir, be acquainted with my masqueraders.   [*To* Fossile.

Foss. Thou female imp of Appollo, more mischievous than Circe, who fed gentlemen of the army in a hog's-stye! What mean you by these gambols? this mummy, this crocodile?   180

Clink. Only a little mummery, uncle?

Foss. What an outragious conceit is this! had you contented yourself with

164 luciferous experiment] An experiment which will afford insight into a subject, throw light upon it.

the metamorphosis of Jupiter, our skill in the classicks might have prevented our terror.

Clink. I glory in the fertility of my invention the more, that it is beyond the imagination of a pagan deity. Besides, it is form'd upon the vraysemblance; for I know you had a mummy and a crocodile to be brought home.

Foss. Dr. Nautilus is an infirm tender gentleman; I wish the sudden concussion of his animal spirits may not kindle him into a fever. I myself, I must confess, have an extreme palpitation.   190

Clink. Dear uncle, be pacified. We are both of us the votaries of our great master Appollo. To you he has assign'd the art of healing: Me he has taught to sing; why then should we jangle in our kindred faculties?

Foss. Appollo, for ought I know, may be a very fine person; but this I am very sure of, that the skill he has given all his physicians is not sufficient to cure the madness of his poets.

Poss. Hark ye, brother Fossile? Your Crocodile has prove a human creature, I wish your wife may not prove a crocodile.

Naut. Hark ye, brother Fossile! Your mummy, as you were saying, seemeth to be hot in the first degree, and is powerful in some diseases of women.

[*Exit* Nautilus *and* Possum.

Foss. You diabolical performers of my niece's masquerade, will it please you to follow those gentlemen?   202

Clink. Nay, Sir, you shall see them dance first.

Foss. Dance! the devil! bring me hither a spit, a fire-fork, I'll try whether the monsters are impenetrable or no.

Plot. I hope, Sir, you will not expose us to the fury of the mob, since we came here upon so courteous a design.

Foss. Good courteous Mr. Mummy, without more ceremony, will it please you to retire to your subterraneous habitation. And you Mr. Crocodile, about your business this moment, or you shall change your Nile for the next horse-pond.   211

Clink. Spare my masqueraders.

Underp. Let it never be said that the famous Dr. Fossile, so renowned for his charity to monsters, should violate the laws of hospitality, and turn a poor alligator naked into the street.

Foss. Deposite your *exuviæ* then, and assume your human shape.

Underp. For that I must beg your excuse. A gentleman would not chuse to be known in these frolicks.

Foss. Then out of my doors. Here footman, out with him; out, thou hypocrite, of an alligator.   [Underplot *is turn'd out*.

Sir, the respect I have for catacombs and pyramids, will not protect you.

[*A noise of mob within*.

Enter Prue.

Prue. Sir, Sir, lock your doors, or else all your monsters will run home again to the Indies. Your crocodile yonder has made his escape; if he get but to Somerset water-gate, he is gone for ever.   [*Exit* Prue.

Enter a Footman.

Foot. The herbwoman swore she knew him to be the devil, for she had met him one dark night in St. Pulchre's church-yard; then the monster call'd a coach, methought with the voice of a christian; but a sailor that came by said he might be a crocodile for all that, for crocodiles could cry like children, and was for killing him outright, for they were good to eat in Egypt, but the constable cry'd take him alive, for what if he be an Egyptian, he is still the king's subject.   [*Exit* Footman.
[*A noise of mob within.*

Enter Prue.

Prue. Then he was hurry'd a way by the mob. A bull-dog ran away with six joints of his tail, and the claw of his near foot before: At last by good fortune, to save his life, he fell in with the Hockley in the Hole bull and bear; the master claim'd him for his monster, and so he is now attended by a vast mob, very solemnly marching to Hockley in the Hole, with the bear in his front, the bull in his rear, and a monkey upon each shoulder.   237

Town. Mr. Mummy, you had best draw the curtains of your chair, or the mob's respect for the dead will scarce protect you.
[*Exit* Plotwell *in a chair.*

Clink. My concern for him obliges me to go see that he gets off safe, lest any further mischief befalls the persons of our masque.   [*Exit* Clinket.

Foss. Sweetly, Horace. *Nunquam satis*, and so forth. A man can never be too cautious. Madam, sit down by me. Pray how long is it since you and I have been married?

Town. Near three hours, Sir.

Foss. And what anxieties has this time produc'd? the dangers of divorce! calumniatory letters! lewd fellows introduc'd by my niece! groundless jealousies on both sides! even thy virginity put to the touch-stone! but this last danger I plung'd thee in myself; to leave thee in the room with two such robust young fellows.   250

Town. Ay, with two young fellows! but my dear, I know you did it ignorantly.

Foss. This is the first blest minute of repose that I have enjoy'd in matrimony. Dost thou know the reason, my dear, why I have chosen thee of all womankind?

234 Hockley in the Hole] A public garden near Clerkenwell Green, famous for bear-baiting and other animal entertainments.

Town. My face, perhaps.

Foss. No.

Town. My wit?

Foss. No.

Town. My virtue and good humour. 260

Foss. No. But for the natural conformity of our constitutions. Because thou art hot and moist in the third degree, and I myself cold and dry in the first.

Town. And so nature has coupled us like the elements.

Foss. Thou hast nothing to do but to submit thy constitution to my regimen.

Town. You shall find me obedient in all things.

Foss. It is strange, yet certain, that the intellects of the infant depend upon the suppers of the parents. Diet must be prescrib'd.

Town. So the wit of one's posterity is determin'd by the choice of one's cook. 270

Foss. Right. You may observe how French cooks, with their high ragousts, have contaminated our plain English understandings. Our supper to night is extracted from the best authors. How delightful is this minute of tranquility! my soul is at ease. How happy shalt thou make me! thou shalt bring me the finest boy! [*A knocking at the door.*

No mortal shall enter these doors this day. [*Knocking again.*] Oh, it must be the news of poor lady Hippokekoana's death. Poor woman! such is the condition of life, some die, and some are born, and I shall now make some reparation for the mortality of my patients by the fecundity of my wife. My dear thou shalt bring me the finest boy! 280

Enter Footman.

Foot. Sir, here's a seaman from Deptford must needs speak with you.

Foss. Let him come in. One of my retale Indian merchants, I suppose, that always brings me some odd thing.

Enter Sailor *with a* Child.

What hast thou brought me, friend, a young drill?

Sail. Look ye d'ye see, master, you know best whether a monkey begot him.

Foss. A meer human child.

Town. Thy carelessness, Sarsnet, has exposed me, I am lost and ruin'd. O heav'n! heav'n! No, impudence assist me. [*Aside.*

Foss. Is the child monstrous? or dost thou bring him here to take physick?

Sail. I care not what he takes so you take him. 291

Foss. What does the fellow mean?

284 drill] A kind of baboon.

Sail. Fellow me no fellows. My name is Jack Capstone of Deptford, and are not you the man that has the raree-show of oyster-shells and pebble-stones?

Foss. What if I am?

Sail. Why, then my invoice is right, I must leave my cargo here.

Town. Miserable woman that I am! how shall I support this sight! thy bastard brought into thy family as soon as thy bride!

Foss. Patience, patience, I beseech you. Indeed I have no posterity.   300

Town. You lascivious brute you.

Foss. Passion is but the tempestuous cloud that obscures reason; be calm and I'll convince you. Friend, how come you to bring the infant hither?

Sail. My wife, poor woman, could give him suck no longer, for she died yesterday morning. There's a long account, master. It was hard to trace him to the fountain-head. I steer'd my course from lane to lane, I spoke to twenty old women, and at last was directed to a ribbon-shop in Covent-Garden, and they sent me hither, and so take the bantling and pay me his clearings.   [*Offers him the* Child.

Foss. I shall find law for you, sirrah. Call my neighbour Possum, he is a justice of peace, as well as a physician.   311

Town. Call the man back. If you have committed one folly, don't expose yourself by a second.

Sail. The gentlewoman says well. Come, master, we all know that there is no boarding a pretty wench, without charges one way or other; you are a doctor, master, and have no surgeons bills to pay; and so can the better afford it.

Town. Rather than you should bring a scandal on your character, I will submit to be a kind mother-in-law.

Enter Justice Possum, *and* Clerk.

Foss. Mr. justice Possum, for now I must so call you, not brother Possum; here is a troublesome fellow with a child, which he would leave in my house.

Poss. Another man's child? he cannot in law.   322

Foss. It seemeth to me to be a child unlawfully begotten.

Poss. A bastard! who does he lay it to?

Foss. To our family.

Poss. Your family, *quatenus* a family, being a body collective, cannot get a bastard. Is this child a bastard, honest friend?

Sail. I was neither by when his mother was stow'd, nor when she was unladen; whether he belong to a fair trader, or be run goods, I cannot tell: In short here I was sent, and here I will leave him.   330

Poss. Dost thou know his mother, friend?

Sail. I am no midwife, master; I did not see him born.

Poss. You had best put up this matter, doctor. A man of your years, when he has been wanton, cannot be too cautious.

Foss. This is all from the purpose. I was married this morning at seven; let any man in the least acquainted with the powers of nature, judge whether that human creature could be conceiv'd and brought to maturity in one fore-noon.

Poss. This is but talk, doctor Fossile. It is well for you, though I say it, that you have fallen into the hands of a person, who has study'd the civil and canon law in the point of bastardy. The child is either yours or not yours.   342

Foss. My child, Mr. Justice!

Poss. Look ye, doctor Fossile, you confound filiation with legitimation. Lawyers are of opinion, that filiation is necessary to legitimation, but not *e contra*.   [*The* Child *cries.*

Foss. I would not starve any of my own species, get the infant some water-pap. But Mr. Justice—

Poss. The proofs, I say, doctor, of filiation are five. Nomination enunci-atively pronounc'd, strong presumptions, and circumstantial proofs—   350

Foss. What is all this to me? I tell you I know nothing of the child.

Poss. Signs of paternal piety, similitude of features, and commerce with the mother. And first of the first, nomination. Has the doctor ever been heard to call the infant, son?

Town. He has call'd him child, since he came into this room. You have indeed, Mr. Fossile.

Poss. Bring hither the doctor's great bible.—Let us examine in the blank leaf whether he be enroll'd among the rest of his children.

Foss. I tell you, I never had any children. I shall grow distracted, I shall—   360

Poss. But did you give any orders against registring the child by the name of Fossile?

Foss. How was it possible?

Poss. Set down that, clerk. He did not prohibit the registring the child in his own name. We our selves have observed one sign of fatherly tenderness; clerk, set down the water-pap he order'd just now. Come we now—

Foss. What a jargon is this!

Poss. Come we now, I say, to that which the lawyers call *magnum naturæ argumentum*, similitude of features. Bring hither the child, friend; Dr. Fossile, look upon me. The unequal circle of the infant's face, somewhat resembles the inequality of the circumference of your countenance; he has also the vituline or calf-like concavity of the profile of your visage.   372

Foss. Pish.

344 filiation] The designation of a person as a son.

Poss. And he is somewhat beetle-brow'd, and his nose will rise with time to an equal prominence with the doctor's.

Town. Indeed he has somewhat of your nose Mr. Fossile.

Foss. Ridiculous!

Town. The child is comely.

Poss. Consider the large aperture of his mouth.

Sail. Nay, the tokens are plain enough. I have the fellow of him at home; but my wife told me two days ago, that this with the wall-eye and splay-foot belong'd to you, Sir.   382

Prue *runs across the stage with letter, which* Fossile *snatches from her.*

Foss. Whither are you going so fast, hussy? I will examine every thing within these walls. [*Exit* Prue. *Reads.*] 'For Richard Plotwell, Esq.' This letter unravels the whole affair: As she is an unfortunate relation of mine, I must beg you would act with discretion.   [*Gives* Possum *the letter.*

Poss. [*Reads.*] 'Sir, the child which you father'd is return'd back upon my 'hands. Your Drury-lane friends have treated me with such rudeness, that 'they told me in plain terms I should be damn'd. How unfortunate soever 'my offspring is, I hope you at least will defend the reputation of the un-'happy

'Phoebe Clinket.'

—As you say, doctor, the case is too plain; every circumstance hits.   393

Enter Clinket.

Clink. 'Tis very uncivil, Sir, to break open one's letters.

Foss. Would I had not; and that the contents of it had been a secret to me and all mankind for ever. Wretched creature, to what a miserable condition has thy poetry reduc'd thee!

Clink. I am not in the least mortified with the accident. I know it has happen'd to many of the most famous daughters of Apollo; and to myself several times.   400

Foss. I am thunderstruck at her impudence! several times!

Clink. I have had one returned upon my hands every winter for these five years past. I may perhaps be excell'd by others in judgment and correctness of manners, but for fertility and readiness of conception, I will yield to nobody.

Foss. Bless me, whence had she this luxuriant constitution!

Poss. Patience, Sir. Perhaps this lady may be married.

Town. 'Tis infamous, Mr. Fossile, to keep her in your house; yet though you turn her out of doors, use her with some humanity; I will take care of the child.   410

Clink. I can find no *Denouement* of all this conversation. Where is the crime, I pray, of writing a tragedy? I sent it to Drury-Lane house to be acted; and here it is return'd by the wrong *gout* of the actors.

Poss. This incident has somewhat embarrassed us. But what mean you here, madam, by this expression? Your offspring.

Clink. My tragedy, the offspring of my brain. One of his majesty's justices of the peace, and not understand the use of the metaphor!

Poss. Doctor, you have used much artifice, and many demurrers; but the child must lie at your door at last. Friend, speak plain what thou knowest of this matter.   420

Foss. Let me relate my story. This morning, I married this lady, and brought her from her lodgings, at Mrs. Chambers's, in King-street, Covent-Garden.

Sail. Mrs. Chambers! To that place I was directed, where liv'd the maid that put the bantling out to be nurs'd by my wife for her lady; and who she was, 'tis none of our business to enquire.

Poss. Dost thou know the name of this maid?

Sail. Let me consider—Lutestring.

Foss. Sarsnet, thou mean'st.

Sail. Sarsnet, that's right.   430

Town. I'll turn her out of my house this moment, filthy creature!

Poss. The evidence is plain. You have cohabitation with the mother, doctor, *currat lex*. And you must keep the child.

Foss. Your decree is unjust, Sir, and I'll seek my remedy at law. As I never was espoused, I never had carnal knowledge of any woman; and my wife, Mrs. Susanna Townley, is a pure virgin at this hour for me.

Poss. Susanna Townley! Susanna Townley! Look how runs the warrant you drew up this morning.   [Clerk *gives him a paper*.

Madam, a word in private with you.   [*Whispers her*.

Doctor, my Lord Chief Justice has some business with this lady.   440

Foss. My Lord Chief Justice business with my wife!

Poss. To be plain with you, doctor Fossile, you have for these three hours entertain'd another man's wife. Her husband, lieutenant Bengal, is just re-turned from the Indies, and this morning took out a warrant from me for an elopement; it will be more for your credit to part with her privately, than to suffer her publickly to be carried off by a tipstaff.

Foss. Surprizing have been the events of this day; but this, the strangest of all, settles my future repose. Let her go—I have not dishonoured the bed of lieutenant Bengal—Hark ye friend! Do you follow her with that badge of her infamy.   450

Poss. By your favour, doctor, I never reverse my judgment. The child is yours: for it cannot belong to a man who has been three years absent in the East-Indies. Leave the child.

Sail. I find you are out of humour, master. So I'll call to-morrow for his clearings.   455

Sailor *lays down the* Child, *and exit with* Possum, Clerk, *and* Townley.

Clink. Uncle, by this day's adventure, every one has got something. Lieutenant Bengal has got his wife again; you a fine child; and I a plot for a comedy; and I'll this moment set about it.   [*Exit* Clinket.

Foss. What must be, must be. [*Takes up the* Child.] Fossile, thou didst want posterity: Here behold thou hast it. A wife thou didst not want; thou hast none. But thou art caressing a child that is not thy own. What then? a thousand, and a thousand husbands are doing the same thing this very instant; and the knowledge of truth is desirable, and makes thy case the better. What signifies whether a man beget his child or not? How rediculous is the act itself, said the great emperor Antoninus! I now look upon myself as a Roman citizen; it is better that the father should adopt the child, than that the wife should adopt the father.   [*Exit* Fossile.

EPILOGUE.

THE ancient Epilogue, as criticks write,
  Was, Clap your hands, excuse us, and good-night.
The modern always was a kind essay
To reconcile the audience to the play:
More polish'd, we of late have learn'd to fly
At parties, treaties, nations, ministry.
Our author more genteelly leaves these brawls
To coffee-houses, and to coblers stalls.
His very monsters are of sweet condition,
None but the Crocodile's a politician;   10
He reaps the blessings of his double nature,
And, Trimmer like, can live on land or water:
Yet this same monster shou'd be kindly treated,
He lik'd a lady's flesh—but not to eat it.

  As for my other spark, my favourite Mummy,
His feats were such, smart youths! as might become ye;
Dead as he seem'd, he had sure signs of life;
His hieroglyphicks pleas'd the doctor's wife.

  Whom can our well-bred poetess displease?
She writ like quality—with wond'rous ease: 20
All her offence was harmless want of wit;
Is that a crime?—ye powers, preserve the pit.

  My doctor too, to give the devil his due,
When every creature did his spouse pursue,
(Men sound and living, bury'd flesh, dry'd fish,)
Was e'en as civil as a wife could wish.
Yet he was somewhat fancy with his vial;
What! put young maids to that unnat'ral trial!
So hard a test! why, if you needs will make it,
Faith, let us marry first,—and then we'll take it.   30

  Who could be angry, though like Fossile teaz'd?
Consider, in three hours, the man was eas'd.
How many of you are for life beguil'd,

And keep as well the mother, as the child!
None but a Tar could be so tender-hearted,
To claim a wife that had been three years parted;
Would you do this, my friends?—believe me, never:
When modishly you part—you part for ever.
   Join then your voices, be the play excus'd
For once, though no one living is abus'd;   40
To that bright circle that commands our duties,
To you superior eighteen-penny beauties,
To the lac'd hat and cockard of the pit, ⎤
To all, in one word, we our cause submit, ⎬
Who think good breeding is a-kin to wit. ⎦

43 *cockard*] Obs. form of 'cockade', a ribbon worn in the hat as a badge of one's party or office.

TOM THUMB

Henry Fielding

1707–1754

Tom Thumb is among the best known and loved of all burlesques, second only to *The Critic* in endurance—and thus in availability. It may not, however, be generally realized that the text reprinted in modern editions* is that of *The Tragedy of Tragedies*, a version of the play revised and enlarged by Fielding in 1731, a year after the original *Tom Thumb* had first been performed at the Little Theatre in the Haymarket. This was the playhouse in which, a few years later, were staged those lampoons against Walpole which brought in their wake theatre censorship and the close of Fielding's career as a dramatist: but in 1730 this career had barely begun, since all that the young playwright had previously written were two unremarkable five-act comedies. He was about to discover—in *Tom Thumb*, and in *The Author's Farce*, a dramatic satire to which the burlesque first served as an afterpiece—two less regular forms in which his theatrical talents really lay.

It was only in his dramatic satires, like *The Author's Farce* and *Pasquin*, that Fielding made use of the rehearsal formula. His true burlesques were entirely self-contained, their parody not dependent upon interpolated comments but upon the language and action of the mock-tragedies themselves. True, the text of the revised *Tragedy of Tragedies* had its pseudo-academic apparatus, but the embellishment was intended for the study, not for the stage. *Tom Thumb* itself, which is here reprinted, lacks the later footnotes. It is, indeed, altogether less polished (though no less robust) than its successor: thus, a comparison reveals, besides much new material, a reshaping of existing passages, to demonstrate more aptly the artificial word-order dictated by a subservience of sense to metre. The earlier version is, however, already distinguished by Fielding's ability to transcend mere parody. True, many of his lines are cheerfully plagiarized from passages bad enough to stand condemned without distortion; but it is the play's strength that it gets its points across to an audience unfamiliar with such sources, and its lack of the textual niceties of *The Tragedy of Tragedies* perhaps better fits it to do so.

* Among them *Eighteenth Century Comedy*, selected by W. D. Taylor, texts newly edited by Simon Trussler (Oxford Paperbacks, 1969).

Tom Thumb is the first burlesque to sustain a successful parodistic attack not in mock-heroic couplets but in blank verse—a less easy but potentially more rewarding idiom to burlesque, and one which gave Fielding greater freedom in his manipulation of verse movement and development of extended similes; in the placing of often devastatingly bathetic emphases; and in the occasional but purposeful use of added syllables. More generally, the play exemplifies 'the profound of Scriblerus'—not least in its embodiment of heroic virtues in the pathetic figure of a midget. The explicit acknowledgment made in the preface to Pope's definition of the 'profound', besides the pseudonymous attribution of the play to Scriblerus Secundus, thus confirms Fielding's indebtedness to Pope's recently published *Art of Sinking in Poetry*—which might itself be described as a handbook of burlesque technique. In its new sense of a toppling from the lofty to the ludicrous, bathos was a remarkably effective weapon in Pope's hands, and in *Tom Thumb* it became equally effective in Fielding's. Perhaps, however, the dramatist stuck too closely in this early play to one characteristic method of his mentor—the demonstration of *unconscious* bathos from the works of other writers. At least, in *The Covent-Garden Tragedy* he was to exploit more fully the possibilities of the *conscious* control of bathos, in the interests of less particularized satire: and it is my own feeling that this later burlesque, which follows *Tom Thumb* in the present collection, is in many ways the better of the two, its actual neglect more accidental than deserved.

TOM THUMB.

A

TRAGEDY.

As it is Acted at the

THEATRE

IN THE

HAY-MARKET.

Written by *Scriblerus Secundus.*

—— *Tragicus plerumque dolet Sermone pedeſtri.*   Hor.

LONDON,

Printed : And Sold by J. Roberts in
Warwick-Lane. 1730.
[Price Six Pence.]

F

PREFACE.

A Preface is become almost as necessary to a Play, as a Prologue: It is a Word of Advice to the Reader, as the other to the Spectator: And as the Business of a Prologue is to commend the Play, so that of the Preface is to Compliment the Actors.

A Preface requires a Style entirely different from all other Writings; A Style for which I can find no Name in either the Sublime of *Longinus*, or the Profound of *Scriblerus*: which I shall therefore venture to call the Supernatural, after the celebrated Author of *Hurlothrumbo*: who, tho' no Writer of Prefaces, is a very great Master of their Style.   9

As *Charon* in *Lucian* suffers none to enter his Boat till stripped of every thing they have about them, so should no Word by any means enter into a Preface till stripped of all its Ideas. Mr. *Lock* complains of confused Ideas in Words, which is entirely amended by suffering them to give none at all: This may be done by adding, diminishing, or changing a Letter, as instead of *Paraphernalia*, writing *Paraphonalia*: For a Man may turn *Greek* into Nonsense, who cannot turn Sense into either *Greek* or *Latin*.

A Second Method of stripping Words of their Ideas is by putting half a dozen incoherent ones together: Such as *when the People of our Age shall be Ancestors*, &c. By which means one discordant Word, like a surly Man in Company, spoils the whole Sentence, and makes it entirely Prefatical.   20

Some imagine this Way of Writing to have been originally introduced by *Plato*, whom *Cicero* observes to have taken especial Pains in wrapping up his Sentiments from the Understandings of the Vulgar. But I can in no wise agree with them in this Conjecture, any more than their deriving the Word Preface, *quasi Plaface, a Plato*: whereas the original Word is *Playface, quasi Players Face*: and sufficiently denotes some Player, who was as remarkable for his *Face*, as his Prefaces, to have been the Inventor of it.

But that the Preface to my Preface be not longer than that to my Play: I shall have done with the Performances of others, and speak a Word or two of my own.   30

This Preface then was writ at the Desire of my Bookseller, who told me that some Elegant Criticks had made three great Objections to this Tragedy:

---

7 the Profound of *Scriblerus*] The allusion is to Pope's *Art of Sinking in Poetry*, included among the *Miscellanies* of Pope and Swift in 1727.   8 *Hurlothrumbo*] A nonsense play by Samuel Johnson of Cheshire, which had preceded *Tom Thumb* at the Haymarket Theatre. 10 *Charon* in *Lucian*] In the *Dialogue of the Dead*.   15 *Paraphonalia*] A spelling mistake of Cibber's, in the preface to his *Provoked Husband*.   18 *when the People of our Age shall be Ancestors*] Another solecism of Cibber's, also in *The Provoked Husband*.

which I shall handle without any Regard to Precedence: And therefore I begin to defend the last Scene of my Play against the third Objection of these *Kriticks, which is, to the destroying all the Characters in it, this I cannot think so unprecedented as these Gentlemen would insinuate, having my-self known it done in the first Act of several Plays: Nay, it is common in modern Tragedy for the Characters to drop, like the Citizens in the first Scene of *OEdipus*, as soon as they come upon the Stage.

Secondly, they Object to the killing a Ghost. This (say they) far exceeds the Rules of Probability; perhaps it may; but I would desire these Gentlemen seriously to recollect, whether they have not seen in several celebrated Plays, such expressions as these, *Kill my Soul, Stab my very Soul, Bleeding Soul, Dying Soul, cum multis aliis*, all which visibly confess that for a Soul or Ghost to be killed is no Impossibility.   45

As for the first Objection which they make, and the last which I answer, *viz.* to the Subject, to this I shall only say, that it is in the Choice of my Subject I have placed my chief Merit.

It is with great Concern that I have observed several of our (the *Grubstreet*) Tragical Writers, to Celebrate in their Immortal Lines the Actions of Heroes recorded in Historians and Poets, such as *Homer* or *Virgil*, *Livy* or *Plutarch*, the Propagation of whose Works is so apparently against the Interest of our Society; when the Romances, Novels, and Histories, *vulgo* call'd Story-Books, of our own People, furnish such abundant and proper Themes for their Pens, such are *Tom Tram*, *Hickathrift*, &c.   55

And here I congratulate my Cotemporary Writers, for their having enlarged the Sphere of Tragedy: The ancient Tragedy seems to have had only two Effects on an Audience, *viz.* It either awakened Terror and Compassion, or composed those and all other uneasy Sensations, by lulling the Audience in an agreeable Slumber. But to provoke the Mirth and Laughter of the Spectators, to join the Sock to the Buskin, is a Praise only due to Modern Tragedy.

Having spoken thus much of the Play, I shall proceed to the Performers, amongst whom if any shone brighter than the rest it was *Tom Thumb*. Indeed such was the Excellence thereof, that no one can believe unless they see its Representation, to which I shall refer the Curious: Nor can I refrain

---

* *Prefatical language.*

---

38 the Citizens in . . . *OEdipus*] The allusion is to a stage direction at the opening of the *Oedipus* of Dryden and Lee (1679).   40 the killing a Ghost] This incident was omitted from *The Tragedy of Tragedies*. Allegedly, it was one of the two events in Swift's life which caused him to laugh.   55 *Tom Tram, Hickathrift*] Heroes of contemporary chapbooks. Thackeray mistakenly attributed the authorship of *Hickathrift* to Fielding.   61 the Sock . . . the Buskin] The former was the low shoe worn by comic actors in the ancient Greek theatre, the latter the high boot worn by tragic actors. Thus, used generically to denote the comic and tragic forms.

from observing how well one of the Mutes set off his Part: So excellent was his Performance, that it out-did even my own Wishes: I gratefully give him my share of Praise, and desire the Audience to refer the whole to his beautiful Action.   70

And now I must return my hearty Thanks to the Musick, who, I believe, played to the best of their Skill, because it was for their own Reputation, and because they are paid for it: So have I thrown little *Tom Thumb* on the Town, and hope they will be favourable to him, and for an Answer to all Censures, take these words of *Martial*,

> *Seria cum possim, quod delectantia malim*
> *Scribere, Tu, Causa es* —————

PROLOGUE.

By no Friend of the Author's.

Spoken by Mr. *JONES.*

*W*ITH *Mirth and Laughter to delight the Mind*
    The modern Tragedy was first design'd:
'Twas this made Farce *with* Tragedy *unite,*
And taught each Scribler in the Town to Write.

   The Glorious Heroes who, in former Years,
Dissolv'd all Athens *and all* Rome *in Tears;*
Who to our Stage, have been transplanted too;
Whom Shakespear *taught to Storm, and* Lee *to Woo,* }
And could to Softness, ev'ry Heart subdue,
Grub-Street *has turned to* Farce.—— *Oh glorious Lane!*   10
O, may thy Authors never write in vain!
May crowded Theatres ne'er give Applause
To any other than the Grub-Street *Cause!*

   Since then, to laugh, to Tragedies you come,
What Heroe is so proper as Tom Thumb?
Tom Thumb! *whose very Name must Mirth incite,*
And fill each merry Briton *with Delight.*

   Britons, *awake!—Let* Greece *and* Rome *no more*
Their Heroes send to our Heroick Shore.
Let home-bred Subjects grace the modern Muse,   20
And Grub-Street *from her Self, her Heroes chuse:*
Her Story-Books *Immortalize in Fame,*
Hickathrift, Jack the Giant-Killer, *and* Tom Tram.
No Venus *shou'd in Sign-Post Painter shine;*
No Roman *Hero in a Scribler's Line:*
The monst'rous Dragon to the Sign belongs,

13 Grub-Street] A street near Moorfields, reputedly the haunt of literary hacks. Used
generically as a term for scribblers.

And Grub-Street's *Heroes best adorn her Songs.*
To-night our Bard, Spectators, *would be* true
To Farce, *to* Tragedy, Tom Thumb, *and* You.
May all the Hissing Audience be struck Dumb;   30
Long live the Man who cries, Long live Tom Thumb.

EPILOGUE.

Sent by an Unknown Hand.

Spoken by Miss *JONES*.

TOM Thumb, *twice Dead, is a third Time Reviv'd,*
And, by your Favour, may be yet long-liv'd.
But, more I fear the snarling Critick's Brow,
Than Grizzle's Dagger, or the Throat of Cow!
Well then——Toupees, I warrant you suppose
I'll be exceeding witty on the Beaus;
But faith! I come with quite a diff'rent View,
To shew there are Tom Thumbs, *as well as you.*
Place me upon the awful Bench, and try
If any Judge can sleep more sound than I.   10
Or let me o'er a Pulpit-Cushion peep,
See who can set you in a sounder Sleep.
Tom Thumb *can feel the Pulse, can give the Pill;*
No Doctor's Feather shall more surely kill.
I'll be a Courtier, give me but a Place;
A Title makes me equal with his Grace:
Lace but my Coat, where is a prettier Spark?
I'll be a Justice—give me but a Clerk.
A Poet too—when I have learnt to read,
And plunder both the Living and the Dead: 20
Any of these, Tom Thumb *with Ease can be,*
For Many such, are nothing more than He.

But, for the Ladies, they, I know, despise
The little Things of my inferior Size.
Their mighty Souls are all of them too large
To take so small a Heroe to their Charge.
Take Pity, Ladies, on a young Beginner;
Faith! I may prove, in time, a thumping Sinner.
Let your kind Smiles our Author's Cause defend;
He fears no Foes, while Beauty is his Friend.   30

Dramatis Personæ.

MEN.

King Arthur,	Mr. *Mullart.*
Tom Thumb,	Miss *Jones.*
Lord Grizzle,	Mr. *Jones.*
Mr. Noodle,	Mr. *Reynolds*
Mr. Doodle,	Mr. *Marshall.*
1 Physician,	Mr. *Hallam.*
2 Physician,	Mr. *Dove.*

WOMEN.

Queen Dollalolla,	Mrs. *Mullart.*
Princess Huncamunca,	Mrs. *Jones.*
Cleora,	Mrs. *Smith.*
Mustacha,	Mrs. *Clark.*

Courtiers, Slaves, Bailiffs, &c.

SCENE *The Court of King* Arthur.

TOM THUMB.

ACT I. SCENE I.

SCENE *The Palace.*

Mr. Doodle, *Mr.* Noodle.

DOODLE.

SURE, such a Day as this was never seen!
The Sun himself, on this auspicious Day,
Shines like a Beau in a new Birth-Day Suit:
All Nature, O my *Noodle!* grins for Joy.
  Nood. This Day, O Mr. *Doodle!* is a Day
Indeed, a Day we never saw before.
The mighty *Thomas Thumb* victorious comes;
Millions of Giants crowd his Chariot Wheels,
Who bite their Chains, and frown and foam like Mad-Dogs.
He rides, regardless of their ugly Looks.   10
So some Cock-Sparrow in a Farmer's Yard,
Hops at the Head of an huge Flock of Turkeys.
  Dood. When Goody *Thumb* first brought this *Thomas* forth,
The *Genius* of our Land triumphant reign'd;
Then, then, O *Arthur!* did thy *Genius* reign.
  Nood. They tell me, it is whisper'd in the Books
Of all our Sages, That this mighty Hero
(By *Merlin*'s Art begot) has not a Bone
Within his Skin, but is a Lump of Gristle.
  Dood. Wou'd *Arthur*'s Subjects were such Gristle, all!   20
He then might break the Bones of ev'ry Foe.
  Nood. But hark! these Trumpets speak the King's Approach.
  Dood. He comes most luckily for my Petition!
Let us retire a little.

---

3 Birth-Day Suit] A form of celebratory dress for the king's birthday.

SCENE II.

King, Queen, *Lord* Grizzle, Doodle, Noodle.

King. Let nothing but a Face of Joy appear;
The Man who frowns this Day, shall lose his Head,
That he may have no Face to frown again.
Smile, *Dollalolla ;*—— Ha! what wrinkled Sorrow
Sits, like some *Mother Demdike*, on thy Brow?
Whence flow those Tears fast down thy blubber'd Cheeks,
Like a swoln Gutter, gushing through the Streets?
  Queen. Excess of Joy, I've heard Folks say,
Gives Tears, as often as Excess of Grief.
  King. If it be so, let all Men cry for Joy,   10
'Till my whole Court be drowned with their Tears;
Nay, 'till they overflow my utmost Land,
And leave me nothing but the Sea to rule.
  Dood. My Liege! I've a Petition——
  King. Petition me no Petitions, Sir, to-day;
Let other Hours be set apart for Bus'ness.
To-day it is our Pleasure to be drunk,
And this our Queen shall be as drunk as Us.
  Queen. If the capacious Goblet overflow
With *Arrack-Punch*— 'fore *George!* I'll see it out;   20
Of *Rum*, or *Brandy*, I'll not taste a Drop.
  King. Tho' *Rack*, in *Punch*, Eight Shillings be a Quart,
And *Rum* and *Brandy* be no more than Six,
Rather than quarrel, you shall have your Will.

[*Trumpets.*

But, ha! the Warrior comes; *Tom Thumb* approaches;
The welcome Hero, Giant-killing Lad,
Preserver of my Kingdom, is arrived.

---

5 *Mother Demdike*] A notorious witch of the early seventeenth century.   20 *Arrack-Punch*] An oriental term for various fermented juices, originally of the date.

SCENE III.

Tom Thumb, *attended;* King, Queen, *Lord* Grizzle,
Doodle, Noodle.

King, O welcome, ever welcome to my Arms,
My dear *Tom Thumb!* How shall I thank thy Merit?
   Thumb. By not b'ing thank'd at all, I'm thank'd enough;
My Duty I have done, and done no more.
   Queen. Was ever such a lovely Creature seen!   [*Aside.*
   King. Thy Modesty's a Candle to thy Merit,
It shines Itself, and shews thy Merit too.
Vain Impudence, if it be ever found
With Virtue, like the Trumpet in a Consort,
Drowns the sweet Musick of the softer Flute.   10
But say, my Boy, where didst thou leave the Giants?
   Thumb. My Liege, without the Castle Gates they stand,
The Castle Gates too low for their Admittance.
   King. What look they like?
   Thumb. Like twenty Things, my Liege;
Like twenty thousand Oaks, by Winter's Hand
Strip'd of their Blossoms, like a Range of Houses,
When Fire has burnt their Timber all away.
   King. Enough: The vast Idea fills my Soul;
I see them, yes, I see them now before me.   20
The monst'rous, ugly, barb'rous Sons of Whores,
Which, like as many rav'nous Wolves, of late
Frown'd grimly o'er the Land, like Lambs look now.
O *Thumb,* what do we to thy Valour owe!
The Princess *Huncamunca* is thy Prize.
   Queen. Ha! Be still, my Soul!
   Thumb. Oh, happy, happy Hearing!
Witness, ye Stars! cou'd *Thumb* have ever set
A Bound to his Ambition—it had been
The Princess *Huncamunca,* in whose Arms   30
Eternity would seem but half an Hour.
   Queen. Consider, Sir, reward your Soldier's Merit,
But give not *Huncamunca* to *Tom Thumb.*
   King. Tom Thumb! Odzooks, my wide extended Realm
Knows not a Name so glorious as *Tom Thumb.*

17 a Range of Houses] A *row* of houses.

Not *Alexander*, in his highest Pride,
Could boast of Merits greater than *Tom Thumb*.
Not *Cæsar*, *Scipio*, all the Flow'rs of *Rome*,
Deserv'd their Triumphs better than *Tom Thumb*.

   Queen. Tho' greater yet his boasted Merit was,   40
He shall not have the Princess, that is Pos'.

   King. Say you so, Madam? We will have a Trial.
When I consent, what Pow'r has your Denyal?
For, when the Wife her Husband over-reaches,
Give him the Petticoat, and her the Breeches.

   Nood. Long Health and Happiness attend the General!
Long may he live, as now, the Publick Joy,
While ev'ry Voice is burthen'd with his Praise.

   Thumb. Whisper, ye Winds! that *Huncamunca*'s mine;
Ecchoes repeat, that *Huncamunca*'s mine!   50
The dreadful Bus'ness of the War is over,
And Beauty, heav'nly Beauty! crowns the Toil.
I've thrown the bloody Garment now aside,
And *Hymeneal* Sweets invite my Bride.
   So when some Chimney-Sweeper, all the Day,
Has through dark Paths pursu'd the Sooty Way,
At Night, to wash his Face and Hands he flies,
And in his t'other Shirt with his *Brickdusta* lies.

SCENE IV.

Lord Grizzle, *Solus.*

   See how the cringing Coxcombs fawn upon him!
The Sun-shine of a Court can, in a Day,
Ripen the vilest Insect to an Eagle:
And ev'ry little Wretch, who but an Hour
Before had scorn'd, and trod him under Feet,
Shall lift his Eyes aloft, to gaze at distance,
And flatter what they scorn'd.

SCENE V.

Enter Queen, *to Lord* Grizzle.

Queen. Well met, my Lord.
You are the Man I sought. Have you not heard
(What ev'ry Corner of the Court resounds)
That little *Thumb* will be a great Man made.
  Griz. I heard it, I confess—for who, alas!
Can always stop his Ears—but would my Teeth,
By grinding Knives, had first been set on Edge.
  Queen. Would I had heard at the still Noon of Night,
The dreadful Cry of Fire in ev'ry Street!
Odsbobs! I could almost destroy my self,   10
To think I should a Grand-mother be made
By such a Rascal.—Sure, the King forgets,
When in a Pudding, by his Mother put,
The Bastard, by a Tinker, on a Stile
Was drop'd.——O, good Lord *Grizzle!* can I bear
To see him, from a Pudding, mount the Throne?
  Griz. Oh Horror! Horror! Horror! cease my Queen,
Thy Voice, like twenty Screech-Owls, wracks my brain.
  Queen. Then rouze thy Spirit—we may yet prevent
This hated Match.——   20
  Griz. We will.—— Not Fate, itself,
Should it conspire with *Thomas Thumb,* should cause it.
I'll swim through Seas; I'll ride upon the Clouds;
I'll dig the Earth; I'll blow out ev'ry Fire;
I'll rave; I'll rant; I'll rush; I'll rise; I'll roar   ⎫
Fierce as the Man whom smiling Dolphins bore,   ⎬
From the Prosaick to Poetick Shore.   ⎭
I'll tear the Scoundrel into twenty Pieces.
  Queen. Oh, no! prevent the Match, but hurt him not;
For, tho' I would not have him have my Daughter,
Yet, can we kill the Man who kill'd the Giants?   30
  Griz. I tell you, Madam, it was all a Trick,
He made the Giants first, and then he kill'd them;
As Fox-hunters bring Foxes to a Wood,

4 a great Man] Probably a casual hit at Sir Robert Walpole, to whom this title was
ironically applied.

And then with Hounds they drive them out again.

    Queen. How! Have you seen no Giants? Are there not
Now, in the Yard, ten thousand proper Giants?

    Griz. Indeed, I cannot positively tell,
But firmly do believe there is not One.

    Queen. Hence! from my Sight! thou Traytor, hie away;   40
By all my Stars! thou enviest *Tom Thumb*.
Go, Sirrah! go; hie away! hie!——thou art
A Setting Dog—and like one I use thee.

    Griz. Madam, I go.
Tom Thumb shall feel the Vengeance you have rais'd.

    So when two Dogs are fighting in the Streets,
With a third Dog, one of the two Dogs meets,
With angry Teeth, he bites him to the Bone,
And this Dog smarts for what that Dog had done.   [*Exit.*

SCENE VI.

Queen, *Sola.*

    And whither shall I go?—— Alack-a-day!
I love *Tom Thumb*—but must not tell him so;
For what's a Woman, when her Virtue's gone?
A Coat without its Lace; Wig out of Buckle;
A Stocking with a Hole in't.—I can't live
Without my Virtue, or without *Tom Thumb*.
Then let me weigh them in two equal Scales,
In this Scale put my Virtue, that, *Tom Thumb*.
Alas! *Tom Thumb* is heavier than my Virtue.
But hold!—— Perhaps I may be left a Widow: 10
This Match prevented, then *Tom Thumb* is mine,
In that dear Hope, I will forget my Pain.

    So when some Wench to *Tothill-Bridewell*'s sent,
With beating Hemp, and Flogging, she's content;
She hopes, in Time, to ease her present Pain;
At length is free, and walks the Streets again.   [*Exit.*

---

13 *Tothill-Bridewell*] A prison to which harlots were often committed.

ACT II. SCENE I.

SCENE *The Street.*

Bailiff, Follower.

Bailiff. COME on, my trusty Follower, inur'd
　　　　To ev'ry kind of Danger; cudgell'd oft;
Often in Blankets toss'd—oft Pump'd upon:
Whose Virtue in a Horse-Pond hath been try'd.
Stand here by me.—— This way must *Noodle* pass.
　Foll. Were he an Half-pay Officer, a Bully,
A Highway-man, or Prize-fighter, I'd nab him.
　Bail. This Day discharge thy Duty, and at Night
A double Mug of Beer and Beer shall glad thee.
Then in an Ale-house may'st thou sit at Ease,　　　　　　　　10
And quite forget the Labours of the Day.
So wearied Oxen to their Stalls retire,
And rest from all the Burthens of the Plough.
　Foll. No more, no more, O Bailiff! ev'ry Word
Inspires my Soul with Virtue.—— O! I long
To meet the Enemy in the Street—and nab him;
To lay arresting Hands upon his Back,
And drag him trembling to the Spunging-House.
　Bail. There, when I have him, I will spunge upon him.
O glorious Thought! By the Sun, Moon, and Stars,　　　　　20
I will enjoy it, tho' it be in Thought!
Yes, yes, my Follower, I will enjoy it.
So Lovers, in Imagination strong,
Enjoy their absent Mistresses in Thought,
And hug their Pillows, as I now do thee:
And as they squeeze its Feathers out—so I
Would from his Pockets squeeze the Money out.
　Foll. Alas! too just your Simile, I fear,
For Courtiers often nothing are but Feathers.
　Bail. Oh, my good Follower! when I reflect　　　　　　30
On the big Hopes I once had entertain'd,
To see the Law, as some devouring Wolf,
Eat up the Land,—'till, like a Garrison,

6 Bully] In the sense of a hired ruffian.　18 Spunging-House] A bailiff's house for the
initial confinement of debtors.

Its whole Provision's gone.—— Lawyers were forc'd,
For want of Food, to feed on one another.
But Oh! fall'n Hope. The Law will be reduc'd
Again to Reason, whence it first arose.
But Ha! our Prey approaches—let us retire.

SCENE II.

Tom Thumb, Noodle, Bailiff, Follower.

Thumb. Trust me, my *Noodle*, I am wond'rous sick;
For tho' I love the gentle *Huncamunca*,
Yet at the Thought of Marriage, I grow pale;
For Oh!—but swear thou'lt keep it ever secret,
I will unfold a Tale will make thee stare.
 Nood. I swear by lovely *Huncamunca*'s Charms.
 Thumb. Then know—My Grand-mamma hath often said—
Tom Thumb, beware of Marriage.——
 Nood. Sir, I blush
To think a Warrior great in Arms as you,   10
Should be affrighted by his Grand-mamma.
Can an old Woman's empty Dreams deter
The blooming Hero from the Virgin's Arms?
Think of the Joy which will your Soul alarm,
When in her fond Embraces clasp'd you lie,
While on her panting Breast dissolv'd in Bliss,
You pour out all *Tom Thumb* in ev'ry Kiss.
 Thumb. Oh, *Noodle!* thou hast fir'd my eager Soul;
Spight of my Grandmother, she shall be mine;
I'll hug, caress, I'll eat her up with Love.   20
Whole Days, and Nights, and Years shall be too short
For our Enjoyment; ev'ry Sun shall rise
Blushing, to see us in our Bed together.
 Nood. Oh, Sir! this Purpose of your Soul pursue.
 Bail. Oh, Sir! I have an Action against you.
 Nood. At whose Suit is it?
 Bail. At your Taylor's, Sir.
Your Taylor put this Warrant in my Hands,
And I arrest you, Sir, at his Commands.
 Thumb. Ha! Dogs! Arrest my Friend before my Face!   30
Think you *Tom Thumb* will swallow this Disgrace!

But let vain Cowards threaten by their Word,
Tom Thumb shall show his Anger by his Sword.   [*Kills the Bailiff.*
  Bail. Oh, I am slain!
  Foll. I'm murdered also,
And to the Shades, the dismal Shades below,
My Bailiff's faithful Follower I go.
  Thumb. Thus perish all the Bailiffs in the Land,
'Till Debtors at Noon-day shall walk the Street,
And no one fear a Bailiff, or his Writ.

                                                           40

SCENE III. *The Princess* Huncamunca's *Apartment.*

Huncamunca, Cleora, Mustacha.

Hunc. Give me some Musick to appease my Soul;
Gentle *Cleora*, sing my fav'rite Song.
                    Cleora *sings.*
            Cupid, *ease a Love-sick Maid,*
            Bring thy Quiver to her Aid;
            With equal Ardor wound the Swain:
            Beauty should never sigh in vain.
            Let him feel the pleasing Smart,
            Drive thy Arrow through his Heart;
            When One you wound, you then destroy;
            When Both you kill, you kill with Joy.   10
  Hunc. O, *Tom Thumb! Tom Thumb!* wherefore art thou *Tom Thumb?*
Why had'st thou not been born of Royal Blood?
Why had not mighty *Bantam* been thy Father?
Or else the King of *Brentford, Old* or *New?*
  Must. I am surprized that your Highness can give your self a Moment's
Uneasiness about that little insignificant Fellow, *Tom Thumb.* One properer
for a Play-thing, than a Husband.—Were he my Husband, his Horns should
be as long as his Body.—If you had fallen in Love with a Grenadier, I
should not have wondered at it. If you had fallen in Love with Something;
but to fall in Love with Nothing!   20
  Hunc. Cease, my *Mustacha*, on your Duty cease.
The *Zephyr*, when in flowry Vales it plays,
Is not so soft, so sweet as *Thummy's* Breath.

13–14 mighty *Bantam . . .* Or else the King of *Brentford*] In his *Author's Farce*, Fielding
had resurrected the royal pair from *The Rehearsal*, in order to marry off the newly-discovered
daughter of the 'exiled' king to the equally newly-discovered heir to the Bantamite throne.

The Dove is not so gentle to its Mate.

Must. The Dove is every bit as proper for a Husband. Alas! Madam, there's not a Beau about the Court that looks so little like a Man. He is a perfect Butterfly, a Thing without Substance, and almost without Shadow too.

Hunc. This Rudeness is unseasonable; desist,
Or I shall think this Railing comes from Love.   30
Tom Thumb's a Creature of that charming Form,
That no one can abuse, unless they love him.

Cle. Madam, the King.

SCENE IV.

King, Huncamunca.

King. Let all but *Huncamunca* leave the Room.

[*Exit* Cleora, *and* Mustacha.

Daughter, I have of late observ'd some Grief
Unusual in your Countenance, your Eyes
That, like two open Windows, us'd to shew
The lovely Beauty of the Room within,
Have now two Blinds before them—What is the Cause?
Say, have you not enough of Meat or Drink?
We've giv'n strict Orders not to have you stinted.

Hunc. Alas! my Lord, a tender Maid may want
What she can neither Eat nor Drink——   10

King. What's that?

Hunc. Oh! Spare my Blushes, but I mean a Husband.

King. If that be all, I have provided one,
A Husband great in Arms, whose Warlike Sword
Streams with the yellow Blood of slaughter'd Giants.
Whose Name in *Terrâ incognitâ* is known,
Whose Valour, Wisdom, Virtue make a Noise,
Great as the Kettle Drums of twenty Armies.

Hunc. Whom does my Royal Father mean?

King. Tom Thumb.   20

Hunc. Is it possible?

King. Ha! the Window-Blinds are gone,
A Country Dance of Joys is in your Face,
Your Eyes spit Fire, your Cheeks grow red as Beef.

Hunc. O, there's a Magick-musick in that Sound,

Enough to turn me into Beef indeed.
Yes, I will own, since licens'd by your Word,
I'll own *Tom Thumb* the Cause of all my Grief.
For him I've Sigh'd, I've Wept, I've gnaw'd my Sheets.

SCENE V.

King, Huncamunca, Doodle.

Dood. Oh! fatal News—the great *Tom Thumb* is dead.
King. How dead!
Dood. Alas! as dead as a Door-Nail.
Help, help, the Princess faints!
King. Fetch her a Dram.
Hunc. Under my Bed you'll find a Quart of Rum.   [*Exit* Doodle.
King. How does my pretty Daughter?
Hunc. Thank you, Papa,
I'm something better now.

Enter Slave.

King. What Slave waits there?   10
Go order the Physicians strait before me,
That did attend *Tom Thumb*—now by my Stars,
Unless they give a full and true Account
Of his Distemper, they shall all be hang'd.
Dood. [*Returns.*] Here is the Bottle, and here is the Glass.
I found them both together——
King. Give them me.   [*Fills the Glass.*
Drink it all off, it will do you no harm.

SCENE VI.

King, Huncamunca, Doodle, Physicians.

1 Phys. We here attend your Majesty's Command.
King. Of what Distemper did *Tom Thumb* demise?
1 Phys. He died, may it please your Majesty, of a Distemper which
Paracelsus calls the *Diaphormane*, *Hippocrates* the *Catecumen*, *Galen* the
Regon—He was taken with a Dizziness in his Head, for which I bled him, and

put on Four Blisters—he then had the Gripes, wherefore I thought it proper to apply a Glister, a Purge, and a Vomit.

2 Phys. Doctor, you mistake the Case; the Distemper was not the *Diaphormane*, as you vainly imagine; it was the *Peripilusis*—and tho' I approve very much of all that you did—let me tell you, you did not do half enough—you know he complained of a Pain in his Arm, I would immediately have cut off his Arm, and have laid open his Head, to which I would have applied some *Trahisick* Plaister; after that I would have proceeded to my *Catharticks*, *Emetics*, and *Diureticks*.   14

1 Phys. In the *Peripilusis* indeed these Methods are not only wholesome but necessary: but in the *Diaphormane* otherwise.

2 Phys. What are the Symptoms of the *Diaphormane*?

1 Phys. They are various—very various and uncertain.

2 Phys. Will you tell me that a Man died of the *Diaphormane* in one Hour—when the Crisis of that Distemper does not rise till the Fourth Day?   20

1 Phys. The Symptoms are various, very various and uncertain.

SCENE VII.

[*To them.*] Tom Thumb *attended.*

Thumb. Where is the Princess? where's my *Huncamunca*?
Lives she? O happy *Thumb!*—for even now
A Murmur humming skips about the Court,
That *Huncamunca* was defunct.
  King. Bless me!
Ye Blazing Stars—sure 'tis Illusion all.
Are you *Tom Thumb*, and are you too alive?
  Thumb. Tom Thumb I am, and eke also alive.
  King. And have you not been dead at all?——
  Thumb. Not I.   10
  1 Phys. I told you, Doctor, that *Cathartick* would do his Business.
  2 Phys. Ay, and I am very much surprized to find it did not.

---

7 Glister] Obs. form of 'clyster', an enema.

SCENE VIII.

King, Thumb, Huncamunca, Physicians, Doodle, Noodle.

Nood. Great News, may it please your Majesty, I bring,
A Traytor is discover'd, who design'd
To kill *Tom Thumb* with Poison.
  King. Ha! say you?
  Nood. A Girl had dress'd her Monkey in his Habit,
And that was poisoned by mistake for *Thumb.*
  King. Here are Physicians for you, whose nice Art
Can take a dress'd up Monkey for a Man.
Come to my Arms, my dearest Son-in-Law!
Happy's the wooing, that's not long a doing;   10
Proceed we to the Temple, there to tye
The burning Bridegroom to the blushing Bride.
And if I guess aright, *Tom Thumb* this Night
Shall give a Being to a new *Tom Thumb.*
  Thumb. It shall be my Endeavour so to do.
  Hunc. O fie upon you, Sir, you make me blush.
  Thumb. It is the Virgin's sign, and suits you well—
I know not where, nor how, nor what I am,
I'm so transported, I have lost my self.
  Hunc. Forbid it, all the Stars; for you're so small,   20
That were you lost, you'd find your self no more.
So the unhappy Sempstress, once, they say,
Her Needle in a Pottle, lost, of Hay.
In vain she look'd, and look'd, and made her Moan;
For ah! the Needle was for ever gone.
  King. Long may ye live, and love, and propagate,
'Till the whole Land be peopled with *Tom Thumbs.*
So when the *Cheshire*-Cheese a Maggot breeds,
Another and another still succeeds;
By thousands and ten thousands they encrease,   30
Till one continu'd Maggot fills the rotten Cheese.

---

23 Pottle . . . of Hay] A bottle or bundle of hay.

SCENE IX.

Manent Physicians.

1 Phys. Pray, Doctor *Church-yard*, what is your *Peripilusis?* I did not care to own my Ignorance to the King; but I never heard of such a Distemper before.

2 Phys. Truly, Doctor *Fillgrave*, it is more nearly allied to the *Diaphormane* than you imagine—and when you know the one, you will not be very far from finding out the other. But it is now past Ten; I must haste to Lord *Weekleys*, for he'll be dead before Eleven, and so I shall lose my Fee.   7

1 Phys. Doctor, your Servant.   [*Exeunt severally.*

SCENE X.

Enter Queen *sola.*

How am I forc'd to wander thus alone,
As if I were the *Phœnix* of my Kind;
Tom Thumb is lost—yet *Hickathrift* remains,
And *Hickathrift*'s as great a Man as *Thumb*.
Be he then our Gallant—but ha! what Noise
Comes trav'ling onward, bellowing as loud
As Thunder rumbling through th' Ætherial Plains?   7

SCENE XI.

King, Queen, Huncamunca, *Courtiers.*

King. Open the Prisons, set the Wretched free,
And bid our Treasurer disburse Six Pounds
To pay their Debts.—Let no one weep to-day.
Come, my fair Consort, sit thee down by me.
Here seated, let us view the Dancers Sport;
Bid them advance.—This is the Wedding-Day
Of Princess *Huncamunca* and *Tom Thumb*.   7

Dance, *Epithalamium*, and Sports.

---

s.d. Sc. xi *Epithalamium*] Celebratory wedding song.

SCENE *The Last*.

Noodle, King, Queen, Huncamunca, *Courtiers*.

Nood. Oh monstrous! dreadful! terrible! Oh! Oh!
Deaf be my Ears, for ever blind my Eyes,
Dumb be my Tongue, Feet lame, all Senses lost.
    King. What does the Blockhead mean?
    Nood. Whilst from my Garret
I look'd abroad into the Street below,
I saw *Tom Thumb* attended by the Mob,
Twice Twenty Shoe-boys, twice two Dozen Links,
Chairmen, and Porters, Hackney-Coachmen, Whores;
When on the sudden through the Streets there came   10
A Cow, of larger than the usual Size,
And in a Moment, guess, oh! guess the rest,
And in a Moment swallow'd up *Tom Thumb*.
    King. Horrible indeed!
    Griz. Swallow'd she him alive?
    Nood. Alive, alive, Lord *Grizzle ;* so the Boys
Of Fishmongers do swallow Gudgeons down.
    Griz. Curse on the Cow that took my Vengeance from me.   [*Aside*.
    King. Shut up again the Prisons, bid my Treasurer
Not give three Farthings out—hang all the *Culprits*,   20
Guilty or not—no matter.—Ravish Virgins,
Go bid the School-masters whip all their Boys;
Let Lawyers, Parsons, and Physicians loose,
To Rob, impose on, and to kill the World.

Ghost of Tom Thumb *rises*.

    Ghost. Thom Thumb I am—but am not eke alive.
My Body's in the Cow, my Ghost is here.
    Griz. Thanks, O ye Stars, my Vengeance is restor'd,
Nor shalt thou fly me—for I'll kill thy Ghost.   [*Kills the Ghost*.
    Hunc. O barbarous Deed!—I will revenge him so.   [*Kills Griz*.
    Dood. Ha! *Grizzle* kill'd—then Murtheress beware.   [*Kills Hunc*.
    Queen. O wretch!—have at thee.   [*Kills Dood*.
    Nood. And have at thee too.   [*Kills the Queen*.
    Cle. Thou'st kill'd the Queen.   [*Kills Nood*.
    Must. And thou hast kill'd my Lover.   [*Kills Cle*.

8 Links] Link-men, those employed to carry torches.

 King. Ha! Murtheress vile, take that.   [*Kills* Must.
And take thou this.   [*Kills himself, and falls.*
So when the Child whom Nurse from Mischief guards,
Sends *Jack* for Mustard with a Pack of Cards;
Kings, Queens and Knaves, throw one another down,
'Till the whole Pack lies scatter'd and o'erthrown;   40
So all our Pack upon the Floor is cast,
And all I boast is, that I fall the last.   [*Dies.*

FINIS.

38 *Jack* for Mustard] J. T. Hillhouse suggests that this may be a reference to a 'child's game, in which cards finally fell into a heap'. An old nursery rhyme, on the other hand, suggests an association between mustard and punishment for naughtiness. The precise sense of the simile remains ambiguous.

THE
COVENT-GARDEN TRAGEDY

Henry Fielding

1707–1754

Fielding's second and last burlesque, *The Covent-Garden Tragedy*, was performed at Drury Lane as an afterpiece to his farce *The Old Debauchees* on 1 June 1732. Publicus reported with satisfaction in *The Grub-Street Journal* that both plays 'met with the universal detestation of the town', and, though *The Debauchees* deservedly survived this initial unpopularity, *The Covent-Garden Tragedy* was withdrawn after its single performance, and never subsequently revived in a legitimate theatre*. In reply to earlier attacks in the *Journal*, Fielding prefaced the published text of his play with an imaginary criticism from that periodical, which, it may be added, constitutes a not unfair parody of its critical style. Ironically, Fielding accused himself of plagiarism. 'As for the characters of Lovegirlo and Kissinda,' his mock-critic asserts, 'they are poor imitations of the characters of Pyrrhus and Andromache in *The Distrest Mother*, as Bilkum and Stormandra are of Orestes and Hermione.' These identifications, suffice it to note, are accurate, though their purpose is not, of course, imitative: but neither is it in any sustained sense satirical. Rather, Fielding uses *The Distrest Mother*, a pseudo-classical tragedy in blank verse by the much abused Ambrose Philips, as a convenient starting-point for a general burlesque of the play's form. More particularly, this enabled him to ridicule the concept of poetic justice, which distorted dramatic probability—as Philips had distorted his Greek and French models—in the interests of a morally fitting climax.

Characteristically, the *Grub-Street Journal's* actual reviewers had made the mistake of identifying Fielding with the bawdy-house philosophy of his characters, and modern critics still tend to refer to the play as 'disagreeably

---

* Since this note was written, a revival of *The Covent-Garden Tragedy* has, in fact, reached the London stage, as part of a 'Triple Bill' presented by the National Theatre at the Old Vic in 1968. After an accident-ridden first night, major cuts were made in the text: and the production was conceived, somewhat apologetically, as a comedy of bad manners rather than as a burlesque. Once more the piece has 'met with the universal detestation of the town', from which it can only be hoped that the present reprint may help, at last, to rescue it.

coarse'. In fact, the setting of his *Covent-Garden Tragedy* in a brothel allowed Fielding to satirize false heroics by attributing them to ignoble characters and causes; to expose the moral falsity of poetic justice by extending its improbable mercy to pimps and whores; and, incidentally, to mock the newly-emergent form of domestic tragedy, that distant ancestor of the nineteenth-century melodrama and problem play, which set out to transform the bourgeoisie into tragic heroes, and their everyday environment into an appropriate setting for tragic conflicts.

Fielding's moral purpose is unobtrusive but uncompromising. The mock-pastoral *What d'ye Call it* and the farcical *Three Hours after Marriage* had both treated the physical aspects of sex with a frankness rare in eighteenth-century drama: but neither had so directly associated sexual with commercial instincts. In this respect—as also in its tangential indebtedness to a single source—the play might seem to resemble *The Mock-Tempest* more closely than Fielding's earlier burlesque. And it is true that, whereas *Tom Thumb* had combined the structural unity of *The What d'ye Call it* with *The Rehearsal's* particularity of allusion, *The Covent-Garden Tragedy* does share certain characteristics with Duffett's play. But Duffett had exploited bawdiness for its own sake. Fielding uses it as a moral and critical correlative, a *reductio ad absurdum* of that inverted moral code which associated virtue in general (and marriageability in particular) with social eminence and financial resource, and which held honour to be a matter rather of military prowess than of personal behaviour.

No wonder that its contemporary audiences found the moral implications of the play so discomfiting that its virtues as a burlesque—its sheer high-spiritedness, its breakneck speed, and its effective abuse of the full range of tragical pomposities—were overlooked. In fact, *The Covent-Garden Tragedy* seems to me no less successful than *Tom Thumb* in achieving what it sets out to achieve—and, in so far as it is less closely parodistic, it relies less on previous acquaintance with a body of forgotten plays. Together, Fielding's two burlesques mount a frontal attack on all three major tragic forms of their period. Thus, in peopling *Tom Thumb* with a shrunken hero, a promiscuous heroine, and a ludicrously middle-class king and queen, Fielding effectively debunks heroic tragedy by counterpointing its assumptions with the fallibilities of ordinary mortals. And in *The Covent-Garden Tragedy* he satirizes both pseudo-classical and domestic tragedy by ironically synthesizing the two forms—by reworking an already debased classical myth, and portraying its perversion in terms of the mercantile morality of the brothel.

THE
COVENT-GARDEN
TRAGEDY.

As it is Acted at the THEATRE-ROYAL
in DRURY-LANE.

By His MAJESTY's Servants.

————*quæ amanti parcet, eadem sibi parcet parum.*
Quasi piscis, itidem est amator lenæ: nequam est nisi recens.
Is habet succum; is suavitatem; eum quovis pacto condias;
Vel patinarium vel assum: verses, quo pacto lubet.
Is dare volt, is se aliquid posci. nam ubi de pleno promitur,
Neque ille scit, quid det, quid damni faciat; illi rei studet:
Volt placere sese amicæ, volt mihi, pedissequæ,
Volt famulis, volt etiam ancillis: & quoque catulo meo.
Subblanditur novus amator, se ut quum videat, gaudeat.
                                          Plautus. Asinar.

LONDON:

Printed for J. WATTS, and Sold by J. ROBERTS
in *Warwick-Lane.*

MDCCXXXII.
[Price One Shilling.]

PROLEGOMENA.

IT hath been customary with Authors of extraordinary Merit, to prefix to their Works certain Commendatory Epistles in Verse and Prose, written by a Friend, or left with the Printer by an unknown Hand; which are of notable Use to an injudicious Reader, and often lead him to the Discovery of Beauties, which might otherwise have escaped his Eye. They stand like Champions at the Head of a Volume, and bid Defiance to an Army of Criticks.

7

As I have not been able to procure any such Panegyricks on the following Scenes from my Friends, nor Leisure to write them myself, I have, in an unprecedented manner, collected such Criticisms as I could meet with on this Tragedy, and have placed them before it; but I must at the same time assure the Reader, that he may shortly expect an Answer to them.

The first of these Pieces, by its Date, appears to be the Production of some fine Gentleman, who plays the Critick for his Diversion, tho' he has not spoil'd his Eyes with too much reading. The latter will be easily discover'd to come from the Hands of one of that Club, which hath determin'd to instruct the World in Arts and Sciences, without understanding any; who

With less Learning than makes Felons 'scape
Less human Genius than God gives an Ape.

Are resolv'd

20

                  —in Spite
Of Nature, and their Stars to write.

DEAR JACK,

"SINCE you have left the Town, and no rational Creature except myself "in it, I have applied myself pretty much to my Books; I have, besides "the *Craftsman* and *Grubstreet Journals*, read a good deal in Mr. *Pope*'s "*Rape of the Lock*, and several Pages in *the History of the King of Sweden*, "which is translated into English; but fancy, I shou'd understand more of it, "if I had a better Map: for I have not been able to find out *Livonia* in mine.

"I believe, you will be surpriz'd to hear, I have not been twice at the "Play-House since your Departure: But alas! what Entertainment can a Man "of Sense find there now? The *Modern Husband*, which we hiss'd the first "Night, had such Success, that I began to think it a good Play, till the

26 the *Craftsman*] The chief journal of the opposition.   32 The *Modern Husband*] A regular comedy by Fielding, which had been attacked in *The Grub-Street Journal*.

"*Grubstreet Journal* assured me it was not. *The Earl of Essex*, which you
"know is my Favourite of all *Shakespeare*'s Plays, was acted the other
"Night; but I was kept from it by a damn'd Farce which I abominate, and
"detest so much, that I have never either seen it, or read it.   37

  "Last *Monday* came out a new Tragedy, called, *The Covent-Garden
"Tragedy*, which I believe, I may affirm to be the worst that ever was
"written. I will not shock your good Judgment by any Quotations out of it.
"To tell you the Truth, I know not what to make of it: One wou'd have
"guess'd from the Audience, it had been a Comedy: For I saw more People
"laugh than cry at it. It adds a very strong Confirmation to your Opinion,
"That it is impossible, any thing worth reading shou'd be written in this
"Age.   45

St. James's Coffee-House.

                                                                            I am, &c.

A CRITICISM *on the* Covent-Garden Tragedy, *originally intended for the*
  Grubstreet Journal.

I HAVE been long sensible, that the Days of Poetry are no more, and that
  there is but one of the Moderns, (who shall be nameless) that can write
either Sense or *English*, or Grammar: For this Reason, I have pass'd by
unremarked, generally unread, the little, quaint, short-lived Productions of
my Contemporaries: For it is a Maxim with my Bookseller, that no Criticism
on any Work can sell, when the Work itself does not.   55

  But when I observe an Author growing into any Reputation, when I see
the same *Play*, which I had liberally hiss'd the first Night, advertised for a
considerable Number of Nights together; I then begin to look about me, and
to think it worth criticizing on: A Play that runs twelve Nights, will support
a temperate Critick as many Days.

  The Success of the *Tragedy of Tragedies*, and the *Modern Husband* did
not only determine me to draw my Pen against those two Performances,
but hath likewise engaged my Criticism on every thing which comes from
the Hands of that Author, of whatever nature it be,

      Seu Graecum sive Latinum.   65

  The *Covent-Garden Tragedy* bears so great an Analogy to the Tragedy of
Tom Thumb, that it needs not the Author's Name to assure us from what
Quarter it had its Original. I shall beg leave therefore to examine this Piece

  51 one of the Moderns] Pope, whose cause and reputation *The Grub-Street Journal*
supported.

a little, even before I am assured what Success it will meet with. Perhaps, what I shall herein say, may prevent its meeting with any.

I shall not here trouble the Reader with a laborious Definition of Tragedy drawn from *Aristuttle* or *Horase*, for which I refer him to those Authors. I shall content myself with the following plain Proposition.

"That a Tragedy is a Thing of five Acts, written Dialogue-wise, consisting "of several fine Similies, Metaphors, and Moral Phrases, with here and there "a Speech upon Liberty. That it must contain an Action, Characters, Senti-"ments, Diction, and a Moral." Whatever falls short of any of these, is by no means worthy the Name of a Tragedy.

> *Quae Genus aut Flexum variant, quaecunque novato*
> *Ritu deficiunt superantve, Heteroclita sunto.*   80

I shall proceed to examine the Piece before us on these Rules, nor do I doubt to prove it deficient in them all,

> *Quae sequitur manca est Numero Casuque Propago.*

As for an Action, I have read it over twice, and do solemnly aver, I can find none, at least none worthy to be called an Action. The Author, indeed, in one Place seems to promise something like an Action, where *Stormandra*, who is enraged with *Lovegirlo*, sends *Bilkum* to destroy him, and at the same time threatens to destroy herself! But alas! what comes of all this Preparation!—Why, *parturiunt montes*—the Audience is deceived according to Custom, and the two murdered People appear in good Health: for all which great Revolution of Fortune, we have no other Reason given, but that the one has been run through the Coat, and the other has hung up her Gown instead of herself.—*Ridiculum!*   93

The Characters, I think, are such as I have not yet met with in Tragedy: I believe all Monsters of the Poet's own Brain. First, for the Character of Mother *Punchbowl*; and, by the way, I cannot conceive why she is called Mother. Is she the Mother of any Body in the Play? No. From one Line one might guess she was a Bawd, *Leathersides* desires her to procure two Whores, &c. but then is she not continually talking of Virtue? How can she be a Bawd? In the third Scene of the second Act she appears to be *Stormandra*'s Mother.   101

> Punchb. *Daughter, you use the Captain too unkind.*

But, if I mistake not in the Scene immediately preceding, *Bilkum* and she have mother'd and son'd it several times. Sure, she cannot be Mother to them both, when she wou'd put them to bed together. Perhaps, she is Mother-in-law to one of them, as being married to her own Child: But of this the Poet shou'd (I think) have given us some better Assurance than

G

barely intimating, that they were going to bed together, which People in
this our Island have been sometimes known to do, without going to Church
together.   110

What is intended by the Character of *Gallono*, is difficult to imagine.
Either he is taken from Life, or he is not. Methinks, I cou'd wish he had been
left out of the Dance,* nothing being more unnatural than to conceive so
great a Sot to be a Lover of Dancing; nay, so great a Lover of Dancing, as to
take that Woman for a Partner whom he had just before been abusing. As
for the Characters of *Lovegirlo* and *Kissinda*, they are poor Imitations of the
Characters of *Pyrrhus* and *Andromache* in the *Distrest Mother*, as *Bilkum* and
Stormandra are of *Orestes* and *Hermione*.

> —*Sed quid morer istis.*

As for Mr. *Leathersides*, he is indeed an Original, and such a one, as I
hope will never have a Copy. We are told (to set him off) that he has learnt
to read, has read Play-Bills, and writ the *Grubstreet Journal*. But how reading
Play-Bills, and writing *Grubstreet* Papers can qualify him to be a Judge of
Plays, I confess, I cannot tell.   124

The only Character I can find entirely faultless, is the Chair-Man: for
first we are assur'd,

> *He asks but for his Fare*,

When the Captain answers him,

> *Thy Fare be damn'd.*

He replies in the gentlest manner imaginable,

> *This is not acting like a Gentleman.*

The Captain upon this threatens to knock his Brains out. He then answers in
a most intrepid and justifiable Manner:

> *Oh! that with me*, &c.   134

I cannot help wishing, this may teach all Gentlemen to pay their Chair-Men.

Proceed we now to the Sentiments. And here, to shew how inclin'd I am
to admire rather than dislike, I shall allow the beautiful Manner wherein
this Play sets out. The first five lines are a mighty pretty Satyr on our Age,
our Country, Statesman, Lawyers, and Physicians: What did I not expect
from such a Beginning? But alas! what follows? No fine Moral Sentences,
not a Word of Liberty and Property, no Insinuations, that Courtiers are

---

* The Critic is out in this Particular, it being notorious *Gallono* is not in the Dance; but
to shew how careful the Author was to maintain his Character throughout, the said *Gallono*
during the whole Dance is employ'd with his Bottle and his Pipe.

Fools, and Statesmen Rogues. You have indeed a few Similies, but they are
very thin sown.   143

> *Apparent rari nantes in Gurgite vasto.*

The Sentiments fall very short of Politeness every where; but those in the
Mouth of Captain *Bilkum* breathe the true Spirit of *Billinsgate*. The Court-
ship that passes between him and *Stormandra* in the second Act is so extremely delicate, sure the Author must have serv'd an Apprenticeship there,
before he cou'd have produced it. How unlike this was the beautiful manner
of making Love in Use among the Ancients, that charming Simplicity of
Manners which shines so apparently in all the * Tragedies of *Plautus*, where

> *—petit & prece blandus amicam.*   152

But alas! how shou'd an illiterate Modern imitate Authors he has never read.
   To say nothing of the Meanness of the Diction, which is some degrees
lower than I have seen in any Modern Tragedy, we very often meet with
Contradictions in the same Line. The Substantive is so far from shewing the
Signification of its Adjective as the latter requires.

> *An Adjective requires some Word to be joined to it to shew its Signification.*
> vid. Accidence.

That it very often takes away its Meaning, as particularly *virtuous Whore*.
Did it ever enter into any Head before, to bring these two Words together.
Indeed, my Friend, I cou'd as soon unite the Idea of your sweet self, and a
good Poet.   163

> *Forth from your empty Head I'll knock your Brains.*

Had you had any Brains in your own Head you never had writ this Line.

> *Yet do not shock it with a Thought so base.*

Ten low Words creep here in a Line indeed.

> *—Monosyllabla nomina quædam,*
> *Sal, sol, ren et splen, car, car, ser, vir, vas.—*

> *Virgal Rod, Grief-stung Soul, &c.*   170

I wou'd recommend to this Author (if he can read) that wholesome little
Treatise, call'd, *Gulielmi Lilii Monita Pædagogica*, where he will find this
Instruction.

---

* I suppose these are lost, there remaining now no more than his Comedies.

---

   167 Ten low Words creep here in a Line] A deliberate echo on the mock-critic's part of
Pope's *Essay on Criticism*, 347.

—Veluti Scopulos, barbara verba fuge.

Much may be said on both sides of this Question;
Let me consider what the Question is;

Mighty pretty, faith! resolving a Question first, and then asking it.

                              —thou hast a Tongue
Might charm a Bailiff to forego his Hold.

Very likely indeed! I fancy, Sir, if ever you were in the Hands of a Bailiff, you
have not escap'd so easily.   181

Hanover-Square *shall come to* Drury-Lane.

Wonderful!

Thou shalt wear Farms and Houses in each Ear.

Oh! *Bavius!* oh! Conundrum, is this true! Sure the Poet exaggerates; What!
a Woman wear Farms and Houses in her Ear, nay, in each Ear, to make it
still the more incredible. I suppose these are poetical Farms and Houses,
which any Woman may carry about her without being the heavier. But I
pass by this and many other Beauties of the like Nature, *quae lectio juxta
docebit*, to come to a little Word which is worth the whole Work.   190

Nor Modesty, nor Pride, nor Fear, nor REP.

Quid sibi vult istud REP?—I have looked over all my Dictionaries, but in
vain,

Nusquam reperitur in usu.

I find indeed such a Word in some of the *Latin* Authors, but as it is not in
the Dictionary, I suppose it to be obsolete. Perhaps it is a proper Name, if so,
it shou'd have been in *Italicks*. I am a little inclined to this Opinion, as we
find several very odd Names in this Piece, such as *Hackabouta*, &c.
   I am weary of raking in this Dirt, and shall therefore pass on to the Moral,
which the Poet very ingenuously tells us, is, he knows not what, nor any
one else I dare swear. I shall however allow him this Merit, that except in
the five Lines abovementioned, I scarce know any Performance more of a
Piece. Either the Author never sleeps, or never wakes throughout.   203

*ASS in praesenti perfectum format in avi.

* *Gul. Lilius* reads this Word with a single *S*.

_____

185 Oh! *Bavius!*] The mock-critic is invoking the assistance of Richard Russel, who, as one
of the chief literary critics of *The Grub-Street Journal*, wrote under this pseudonym.

PROLOGUE.

Spoken by Mr. *THEOPHILUS CIBBER.*

IN Athens *first* (*as Dictionaries write*)
  The Tragick Muse was midwif'd into Light;
Rome *knew her next, and next she took a Dance,*
Some say to England, *others say to* France.
But when, or whence, the tuneful Goddess came,
Since she is here, I think, is much the same:
Oft have you seen the King and Hero rage,
Oft has the Virgin's Passion fill'd the Stage;
To-night, nor King, nor Hero shall you spy,
Nor Virgin's Love shall fill the Virgin's Eye.   10
Our Poet from unknown, untasted Springs,
A curious Draught of Tragic Nectar brings.
From Covent-Garden, *culls delicious Stores,*
Of Bullies, Bawds, and Sots, and Rakes, and Whores.
Examples of the Great can serve but few,
For what are Kings and Heroes Faults to you?
But these Examples are of general Use.
What Rake is ignorant of * King's Coffee-House?
Here the old Rake may view the Crime's h'as known,
And Boys hence dread the Vices of the Town: 20
Here Nymphs seduc'd may mourn their Pleasures past,
And Maids, who have their Virtue, learn to hold it fast.

---

* A Place in *Covent-Garden* Market, well known to all Gentlemen to whom Beds are unknown.

---

14 *Bullies*] Here the word signifies a protector of whores, a function discussed at length by Mother Punchbowl in Act II, Scene iii.

EPILOGUE.

Spoken by Miss *RAFTOR*, who acted the Parts of *Isabel* in the *Old Debauchees,* and of *Kissinda* in this Tragedy.

*I*N various Lights this Night you've seen me drest.
  A virtuous Lady, and a Miss confest.
Pray tell me, Sirs, in which you like me best?
Neither averse to Love's soft Joys you find,
'Tis hard to say, which is the best inclin'd;
The Priest makes all the Diff'rence in the Case;
Kissinda's *always ready to embrace,*
And Isabel *stays only to say Grace.*
For several Prices ready both to treat,
This takes a Guinea, that your whole Estate.   10
Gallants, believe our Passions are the same,
And virtuous Women, tho' they dread the Shame,
Let 'em but play secure, all love the Game.
For tho' some Prude her Lover long may vex,
Her Coyness is put on, she loves your Sex;
At you, the pretty things, their Airs display;
For you we dance, we sing, we smile, we pray;
On you we dream all Night, we think all Day.
For you the Mall and Ring with Beauties swarm;
You teach soft Senefino's *Airs to charm.*   20
For thin wou'd be th'Assembly of the Fair
At Operas—were none but Eunuchs there.
In short, you are the Business of our Lives,
To be a Mistress kept, the Strumpet strives,
And all the modest Virgins to be Wives.
For Prudes may cant of Virtues and of Vices,
But faith! we only differ in our Prices.

---

8 Isabel] The virtuous heroine of *The Old Debauchees*, to which *The Covent-Garden Tragedy* was performed as an afterpiece.

Dramatis Personæ.

GENTLEMEN.

Captain *Bilkum*.
Lovegirlo.
Gallono.
Leathersides.
Chairman.

Mr. *Mullart.*
Mr. *Cibber*, jun.
Mr. *Paget.*
Mr. *Roberts.*
Mr. *Jones.*

LADIES.

Mother *Punchbowl.*
Kissinda.
Stormandra.
Nonparel.

Mr. *Bridgewater.*
Miss *Raftor.*
Mrs. *Mullart.*
Miss *Mears.*

SCENE *An Antichamber, or rather Back-Parlour in*
Mother Punchbowl's *House.*

THE
COVENT-GARDEN
TRAGEDY.

ACT I. SCENE I.

SCENE *An Antichamber.*

MOTHER PUNCHBOWL, LEATHERSIDES, NONPAREL,
INDUSTRIOUS JENNY.

MOTHER.

WHO'D be a Bawd in this degen'rate Age!
Who'd for her Country unrewarded toil!
Not so the Statesman scrubs his plotful Head,
Not so the Lawyer shakes his unfeed Tongue,
Not so the Doctor guides the doseful Quill.
Say *Nonparel*, industrious *Jenny*, say,
Is the Play done and yet no Cull appears?

NONPAREL.

The Play is done: For from the Pigeon-hole
I heard them hiss the Curtain as it fell.

MOTHER.

Ha, did they hiss? Why then the Play is damn'd,
And I shall see the Poet's Face no more.
Say, *Leathersides*, 'tis thou that best canst tell:
For thou hast learnt to read, hast Play-bills read,
The *Grubstreet Journal* thou hast known to write,
Thou art a Judge; say, wherefore was it damn'd?

10

8 Pigeon-hole] A seat at the very back of the theatre gallery.

LEATHERSIDES.

I heard a Tailor sitting by my side,
Play on his Catcal, and cry out, *sad Stuff*.
A little farther an Apprentice sat,
And he too hiss'd, and he too cry'd, *'twas low*.
Then o'er the Pit I downward cast my Eye,   20
The Pit all hiss'd, all whistled, and all groan'd.

MOTHER.

Enough. The Poet's lost, and so's his Bill.
Oh! 'tis the Tradesman, not the Poet's Hurt:
For him the Washerwoman toils in vain,
For him in vain the Taylor sits cross'd-legg'd,
He runs away and leaves all Debts unpaid.

LEATHERSIDES.

The mighty Captain *Bilkum* this way comes.
I left him in the Entry with his Chairman
Wrangling about his Fare.

MOTHER.

Leathersides, 'tis well.   30
Retire, my Girls, and patient wait for Culls.

SCENE II.

MOTHER PUNCHBOWL, CAPTAIN BILKUM, CHAIRMAN.

CHAIRMAN.

Your Honour, Sir, has paid but half my Fare.
I ask but for my Fare.

CAPTAIN BILKUM.

Thy Fare be damn'd.

CHAIRMAN.

This is not acting like a Gentleman.

31 Culls] Dupes, simpletons.

CAPTAIN BILKUM.

Begone, or by the Powers of Dice I swear,
Were there no other Chairman in the World,
From out thy empty Head, I'd knock thy Brains.

CHAIRMAN.

Oh, that with me, all Chairmen would conspire,
No more to carry such sad Dogs for Hire,
But let the lazy Rascals straddle thro' the Mire.   10

SCENE III.

CAPTAIN BILKUM, MOTHER PUNCHBOWL.

MOTHER.

What is the Reason, Captain, that you make
This Noise within my House? Do you intend
To arm reforming Constables against me?
Wou'd it delight your Eyes to see me dragg'd
By base *Plebeian* Hands to *Westminster*,
The Scoff of Serjeants and Attornies Clerks,
And then exalted on the Pillory,
To stand the sneer of ev'ry virtuous Whore?
Oh! cou'dst thou bear to see the rotten Egg
Mix with my Tears, and trickle down my Cheeks,   10
Like Dew distilling from the full blown Rose:
Or see me follow the attractive Cart,
To see the Hangman lift the Virgal Rod,
That Hangman you so narrowly escap'd!

CAPTAIN BILKUM.

Ha! that last Thought has strung me to the Soul;
Damnation on all Laws and Lawyers too:
Behold thee carted—oh! forefend that Sight,
May *Bilkum*'s Neck be stretch'd before that Day.

12 attractive Cart] The cart which is a great public attraction.   13 Virgal Rod] Rod made
of bound twigs.

MOTHER.

Come to my Arms, thou best belov'd of Sons,
Forgive the Weakness of thy Mother's Fears: 20
Oh! may I never, never see thee hang'd!

CAPTAIN BILKUM.

If born to swing, I never shall be drown'd:
Far be it from me, with too curious Mind,
To search the Office whence eternal Fate
Issues her Writs of various Ills to Men;
Too soon arrested we shall know our Doom,
And now a present Evil gnaws my Heart.
Oh! Mother, Mother—

MOTHER.

Say, what wou'd my Son?

CAPTAIN BILKUM.

Get me a Wench, and lend me half a Crown.   30

MOTHER.

Thou shalt have both.

CAPTAIN BILKUM.

Oh! Goodness most unmatch'd,
What are your 'Nelope's compar'd to thee?
In vain we'd search the Hundreds of the Town,
From where, in Goodman's-Fields, the City Dame
Emboxed sits, for two times Eighteen Pence.
To where at Midnight Hours, the nobler Race
In borrow'd Voice, and mimick Habit squeak.
Yet where, oh where is such a Bawd as thou?

MOTHER.

Oh! deal not Praise with such a lavish Tongue;   40
If I excel all others of my Trade,
Thanks to those Stars that taught me to excel!

---

35 Goodman's-Fields] A theatre much frequented by city merchants and their wives.
37 To where at Midnight Hours . . .] That is, at the masquerade.

SCENE IV.

MOTHER PUNCHBOWL, CAPTAIN BILKUM, LEATHERSIDES.

LEATHERSIDES.

A Porter from *Lovegirlo* is arriv'd,
If in your Train one Harlot can be found,
That has not been a Month upon the Town;
Her, he expects to find in Bed by two.

MOTHER.

Thou, *Leathersides*, best know'st such Nymphs to find,
To thee, their Lodgings they communicate.
Go, thou procure the Girl, I'll make the Punch,
Which she must call for when she first arrives.
Oh! *Bilkum*, when I backward cast my Thoughts,
When I resolve the glorious Days I've seen,   10
(Days I shall see no more)—it tears my Brain.
When Culls sent frequent, and were sent away.
When Col'nels, Majors, Captains, and Lieutenants,
Here spent the Issue of their glorious Toils;
These were the Men, my *Bilkum*, that subdu'd
The haughty Foe, and paid for Beauty here.
Now we are sunk to a low Race of Beaus,
Fellows unfit for Women or for War;
And one poor Cull is all the Guests I have.

SCENE V.

LEATHERSIDES, MOTHER PUNCHBOWL, BILKUM.

LEATHERSIDES.

Two Whores, great Madam, must be straight prepar'd,
A fat one for the 'Squire, and for my Lord a lean.

MOTHER.

Be that thy Care. This weighty Bus'ness done,
A Bowl of humming Punch shall glad my Son.

4, Sc. v humming] Strongly alcoholic.

SCENE VI.

BILKUM solus.

Oh! 'tis not in the Pow'r of Punch to ease
My Grief-stung Soul, since Hecatissa's false,
Since she could hide a poor half Guinea from me.
Oh! had I search'd her Pockets ere I rose,
I had not left a single Shilling in them.
But lo! *Lovegirlo* comes, I will retire.

SCENE VII.

LOVEGIRLO, GALLONO.

GALLONO.

And wilt thou leave us for a Woman thus!
Art thou *Lovegirlo*? Tell me, art thou he,
Whom I have seen the Saffron-colour'd Morn
With rosy Fingers beckon home in vain?
Than whom none oftner pull'd the pendent Bell,
None oftner cry'd, *another Bottle bring*;
And canst thou leave us for a worthless Woman?

LOVEGIRLO.

I charge thee, my *Gallono*, do not speak
Ought against Woman; by *Kissinda*'s Smiles,
(Those Smiles more worth than all the *Cornwall* Mines)   10
When I drank most, 'twas Woman made me drink,
The Toast was to the Wine an Orange-Peel.

GALLONO.

Oh! wou'd they spur us on to noble Drink,
I too wou'd be a Lover of the Sex.
And sure for nothing else they were design'd,
Woman was only born to be a Toast.

LOVEGIRLO.

What Madness moves thy slander-hurling Tongue?
Woman! What is there in the World like Woman?
Man without Woman is a single Boot,
Is half a Pair of Sheers. Her wanton Smiles   20

Are sweeter than a Draught of cool small Beer
To the scorch'd Palate of a waking Sot.
Man is a Puppet which a Woman moves
And dances as she will—Oh! had it not
Been for a Woman, thou hadst not been here.

GALLONO.

And were it not for Wine—I wou'd not be.
Wine makes a Cobler greater than a King;
Wine gives Mankind the Preference to Beasts,
Thirst teaches all the Animals to drink,
But Drunkenness belongs to only Man.   30

LOVEGIRLO.

If Woman were not, my *Gallono*, Man
Wou'd make a silly Figure in the World.

GALLONO.

And without Wine all Human-kind wou'd be
One stupid, sniveling, sneaking, sober Fellow.

LOVEGIRLO.

What does the Pleasures of our Life refine?
'Tis charming Woman.

GALLONO.

Wine.

LOVEGIRLO.

'Tis Woman.

GALLONO.

Wine.

SCENE VIII.

BILKUM.

Much may be said on both sides of this Question;
Let me consider what the Question is:
If Wine or Woman be our greater Good,
Wine is a Good—and so is Woman too,

But which the greater Good [*A long Pause*] I cannot tell.
Either to other to prefer I'm loth,
But he does wisest who takes most of both.

SCENE IX.

LOVEGIRLO, KISSINDA.

LOVEGIRLO.

Oh! my *Kissinda!* oh! how sweet art thou?
Nor *Covent-Garden*, nor *Stocks-Market* knows
A Flower like thee; less sweet the *Sunday* Rose,
With which, in Country Church, the Milk-maid decks
Her ruddy Breast: Ne'er wash'd the courtly Dame
Her Neck with Honey-water half so sweet.
Oh! thou art Perfume all; a Perfume Shop.

KISSINDA.

Cease, my *Lovegirlo*, oh! thou hast a Tongue
Might charm a Bailiff to forego his Hold.
Oh! I cou'd hear thee ever, cou'd with Joy   10
Live a whole Day upon a Dish of Tea,
And listen to the Bagpipes in thy Voice.

LOVEGIRLO.

Hear this, ye Harlots, hear her and reform;
Not so the Miser loves to see his Gold,
Not so the Poet loves to see his Play,
Not so the Critick loves to see a Fault,
Not so the Beauty loves to see herself,
As I delight to see *Kissinda* smile.

KISSINDA.

Oh! my *Lovegirlo*, I must hear no more,
Thy Words are strongest Poison to my Soul;   20
I shall forget my Trade and learn to dote.

LOVEGIRLO.

Oh! give a Loose to all the Warmth of Love.
Love like a Bride upon the Second Night;
I like a ravish'd Bridegroom on the First.

KISSINDA.

Thou know'st too well a Lady of the Town
If she give way to Love must be undone.

LOVEGIRLO.

The Town! thou shalt be on the Town no more,
I'll take thee into Keeping, take thee Rooms
So large, so furnish'd, in so fine a Street,
The Mistress of a *Jew* shall envy thee,   30
By *Jove*, I'll force the sooty Tribe to own,
A Christian keeps a Whore as well as they.

KISSINDA.

And wilt thou take me into Keeping—?

LOVEGIRLO.

Yes.

KISSINDA.

Then I am blest indeed—and I will be
The kindest, gentlest, and the cheapest Girl.
A Joint of Meat a Day is all I ask,
And that I'll dress my self—A Pot of Beer
When thou din'st from me, shall be all my Wine;
Few Clothes I'll have, and those too Second-hand;   40
Then when a Hole within thy Stocking's seen,
(For Stockings will have Holes) I'll darn it for thee,
With my own Hands I'll wash thy soapen'd Shirt,
And make the Bed I have unmade with thee.

LOVEGIRLO.

Do virtuous Women use their Husbands so?
Who but a Fool wou'd marry that can keep——
What is this Virtue that Mankind adore?
Sounds less the scolding of a virtuous Tongue!
Or who remembers, to increase his Joy,
In the last Moments of excessive Bliss,   50
The Ring, the License, Parson, or his Clerk?
Besides, whene'er my Mistress plays me foul,
I cast her, like a dirty Shirt, away.
But oh! a Wife sticks like a Plaister fast,
Like a perpetual Blister to the Pole.

KISSINDA.

And wilt thou never throw me off——?

LOVEGIRLO.

Never,
'Till thou art soil'd.

KISSINDA.

Then turn me to the Streets,
Those Streets you took me from.   60

LOVEGIRLO.

Forbid it all
Ye Powers propitious to unlawful Love.
Oh! my *Kissinda*, by this Kiss I swear,
(This Kiss, which at a Shilling is not dear)
I wou'd not quit the Joys this Night shall give,
For all the virtuous Wives or Maids alive.
Oh! I am all on Fire, thou lovely Wench,
Torrents of Joy my burning Soul must quench,
Reiterated Joys!
Thus burning from the Fire, the Washer lifts   70
The red-hot Iron to make smooth her Shifts,
With Arm impetuous rubs her Shift amain,
And rubs, and rubs, and rubs it oe'r again;
Nor sooner does her rubbing Arm withhold,
'Till she grows warm, and the hot Iron cold.

ACT II. SCENE I.

STORMANDRA, CAPTAIN BILKUM.

STORMANDRA.

NOT, tho' you were the best Man in the Land,
Shou'd you, unpaid for, have from me a Favour?
Therefore come down the Ready, or I go.

BILKUM.

Forbid it, *Venus*, I shou'd ever set
So cursed an Example to the World:

3 come down the Ready] Produce the ready money, the hard cash.

Forbid, the Rake, in full Pursuit of Joy
Requir'd the unready Ready to come down,
Shou'd curse my Name, and cry, *thus* Bilkum *did*;
To him this cursed Precedent we owe.

STORMANDRA.

Rather forbid, that, bilk'd in after-time,   10
The Chair-less Girl should curse *Stormandra*'s Name,
That as she walks with draggled Coats the Street,
(Coats shortly to be pawn'd) the hungry Wretch
Shou'd bellow out, *for this, I thank Stormandra!*

BILKUM.

Trust me to-night and never trust me more,
If I do not come down when I get up.

STORMANDRA.

And dost thou think I have a Soul so mean?
Trust thee! dost thou think I came last Week to Town,
The Waggon Straws yet hanging to my Tail?
Trust thee! oh! when I trust thee for a Groat,   20
Hanover-Square shall come to *Drury-Lane*.

BILKUM.

Madam, 'tis well, your Mother may perhaps,
Teach your rude Tongue to know a softer Tone.
And see, she comes, the smiling Brightness comes.

SCENE II.

MOTHER PUNCHBOWL, CAPTAIN BILKUM, STORMANDRA.

STORMANDRA.

Oh! Mother *Punchbowl*, teach me how to rail;
Oh! teach me to abuse this monstrous Man.

MOTHER.

What has he done?

STORMANDRA.

Sure a Design so base,
Turk never yet conceiv'd.

MOTHER.

Forbid it, Virtue.

STORMANDRA.

It wounds me to the Soul—he wou'd have bilk'd me.

MOTHER.

Ha! in my House! oh! *Bilkum*, is this true?
Who set thee on, thou Traitor, to undo me,
Is it some envious Sister, such may be;   10
For even Bawds, I own it with a Blush,
May be dishonest in this vicious Age.
Perhaps, thou art an Enemy to us all,
Wilt join malicious Justices against us.
Oh! think not thus to bribe th'ungrateful Tribe,
The Hand to *Bridewel* which thy Mother sends,
May one Day send thee to more fatal Goal;
And oh! (avert the Omen all ye Stars)
The very Hemp I beat may hang my Son.

BILKUM.

Mother, you know the Passage to my Heart,   20
But do not shock it with a Thought so base.
Sooner *Fleet-Ditch* like Silver *Thames* shall flow,
The *New-Exchange* shall with the *Royal* vye,
Or *Covent-Garden*'s with St. *Paul*'s great Bell:
Give no Belief to that ungrateful Woman;
Gods! who wou'd be a Bully to a Woman?
Canst thou forget—(it is too plain thou canst)
When at the *Rummer*, at the Noon of Night,
I found thee with a base Apprentice boxing?
And tho' none better dart the clinched Fist,   30
Yet wast thou over-match'd, and on the Ground.
Then like a Bull-Dog in *Hockleian* Holes,
Rush'd I tremendous on the snotty Foe,
I took him by the Throat and kick'd him down the Stairs.

STORMANDRA.

Dost thou recount thy Services, base Wretch,
Forgetting mine? Dost thou forget the Time,

28 at the *Rummer*] I.e. hitting the drink. 32 *Hockleian* Holes] Hockley-in-the-Hole,
famous for various kinds of contests and entertainments involving animals.

When shiv'ring on a Winter's icy Morn,
I found thy coatless Carcase at the Roundhouse,
Did I not then forget my proper Woes,
Did I not send for half a Pint of Gin,   40
To warm th'ungrateful Guts? pull'd I not off
A Quilted-Petticoat to clothe thy Back?
That unskinn'd Back, which Rods had dress'd in red,
Thy only Title to the Name of Captain?
Did I not pick a Pocket of a Watch,
A Pocket pick for thee?

BILKUM.

Dost thou mention
So slight a Favour? Have I not for thee
Fled from the Feather-bed of soft Repose,
And as the Watch proclaim'd approaching Day,   50
Robb'd the Stage-Coach?—Again, when Puddings hot,
And *Well-fleet* Oisters cry'd, the Evening come,
Have I not been a Foot-pad for thy Pride!

MOTHER.

Enough, my Children, let this Discord cease,
Had both your Merits had, you both deserve
The Fate of greater Persons—Go, my Son,
Retire to rest—gentle *Stormandra* soon
Will follow you. See kind Consent appear,
In softest Smiles upon her lovely Brow.

BILKUM.

And can I think *Stormandra* will be mine!   60
Once more, unpaid for mine! then I again
Am blest, am paid for all her former Scorn.
So when the doating Hen-peck'd Husband long
Hath stood the Thunder of his Deary's Tongue;
If, Supper over, she attempt to toy,
And laugh and languish for approaching Joy,
His raptur'd Fancy runs her Charms all o'er,
While Transport dances Jiggs thro' ev'ry Pore,
He hears the Thunder of her Tongue no more.

---

38 Roundhouse] Place for the preliminary detention of criminals.

SCENE III.

STORMANDRA, MOTHER PUNCHBOWL.

MOTHER.

Daughter, you use the Captain too unkind,
Forbid it, Virtue, I shou'd ever think
A Woman squeezes any Cull too much,
But Bullies never shou'd be us'd as Culls.
With Caution still preserve the Bully's Love,
A House like this, without a Bully left,
Is like a Puppet-Show without a Punch.
When you shall be a Bawd, and sure that Day
Is written in the Almanack of Fate,
You'll own the mighty Truth of what I say.   10
So the gay Girl whose Head Romances fill,
By Mother married well against her Will;
Once past the Age that pants for Love's Delight,
Herself a Mother, own her Mother in the Right.

SCENE IV.

STORMANDRA sola.

What shall I do? Shall I unpaid to Bed?
Oh! my *Lovegirlo!* oh! that thou wert here;
How my Heart dotes upon *Lovegirlo*'s Name,
For no one ever paid his Girls like him.
She, with *Lovegirlo* who had spent the Night,
Sighs not in vain for next Day's Masquerade,
Sure of a Ticket from him—Ha! ye Powers,
What is't I see? Is it a Ghost I see?
It is a Ghost. It is *Lovegirlo*'s Ghost.
Lovegirlo's dead; for if he were not dead,   10
How cou'd his living Ghost be walking here?

SCENE V.

LOVEGIRLO, STORMANDRA.

LOVEGIRLO.

Surely this is some Holiday in Hell,
And Ghosts are let abroad to take the Air,
For I have seen a Dozen Ghosts to-night
Dancing in merry Mood and winding Hayes,
If Ghosts all lead such merry Lives as these,
Who wou'd not be a Ghost!

STORMANDRA.

Art thou not one?

LOVEGIRLO.

What do I see, ye Stars? Is it *Stormandra?*

STORMANDRA.

Art thou *Lovegirlo?*—oh! I see thou art.
But tell me, I conjure, art thou not dead?   10

LOVEGIRLO.

No, by my Soul I am not.

STORMANDRA.

May I trust thee?
Yet if thou art alive, what dost thou here
Without *Stormandra?*—but thou needst not say,
I know thy Falshood, yes, perfidious Fellow,
I know thee false as Water or as Hell;
Falser than any thing but thy self——

LOVEGIRLO.

Or thee.
Dares thus the Devil to rebuke our Sin!
Dares thus the Kettle say the Pot is black!   20
Canst thou upbraid my Falshood! thou! who still
Art ready to obey the Porter's Call,
At any Hour, to any sort of Guest;
Thy Person is as common as the Dirt,
Which *Pickadilly* leaves on ev'ry Heel.

STORMANDRA.

Can I hear this, ye Stars! injurious Man!
May I be ever bilk'd!—May I ne'er fetch
My Watch from Pawn, if I've been false to you.

LOVEGIRLO.

Oh! Impudence unmatch'd! canst thou deny
That thou hast had a thousand diff'rent Men?   30

STORMANDRA.

If that be Falshood, I indeed am false,
And never Lady of the Town was true;
But tho' my Person be upon the Town,
My Heart has still been fix'd on only you.

SCENE VI.

LOVEGIRLO, STORMANDRA, KISSINDA.

KISSINDA.

Where's my *Lovegirlo?* point him out, ye Stars,
Restore him panting to *Kissinda*'s Arms.
Ha! do I see!

STORMANDRA.

Hast thou forgot to rail?
Now call me false, perfidious, and Ingrate,
Common as Air, as Dirt, or as thy self.
Beneath my Rage, hast thou forsaken me?
All my full Meals of luscious Love, to starve
At the lean Table of a Girl like that?

KISSINDA.

That Girl you mention with so forc'd a Scorn,   10
Envies not all the large Repasts you boast,
A little Dish oft furnishes enough;
And sure Enough is equal to a Feast.

STORMANDRA.

The puny Wretch such little Plates may choose,
Give me the Man who knows a stronger Taste.

KISSINDA.

Sensual and base! to such as you we owe
That Harlot is a Title of Disgrace,
The worst of Scandals on the best of Trades.

STORMANDRA.

That Shame more justly to the Wretch belongs,
Who gives those Favours which she cannot sell.   20

KISSINDA.

But harder is the wretched Harlot's Lot,
Who offers them for nothing and in vain.

STORMANDRA.

Shew me the Man, who thus accuses me,
I own I chose *Lovegirlo*, own I lov'd him,
But then I chose and lov'd him as a Cull;
Therefore prefer'd him to all other Men,
Because he better paid his Girls than they.
Oh! I despise all Love but that of Gold,
Throw that aside and all Men are alike.

KISSINDA.

And I despise all other Charms but Love.   30
Nothing could bribe me from *Lovegirlo*'s Arms;
Him, in a Cellar, wou'd my Love prefer
To Lords in Houses of six Rooms a Floor.
Oh! had I in the World a hundred Pound,
I'd give him all. Or did he, (Fate forbid!)
Want three half Crowns his Reckoning to pay,
I'd pawn my Under-petticoat to lend them.

LOVEGIRLO.

Wou'dst thou, my Sweet? Now by the Powers of Love,
I'll mortgage all my Lands to deck thee fine.
Thou shalt wear Farms and Houses in each Ear,   40
Ten thousand Load of Timber shall embrace
Thy necklac'd Neck. I'll make thy glitt'ring Form
Shine thro' th'admiring Mall a blazing Star.

Neglected Virtue shall with Envy die,
The Town shall know no other Toast but thee.
So have I seen upon my Lord-Mayor's Day,
While Coaches after Coaches roll away,
The gazing Crowd admire by Turns and cry,
See such and such an Alderman pass by;
But when the mighty Magistrate appears,   50
No other Name is sounded in your Ears;
The Crowd all cry unanimous—*see there*,
Ye Citizens, behold the Coach of the Lord Mayor.

SCENE VII.

STORMANDRA, CAPTAIN BILKUM.

BILKUM.

Why comes not my *Stormandra*? Twice and once
I've told the striking Clock's increasing Sound,
And yet unkind *Stormandra* stays away.

STORMANDRA.

Captain, are you a Man?

BILKUM.

I think I am;
The Time has been when you have thought so too,
Try me again in the soft Fields of Love.

STORMANDRA.

'Tis War not Love must try your Manhood now,
By Gin, I swear, ne'er to receive thee more,
'Till curs'd *Lovegirlo*'s Blood has dy'd thy Sword.   10

BILKUM.

Lovegirlo! Whence this Fury bent on him?

STORMANDRA.

Ha! dost thou question, coward?—Ask again,
And I will never call thee Captain more.
Instant obey my Purpose, or by Hemp
Rods, all the Horrors *Bridewel* ever knew,

I will arrest thee for the Note of Hand,
Which thou hast given me for twice one Pound;
But if thou dost, I call my sacred Honour
To witness, thy Reward shall be my Love.

BILKUM.

   Lovegirlo is no more. Yet wrong me not,   20
It is your Promise, not your Threat, prevails.
So when some Parent of Indulgence mild,
Wou'd to the nauseous Potion bring the Child;
In vain to win or frighten to its good,
He cries, *my Dear*, or lifts the useless Rod;
But if by chance, the Sugar Plumb he shows,
The simp'ring Child no more Reluctance knows;
It stretches out its Finger and its Thumb,
It swallow first, the Potion, then the Sugar Plumb.

SCENE VIII.

STORMANDRA *sola.*

   Go, act my just Revenge, and then be hang'd,
While I retire and gently hang my self.
May Women be by my Example taught,
Still to be good, and never to be naught;
Never from Virtue's Rules to go astray,
Nor ever to believe what Man can say.
She who believes a Man, I am afraid,
May be a Woman long, but not a Maid.
If such blest Harvest my Example bring,
The female World shall with my Praises ring,   } 10
And say, that when I hang'd my self, I did a noble thing. }

SCENE IX.

MOTHER PUNCHBOWL, KISSINDA, NONPAREL.

MOTHER.

   Oh! *Nonparel*, thou loveliest of Girls,
Thou latest Darlings of thy Mother's Years;

Let thy Tongue know no Commerce with thy Heart,
For if thou tellest Truth thou art undone.

NONPAREL.

Forgive me, Madam, this first Fault—henceforth
I'll learn with utmost Diligence to fib.

MOTHER.

Oh! never give your easy Mind to Love,
But poise the Scales of your Affection so,
That a bare Six-pence added to his Scale,
Might make the Cit Apprentice or the Clerk   10
Outweigh a flaming Col'nel of the Guards.
Oh! never give your Mind to Officers,
Whose Gold is on the outside of the Pocket.
But fly a Poet as the worst of Plagues,
Who never pays with any thing but Words.
Oh! had *Kissinda* taken this Advice,
She had not now been bilk'd.—

KISSINDA.

Think me not so,
Some hasty Business has *Lovegirlo* drawn
To leave me thus—but I will hold a Crown   20
To Eighteen-pence, he's here within an Hour.

SCENE X.

To them LEATHERSIDES.

MOTHER.

Oh! *Leathersides*, what means this newsful Look?

LEATHERSIDES.

Through the *Piaches* as I took my way
To fetch a Girl, I at a distance view'd
Lovegirlo, with great Captain *Bilkum* fighting,
Lovegirlo push'd, the Captain parry'd, thus
Lovegirlo push'd, he parried again;

10 Cit] Townsman, of low or bourgeois breeding.

Oft did he push, and oft was push'd aside.
At length the Captain with his Body thus,
Threw in a cursed Thrust in Flanconade.
'Twas then—oh! dreadful Horror to relate!   10
I at a Distance saw *Lovegirlo* fall,
And look as if he cry'd—*oh! I am slain.*

[Kissinda *sinks into* Nonparel's *Arms.*]

SCENE XI.

To them GALLONO.

GALLONO.

Give me my Friend, thou most accursed Bawd,
Restore him to me drunken as he was,
Ere thy vile Arts seduc'd him from the Glass.

MOTHER.

Oh! that I cou'd restore him—but alas!
Or drunk or sober, you'll ne'er see him more,
Unless you see his Ghost—his Ghost, perhaps,
May have escap'd from Captain *Bilkum*'s Sword.

GALLONO.

What do I hear!—oh damn'd accursed Jade,
Thou art the Cause of all—With artful Smiles
Thou didst seduce him to go home ere Morn.   10
Bridewel shall be thy Fate, I'll give a Crown
To some poor Justice to commit thee thither,
Where I will come and see thee flogg'd my self.

KISSINDA.

One flogg'd as I am can be flogg'd no more;
In her *Lovegirlo*, Miss *Kissinda* liv'd:
The Sword that pass'd thro' poor *Lovegirlo*'s Heart,
Pass'd eke thro' mine, he was three fifths off me.

9, Sc. x Flanconade] A sword wound in the thigh.

SCENE XII.

To them BILKUM.

BILKUM.

Behold the most accursed of humankind,
I for a Woman with a Man have fought;
She, for I know not what, has hang'd herself,
And now *Jack-Ketch* may do the same for me.
Oh! my *Stormandra!*

MOTHER.

What of her?

BILKUM.

Alas!
She's hang'd herself all to her Curtain's Rod,
I saw her swinging and I ran away.
Oh! if you lov'd *Stormandra*, come with me;   10
Skin of your Flesh, and bite away your Eyes;
Lug out your Heart, and dry it in your Hands;
Grind it to Powder, make it into Pills,
And take it down your Throat.

MOTHER.

Stormandra's gone!
Weep all ye Sister-Harlots of the Town;
Pawn your best Clothes, and clothe your selves in Rags.
Oh! my *Stormandra!*

KISSINDA.

Poor *Lovegirlo*'s slain.
Oh! give me way, come all your Furies, come,   20
Lodge in th'unfurnish'd Chambers of my Heart,
My Heart which never shall be let again
To any Guest but endless Misery,
Never shall have a Bill upon it more.
Oh! I am mad methinks, I swim in Air,
In Seas of Sulphur and eternal Fire,
And see *Lovegirlo* too.

GALLONO.

Ha! see him! where?
Where is the much-lov'd Youth—oh! never more
Shall I behold him. Ha! Distraction wild   30
Begins to wanton in my unhing'd Brain:
Methinks I'm mad, mad as a wild *March* Hare;
My muddy Brain is addled like an Egg,
My Teeth, like Magpies, chatter in my Head;
My reeling Head! which akes like any mad.

OMNES.

Oh!

LEATHERSIDES.

Was ever such a dismal Scene of Woe?

SCENE *the last.*

To them LOVEGIRLO, STORMANDRA, and a FIDLER.

LOVEGIRLO.

Where's my *Kissinda?*—bear me to her Arms,
Ye winged Winds—and let me perish there.

KISSINDA.

Lovegirlo lives—oh! let my eager Arms
Press him to Death upon my panting Breast.

BILKUM.

Oh! all ye Powers of Gin, *Stormandra* lives.

STORMANDRA.

Nor Modesty, nor Pride, nor Fear, nor Rep,
Shall now forbid this tender chaste Embrace.
Henceforth I'm thine as long as e'er thou wilt.

GALLONO.

Lovegirlo!

LOVEGIRLO.

Oh, Joy unknown, *Gallono.*   10

6 Rep] Obs. abbreviation for 'reputation'.

MOTHER.

Come all at once to my capacious Arms,
I know not where I shou'd th'Embrace begin;
My Children! oh! with what tumultuous Joy
Do I behold your almost virtuous Loves.
But say, *Lovegirlo*, when we thought you dead;
Say, by what lucky Chance we see you here?

LOVEGIRLO.

In a few Words I'll satisfy your Doubt,
I through the Coat was, not the Body, run.

BILKUM.

But say, *Stormandra*, did I not behold
Thee hanging to the Curtains of thy Bed?   20

STORMANDRA.

No, my dear Love, it was my Gown, not me,
I did intend to hang my self, but ere
The Knot was ty'd, repented my Design.

KISSINDA.

Henceforth, *Stormandra*, never rivals more,
By *Bilkum* you, I by *Lovegirlo* kept.

LOVEGIRLO.

Foreseeing all this sudden Turn of Joy,
I've brought a Fidler to play forth the same.

MOTHER.

I too will shake a Foot on this blest Day.

LOVEGIRLO.

From such Examples as of this and that,
We are all taught to know I know not what.   30

FINIS.

CHRONONHOTONTHOLOGOS

Henry Carey

Died 1743

Henry Carey was reputed to be an illegitimate son of the Marquis of Halifax: but obscurity has continued to cloud the early years of his life, as it has the causes of a premature death at his own hands. 'A musician by profession, and one of the lower order of poets', he possessed, according to the *Biographia Dramatica*, 'a good deal of low humour'. This contemporary estimate still holds good in most respects, for of his collected verses and songs only *Sally in our Alley* has its claim to immortality—though *Namby Pamby* enjoys the fortuitous renown of having coined the nickname for Ambrose Philips later adopted in Pope's *Dunciad*. But such grounds for faint praise of Carey fail to do justice to the note of wild inventiveness which distinguishes his *Chrononhotonthologos*, and which foreshadows a nineteenth-century tradition of controlled nonsense in verse and in drama.

Carey attempted, without much success, some serious librettos in the Italian manner, before striking an original vein of burlesque in *Chrononhotonthologos*. The play, which was first performed in 1734, is obviously indebted to Fielding's *Tom Thumb*, both in its mixture of blank-verse and heroic couplets, and in its choice of an unlovely object for its adulterous queen's affections—in this case, a defeated antipodean invader, of topsy-turvy habits. But Carey does not attempt close parody—nor is even a general burlesquing of bombast his chief concern, though he hits off the tricks of tragic ranting nicely enough. 'If the young fellow is right,' Quin is said to have remarked, 'we are all in the wrong.' But Carey's tongue-twisting nomenclature, to cite only his play's most obvious claim to originality, is too incredible to serve more than incidentally a satiric purpose: and as burlesque, it bludgeons rather than pierces its target. Similarly, Carey's verbal virtuosity reflects a sheer delight in the manipulation of language rather than a careful distortion of heroic hyperbole. *Chrononhotonthologos* is, in short, that dramatic rarity, an extravaganza in firm control of its extravagence.

The plotting of *Chrononhotonthologos* compares unfavourably with that of Fielding's pair of self-contained burlesques, for Carey's play is virtually split down its middle—half its episodes being devoted to the king's successive conflicts, and half to the amours of the queen (whose climactic double-marriage makes prophetic parody of Goethe's *Stella*). The royal pair, it may be observed, meet not once in the course of the action: their marriage is one of structural convenience. However, even Carey's arbitrariness in fitting together the jigsaw-puzzle of his play's events achieves a surreal consistency of its own. And this impression must surely have been strengthened in performance—at once spaced out and knitted together as the action would have been by the songs, dances, and other entertainments (the antipodean king's acrobatics no doubt among them) specified in the stage-directions. All contribute to the development of an atmosphere of fantasy—closer, perhaps, to that of Jarry's *Ubu* plays than to the theatrical self-consciousness of the earlier tradition of burlesque. *Chrononhotonthologos* represents, in fact, an interesting combination of the critical and the creative functions of its burlesque form.

THE
TRAGEDY

OF

Chrononhotonthologos:

BEING

The moſt Tragical Tragedy, that ever
was Tragediz'd by any Company of
TRAGEDIANS.

Written by BENJAMIN BOUNCE, Eſq;

Qui capit ille facit.

LONDON:

Printed for *J. Shuckburgh*, and *L. Gilliver*, in *Fleet-
Street*, *J. Jackson*, in *Pall-Mall*; and ſold by
A. Dodd, without *Temple-Bar*, and *E. Nutt*, at
the *Royal-Exchange.*   [Price Six Pence.]

PROLOGUE.

Spoken by Mr. *W. MILLS*.

*T*O Night our comic Muse *the Buskin wears,*
    And gives her self no small Romantic Airs;
Struts in Heroics, and in pompous Verse,
Does the minutest Incidents rehearse;
In Ridicule's strict Retrospect displays,
The Poetasters of these modern Days:
When the big bellowing Bombast rends our Ears,
Which stript of Sound, quite void of Sense appears;
Or when the Fiddle Faddle Numbers flow,
Serenely dull, Elaborately low: 10
Either Extreme, when vain Pretenders take,
The Actor suffers for the Author's sake.
The quite tir'd Audience lose whole Hours, yet pay
To go un-pleas'd and un-improv'd away:
This being our Scheme, we hope you will excuse
The wild Excursion of the wanton Muse;
Who out of Frolic wears a mimic Mask,
And sets herself so whimsical a Task:
'Tis meant to please, but if it should offend,
It's very short, and soon will have an End.   20

Dramatis Personæ.

Chrononhotonthologos, *King of Queerumania*,	*Mr.* Winstone.
Bombardinion, *his General*,	*Mr.* Ridout.
Aldiborontiphoscophornio, } *Courtiers*,	{ *Mr.* Cross.
Rigdum Funnidos, }	{ *Mr.* Oates.
Captain of the Guards,	*Mr.* Woodburn.
Doctor,	*Mr.* Gray.
Cook,	*Mr.* H. Tench.
King of the Fidlers,	*Mr.* Davis.
King of the Antipodes,	*Mr.* Jannot.
Dumb, *Master of the Ceremonies*,	*Mr.* Gray.
Signor Scacciatinello,	*Master* Arne.
Signora Sicarina,	*Miss* Jones.
Fadladinida, *Queen of Queerumania*,	*Mrs.* Shireburne.
Tatlanthe, *her Favourite*,	*Mrs.* Charke.
Two Ladies of the Court,	{ *Miss* Oates.
	{ *Miss* Dancy.
Venus,	*Mrs.* Clark.
Cupid,	*Master* Arne.

SCENE *Queerumania*.

The Tunes of ẏ Songs.
See Venus does attend thee.
(My Dilding my Dolding.)

Take this Magic Wand in Hand.
(Dance o'er the Lady Lee.)

Are you a Widow or are you a Wife.
(Gilly flower gentle Rosemary.)

Marriage may become a Curse.
(Swedes March.)

Da Capo

THE
TRAGEDY
OF
Chrononhotonthologos, &c.

SCENE *An Antichamber in the Palace.*

Enter Rigdum-Funnidos, *and* Aldiborontiphoscophornio.

Rigdum-Funnidos.

*A*LDIBORONTIPHOSCOPHORNIO!
Where left you *Chrononhotonthologos?*

Aldiborontiphoscophornio.

Fatigu'd with the tremendous Toils of War,
Within his Tent, on downy Couch succumbent,
Himself he unfatigues with gentle Slumbers;
Lull'd by the chearful Trumpets gladsome Clangor,
The Noise of Drums and Thunder of Artillery,
He sleeps Supine amidst the Din of War:
And yet 'tis not definitively Sleep;
Rather a kind of Doze, a waking Slumber,   10
That sheds a Stupefaction o'er his Senses;
For now He nods and snores; anon he starts,
Then nods and snores again: If this be Sleep,
Tell me, ye Gods! what mortal Man's awake!
What says my Friend to this?

Rigdum.

—Say! I say he sleeps Dog-sleep, what a Plague wou'd you have me say?

16 Dog-sleep] Light sleep, pretended sleep.

Aldiboronti.

O impious Thought! O curst Insinuation!
As if great *Chrononhotonthologos*
To Animals detestable and vile,
Had ought the least Similitude!   20

Rigdum.

My dear Friend! you entirely misapprehend me; I did not call the King,
Dog by Craft, I was only going to tell you the Soldiers have just receiv'd their
Pay, and are all as drunk as so many Swabbers.

Aldiboronti.

Give Orders instantly, that no more Money
Be issued to the Troops: Mean time, my Friend!
Let all the Baths be fill'd with Seas of Coffee,
To stupify their Souls into Sobriety.

Rigdum.

I fancy you had better banish the Sutlers, and blow the *Geneva* Casks to
the Devil.

Aldiboronti.

Thou counsel'st well, my *Rigdum-Funnidos*,   30
And Reason seems to father thy Advice:
But soft!—The King in pensive Contemplation
Seems to resolve on some important Doubt;
His Soul, too copious for his Earthly Fabrick,
Starts forth spontaneous in Soliloquy,
And makes his Tongue the Midwife of his Mind.
Let us retire, lest we disturb his Solitude.   [*They retire.*

Enter King.

King.

This God of Sleep is watchful to torment me,
And Rest is grown a Stranger to my Eyes:
Sport not with *Chrononhotonthologos*,   40
Thou idle Slumb'rer, thou detested *Somnus*:
For if thou dost, by all the waking Pow'rs,
I'll tear thine Eye Balls from their leaden Sockets,
And force thee to out-stare Eternity.   [*Exit in a Huff.*

23 Swabbers] Swabbers of a ship's deck, hence persons of low employment or behaviour.
28 Sutlers] Tradesmen following and living off an army.   28 *Geneva* Casks] Casks of gin.

Re-enter Rigdum-Funnidos *and* Aldiborontiphoscophornio.

Rigdum.

The King's in a cursed Passion: Pray who is this Mr. *Somnus* he's so angry withal?

Aldiboronti.

The Son of *Chaos* and of *Erebus*,
Incestuous Pair! Brother of *Mors* relentless,
Whose speckled Robe and Wings of blackest Hue,
Astonish all Mankind with hideous Glare;   50
Himself with sable Plumes to Men benevolent
Brings downy Slumbers and refreshing Sleep.

Rigdum.

This Gentleman may come of a very good Family, for aught I know; but I wou'd not be in his Place for the World.

Aldiboronti.

But lo! the King his Footsteps this Way bends,
His cogitative Faculties immers'd
In Cogibundity of Cogitation;
Let Silence close our folding Doors of Speech,
Till apt Attention tell our Heart the Purport
Of this profound Profundity of Thought.   60

Re-enter King *and* Attendants.

King.

It is resolv'd—Now *Somnus* I defy thee,
And from Mankind ampute thy curs'd Dominion.
These Royal Eyes thou never more shall close.
Henceforth let no Man sleep, on Pain of Death:
Instead of Sleep, let pompous Pageantry,
And solemn Show, with sonorous Solemnity,
Keep all Mankind eternally awake.
Bid *Harlequino* decorate the Stage
With all Magnificence of Decoration:
Giants and Giantesses, Dwarfs and Pigmies,   70
Songs, Dances, Musick in its amplest Order,
Mimes, Pantomimes, and all the magick Motion
Of Scene deceptiovisive and sublime.

47 *Erebus*] Son and husband of Chaos. Hence the 'incestuous pair' of the next line.
48 *Mors*] Death, twin brother of Somnus, with whom he dwelt in Hades.

An Entertainment of Singing, after the Italian Manner,
by Signor Scacciatinello *and Signora* Sicarina.

Enter Captain of the Guards.

Captain.

To Arms! to Arms! great *Chrononhotonthologos*!
Th'*Antipodean* Pow'rs, from Realms below,
Have burst the solid Entrails of the Earth.
Gushing such *Cataracts* of *Forces* forth,
This World is too incopious to contain 'em:
Armies, on Armies, march in Form stupendous;
Not like our Earthly Legions, Rank by Rank,   80
But Teer o'er Teer, high pil'd from Earth to Heaven:
A blazing Bullet, Bigger than the Sun,
Shot from a huge and monstrous Culverin,
Has laid your Royal *Citadel* in Ashes.

King.

Peace Coward! were they wedg'd like Golden Ingots,
Or pent so close, as to admit no *Vacuum.*
One look from *Chrononhotonthologos*
Shall scare them into Nothing. *Rigdum Funnidos*,
Bid *Bombardinion* draw his Legions forth,
And meet us in the Plains of *Queerumania.*   90
This very now ourselves shall there conjoin him;
Mean Time, bid all the Priests prepare their Temples
For Rites of Triumph: Let the Singing Singers,
With vocal Voices, most Vociferous,
In sweet Vociferation, out vociferize
Ev'n Sound itself; So be it as we have order'd.   [*Exeunt.*

SCENE *A magnificent Apartment.*

Enter Queen Fadladinida, Tatlanthe, *and two* Ladies.

Queen.

—Day's Curtain drawn, the Morn begins to rise,
And waking Nature rubs her sleepy Eyes.
The pretty little fleecy bleating Flocks,

In Baa's harmonious warble thro' the Rocks:
Night gathers up her Shades in sable Shrouds,
And whispering Oziers tattle to the Clouds.
What think you, Ladies, if an Hour we kill,
At Basset, Ombre, Picquet or Quadrille.

Tatlanthe.

—Your Majesty was pleas'd to order Tea.

Queen.

—My Mind is alter'd: Bring some Ratafia.   10
                  [*They are serv'd round with a Dram.*
I have a famous Fidler sent from *France*,
Bid him come in, What think ye of a Dance?

Enter King of the Fidlers.

King of the Fidlers.

—Thus to your Majesty says the suppliant Muse:
Would you a *Solo*, or *Sonata* chuse
Or bold *Concerto*, or soft *Siciliana*,
Alla Francese overo in Gusto Romano?
When you Command, 'tis done as soon as spoke.

Queen.

  A civil Fellow!—play us the *Black Joak.*
             [Queen *and* Ladies *Dance the* Black Joak.
So much for Dancing; now lets rest a while.
Bring in the Tea-Things, does the Kettle boil?   20

Tatlanthe.

—The Water bubbles and the Tea-Cups skip
Through eager Hope to kiss your Royal Lip.   [*Tea brought in.*

Queen.

—Come Ladies, will you please to chuse your Tea;
Or Green Imperial, or *Pekoe* Bohea?

1st Lady.

—Never, no, never sure on Earth was seen,
So *gracious*, *sweet* and *affable* a Queen.

6 Oziers] A kind of willow.

2d Lady.

—She is an *Angel*.

1st Lady.

—She's a *Goddess* rather.

Tatlanthe.

She's *Angel*, *Queen*, and *Goddess* altogether.

Queen.

—Away! you Flatter me.

1st Lady.

—We don't indeed,
Your *Merit* does our *Praise* by far exceed.   30

Queen.

—You make me blush: Pray help me to a *Fan*.

1st Lady.

—That Blush becomes you.

Tatlanthe.

—Would I were a *Man*.

Queen.

I'll hear no more of this as I'm a *Sinner*.
[*Enter* Dumb Master of the Ceremonies, *makes Signs of Eating*.
Dear me! that's true, I never thought of *Dinner*:
But 'twill be over Ladies very soon,
Mean time, my Friend, play t'other little Tune.
[*Musick plays, they all Dance off.*

SCENE *Another Apartment.*

Enter Rigdum Funnidos *and* Aldiboronti, *&c.*

Rigdum.

—'Egad we're in the wrong Box! Who the Devil wou'd have thought that
this same *Chrononhotonthologos* shou'd beat that mortal sight of *Tippodeans*;

1 in the wrong Box] In a false or untenable position.

why, there's not a Mother's Child of 'em to be seen. 'Egad they *footed* it away
as fast as their *Hands* cou'd carry 'em; but they have left their *King* behind
'em, we have *him* safe, that's one Comfort.

Aldiboronti.

—Would he were still at amplest Liberty.
For, O! my dearest *Rigdum Funnidos*,
I have a *Riddle* to *unriddle* to thee,
Shall make thee *stare* thy self into a *Statue*.
Our Queen's in *Love* with this *Antipodean*.   10

Rigdum.

—The Devil she is? Well, I see Mischief is going forward with a Vengeance.

Aldiboronti.

But lo! the Conqueror comes all crown'd with Conquest.
A solemn Triumph graces his Return:
Let's grasp the Forelock of this apt Occasion.
To greet the *Victor*, is his Flow of *Glory*.

A Grand Triumph.

Enter King *in Triumph, &c. met by* Rigdum *and* Aldiboronti.

Aldiboronti.

—All hail! to *Chrononhotonthologos*,
Thrice trebly welcome to your Loyal Subjects
My self and faithful *Rigdum Funnidos*
Lost in a Labyrinth of Love and Loyalty,   20
Intreat you to inspect our inmost Souls,
And read in them what Tongue can never utter.

King.

—*Aldiborontiphoscophornio*,
To thee and gentle *Rigdum Funnidos*;
Our Gratulations flow in streams unbounded:
Our bounty's Debtor to your Loyalty,
Which shall with Int'rest be repaid, e'er long,
But where's our Queen? where's *Fadladinida*;
She should be foremost in this gladsome Train,
To grace our Triumph; but I see she slights me,   30
This haughty Queen shall be no longer mine,
I'll have a *sweet* and *gentle Concubine*.

Rigdum. [*Aside.*

—Now my dear sweet *Phoscophorny*, for a swinging Lye to bring the Queen off: and I'll run with it this Minute to her, that we may be all in a Story.
[*They whisper importantly*, *and* Rigdum Funnidos *goes out.*

Aldiboronti.

—Speak not, great *Chrononhotonthologos*,
In Accents so injuriously severe
Of *Fadladinida*, your faithful Queen:
By me she sends an Embassy of Love,
Sweet Blandishments and kind Congratulations;
But, cannot, O! she cannot come Her self.   40

King.

—Our Rage is turn'd to Fear: What ails the Queen?

Aldiboronti.

A sudden *Diarrhœa*'s rapid Force,
So stimulates the Peristtaltic Motion,
That all conclude her Royal Life in danger.

King.

Bid the Physicians of the Earth assemble,
In Consultation solemn and sedate:
More to corroborate their sage Resolves,
Call from their Graves the Learned Men of old:
Galen, *Hipocrates*, and *Paracelsus*;
Doctors, Apothecaries, Surgeons, Chymists,   50
All! all! attend and see they bring their Med'cines,
Whole Magazines of gallipotted Nostrums.
Materializ'd in *Pharmaceutic* Order.
The Man that cures our Queen shall have our Empire.
[*Exeunt Omnes.*

Enter Tatlanthe, *and* Queen.

Queen.

—Hey ho! my Heart.

43 Peristtaltic Motion] Natural contractions.   52 gallipotted Nostrums] Medicines contained in the earthen pots used by apothecaries.

Tatlanthe.
—What ails my gracious Queen?

Queen.
—O would to *Venus* I had never seen.

Tatlanthe.
—Seen what, my Royal Mistress!

Queen.
—Too! too much.

Tatlanthe.
—Did it affright you?

Queen.
—No, 'tis nothing such.

Tatlanthe.
—What was it, Madam?

Queen.
—Really I don't know.

Tatlanthe.
—It must be something!

Queen.
—No;

Tatlanthe.
—Or, nothing;

Queen.
—No.

—O, my *Tatlanthe*, have you never seen?   60

Tatlanthe.
—Can I guess what, unless you tell? my Queen!

Queen.
—The King I mean.

Tatlanthe.

—Just now return'd from War:
He rides like *Mars* in his Triumphal Car.
Conquest precedes with Laurels in his Hand,
Behind him Fame does on her Tripos stand.
Her Golden Trump shrill thro' the Air she sounds,
Which rends the Earth, and thence to Heaven rebounds.
Trophies and Spoils innumerable grace,
This Triumph which all Triumphs does deface: 70
Haste then, great Queen! your Hero thus to meet,
Who longs to lay His Laurels at your Feet.

Queen.

—Art mad, *Tatlanthe*, I meant no such thing,
Your Talk's distasteful.

Tatlanthe.

                    —Didn't you name the King?

Queen.

—I did, *Tatlanthe*, but it was not thine,
The charming King, I mean, is only mine.

Tatlanthe.

—Who else, who else, but such a charming Fair
In *Chrononhotonthologos* should share:
The Queen of Beauty, and the God of Arms,
In him and you united blend their Charms.   80
Oh! had you seen him, how he dealt out Death,
And at one stroke robb'd Thousands of their Breath.
While on the Slaughter'd Heaps himself did rise,
In Pyramids of Conquest to the Skies;
The Gods all hail'd, and fain would have him stay;
But your bright Charms have call'd him thence away.

Queen.

—This does my utmost Indignation raise,
You are too pertly Lavish in his Praise;
Leave me for ever!

Tatlanthe.   [*Kneeling.*
                    —O what shall I say?
Do not, great Queen, your Anger thus display,   90

O frown me dead, let me not live to hear
My gracious Queen, and Mistress so severe;
I've made some horrible Mistake, no doubt,
Oh! tell me what it is!

Queen.

No, find it out.

Tatlanthe.

—No, I will never leave you, here I'll grow,
'Till you some Token of Forgiveness show:
O all ye Powers above, come down, come down!
And from her Brow dispel that angry Frown.

Queen.

—*Tatlanthe* rise, you have prevail'd at last,
Offend no more, and I'll excuse what's past.   100

Tatlanthe.   [*Aside.*

Why what a Fool was I not to perceive her Passion for the topsy turvy
King, the Gentleman that carries his Head where his Pocket should be; but I
must tack about I see.

[*To the* Queen.

Excuse me, *gracious* Madam! if *my* Heart
Bears Sympathy with yours in ev'ry Part;
With you alike, I sorrow, and rejoice,
Approve your Passion, and commend your Choice,
The Captive King.

Queen.

—That's he! that's he! that's he!
I'd die ten Thousand Deaths to set him free:
Oh! my *Tatlanthe!* have you seen his Face;   110
His Air, his Shape, his Mein, with what a Grace,
Quite upside down, in a new way he stands,
How prettily he foots it with his Hands!
Well, I must have him if I Live or die,
To Prison, and his Charming Arms I fly.   [*Exeunt.*

SCENE *A Prison*.

The King of the Antipodes *discover'd sleeping on a Couch*.

Enter Queen.

Is this a Place, Oh! all ye Gods above,
This a Reception for the Man I love?
See in what charming Attitude he sleeps,
While Nature's Self at his Confinement weeps.
Rise, Lovely Monarch! see your Friend appear,
No *Chrononhotonthologos* is here;
Command your Freedom, by this sacred Ring,
Then command me; what says my charming King.

She puts the Ring in his Mouth; he makes an odd Kind of Noise.

Ah! wretched Queen! how hapless is thy Lot,
To love a Man that understands thee not!   10
O lovely *Venus*, Goddess all Divine;
And gentle *Cupid*, that sweet Son of thine.
Assist, assist me, with your sacred Art,
And teach me to obtain this Stranger's Heart.

Venus descends in her Chariot with *Cupid*, *and Sings*.

See *Venus* does attend thee
        My Dilding, my Dolding,
Love's Goddess will befriend thee,
        Lilly bright and shinee.
With Pity and Compassion,
        My Dilding, my Dolding,   20
She sees thy tender Passion,
        Lilly, &c. Da Capo.

Air Changes.

To thee I yield my Pow'r divine,
        Dance over the Lady Lee,
Demand what e'er thou wilt, 'tis thine,
        My gay Lady.
Take this magic Wand in Hand,
        Dance, &c.
All the World's at thy Command,
        My gay, &c. Da Capo.   30

Cupid *sings*.

Are you a Widow, or are you a Wife,
> *Gilly Flow'r, gentle Rosemary.*
Or are you a Maiden, so fair and so bright,
> *As the Dew that flies over the Mulberry Tree.*

Queen.

Would I were a Widow, as I am a Wife.
> *Gilly Flow'r, &c.*
For I'm to my Sorrow a Maiden as bright,
> *As the Dew, &c.*

Cupid.

You shall be a Widow before it is Night,
> *Gilly Flow'r, &c.*   40
No longer a Maiden, so fair and so bright,
> *As the Dew, &c.*
Two jolly Young Husbands your Person shall share,
> *Gilly Flow'r, &c.*
And twenty fine Babies your Body shall bear,
> *As the Dew, &c.*

Queen.

O thanks Mr. *Cupid*! for this your good News,
> *Gilly Flow'r, &c.*
What Woman alive would such Offers refuse,
> *While the Dew, &c.*   50
> [Venus *and* Cupid *re-ascend*.

SCENE *Bombardinions Tent*.

King, *and* Bombardinion *at a Banquet*.

Bomb.

This Honour, Royal Sir! so royalizes
The Royalty of your most Royal Actions,
The Dumb can only utter forth your Praise,
For we who speak, want Words to tell our Meaning.
Here! fill the Goblet with *Phalernian* Wine,
And while our Monarch drinks, bid the shrill Trumpet
Tell all the Gods that we propine their Healths. [*Trumpets sound*.

7 propine] Offer up drinks to.

King.

—Hold *Bombardinion*, I esteem it fit,
With so much Wine, to eat a little Bit.

Bomb.

See that the Table instantly be spread,   10
With all that Art and Nature can produce.
Traverse from Pole to Pole; sail round the World,
Bring every Eatable that can be eat:
The King shall eat, tho' all Mankind be starv'd.

Cook.

And it please your Honour, there's some cold Pork in the Pantry, I'll hash
it for his Majesty in a Minute.   [*Exit in a Hurry.*

King.

Hash'd Pork! shall *Chrononhotonthologos*
Be fed with Swine's Flesh, and at second Hand?
Now, by the Gods! Thou dost insult us, General!

Bomb.

The Gods can Witness, that I little thought   20
Your Majesty, to Pork, had such aversion.

King.

Away thou Traytor! Dost thou mock thy Master? [*Strikes him.*

Bomb.

A Blow! Shall *Bombardinion* take a Blow?
Blush! Blush thou Sun! start back thou rapid Ocean:
Hills! Vales! Seas! Mountains! all commixing crumble,
And into *Chaos* pulverize the World:
For *Bombardinion* has receiv'd a Blow,
And *Chrononhotonthologos* shall Die.   [*Draws.*

King.

What means the Traytor?   [*Draws.*

Bomb.

                              —Traytor in thy Teeth,
Thus I defy Thee!

                              [*They fight, he kills the* King.

—Ha! What have I done?   30
Go, call a Coach, and let a Coach be call'd,
And let the Man that calls it be the Caller;
And, in his calling, let him nothing call,
But Coach! Coach! Coach! O for a Coach ye Gods!
                    [*Exit Raving. Returns with a* Doctor.
—How fares your Majesty?

Doctor.

          My Lord he's Dead.

Bomb.

   Ha! Dead! impossible! it cannot be;
I'd not believe it tho' himself should Swear it.
Go join his Body to his Soul again,
Or, by this Hand, thy Soul shall quit thy Body.

Doctor.

   My Lord, he is past the power of Physick,   40
His Soul has left this World.

Bomb.

   Then go to t'other World and fetch it back.   [*Kills him.*
And if I find thou triflest with me there,
I'll chace thy Shade through Myriads of Orbs,
And drive thee far beyond the Verge of Nature.
Ha!—Call'st thou *Chrononhotonthologos?*
I come! your Faithful *Bombardinion* comes:
He comes in Worlds unknown to make new Wars
And gain thee Empires, num'rous as the Stars.   [*Kills himself.*

Enter Queen *and others.*

Aldiboronti.

—O horrid! horrible, and horrid'st horror!   50
Our King, our General: Our Doctor dead.
All dead! Stone dead, irrecoverably dead!
Oh!—   [*All Groan a Tragedy Groan.*

Queen.

   My Husband dead! Ye Gods, what is't you mean,
To make a Widow of a Virgin Queen?
For, to my great Misfortune, he, poor King,
Has left me so, and that's a wretched Thing.   [*To* Tatlanthe.

Tatlanthe.

Why then, dear Madam! make no farther Pother,
Were I your Majesty, I'd try another.

Queen.

I think 'tis best to follow thy Advice.   [*Simp'ring.*

Tatlanthe.

I'll fit you with a Husband in a Trice: 61
Here's *Rigdum Funnidos*, a proper Man,
If any one can please a Queen, he can.

Rigdum.

Ay, that I can, and please your Majesty; so Ceremonies apart. Let's proceed to Business.   [*Kisses the* Queen.

Queen.

Oh! but the Mourning takes up all my Care:
I'm at a Loss what colour'd Weeds to wear.

Rigdum.

Never talk of Mourning, Madam,
One Ounce of Mirth is worth a Pound of Sorrow,
Let's bed to Night and then we'll wed to Morrow.   70
I'll make thee a great Man, my little *Phoscophorny*.
                            [*To* Aldiboronti. *aside.*

Aldiboronti.

I scorn thy Bounty, I'll be King, or nothing.
Draw Miscreant! Draw!   [Rigdum *runs behind the* Queen.

Queen.

Well, Gentlemen, to make the Matter easy,
I'll have you both, and that, I hope, will please ye.
                            [*Takes each by the Hand.*
And now, *Tatlanthe* thou art all my care:
Where shall I find thee such another Pair.
Pity, that one has serv'd so long, so well,
Shou'd die a Virgin, and lead Apes in Hell.
Chuse for your self, dear Girl, our Empire round,   80
Your Portion is Twelve Hundred Thousand Pound.

79 lead Apes in Hell] Legendary occupation of a woman who died a spinster.

Tatlanthe.

Thanks to your Majesty, give me the Money,
Let me alone to find myself a Honey.

Tatlanthe Sings.

Marriage may become a Curse,
Husbands may but teaze me;
So, for better or for worse,
No Man e'er shall seize me.
Changing, Ranging at my Pleasure,
Men in Plenty for my Treasure.
I myself, will keep the Purse,   90
And pay them as they please me.

Queen Sings.

Troth, my Girl, thou'rt in the Right,
And thy Scheme I'll borrow;
'Tis a Thought that's new and bright,
Wedlock brings but Sorrow.

                         [*To* Aldiboronti. *and* Rigdum.

Gentlemen! I'm not for Marriage,
But, according to your Carriage,
As you both behave to Night,
You shall be paid to Morrow.

FINIS.

EPILOGUE.

Spoken by Mrs. *SHIREBURNE*.

CUSTOM commands that I should something say
In Favour of the Poet, and the Play:
Criticks! on you, our Author does depend,
Be you his Champions, and his Cause defend;
You know his Drift, if wrongheads should misplace it;
I'm bid to say, Qui capit ille facit.
Whate'er you please to censure or correct,
We shall amend with Pleasure and Respect:
But to our Failings, some Indulgence give,
And with one gen'rous Plaudit, bid us live.   10

THE
DRAGON OF WANTLEY

Henry Carey

Died 1743

The Dragon of Wantley is the only burlesque in this collection of a musical rather than a 'legitimate' form of drama: and it was among the first of its kind. For Gay's *Beggar's Opera* and its several successors were not really musical burlesques. True, they parodied prevailing operatic plot-conventions, but they tried to correct the taste for opera in a more exemplary manner, by *substituting* English ballads for Italian arias. There is little of such didacticism, and less ill-nature, in Carey's burlesque, in spite of his dedicatory remarks about the 'beauty of nonsense, so prevailing in the Italian operas'. The production of *The Dragon of Wantley* in 1737 may, indeed, have been suggested by the failure of Handel's *Justin*—replete with dragons of its own—a few months earlier: be that as it may, Handel himself enjoyed the piece, and continued to hold it in affectionate regard. Carey's method of burlesque was thus similar to Gay's in *The What d'ye Call it*—his purpose not so much to abuse as to make *original* use of a parent form, by peopling it with the lowly and the ill-bred, and by substituting commonplace for idealized behaviour. *The Dragon of Wantley* is, in fact, close to mock-pastoral in the rough realism it infuses into its artificial medium.

John Frederick Lampe, an eminent bassoonist often employed by Rich to compose music for his irregular entertainments at Covent Garden, wrote the score for the piece, as he had for Carey's unsuccessful *Amelia* in 1732. For both plays he appears to have provided an accompaniment straightforwardly imitative of the Italian manner. His music was, as Carey put it in his dedicatory letter, 'as grand and pompous as possible, by which means the *contrast* is the stronger'. The bathetic effect of setting the rustic effusions of Carey's characters to the formal strains of Lampe's music can well be imagined. Certainly the result appealed to the audiences at Covent Garden, who flocked to see the piece nearly seventy times in its first season—an immediate popularity greater even than that accorded *The Beggar's Opera*.

The Dragon of Wantley is a slighter piece than *Chrononhotonthologos*—indeed, not very much longer than the burlesque ballad which prefaces the printed text—and structurally it is not much better organized. The battle with the dragon itself is over in seven lines and a couple of curt stage directions—evidence that Carey was not particularly interested in satirizing spectacular stage effects such as Rich loved to exploit. The play reads less easily than its predecessor, moreover, because so much of its force was dependent on the contrast in performance between its low action and Lampe's pompous musical setting. What can still be relished in print is the free rein Carey allows—and is better able to allow than in *Chrononhotonthologos*—to his particular tricks of versification. Double and treble-rhyming couplets contribute to a kind of rhythmic verve that Carey also achieved in *Namby Pamby*, and his spoken dialogue rattles along nicely in breathless exchanges which often approach the intended 'sublimity of burlesque'. *The Dragon of Wantley* is no masterpiece: but it is a pleasing *jeu d'esprit* with a sure sense of the ridiculous, a rare thing of its own kind.

THE
DRAGON
OF
WANTLEY.
A
BURLESQUE OPERA.

The MUSICK
By Mr. JOHN FREDERICK LAMPE,

And Performed at the

THEATRE-ROYAL in *Covent-Garden.*

Moderniz'd from the OLD BALLAD *after
the* Italian *Manner, by Sig.* CARINI.

The TWELFTH EDITION, with Additions.
To which is prefix'd, the Original BALLAD *(cum Notis variorum)*
by way of Argument, *&c. &c. &c.*

———————— *Ridiculum acri*
Fortius & melius.   HOR.

LONDON;
Printed for J. SHUCKBURGH, at the *Sun* near the
Inner-Temple-Gate in *Fleet-street,* 1738.
(Price Six-pence.)

TO

Mr. *John-Frederick Lampe*.

Dear JACK,

TO whom should I dedicate this *Opera* but to You, for whose Interest it was calculated, and at whose Request it was compleated: Many joyous Hours have we shared during its Composition, chopping and changing, lopping, eking out, and coining of Words, Syllables, and Jingle, to display in *English* the Beauty of Nonsense, so prevailing in the *Italian Operas*.

This Pleasure has been since transmitted to the gay, the good-natur'd, and jocular Part of Mankind, who have tasted the Joke and enjoy'd the Laugh; while the Morose, the Supercilious, and Asinine, have been fairly taken in, so far as to be downright angry; they say 'tis low, very low; now (begging their Worships Pardon) I affirm it to be sublime, very sublime.—   10

> *It is a Burlesque Opera:*
> *And Burlesque cannot be too low.*

Lowness (figuratively speaking) is the Sublimity of Burlesque: If so, *this Opera* is, consequently, the tip-top Sublime of its Kind.

Your Musick, on the other hand, is as grand and pompous as possible, by which Means the *Contrast* is the stronger, and has succeeded accordingly.

The following Prediction made by my Cousin *Harry* in the Year 1726, is now, I think, amply verified in Your Favour:

> *Call not my* Lampe *obscure, because unknown;*
> *He shines in Secret now, to Friends alone:*   20
> *Light him but up, let him in Publick blaze,*
> *He will delight not only, but amaze.*

We must both confess our-selves obliged to the Performers, particularly to Mr. *Salway* and the two Miss *Youngs*, not forgetting Signor *Laguerrini*, and Mynheer *Reinhold*, who have given Life and Spirit to our Compositions, and Pleasure to the Publick; but in a more singular Sense we stand indebted to Mr. *Rich*, who received our poor disconsolate *Dragon* with Pleasure, after it had lain several Years dormant in the Repository, and under the Inspection,

17 my Cousin *Harry*] Henry Carey himself, in his *Poems*, p. 115. The authorship of *The Dragon of Wantley* was ascribed pseudonymously to Signor Carini, who thus signs the Dedication.   27 Mr. *Rich*] Manager successively of the theatre in Lincoln's Inn Fields, where *The Beggar's Opera* was staged, and of the new Theatre Royal in Covent Garden.

of the most wise, most learned, and judicious, 'Squire *What-d'ye-call-him*,
Master of *Drury-Lane* Play-house.   30

                              I am,
                                Your Affectionate Friend,
                                  And Fellow-Student,

                                                        CARINI.

  Pall-mall, Jan. 3,
    1738.

A Critical REMARK on the Old Ballad, called *The Dragon of Wantley*
by the late Mr. *Rousillon*.

*T*HIS Ballad *does not properly fall under the Denomination of Historical, it
having been ever look'd upon as a Criticism or Ridicule upon St.* George,
The Seven Champions, Guy *of* Warwick, *and several other Songs of the like
Nature, and is the same to Ballads of Chivalry, as Don* Quixot *is to Books of
that Kind: However, there are some People who will, by no means, allow this to
be the Design of the Poet, nor the Song to be a Piece of Criticism, but a Satyr:
And to prove this, they tell you, That in Days of old, a certain Gentleman,* a
Member of the Law, *and here represented by the* Dragon, *being left Guardian to
three Orphans, and finding some little Flaw in their Titles, put in his Claim,
depriv'd them of their Estate, took Possession of it himself, and turn'd them over
to the Parish. Upon which another (here called* Moore *of* Moore-hall) *took up
their Cause, sued the unjust Guardian, cast him, and recover'd the Estate for the
Children. I shall not pretend to decide any thing in a Dispute of this Importance:
the Hypotheses are both probable; but which may be the justest, I shall leave the
Learned to determine.*

I

An Excellent
BALLAD

Of a most Dreadful COMBAT, fought between MOORE of *Moore-hall*,
and the DRAGON of *Wantley*.

To a pleasant Tune much in Request.

OLD Stories tell, how *Hercules*
 A Dragon slew at *Lerna*,
With seven Heads and fourteen Eyes
 To see and well discern-a:
But he had a Club this Dragon to drub,
 Or he had ne'er don't, I warrant ye:
But *Moore* of *Moore-hall* with nothing at all,
 He slew the Dragon of *Wantley*.

This Dragon had two furious Wings,
 Each one upon each Shoulder;   10
With a Sting in his Tail as long as a Flail,
 Which made him bolder and bolder.
He had long Claws, and in his Jaws
 Four and forty Teeth of Iron,
With a Hide as tough as any Buff,
 Which did him round environ.

Have you not heard of the *Trojan* Horse,
 With seventy Men in his Belly?
This Dragon was not quite so big,
 But very near, I'll tell you: 20
Devoured he poor Children three,
 That could not with him grapple;
And at one sup he eat them up,
 As one would eat an Apple.

2 *Lerna*] The lake at which Hercules destroyed the hydra.

All sorts of Cattle this Dragon did eat,
  Some say he ate up Trees,
And that the Forest sure he would
  Devour by degrees:
For Houses and Churches, were to him Geese and Turkies;
  He eat all, and left none behind,   30
But some Stones, dear *Jack*, which he could not crack,
  Which on the Hills you'll find.

In *Yorkshire*, near fair *Rotherham*,
  The Place I know it well,
Some two or three Miles, or thereabouts,
  I vow I cannot tell;
But there is a Hedge just on the Hill edge,
  And *Matthew*'s House hard by't;
O there and then was this Dragon's Den,
  You could not chuse but spy it.   40

Some say this Dragon was a Witch;
  Some say he was a Devil,
For from his Nose a Smoke arose,
  And with it burning Snivel;
Which he cast off, when he did cough,
  Into a Well that stands by;
Which made it look just like a Brook,
  Running with burning Brandy.

Hard by a furious Knight there dwelt,
  Of whom all Towns did ring;   50
For he could wrestle, play at Quarter-staff,
  Kick, cuff, and huff,
Call Son of a Whore, do any kind of thing:
By the Tail and the Main, with his Hands twain,
  He swung a Horse 'till he was dead;
And what is stranger, he for very Anger,
  Eat him all up but his Head.

These Children, as I told, being eat;
  Men, Women, Girls, and Boys,
Sighing and sobbing, came to his Lodging,   60
  And made a hideous Noise:
O save us all, *Moore* of *Moore-hall*,
  Thou peerless Knight of these Woods;

Do but slay this Dragon, who won't leave us a Rag on,
   We'll give thee all our Goods.

Tut, tut, quoth he, no Goods I want,
   But I want, I want in sooth,
A fair Maid of sixteen, that's brisk,
   And smiles about the Mouth;
Hair black as a Sloe, and a Skin white as Snow,   70
   With Blushes her Cheeks adorning;
To 'noint me o'er Night, e'er I go to fight,
   And to dress me in the Morning.

This being done, he did engage
   To hew the Dragon down;
But first he went new Armour to
   Bespeak at *Sheffield* Town,
With Spikes all about, not within but without,
   Of Steel so sharp and strong,
Both behind and before, Arms, Legs, and all o'er,   80
   Some five or six Inches long.

Had you see him in this Dress,
   How fierce he look'd and how big,
You would have thought him for to be
   Some *Egyptian* Porcupig:
He frighted all, Cats, Dogs, and all,
   Each Cow, each Horse, and each Hog;
For fear they did flee, for they took him to be
   Some strange out-landish Hedge-hog.

To see the Fight all People then   90
   Got upon Trees and Houses,
On Churches some, and Chimnies too;
   But they put on their Trowses,
Not to spoil their Hose. As soon as he arose,
   To make him strong and mighty,
He drank by the tale six Pots of Ale,
   And a Quart of *Aqua Vitæ*.

It is not Strength that always wins,
   For Wit does Strength excel;
Which made our cunning Champion   100
   Creep down into a Well;

Where he did think this Dragon would drink,
   And so he did in truth;
And as he stoop'd low, he rose up and cry'd Boh!
   And hit him on the Mouth.

Oh, quoth the Dragon, Pox take you, come out,
   Thou that disturb'st me in my Drink:
With that he turn'd, and sh-t at him;
   Good lack, how he did stink!
Beshrew thy Soul, thy Body is foul,   110
   Thy Dung smells not like Balsam;
Thou Son of a Whore, thou stink'st so sore,
   Sure thy Diet is unwholesome.

Our politick Knight, on the other side,
   Crept out upon the Brink,
And gave the Dragon such a Douse,
   He knew not what to think:
By cock, quoth he, say you so; do you see?
   And then at him he let fly,
With Hand, with Foot, and so they went to't,   120
   And the Word it was, Hey, Boys, hey!

Your Words, quoth the Dragon, I don't understand:
   Then to it they fell at all,
Like two wild Boars so fierce, I may
   Compare great Things with small.
Two Days and a Night with this Dragon did fight
   Our Champion on the Ground;
Tho' their Strength it was great, their Skill it was neat,
   They never had one Wound.

At length the hard Earth began to quake,   130
   The Dragon gave him such a Knock,
Which made him to reel, and strait he thought
   To lift him high as a Rock,
And then let him fall: But *Moore* of *Moore-hall*,
   Like a valiant Son of *Mars*,
As he came like a Lout, so he turn'd him about,
   And hit him a kick on the Back-side.

Oh! quoth the Dragon, with a deep Sigh,
   And turn'd six times together,

Sobbing and tearing, cursing and swearing   140
  Out of his Throat of Leather;
Moore of *Moore-hall*, O thou Rascal!
  Would I had seen thee never;
With the thing at thy Foot thou hast prickt my A-se-gut,
  And I'm quite undone for ever.

Murder, Murder, the Dragon cry'd,
  Alack, alack, for Grief;
Had you but miss'd that Place, you could
  Have done me no Mischief.
Then his Head he shak'd, trembled and quak'd,   150
  And down he laid and cry'd;
First on one Knee, then on Back tumbled he,
  So groan'd, kick'd, sh-t, and died.

PUFF.

The Opinion of a Grave and Learned *Pædagogue* concerning the following OPERA.

EXCLUSIVE of the Pleasure this Opera *has given the Adult, I have found it to be of infinite Use in alluring little Children to learn to read, when other Books have been found ineffectual. For which Reason I hereby exhort and advise all Fathers and Mothers, Godfathers, &c. to buy this Book by way of New-years Gift, as they would an* Anodyne Necklace *for the Improvement of this Generation, and the Advantage of the future.*

P. ANDERSON.

Westminster, Jan. 1,
1738.

Anodyne Necklace] An amulet supposed to have therapeutic properties.

DRAMATIS PERSONÆ.

The Dragon,

Moore *of* Moore-Hall,

Gaffer Gubbins, *Father to* Margery,

Margery,

Mauxalinda,

Mr. REINHOLD.

Mr. SALWAY.

Mr. LAGUERRE.

Miss ISABELLA YOUNG.

Miss ESTHER YOUNG.

CHORUS *of Nymphs and Swains.*

SCENE *that Part of* Yorkshire *near* Rotherham.

THE
DRAGON of *WANTLEY*.

ACT I. SCENE I.

A Rural Prospect.

CHORUS.

*F*LY, *Neighbours, fly,*
    The Dragon's nigh,
Save your Lives and fly;
    Away, away,
    For if you stay,
Sure as a Gun you die.
             Fly, &c.   *[Exeunt.*
                 [The Dragon crosses the Stage.

SCENE, *A Hall.*

GUBBINS, MAUXALINDA, *and* CHORUS.

Gub. What wretched Havock does this Dragon make!
  He sticks at nothing for his Belly's Sake:
  Feeding but makes his Appetite the stronger,
  He'll eat us all, if he 'bides here much longer!

AIR.

Poor Children three,
  Devoured he,
That could not with him grapple;
  And at one sup,
  He eat them up,
As one would eat an Apple.

CHORUS.

Houses and Churches,
To Him are Geese and Turkies.

10

To them MARGERY.

Marg. O Father! Father! as our noble 'Squire
  Was sate at Breakfast by his Parlour Fire,
  With Wife and Children, all in pleasant Tattle,
  The Table shook, the Cups began to rattle;
  A dismal Noise was heard within the Hall,
  Away they flew, the Dragon scar'd them all:
  He drank up all their Coffee at a Sup,
  And next devour'd their Toast and Butter up.   20

AIR.

  But to hear the Children mutter,
  When they lost their Toast and Butter,
      And to see my Lady moan,
  Oh! 'twould melt a Heart of Stone.

  Here the 'Squire with Servants wrangling;
  There the Maids and Mistress jangling,
  And the pretty hungry Dears
  All together by the Ears,
      Scrambling for a Barley Cake:
      Oh! 'twould make one's Heart to ake.   30
                      But to hear, &c.

Gub. This Dragon very modish, sure, and nice is:
  What shall we do in this disast'rous Crisis?
Marg. A Thought, to quell him, comes into my Head;
  No way more proper than to kill him dead.
Gub. O Miracle of Wisdom! rare Suggestion!
  But how, or who to do it, that's the Question.
Marg. Not far from hence there lives a valiant Knight,
  A Man of Prowess great, and mickle Might:
  He has done Deeds St. *George* himself might brag on;   40
Maux. This very Man is he shall kill the Dragon.

AIR.

  He's a Man ev'ry Inch, I assure you,
      Stout, vig'rous, active and tall;
  There's none can from Danger secure you,
      Like brave gallant Moore *of* Moore-Hall.
  No Giant or Knight e'er quell'd him,
      He fills all their Hearts with Alarms;

No Virgin yet ever beheld him,
But wish'd herself clasp'd in his Arms.

CHORUS.

Let's go to his Dwelling,   50
  With Yelping and Yelling;
And tell him a sorrowful Ditty.
Who knows but the Knight,
With this Dragon may fight,
  If he has but a Morsel of Pity.   [*Exeunt.*

SCENE, *Moore-Hall.*

Symphony.

MOORE *and his Companions.*

Moore. Come, Friends, let's circulate the chearful Glass;
Let each true Toper toast his favourite Lass.
Sound all your Instruments of Joy, and play:
Let's drink and sing, and pass the Time away.

AIR.

Zeno, Plato, Aristotle,
  All were Lovers of the Bottle;
Poets, Painters and Musicians,
Churchmen, Lawyers and Physicians,
   All admire a pretty Lass,
   All require a cheerful Glass.   10
   Ev'ry Pleasure has its Season,
  Love and Drinking are no Treason.   [*Zeno, &c.*

Enter GUBBINS, MARGERY, MAUXALINDA, *and others.*

CHORUS.

O save us all!   [*Kneeling.*
Moore *of* Moore-Hall!
Or else this cursed Dragon   [*They rise.*
Will plunder our Houses,
Our Daughters and Spouses,
And leave us the Devil a Rag on.
       O save, &c. [*They Kneel again.*

AIR.

Marg. [*Rising.*] *Gentle Knight! all Knights exceeding,*   20
           Pink of Prowess, and good Breeding,
           Let a Virgin's Tears inspire thee;
           Let a Maiden's Blushes fire thee.
           For my Father and my Mother,
           For my Sisters and my Brother,
           For my Friends that stand before thee,
           Thus I sue thee, thus implore thee;
           Thus I kiss thy valiant Garment,
           Humbly hoping there's no Harm in't.

Moore. [*Aside.*] Her looks shoot thro' my Soul, her Eyes strike Fire;   30
     I'm all a Conflagration of Desire.
     [*To her.*] Fair Maid, I grant whatever you can ask,
     The Deed is done, when once you name the Task.
Marg. The Dragon, Sir! the Dragon!
Moore.   Say no more,
     You soon shall see him weltring in his Gore.
Marg. Most mighty *Moore!* do but this Dragon kill,
     All that we have is wholly at your Will.
Moore. The only Bounty I require, is this,
     That thou may'st fire me with an ardent Kiss;
     That thy soft Hands may 'noint me over Night,   40
     And dress me in the Morning e'er I fight.

AIR.

Marg.   *If that's all you ask,*
                        My Sweetest,
                        My Featest,
                        Compleatest,
                        And Neatest,
                    I'm proud of the Task.
                    Of Love take your fill,
                        Past measure,
                        My Treasure,   50
                        Sole Spring of my Pleasure,
                    As long as you will.
                            If that's all, &c.

Maux. [*Overhearing.*] A forward Lady! she grows fond apace;
     But I shall catch her in a proper Place.

Moore. Leave her with me; conclude the Dragon dead:
   If I don't maul the Dog, I'll lose my Head.

> [*All go off but* Moore *and* Margery.

DUETTO.

> *Moore. Let my Dearest be near me;*
> *Marg. I'll ever be near thee,*
> *Moore. To warm me, to cheer me;*   60
> *Marg. To warm thee, to cheer thee.*
> *Moore. To fire me, inspire me;*
> *Marg. To fire thee, inspire thee*
>   *Both. With Kisses and Ale.*
> *Moore. Your Fears I'll abolish;*
> *Marg. This Dragon demolish.*
> *Moore. I'll work him.*
> *Marg. Ay, work him.*
> *Moore. I'll jerk him,*
> *Marg. Ay, jerk him*   70
>   *Both. From Nostril to Tail.*

> [*Let my, &c.*

MOORE *leads off* MARGERY; MAUXALINDA *enters, and
   pulls him back by the Sleeve.*

Maux. O Villain! Monster! Devil! Basely base!
   How can you dare to look me in the Face?
   Did you not swear last *Christmass* we should marry?
   Oh, 'tis enough to make a Maid miscarry!
   Witness this Piece of Six-pence, certain Token
   Of my true Heart, and your false Promise broken.
Moore. The Devil's in the Woman! What's the Matter?
Maux. Now you insult me; Time was you cou'd flatter.
Moore. Upon my Soul, I don't know what you mean!   80
Maux. Don't you know *Margery* of *Roth'ram-Green*?
Moore. Not I, upon my Honour.
Maux.   That's a Lie.
   What do you think I've neither Ear or Eye?
   Villain! I will believe my Eyes and Ears!
   She whom you kiss'd, and call'd ten thousand Dears.
   [*Sings mockingly.*] *Let my Dearest be near me,* &c.
Moore. [*Aside.*] By Jove! I'm blown. Z——ds! how came this about?
   However, I'm resolv'd to stand it out.
   [*To Maux.*] I only out of Policy was civil;

But, 'faith, I hate her as I hate the Devil.   90
You're all I value, witness this close Hug,
I'm yours, and only yours—
Maux.   Ah coaxing Pug!
Moore. My pretty *Mauxy*, prithee don't be jealous.
Maux. Dear me! you Men are such bewitching Fellows;
    You steal into our Hearts by sly Degrees,
    Then make poor Girls believe just what you please.

AIR.

Moore.   *By the Beer, as brown as Berry,*
                            By the Cyder and the Perry,
                            Which so oft has made us merry,
                            With a Hy-down, Ho-down-derry,   100
                            Mauxalinda's I'll remain,
                            True Blue will never stain.
                                        By the Beer, &c.

Maux. But do you really love me?
Moore.   By this Kiss,
    By Raptures past, and Hopes of future Bliss.

DUETTO.

                    Pigs shall not be
                    So fond as we ;
            We will out-cooe the Turtle Dove.
                    Fondly toying,
                    Still enjoying,   110
            Sporting Sparrows we'll out-love.
                            Pigs shall not, &c.

    End of the First ACT.

ACT II. SCENE I.

A Garden.

MARGERY *sola.*

AIR.

*S*URE *my Stays will burst with sobbing,*
     And my Heart quite crack with throbbing.
My poor Eyes are red as Ferrets,
And I ha'n't a Grain of Spirits.
O I wou'dn't for any Money,
This vile Beast shou'd kill my Honey;
Better kiss me, gentle Knight,
Than with Dragons fierce to fight.
                         Sure my Stays, &c.

                                                    [*To her* Moore.

Moore. My *Madge!* my Honey-suckle, in the Dumps!   10
Marg. Put your Hand here, and feel my Heart how't thumps.
Moore. Good lack a day! how great a Palpitation!
    Tell me, my Dear! the Cause of this Vexation.
Marg. An ugly Dream has put me in a Fright;
    I dreamt the Dragon slew my gentle Knight:
    If such a thing should happen unto thee,
    O miserable, miserable, *Margery!*
Moore. Don't fright thy self with Dreams, my Girl, ne'er fear him,
    I'll work his Buff, if ever I come near him.
    I've such a Suit of spiked Armour bought,   20
    Bears, Lions, Dragons, it sets all at nought:
    In which, when I'm equip'd, my *Madge* shall see,
    I'll scare the Dragon, not the Dragon me.
    But Time grows short, I must a while away.
Marg. Make haste, my Dear!
Moore.   My Duck! I will not stay.   [*Exit.*

Enter MAUXALINDA *to* MARGERY.

Maux. So Madam! have I found you out at last?
    You now shall pay full dear for all that's past.
    Were you as fine as e'er wore Silk or Sattin,
    I'd beat your Harlot's Brains out with my Patten,

29 Patten] A kind of wooden overshoe, resembling a clog.

Before you shall delude a Man of mine.   30
Marg. Who in the Name of Wonder made him thine?
Maux. D'ye laugh; you Minx! I'll make you change your Note,
   Or drive your grinning Grinders down your Throat.

DUETTO.

Insulting Gipsey,
You're surely tipsy,
Or non se ipse,
   To chatter so.
Your too much feeding,
All Rules exceeding,
Has spoil'd your Breeding,   40
   Go, Trollop, go.
      Insulting, &c.

Marg. Lauk! what a monstrous Tail our Cat has got?
Maux. Nay, if you brave me, then you go to pot.
   Come, Bodkin, come! take *Mauxalinda's* Part,
   And stab her hated Rival to the Heart.

           [*Goes to kill* Margery, *she swoons.*

Enter MOORE, *takes away the Bodkin.*

Moore. Why, what the Devil is the Woman doing!
Maux. To put an End to all your Worship's Wooing.
Moore. 'Tis well I came, before the Whim went further;
   Had I stay'd longer, here had sure been Murder.   50
   This cursed Jade has thrown the Girl in Fits.
   How do'st, my Dear?   [Margery *recovers.*
Marg.   Frighted out of my Wits.
Moore. But fear her not, for by her own Confession,
   I'll bind her over to the Quarter-Session.

AIR.

Maux.   *O give me not up to the Law,*
           I'd much rather beg upon Crutches;
           Once in a Sollicitor's *Paw,*
           You never get out of his Clutches.

Marg. Come, come, forgive her!
Moore.   Here my Anger ends.
Maux. And so does mine.
Moore.   Why then let's buss and Friends.   [*Kiss round.*

TRIO.

Maux. *Oh how easy is a Woman,*   61
    How deluding are you Men!
    Oh how rare, to find a true Man,
    Not so oft as one in ten.
Moore. *Oh how charming is a Woman,*
    Form'd to captivate us Men;
    Yet so eager to subdue Man,
    For each one she covets ten.
Marg. *Let's reward them as they treat us,*
    Women prove sincere as Men;   70
    But if they deceive and cheat us,
    Let us e'en cheat them again.
Omnes. *Let's reward them as they treat us, &c.*

Enter GUBBINS.

Gub. Now, now, or never save us, valiant *Moore!*
  The Dragon's coming, don't you hear him roar?
Moore. Why let him roar his Heart out, 'tis no matter:
  Stand clear, my Friends, this is no Time to chatter.
Gub. Here take your Spear.
Moore.   —I scorn Sword, Spear, or Dart;
  I'm arm'd compleatly in a valiant Heart.
  But first I'll drink, to make me strong and mighty,   80
  Six Quarts of Ale, and one of *Aqua Vitae.*
    Fill, fill, fill a mighty Flagon,
    Then I'll kill this monstrous Dragon.   [*Drinks.*

CHORUS.

    Fill, fill, fill the mighty Flagon,
    Kill, kill, kill this monstrous Dragon.   [*Exeunt.*

ACT III. SCENE I.

A rural Prospect near the Dragon's Den.

Enter MOORE *in Armour, and* MARGERY.

Moore. ONE Buss, dear *Margery*, and then away.
  Marg. I cannot go, my Love!

Moore.   You must not stay.
 Get up, sweet Wench, get up in yonder Tree,
 And there securely you may hear and see.

       [Margery *gets up into the Tree.*

 Come, Mr. *Dragon*, or by *Jove* I'll fetch you;
 I'll trim your Rascal's Jacket, if I catch you.

AIR.

Moore.   *Dragon! Dragon! thus I dare thee:*
      Soon to Atoms thus I'll tear thee;
       Thus thy Insolence subdue.
       But regarding where my Dear is,   10
       Then, alas! I feel what Fear is,
       Sweetest Margery *for you.*

          Dragon! &c.

           [*Dragon roars.*

Moore. It is not Strength that always wins;
 Good Wit does Strength excel.—
 Confound the Rascal, how he grins,—
 I'll creep into this Well.

          [*Gets into the Well.*
    [*Enter Dragon, and goes to the Well, as to drink.*

Dragon. What nasty Dog has got into the Well,
 Disturbs my Drink, and makes the Water smell.

         [Moore *within, cries* Boh!

AIR.

Dragon.   *Oh ho! Mr.* Moore,   20
       You Son of a Whore,
     I wish I'd known your Tricks before.
    [*Moore gets out of the Well, encounters the Dragon, and*
       kills him by a kick on the Back-side.

Dragon. Oh! oh! oh!
  The Devil take your Toe.   *[Dies.*

To him MARGERY, *in a Rapture.*

Marg. Oh, my Champion! how d'ye do?
Moore. Oh, my Charmer! how are you?
Marg. Very well, thank you;
Moore.   I'm so too.
  Your Eyes were livid, and your Cheeks were pale;
  But now you look as brisk as bottled Ale.
  Give me a Buss.
Marg.   Ah, twenty if you please.   30
Moore. With all my heart, and twenty after these.

DUETT.

> *My sweet Honey suckle, my Joy and Delight,*
> *I'll kiss thee all Day, and I'll hug thee all Night.*
> *My Dearest is made of such excellent Stuff,*
> *I think I shall never have Kissing enough.*
>   *My sweet,* &c.

Gub. Most mighty *Moore,* what Wonders hast thou done?
  Destroy'd the Dragon, and my *Marg'ry* won.
  The Loves of this brave Knight, and my fair Daughter,
  In *Roratorios* shall be sung hereafter.   40
  Begin your Songs of Joy; begin, begin.
  And rend the *Welkin* with harmonious Din.

CHORUS.

> *Sing, sing, and rorio,*
> *An* Oratorio
> *To gallant* Morio,
>   *Of* Moore-Hall.
> *To* Margerenia
> *Of* Roth'ram Greenia,
> *Beauty's bright Queenia,*
>   *Bellow and bawl.*   50
>   *Sing, sing,* &c.

42 rend the *Welkin*] Split the heavens.

CHORUS of CHORUSES.

HUZZA!

Marg.
Maux. } Huz——za!

Omnes. HUZZA! HUZZA! HUZZA!

FINIS.

DISTRESS UPON DISTRESS

George Alexander Stevens

1710–1784

The critical purpose of burlesque usually militates against an over-involvement of the dramatist in his work: he, like his audience, is distanced from the play by a cerebral awareness of its satiric content. One personal feeling which may still intrude is the contempt, indignation, or simple amusement which has determined the dramatist's particular target: and it is thus in part a pervasive scorn for pedantry which gives bite to George Alexander Stevens's only essay in burlesque, *Distress upon Distress*. But Stevens's prematurely subtitled *Religion, or the Libertine Repentent*, written in the aftermath of severe illness in 1751, had been more deeply rooted in his own experience: and *Distress upon Distress*, published just a year later, also makes occasional echo of its author's state of mind. Stevens was an actor—not over talented, it seems, but popular with his fellows, and somewhat intemperate in his habits. Hence the personal implications of his dedicatory references to broken resolutions—which almost plunge him 'into a fit of the vapours'. Hence, too, the tame repentance of Squire Fanfly at the climax of the play, and the recurrent motif of drunkenness and its consequences. Stevens's own morbid guilt sustains this undertone of melancholy, strangely counterpointing the more dominant note of objective indignation, which prompts, for example, the annotative outbursts against Warburton in the second act.

Distress upon Distress declares itself to be a heroi-comi-parodi-tragedi-farcical burlesque; and within its two acts, thickly cushioned with footnotes, generic confusion certainly reigns—a confusion assisted, one feels, by Stevens's own changes of course. The plotting is arbitrary, the action disjointed, the characterization random. The author's interest—and thus the felt emphasis of the printed text—switches from play to footnotes and back again. The footnotes themselves begin as almost 'pataphysical assaults upon language and logic, then develop a closely critical attack on the pedantry of Shakespearian editors, and finally peter out altogether. The dialogue is complicated by its combination of parody and moral reflection—as in Fanfly's *Hamlet*-based soliloquy upon intemperance. The Swiftian digressions on the art of humming in the dedication and early footnotes bear no organic relationship to the rest of the play. And the play itself concludes with an interlude in the madhouse unrelated to its preceding action, and closer to dramatic satire than burlesque. All this suggests a writer uncertain of his direction: but it also gives to *Distress upon Distress* an intriguing density alike in structure and content.

Stevens felt, it may finally be noted, no need to claim a pedigree or provide a theoretical justification for his play. The burlesque form—the decades of its fullest exploitation only just at a close—was well-established: it was as 'legitimate' as an irregular dramatic mode could ever be. *Distress upon Distress* is thus among the least self-conscious of burlesques: its author chose the form as freely as he might have chosen any other, and put it to a highly personal use—fortunately oblivious of the boundaries by which the present or any other critic might attempt to hem it in.

Distress upon Distress:

OR,

TRAGEDY

IN TRUE TASTE.

A Heroi-Comi-Parodi-Tragedi-Farcical BURLESQUE.

IN TWO ACTS.

By *George Alexander Stevens*

WITH

All the Similies, Rants, Groans, Sighs, &c.
entirely New.

WITH

Annotations, Diſſertations, Explanations, Obſer-
vations, Emendations, Quotations, Reſtorations, &c.

By Sir *HENRY HUMM.*

AND

NOTES Critical, Classical and Historical,

By *Paulus Purgantius Pedaſculus.*

Who has carefully Reviſed, Corrected and Amended it ; Expunged the ſeveral Errors and Inter-
polations ; Reconciled the various Readings,
and Reſtored the AUTHOR to himſelf.

LONDON:

Reprinted from the *Dublin* Edition, for
R. Griffiths in St. *Paul*'s Church-yard,
1752. Price 1 *s.* 6 *d.*

To the RIGHT COMICAL
* Lord Chief Justice *SPARKS*, &c.

May it please Your Lordship,

LIFE, as SHAKESPEAR says, is like a poor Player, and a poor Player is like to be a poor Life; nay, any Life, unless tolerably acted, is like to be a poor one.

THE World's a Stage, Life an irregular Drama, our Passions are the Players, our Senses the Scenes, and Reason a drowsy Part of the Audience, that cannot, or will not, mind what's performing around him.

> *Life is but a Joke—and our Art at the best,*
> *Is solely in making the most of the Jest.*

To help the Joke on, you greatly contribute, and I sometimes am allow'd to play an under Part to you.   11

LET me not rake up the Ashes of the Dead; disturb the *Manes* of the Great deceased, or disfurnish the Trophies of ancient Law-Givers, to make a Panegyric on your Lord Chief Justiceship. Come ye Sons of sterling Humour, *Lucian, Rablais, Cervantes,* and THOU, the most witty, most worthy of all, immortal *SWIFT*, inspire me. Teach me to paint THEE and thy Court—It will not be—not one Ray of all their mighty Power will they beam on me— unhappy Rustic.

SUFFER me then, as Your *Attorney-General*, to address You, and offer a Case to Your Lordship, which comes immediately under Your Jurisdiction.

IT is the whole Art and Mystery of

HUM-BUGGING.   21

This is a very ancient Science, and, as *Maimonedes* reports in the *Munster* MSS. was first taught by the *Ægyptians*.

Hermes Trismegistus, and *Zoroaster*, were *Hieroglyphical Hummers.*

THE first found out the *Philosopher's Stone,* the other invented *Oracles.*

IT is very difficult to come to a right Account of those dark and fabulous

---

* A Club of Gentlemen met every *Sunday* Night for the Winter Season, where Mr. *Sparks* presided as Judge for the Tryal of Offences committed in that Society.

Lord Chief Justice *Sparks*] Isaac Sparks, described by Stevens's biographer Thomas Seccombe as a 'dissolute humorist'. Stevens and Sparks founded the so-called Nassau Court in Dublin, to the mock-procedures of which the dedication refers.   12 *Manes*] Benevolent spirits of the dead.

Ages. The first Authors of Antiquity to be depended upon for their Veracity, are, *Herodotus*, *Ælian*, *Pliny* the *Naturalist*, and Sir *John Mandevile*.

IN the Life of *Thersites*, *Herodotus* gives us an Account of a very remarkable *Hum*. It was called, *The Trojan Horse*; though some Authors will tell you it was a *Mare*; others, that it was a *Cow*; and that the Model of it being preserved in the *Cretan Musæum*, gave *Dædalus* the Hint for carrying on the Intrigue for Madam *Pasiphaæ* with *Europa's Galloway*.   33

ULYSSES we may set down as a tolerable *Hummer*; *vide* the Reports, Cases, and Tryals, of *Rhesus*, *Achilles*, *Palamedes*, *Philoctetes*, *Ajax*, *Circe*, *Calipso*, &c. &c.

LADY *Penelope*, his Spouse, was not a Jot behind Hand with him. She carried on a good Sort of a *Joke* on her Side the Water. Ah, my LORD, that undoing at *Night* what has been done in the *Day*, is too often the Case at present with most of the Male and Female Descendants from *Adam*.   40

HER Web is a good Emblem of the Morning Resolves of Sobriety, and the Evening Temptations to break them.

IN vain may we reason dispassionately, declare for Abstinence and good Hours. It is all but a Web. At Night, Claret and good Company unravel all our Resolutions.

AND Faith, *entre nous*, I think we are in the Right of it. Time will not stay for us, why should we stay for Time. The future Moments are scarcely worth reflecting on, the past too painful to remember, and the present only fit for Laughter. Let us then socially sacrifice to *Mirth* and *true Humour*: As in the ancient Days of Pleasantry our Forefathers tasted the Sweets of joyful Society.   51

THE *Spirit of Hospitality* presided at their Tables; *Wit* and *good Humour* were their Companions; and *Fancy* furnish'd out the Feast.

BUT to return to my History.

ALEXANDER the Great was a famous *Hummer*; he persuaded the *Macedonians* into a Belief he was the Son of *Jupiter*; but he carried the Joke rather too far, for he believed it himself at last; so may properly be said to be *self-hum'd*: Like the Miser who pick'd his own Pocket.

ALCIBIADES was certainly a very great Master of this Science: But why should I disturb the tawny Mold of these Dust-converted Heroes; not but there were some very pretty Fellows formerly to be sure. For Instance;

SCIPIO was a very modest Fellow; yet I take *Lælius* to be but a led *Captain*, and *Socrates* little better than a *Putt*: *Demosthenes* said a great many good Things, and *Cæsar* had certainly something very smart about him: *Mark Anthony* was a very *jemmy Fellow*, and *Cleopatra* quite the Thing to be sure; *Lucretia* was a Fright, and *Virginius* a Beast of a Fellow: *Virgil* had a good deal of the Gentleman about him, and *Horace* was a very honest Fellow:

64 *jemmy*] Smart, neatly attired.

Ovid was a good Woman's Man, and *Cicero* tolerable Company: But what's all this to the Purpose, if the fine Fellows of former Ages were alive now, they would be looked on little better than *Tramontanes*.   70

FOR pray, what Figure would *Phocion* cut in a *Pump-Room*, or how would *Hannibal* behave in a *Minuet*. *Ulysses* might do something at *Broughton*'s perhaps, but what would become of *Aristides* at a *Masquerade*, or who would take *Epaminondas* for a Partner at a *Card-Table*?

IT is not by slaying of Monsters, founding of Empires, or being Tempest-toss'd for half a Score Years, we now become great. The System of Life is entirely altered. If we must give Battle, what can we better kill than our Time. And if we would do any Thing for Posterity, we may endeavour to increase the Infant Inhabitants of the *Foundling-Hospital*; and as to encountr-ing Fatigues, the rude Jolts of a Hackney-Coach over the rough irregular Streets, and broken Pavement, is enough to discompose the Oeconomy of both Limbs and Linnen of the prettiest Fellow existing.   82

I BEG Pardon for this Digression, and shall leave the Ancients to their Commentators, and look into our own Times, see how far this *Humbugg*, (or *Humbuzz*, as *Ben Johnson* calls it:) I say, see how far it has spread.

ITS Etymology is difficult to ascertain; though *Machaon*, in his *Tuscan* Treatise upon *Muscular Motion*, derives it from the Sounds which issued from the Nostrils of the *Phœnician Fanatics*, when they pretended to undergo the Operation of the Spirit. No bad *Hum* that, nor badly propagated since. It became general in *Cromwel*'s Time, who must be allowed a *Hero in Humming*.

IN the merry Days of King *Charles* the Second, all these formal Fashions were banish'd, and a new Branch of this Science was introduced by *Jack Bite* and Miss *Quibble*, who lived very handsomely at the Court by selling Bargains.   94

THEY have continued, Courtiers-like, in Esteem and out, as Caprice and Constitution commanded, till a younger Brother, tired of *Levee* Dependance, struck a bold Stroke, and set up for himself.—The Story is thus:

YOUNG HUMM, the Buck I speak of, is a collateral Descendant from the House of *Legend*: A long Time he had been put to his Shifts, rambling about sometimes as a *Gipsy*, a *Mountebank Doctor*, a *Methodist Preacher*, an *Italian Count*, a *Fortune Hunter*, a *decay'd Gentleman*, an *Oculist*, &c. At last he struck at the Stage, and resolved to commence *Actor*. He made his first Appearance in the little Theatre in the *Haymarket*, in the Character of a *Bottle Conjurer*.

WHAT became of him afterwards I could never learn, till by the late Advertisement for *Macklin*'s Benefit, we find that *Actor* has employed him to fill his House for him.   106

70 *Tramontanes*] Those from 'across the mountains', i.e. barbarous.   72 at *Broughton*'s] At the boxer John Broughton's pugilistic displays.   103 *Bottle Conjurer*] See Stevens's own note to page 294.

I wish Your Lordship would lay a Fine on all such Pretenders to Wit, Science, &c. That no Pedlar in Poetry, no plagiary Humourist, no unclassical Critic, shall have Liberty to vend his Dregs for true Doctrine.

For my own Part, I shall, as Your *Attorney-General*, prefer a Bill against all Pretenders to *Hum*, who dare practise without being able to shew a sensible Diploma; or, at least a Deputation from the Court of good Humour.

That is the Court which all Men ought to practise in, especially all those who with natural or acquired Qualifications are capable of taking upon them the Character of fine Companions.   115

With Submission to Your Lordship's Judgment, I cannot help giving it as my Opinion, that however Fame-worthy Wit, Wisdom, and Learning are, Good-nature is much their superior.

My esteeming Good-nature before Wit, &c. may be thought in me to proceed from the common Vice of railing at what I cannot enjoy.   120

I allow it; yet must beg Leave to observe, that although Wit is very pleasing, it is sometimes as hurtful; it often raises up a Foe, seldom makes a Friend.

A man of Wit and Humour may justly be compared to a beautiful Girl without a Fortune; they both attract many Admirers, who pay strong Court for Possession; but it is momentary Self-Gratification only they aim at. After, long Enjoyment blunts the Edge of Appetite, and Familiarity renders every wish'd-for Perfection common. Satiety succeeds Desire, and the former Lovers are no longer anxious after Enjoyment. What is then to become of those Victims to Frolic? The Girl languishes out her Disease-shorten'd Days in an Hospital; and the Man of Wit, broken-hearted, perishes in Goal, under the miserable Reflections of mispent Time and baseless Friendships.

But, Mr. Sparks, give me Leave seriously to address you, and in this public Manner declare, That if every one, who likes you as an Actor, was to be a Witness, like me, of your Behaviour in private Life, You would, if *possible*, be much more respected than You are at present. You are very pleasing as an Actor, highly diverting as a Companion, but more Praise-worthy as *a Man*. I know You to be a sensible Friend, an indulgent Father, and an affectionate Husband. These are Qualities none can exceed, few come up to. When the Sallies of Wit and Humour shall decay, when the Grape's enlivening Juice becomes tasteless, and when the best Company ceases to be entertaining, this Character shall remain. Then in Your last, in Your latest Moments, shall You enjoy the secret Satisfaction of an honest well-spent Life.   144

Long may those Moments be distant.

I have almost thought myself into a Fit of the Vapours, and, I believe, at this present Reading, You are not much better; therefore, if Your Lordship

131 Goal] Obs. form of 'gaol'.

pleases, I'll call a new Cause, and consider of—what—why myself, tho' that is a Topic hardly worth Consideration, and what, indeed, I am very unfit for.

METHINKS some hasty Readers may cry out, What is all this about, this *Humdrum*? What a Plague does this *Stevens* trouble us with himself and such Stuff? Why, that's true, faith, I can plead nothing in Defence of this Paper-wasting Practice, this CACOETHES SCRIBENDI, (there's Learning, my Lord) I say, I can plead nothing in Defence of myself but Idleness and the Fashion; and if they don't acquit me—why I'm undone, that's all. 155

YOU say in Your EPILOGUE, that the Town is the Jury: To them therefore I submit; and if any Performance of mine, either as an Author, or Actor, can amuse them, my End is answered, my Labour paid: But if, on the Contrary, I'm condemned, why, Silk-worm like, I'll wrap myself up in my own Labours, and dose out the rest of my Days in Dirt and Despair; a miserable *Momento* to all wou'd-be Wits my Cotemporaries. 161

IT is very hard to be witty, and a melancholy Thing, very melancholy indeed, when we want to arrive at Wit: And Dulness (fast Friend to us Rhime-makers) claps an Embargo on our Understandings. But though I can't come at Wit, I may at Sincerity; and, possessed of that, dare say, if a single Page in the following Burlesque meets with Approbation from the Readers of Taste in this Metropolis, I shall from thenceforth begin to have a good Opinion of a certain Son of Indiscretion, called,

Geo. Alex. Stevens.

Dublin, May 1,
1752.

N.B. *For the Benefit of all Theatrical Puffers, Hummers, &c. here is a Copy of Mr.* MACKLIN's *last Advertisement.*

For the Benefit of Mr. MACKLIN.

AT THE

THEATRE Royal in *Covent-Garden,* on *Wednesday* the 8th of *April,* will be presented a Comedy————

After which will be exhibited, a new Dramatic Satire of two Acts, called

Covent-Garden Theatre :

OR,

PASQUIN turn'd *DRAWCANSIR,*

Censor of *Great-Britain.*

Written in the Model of the Comedies of Aristophanes, *and the* Pasquinades *of the* Italian *Theatre in* Paris.

With Chorusses of the People after the Manner of the *Greek* Drama.
The Parts of the Pit, the Boxes, the Galleries, the Stage, and the Town, to be performed
By THEMSELVES for their Diversion;
The Parts of several dull disorderly Characters in and about St. *James*'s, to be perform'd
By CERTAIN PERSONS, for Example;
And the Part of *Pasquin-Drawcansir* to be performed
By his CENSORIAL HIGHNESS,
For his Interest.

The Satire to be introduced by an Oration, and to conclude by a Peroration: Both to be spoken from the *Rostrum,* in the Manner of certain Orators,
By Signior *PASQUIN.*

THE
GENEALOGY
OF THE
AUTHOR.

I OWEN LLWYDDGMACH DUOLLCHYRFDSFITH, Genealogist, Having well and
faithfully examined all the Records relating to the Family of our AUTHOR,
find him duly and truly poetically begot, being a Descendant, in a Right
Line, from the famous,

Joan la Pucelle, commonly call'd the Maid of *Orleans*.

She falling in Love with Mons. *Rondeau*, Madrigall Maker to the Court,
bore him one Son, who for the Incontinency of his Mother, was forced to
take the Vow of Celibacy upon him and turn Monk.
He invented those Rhymes, afterwards called
Leonine Verses.   10
But eloping from the Monastery, he hired himself
to a *German* Anagrammatist,
Whose Daughter he married, and she bare him a
Son called *Johannes Initialis*, Inventor of Acrostics.
Signiora Cramboni, Rebus-Maker to the *Basso-Relievo* College at *Padua*,
married *Johannes*, and they had one Child call'd

DORMIO DRAMMATICO.

He first added Verses to the Ends of Acts of heroic Plays, vulgarly called
Tragedy Taggs.
From him came *Tom Travesty*, *Dubartas*, and *Elkannah Settle*, Motto-
Maker and Professor of Poetry to my Lord-Mayors Pageants. He wrote a
Play call'd *Pope Joan*, and taking a Fancy to the Lady who acted the
Heroine, he married her, and she bore him a Son, the original Composer of
Bellmen's *Verses*; his Name was *Dactyle*, he married into the *Spondee*
Family, a Sister of the House of *Pindarics*,   25

Who put the *London Cries* into *Metre*.

These were Great Grand-Father and Mother to our AUTHOR.
His Grand-Father was Prologue-Writer to *Powel*'s Puppet-Show; and his

28 *Powel*'s Puppet-Show] The allusion is to a famous puppet show managed by Martin
Powell in the early eighteenth century.

Grand-mother Poesy-Poetess for Wedding-Rings.

His own Father was Distich-maker to Sign Painters, and his Mother made St. *Giles*'s best Ballads. 31

As to himself, he never before this Attempt arrived at any Thing greater than writing Couplets for Astrologers to decorate Almanacks with, or now-and-then assisting at an *Ænigma* for the Magazine.

He has met with great Success in composing *Valentines*: And once put up for the Place of Epitaph Maker to the Company of Tombstone-Cutters.

This Publication is therefore made to enable him to stand Candidate for the Employment of HISTORIOGRAPHER to the *HOTTENTOTS*. Which Place now being vacant, he hopes to fill with Reputation, as he happens to be related to the chief Families in that Kingdom.

K

Dramatis Personæ.

MEN.

'Squire *Fanfly*.
Beverage, a *Vintner*.
Spunge, *a led Captain*.
Gamble, *a Sharper*.
Phlebotome, *a mad Doctor*.
Scarebabe, *his Man*.
Caustic, *a Corn-Cutter*.
Jack Handy, *the 'Squire's Gentleman*.

WOMEN.

Capriola, *a Ropedancer*.
Arietta, *an Opera Singer*.
Miss Languish, *an Heiress*.
Sybilla, *her Governess*.
The 'Squire's Mama.

Constable, Watch, Ghost, Attendants.

Distress upon Distress.

ACT I.

SCENE I. AIR I.

Enter GAMBLE *in a Passion.*[*]

Sings.

WOE heap'd on Woe, as Wave on Wave,
 A Sea of Sorrows fills my Breast[†],
Can mortal Man more Trouble have?
 By Love and Debt at once oppress'd[‡].

Enter SPUNGE *in a Fury, and trips up* GAMBLE[§].

GAMBLE.

Whence this Insult?

SPUNGE.

Insult, Sir?

GAMBLE.

Ay, Insult!

---

 [*] This Passage has occasioned many Disputes among the Learned, how a Man could sing, if he was in a Passion? But it is easily set to rights, by supposing GAMBLE to be a *Welchman*. PAULUS PURGANTIUS.

 [†] This is a very just Metaphor: For as Tears are of a very briny or salt Nature, they are aptly expressed by the Sea.

 [‡] These are very natural Distresses, and I believe one Way or other affect every Reader. HENRY HUM.

It is necessary here to premise the Art of the Author, in so well opening of his Poem, consonant to his Title-Page. For it is *Distress upon Distress*, for a Man to be in Love and Debt at the same Time.

 [§] This tripping up is perfectly pantomimical, and has been used with very great Success in several dramatic Entertainments, particularly King LEAR, where *Kent* trips up the Gentleman-Usher with a very good Grace; and the Audience, as well as the several royal Personages it is done before, is convinced, that the old Nobleman is a very good Wrestler. H.H.

SPUNGE.

Be calm a Moment, and a Moment mind,
Attentive list with philosophic Ear*,
From Passion purged.   10

AIR II.

GAMBLE.

Sir, you're a Scoundrel—   [*Loud Symphony.*
Sir, a Scoundrel, Damme†—   [*Da Capo.*

SPUNGE.

Thy boiling Rage in frothy Phrase reeks out:
Repell'd by Reason's Shield, condens'd, the Steam,
In dribbling Drops, falls down—‡my Wrath subsides.

GAMBLE.

Sir, I'll be damn'd—

SPUNGE.

You may;§

GAMBLE.

I say I will, before I'll put this up;
Therefore be quick, and give me Satisfaction.

Enter BEVERAGE.

* *And philosophic hear.*—This is the true reading. Ear is a pedantic Interpolation,
alluding to an old Maxim in the Schools. H *non est Litera. P.P.*

† *Dam me quasi da me, pro mihi, vel redde mihi,* or give me, or unto me, Satisfaction; *Porphyrius Torrentius,* and *Lambinus,* concur with me in the reading; for
we cannot suppose, in a dramatic Performance, the Author would allow any
Personages of the Drama to swear.

‡ This is a fine physical, hydrostatical Metaphor.

For any Fluid rarified by Heat, when it meets with a cold Medium immediately
condensing, conglobes in pearly Particles, adhesing to the chilly metalline, or
lignified Superficies. *H.H.*

What Body it was that the elemental Effluvias adhered to, I was long unable to
determine; but fancy the Annotator must mean, by the Word Superficies, a Kettle's
Covering, commonly called a Pot-lid; and the Words, metalline and lignified, I
take to relate to the essential Quality of Matter it was made out of. *P.P.*

§ This is wrong pointed: He has stopped this Line with a Semicolon, and it
should be with a Colon.

BEVERAGE.

Be quiet, Puppies, are you drunk,   20
Or dreaming? Is this a Day to fight on?
This brave Day, when our young Landlord
Fanfly's come of Age.

SPUNGE.

No, I was wrong, I'll take another Time.

BEVERAGE.

Another Time, what Time? Hark ye, my Friend,
Since you're for Time, pray give me Leave to Speak*,
What Time to pay this Bill off, will you take?

GAMBLE.

We have gone too far.

BEVERAGE.

Yes, in my Debt you have.
So I have seen, in an unfurnish'd Room†,   30
A needy Spider raise his air-spread Loom;
From one poor Speck at first his Web begins,
Thread after Thread, the Tax-free Tenant spins.
Day after Day, thus you've increas'd your Score,
You've spun your Threads out, and I'll trust no more.

SPUNGE.

Either I dream, or else I am awake‡,
Did not I hear my dear Miss *Molly* speak?
So have I seen—I can't tell what at present,
But something, somewhere, very like her.

BEVERAGE.

Come, leave your Ogling, let's attend the Squire.   40
For him, the Sparkling Glass shall oft go round,

* Here is a Quibling on the Word *Time*, which is beneath the Dignity of a
Tragedy Writer. To be sure, the Man had a Right to ask for his Money; but as the
other does not seem ready to comply, the Demand was certainly not well *timed*. *P.P.*

† So I have seen—very unclassical—*Lege*, So have I seen. *P.P.*

‡ He is either one or t'other. This is reducing Things to a Certainty, and indeed
I wish all our modern Tragedy Writers would be as explicit; for it is impossible
sometimes to tell by their Writings, whether they are asleep or awake.

For him, our Streets in strong *October*'s drown'd,
For him, each pimpled Cheek shall redder grow,
For us he comes; and therefore Friends we'll go.

[*Exeunt* BEVERAGE *and* GAMBLE.

SPUNGE.

I will but make a Simile and follow:
So—so—so,
I don't know how to stay, or how to go,
Like some poor spunging Guest, who drinks his Part,
But when the Reck'ning's call'd, sleeps o'er the Quart,
When waked and question'd what he has to pay, ⎫   50
His Money gone, he don't know what to say,   ⎬
*But like me, softly takes himself away.   ⎭

[*Exit on Tiptoe.*

SCENE II.

Enter Miss MOLLY *and her* GOVERNESS.

MISS.

How long, Mama, must I request in vain?
Sigh for Delights, yet ne'er Delights obtain†.
Want, wish, and whimper, whimper, wish, and want,
I will not bear it longer, no nor can't.

GOVERNESS.

These sixty Years come *Lammas*, I ne'er knew,
A Miss so mad, so Husband-mad as you.

MISS.

Within my Trunk, I secretly have hid,
'Tis yet untouch'd, a Pot of Marmalade:
To you I'll give it, grant me?

* I do not understand how a Man can take himself away; yet it is a common
Phrase among the love-selling Ladies of *Covent-Garden*, *Drury-Lane*, the *Strand*,
&c. &c. &c. &c. &c. &c.
† More Distress.

GOVERNESS.

Never speak it.

MISS.

Why then the Devil fetch me but I'll break it*.   10
Shall I still Samplers stitch, or all the Day,
Like a mere Child, with jointed Babies play?
You'll break my Heart, dear Ma'am, what do you mean?
I'm now no Girl, this Month I've been fourteen,
Soon I'll be wed, I hope, and bedded too,
I am old enough, tho' not so old as you.

GOVERNESS.

Long have I hobbled, wrinkled, thro' this Life,
A Virgin, Widow, and a widow'd Wife†.
I've try'd all Troubles, I have felt the Jars
Of Cholics, Cramps, Hysterics, and Catarrhs‡.   20
Yet never grumbled, never look'd awry,
Till now you force me—fye upon ye fye.

§*Enter* ARIETTA, *with two* Tragedy Handkerchiefs.

ARIETTA.

Oh, who wou'd put their Trust in faithless Man?
Have I for him refused the Lord knows who,
Pensions and Placemen, Dukes, *Et Cetera*‖.

* Here Reader, in this Speech there is an Antitheses worthy Observation. It consists of the different *Modus* which Miss MOLLY makes use of, in applying the Verb *Break*.

> First, as breaking the Pot of Marmalade.
> Secondly, as breaking her own Heart.

I could have been better pleased with it, had the Verb been both Times used in the first Person. *H.H.*

† By way of Ænigma. *H.H.*

‡ Distress again. *P.P.*

§ Common Distress is represented by one Tragedy Handkerchief; but as this is uncommon Distress, and two-fold, the Author has judiciously doubled the Hieroglyphic. *P.P.*

‖ *Plotinus*, in his Dissertation upon Semi-colons, mightily recommends the Use of an *Et Cetera*. And *Gerard Van Bergen*, in the six Volumes he has published upon the Use and Antiquity of an Hyphen, has given us its Etymology and Cuts, how it is used by various Nations. *H.H.*

Oh I cou'd tear my Tucker, burn my Tete, ⎫
Let me have Room to rave in, now I fret, ⎬
Pray let me fan myself—Lord, how I sweat.* ⎭

MISS.

Ma'am, with Submission, but I beg to know, ⎫
If you think fit to sit a Bit or so,   ⎬   30
If Love, it is the Cause of your o'erthrow? ⎭

ARIETTA.

Madam, your Servant, but pray now be seated,
Heigh, ho! Lord help me, I'm so tosticated†.
Know ye, young *Fanfly*'s Lady?

MISS.

Very well.—

ARIETTA.

Miss, you'll excuse me, but I think it 'tant.

MISS.

Dear, Ma'am, proceed, I vow I meant no Harm.

GOVERNESS.

No, that I'll swear for, pray, Ma'am, don't be warm.

---

* Though this may seem somewhat indelicate, it is very natural. For to be in a Passion, or be in a Heat, are compatible, nay sometimes synonymous. Now it is not at all contradictory to the animal System to suppose, that when any one is in a Heat, Perspiration may ensue. *P.P.*

† *Pro* intoxicated, *aude* common Conversation.

To mutilate, metamorphise, and transmigrate the *English* Language, is at present the polite Taste, while on the contrary, the Under-bred, instead of curtailing out of an unwonted Generosity, add to their Dialect. *E.g. Mem* pro *Madam* at *St.* James's *Misturs* pro *Madam*, *St.* Giles's. *H.H.*

Here I cannot help observing the Particularity of Stile used by Tradesmen, Brokers, &c. of the Metropolis of *Great Britain*. They look on the Pronouns *He* or *I* to be no ways essential in their Advertisements, but think the Word *Said* sufficient.

And I hear there is a Complaint lodged in *Nassau* Court, by said Pronouns, backed by Particle *The*, against *Dublin* News Printers, for same Fault. Said printers not given said Words fair Play in Advertisements.

---

26 Tete] An elaborately dressed wig.

ARIETTA.

Then Ladies know I was, but what of that?
I am at present, but I don't know what*.
On that fam'd Stage, where *Perseus* oft has flew,
Where *Faustus* conjur'd, and where *Orpheus* play'd,
With warbling Songs, I've charm'd attentive Crouds,
And Lords done Homage round me as at Court.
The Levee-throng'd Dependants watch their Prince,
To catch the secret Whisper, snatch his Smiles,
And then strut happy Home, big grown with Hope.
At length, one fatal Eve the Squire came,
Protested Love, presented, but, O Gods!
His Words were weighty, for his Gifts were large.
He begg'd, I granted, but I can no more:
He's lost, I'm left, and all my Splendour's o'er†.

40

50

MISS.

Madam, for once, a Girl's Advice receive,
No longer for the unconstant *Fanfly* grieve.
Were I like you, I'd all Resentment smother,
And since I've lost one Love, I'd get another‡.

GOVERNESS.

Be ruled, good Madam, think how old I am,
Take my Advice, my Dear, and drink a Dram§.

ARIETTA.

Wou'd I were drunk; nay, drunk I will be too,
And when I am I'll make the Devil to do‖.
Ye gilded Chariot, and ye rich Brocade,
And the dear¶ Joys of midnight Masquerade,

60

---

* *Don't know what.*
This Line is perfectly metaphysical. For her Ideas being certainly too circumstantially disturbed, *i.e.* (disturbed by her present Circumstances) it was impossible by this Parity of Reasoning, she could form a proper Assemblage of them, or range them in a just Order, to think what she was.
† More Distress. *H.H.*   ‡ Natural enough. *P.P.*
§ Very natural that too. *H.H.*   ‖ Clymax of Naturalities. *H.P.*
¶ I am at a Loss how to understand the Adjective *dear*, whether it relates to the Dearness of the Ticket, or whether the Joys she had there were dear *pro* endear'd to her.

A long Adieu, now thro' the filthy Town,
In dirty Hackney, and in plain silk Gown,
Must I be drove; perhaps 'tis worse decreed,
And thro' the Streets in Pattens I must tread.
Perhaps mend Stockings; O, ye cruel Gods!
Or scrub my Flesh off in the sharp Soap-Suds.

GOVERNESS.

Hope for the best, my Dear, send for the Squire.

ARIETTA.

I to the Creature send, excuse me Ma'am,
What like a Wife petition? if I do;   70
And now, I think on't, I will make a Vow*.
†Hear me ye Naiads, Fairies, Nymphs and Fawns,

* *Make a Vow*—This vow is made with Premeditation, and as it ought to be;
for tho' Swearing is at present in tip top Taste, and *quite the Thing*, I don't believe
the Generality of Gentlemen Cursers take a sufficient Time to recollect what they
are going to do when they swear; for it is proper to consider, that an Oath may be
sometimes used *periodically*, sometimes *expletively*, at other Times by way of
Corroboration.

Further, I must needs say, that tho' there are some Persons, called Clergymen,
who will make a Bustle about Duty, Decency, and Religion, and pretend, indeed,
to have Swearing abolish'd, it would be as pernicious to Conversation, as the
Prohibition of Spirits would be to Dram-Drinkers; For as Oaths not only interlard
but make up two Parts in three of several Persons Conversation, what could those
choice Spirits say if they were not to swear. Why, upon the nicest Calculation,
according to *de Moivre, Sympson Leibnitz*, &c. it therefore follows, that they must
be condemned to sit silent two Thirds of that Time they now fill up with such
elegant Volubility. *P.P.   H.H.*

There is something so daringly wicked in this calling upon GOD to confirm a
momentous Relation, or upon the least Affront received, commanding a Deity to
condemn them to eternal Perdition, that I cannot think common Swearers believe
there is a GOD that hears them; or, perhaps, more modest, imagine the Deity thinks
such Reptiles too much below his Notice to punish.

† Here is a long Speech, which, I believe, was introduced for no other Design
than to show the Author was deep read in Romance, and had a tolerable or in-
tolerable Knack at Description. *P.P.*

He is to be commended for it, since as every Reader is look'd on as a Guest,
and an Author is to furnish out as good a Feast as he can for the Reader's Entertainment; and, as at Gentlemen's Houses vast Pieces of Plate, ornamented, tho' useless
adorn the Side-board; so, as Authors can seldom, that way, please their Guests,
they are right to open the Richness of their Fancy for them. *H.H.*

---

65 Pattens] Cheap, clog-like shoes.

Who wanton lave amidst the chrystal Streams;
That o'er the smooth-worn Pebbles plays
Thro' flow'ry Vales, and daisy-sprinkled Meads:
And ye who govern the high-waving Woods;
Who secret dwell in sun-sequestred Groves,
And nightly dance thro' arch-embower'd Walks.
Ye Hamadryads hear! Ye sullen Gnomes
That flit on foggy Clouds from Earth uprais'd: 80
Ye purer Sylphs, that skim the midway Air;
And all ye Genii of the Deep attend.
If I request, petition, send, or sue,
May Thunder split my Snuff-box all to pieces,
And Lightnings burn my *Brussels* Mob to Ashes.

MISS.

But you'll see him Madam.

ARIETTA.

I'll be blind first truly; no, I'll now,
With weary, wandring, melancholy, tread;
Goaded by Griefs, disconsolately creep:
On the soft Pillow rest my aching Head,   90
Sob like a Child, and sigh my self to sleep,
Snore out my Wrongs and dream—the Lord knows what.
What I in Vision see, that I'll fullfil,
If 'tis my Blood, or Pen-dipt-Ink to spill:
To end my Woes at once by well-set Knife*,
Or vindicate my Wrongs, and write my Life†.

[*Exit curt'sying.*

SCENE *Moorefields. Enter* PHLEBOTOME.

PHLEBOTOME.

The Morning rises black, as black as Ink;
Perhaps *Apollo* has a dirty Shirt on:
It looks as if 'twou'd Rain, or Hail, or Snow;
It looks, methinks, it looks I don't know how;
Hah! Who comes here? Are you, or are you not‡.

---

* This was once in Vogue.   † This is at present the Taste.
‡ By this Speech we learn that *Phlebotome* was one of those Philosophers called
Sceptics. They were remarkable for doubting if they could see, or doubting the

Enter SCAREBABE.

SCAREBABE.

I am Sir.

PHLEBOTOME.

What?

SCAREBABE.

Your humble Servant.

PHLEBOTOME.

Either my Optics err, the visual Ray
Refracted, densely beams obliquely forth*,
Or thou art Scarebabe.

SCAREBABE.

Sir; the same.
A† Letter, Sir, from Squire *Fanfly*'s Mother.   10
She says he's mad, and therefore begs your Worship
Will seize her Son, and put him into *Bedlam*,
'Till by your Discipline he's gain'd his Senses.

PHLEBOTOME.

She writes me here, bad *English*; but no Matter,
I'll seize the Squire, and give him Castigation.
Conclude it done—have you more Bus'ness with me.

Enter CAUSTIC *with a black Eye.*

Existence of whatever they did see; like some Moderns who cannot, will not, or must not believe their Eyes, nor too critically attend to the Evidence and Examination of any of their other Senses. *H.H.*

* *Obliquely forth*—That is, the Rays of Light don't come in a direct Line but oblique. For Rays are made to converge when they are refracted towards each other by their being drawn from the Centre of Convexity on the other Side, as by this Proposition will more plainly appear.

AB is to CD as the Lines of Refraction by Convexion, *i.e.* as q is to p, or p to q; and as AB to EF so CD $= \frac{p}{q}$ or $\frac{q}{p}$, AB to $\frac{p}{q}$ or $\frac{q}{p}$ NO; and, so is K:L to M:N; and, so is WX to YZ. *Ergo*, AB $\frac{pq}{qp}$ is as the Side of Refraction to the Angle of Incidence C:D::E. *H.H.*

† The Messenger telling the Purport of the Letter is very natural, for he might have looked over as she wrote, or read it before she sent it.

CAUSTIC.

Seek not for Business; shun the rash Pursuit;
Behold, by Business, what to me's befallen.
Had I been born but rich I had been bless'd.
Safe then each Day in indolentic Ease;   20
Supine, my Life insipidly had slid.
Thro' the throng'd Park, I'd lazy lownge along,
Arm linked in Arm with my laced Coat compeers,
And dawdling dangle with affected Limp.
Or big with pleasing Contemplation stand
'Gainst the Pier-Glass, and look whole Hours away*:
Then nightly trifle round Theatric Scenes,
Retailing remnants of stale Repartee.
Or o'er the exhilerating Coffee join,
In Speculations for the Nation's Good;   30
Or with harmonious Taste, or clenched Fist,
Direct† *Jack Broughton*'s, or the Opera rule.

PHLEBOTOME.

Permit me, Friend, by mild Request, to probe
Thy febrile Mind: I view thy Eye contus'd;
Fist-swol'n, perhaps; exhibit thou the Cause.

CAUSTIC.

Ask thou the Cause: 'Twas Squire *Fanfly* did it;
If I forgive it; but it is no Matter;
Few Words are best; so I'll relate it briefly.
   As Yesternoon I thro' *St. James*'s walk'd,
With tuneful Sound, enquiring, as I past,   40

* The Meaning of this is an Allusion to *Narcissus* looking at himself, till, according
to the Author of *Henry* VII, or the *Popish Imposter*, *he vanished into nothing*. *H.H.*
   † *John Broughton*, formerly a Waterman, but for some Years last past remarkable
for his Skill in the Science of *Offence*, called Boxing; and for the teaching of which
he established an Athletical Academy to instruct the polite Youth of *London* in the
Exercise of the Fist, and all the Dexterity of Cross-Buttocks. But as there are some
too delicate to be taught with the naked Hand, he has Gloves lin'd with Hair, and
quilted Breast-Plates, for the very fine Gentlemen to practise in.
   Non his Juventus orta parentibus, &c. HOR. Lib. iii. Od.6.
   There are also several more heroical Bruisers, who fight pitch'd Combats on his
Stage, and to see which Half-Guineas, and Crowns, are given for Tickets. *P.P.*

---

26 Pier-Glass] Tall mirror, usually situated between two windows.

Who wanted Ease from the toe-troubling Corn,
A neat white-stocking'd Footman, down whose Ears
Two twisted Papers dangled (pendant thus
The String tied Cherry vibrates: Infant play)
In Squire *Fanfly*'s Name, with courteous Air,
Requested my Attendance; hapless Jobb.
Within th'unrefreshing Hall, high hung
With steely Trophies*, and the Huntsman's Spoil:
Chilly I wait; at length my Patient's brought,
On Couch reclin'd, his Legs in Flannel wrapp'd†:   50
With tender Care, as I one Foot uncloath'd,
Full in my Breast the other he discharg'd;
Prone‡ on the Ground I fell. As I uprose;
Thro' the resistless Air, with agile Whirl
His Slipper, wooden-heel'd, he threw direct,
Luckless my Eye received it, flashing Fire.

PHLEBOTOME.

These Symptoms indicate the Youth is mad.
As creaking Signs, or the thick throbbing Corn,
Or Sink offensive, bode impending Showers;
So the prognosticating Symptoms shew,   60
The State morbific. Diagnostics are
Signals which Nature holds out in Distress:
Then the Physician, as a Pilot, acts
To steer the Body from the Rocks of Death,
And tide it safely to the Bay of Health.

SCAREBABE.

A Set of Sharpers now attend the Squire,
And Leech-like live upon him: 'Tis To-day

---

* *Steely Trophies*—Read it *stilly* Trophies; Weapons that were silent and unus'd.
Richard III. The Hum of either Army *stilly* sounds. *P.P.*

† Wrapp'd—Read it *lapp'd*; the Word *wrapp'd* is an Interpolation: To be
wrapp'd is to be bound tight, which was not proper in the Gout, as we suppose to
be the Case with the Squire. *P.P.*

‡ *Prone*—He could not fall *prone*; for when a Man has a Blow on the Breast he
falls backward. Vide *Slack* upon *Broughton*. I therefore read, *Thrown on the Ground*,
I fell.

As I uprose—Erroneous. It should be, *as I suppose*; for we may suppose he was
senseless by the Blow. *P.P.*

He's come to Age, &* open House he keeps
At *Beverage* the Vintner's.

CAUSTIC.

So, he may.
No more of that for me, I spunge no more.—   70
Who'd be that sordid sycophantic Wretch,
To cringe, be kick'd, or flatter for a Dinner,
And turn led Captain. No, if e'er I do,
May I be bruised in every aching Limb,
In the strong Blanket toss'd 'twixt Earth and Air,
By 'Jaculation dire,—sickly Sport:
So poor *Jack Needy* suffer'd†. Luckless Youth.

SCAREBABE.

I saw him toss'd.
A Sight, so dirty-sad, my Eyes did ne'er behold.

PHLEBOTOME.

So dirty, peace;
It is unutterable; yet I'll tell it‡.
In that wet Season, when descending Rains   80
Stream thro' the Streets, and swell along the Lanes.
When Mud obnoxious o'er the Pavement spread,
Soils the white Stocking at each mirey Tread.
When the shrill Link-boy plies the Playhouse Door,
And Mack'rel pleasing Cry, is heard no more.
When Strength-restoring Oysters are in prime;
Or, in plain *English*, it was Winter-Time;
Then was *Peel Garlick* toss'd.

CAUSTIC.

How did he bear it?

PHLEBOTOME.

At the first Toss he puked, then loudly swore, ⎫
But when the Blanket burst, he said no more; ⎬   90
But dropt down swift into the common Shore. ⎭

* This should be wrote *and* at full, and not, &. *P.P.*

† *So poor* John Needy *suffered*—it must be read: For, if you read it *Jack Needy*, the Sound of Jaculation in the preceding Line, and the Sound of *Jack* in the succeeding one, breaks all Hexameter Harmony. *H.H.*

‡ *Vide* modern Tragedies for Precedents of this Stile and Manner.

O'erwhelm'd with Filth, he wallow'd in the Mud,
And groap'd his Way out, flound'ring thro' the Flood.

CAUSTIC.

Why must the Great have Privilege to kick,
And not the Poor return it? Partial Fate!
Domitian thus the Spider's Prey purloined*,
And tilted Flies for Pastime. Cruel Sport!
Ye Gods, why gave ye me a Monarch's Soul,
And wrapp'd it up in such a wretched Case!

PHLEBOTOME.

But see, who's this approaches? With what State   100
She seems to tread, and side-long how she holds
Her Hoop wide op'ning, O *Circean Cave*†.
Know ye the Dame?

SCAREBABE.

Yes, 'tis *Capriola*.
A Mistress *Fanfly* keeps, let us go seek the Squire.

CAUSTIC.

I know where to find him.

PHLEBOTOME.

Go you before, and I will follow after‡.
Methinks I walk in Stilts, I'm so elated,

* *Domitian*, the *Roman* Emperor, used to amuse himself with killing Flies, till he had destroyed the Maggot-bred Progeny, upon which it was *wittily* said, by a Philosopher, (who was asked if the Emperor had any one with him) no, not so much as a Fly.

† This is an odd Epithet, and I am convinced the Author never designed it so; but by the Blunder of some ignorant Transcriber, it has crept into the Text. In the first Place, *Circe* never wore a Hoop. Secondly, she lived not in a Cave. Thirdly, but enough has been said to prove what it is not; let us consider what it is. This Doctor is a learned Man; he there speaks *Latin*, *Cave* beware; and the other Word is either calling her by her Name, which was *Cecilia*; as for Instance, Oh *Cicely*, beware, don't stumble; for she might hold her Hoop so high, that she could not look before her: Or else it is, Oh *Silesian* Cave; her Hoop might be made of that Sort of Stuff. *P.P.*

‡ This is very natural; for if one goes before, the other must follow after, unless, as it sometimes happens, on the Stage, for one to pull the other back, and so go out

To have a wealthy Patient: o'the Rapture!
As *Gallen* has it in his second Chapter.
Cathartics and Narcotics I'll apply,   ⎫   110
Nephretics and Emetics we must try,   ⎬
And drain for Drugs the Dispensary dry.   ⎭
The Attorney thus to lengthen out his Suit,
Forbids Peace-making, and foments Dispute;
Incessant watches o'er his Client's Purse,
Makes good Things bad, and bad he makes much worse.
So Squire *Fanfly*, if I can allure him,
I'll make him mad, and afterwards I'll cure him.

SCENE *Covent-Garden.*

Enter CAPRIOLA, *and Servant.*

CAPRIOLA.

Away; go troop, or I will tread your Guts out.
Arietta, o'the Sing-song dirty Trull,
For her neglected?

SERVANT.

Be but easy, Madam.

CAPRIOLA.

And shall a bunting Ballad-singer hold him?
Sooner shall Spaws with Kennel Water flow;
Sooner shall Modesty Preferment gain;
Sooner I'll hang myself, and there's an End on't.

SERVANT.

Here comes the Lady.

---

first, according to the old Proverb, he is *first* at last, though he was behind before.
P.P.

Mr. *Pedasculus* has a Mind to be merry with his Proverb, and wrest the Author's
Meaning to an Explanation never intended. To pull one back, and step in his Place,
or get before him, is an Action common to all Men, as well off, as on the Stage, and
may be properly called, the Art of Supplanting. *H.H.*

---

4 bunting] Fat and tawdry.   5 Spaws] Spas, mineral springs.

CAPRIOLA.

O! the dirty Minx.

Enter ARIETTA*.

ARIETTA.

Are you the Wench whom they *Capriola* call?

CAPRIOLA.

Yes, Miss Mock-modesty, what then?

ARIETTA.

——That's all.   10
Some People are impertinent, 'tis true,
And wou'd rob other People of their Due,
But, Ma'am, excuse me, I don't think 'tis you.

CAPRIOLA.

Good lack-a-day, and so they bid me tell you.
Lord, I shall faint, but I despise such Creatures†,
If I must talk, it shall be to your Betters.
Your Impudence, all *Billingsgate* exceeding,
Declares you know not what belongs to Breeding.

ARIETTA.

Madam, you're humble, but you're so notorious,
I dare not talk, you know the World's censorious.   20
Shou'd my Friends see me hold you in Discourse‡,
I shou'd be thought as bad as you, or worse.

CAPRIOLA.

As bad as me! Ill Manners I detest,
Begging your Pardon, you're a nasty Beast.

* This is a Scene of Altercation. I cannot help reminding the Reader of the Diversity of Scenes, Stiles, and Similes in this elaborate Performance. And herein I follow the Steps of the Editor of Mr. *Pope*'s Works, who has pointed out to every Reader, all the Species of Writing, the Author of *the Essay on Man* used in the latter Part of that Poem, doubting, or despising the Capacities of his Readers; or else imagining, that Philosophy and Poetry are always to be examined by classical Scale and Compass, like the Mathematician, who only read *Virgil*, to examine by the Map, how, Navigator-like, he had conducted *Æneas* in his Voyage. *H.H.*

† It is pronounced Creters. *P.P.*

‡ To hold you in Discourse—or to force Discourse, Phrases of Course.

Have you forgot how high in *Drury-Lane*,
Drench'd by the Drippings of the drizzling Rain,
On broken Bedstead, deck'd by dirty Rugs,
You nightly snor'd, bit by Blood-loving Bugs?
At Morning's Dawn you left your stinking Flocks,
To foot Silk Stockings, and to mend old Socks;   30
In Winter Evening, you'd the Parish teaze,
With bak'd Ox Cheek, or calling out grey Pease.
At Midnight strole along the silent Lane,
And draggled, sneak to Garret back again.

ARIETTA.

Methinks, Ma'am, you are drest in a delicate Taste,
What a Pity it is your Complexion won't last?
How her Cloaths are hung on, and how set is each Feature,
Let me die, but I think you're a comical Creature.
But least the Dispute, by bad Words, should grow long,
I'll the Argument end, Child, and give you a Song.   40

Enter JACK HANDY.

JACK HANDY.

Stand clear, make way, bear back, get farther off*.

CAPRIOLA.

Why, what's the Matter, pray good Captain *Puff*?

JACK HANDY.

Young Squire *Fanfly*'s coming, that's enough.

Enter Squire FANFLY. BEVERAGE *kicking his Drawer*†.

---

* Here you have in this Line, the whole Exercise of the Levee.
1st. *Stand clear*. The great Man rises to go to his Coach.
2d. *Make way*. The Dependants are drawn up on each Side.
3d. *Bear back*. They squeeze against the Wainscot.

4th. *Get farther off*. Those who have forgot to see the Porter, and forced to stand on the Outside of the Door, now must leave lounging against the Rails.

† However queer it is to be kicked, and though it may not be pleasing to feel, it is to see, since it is practised on the Stage with great Applause. *H.H.*

Think not, Reader, I am intending to ridicule the Tastes of an Audience, or imagine they cannot distinguish. Far be it from me, to hint at such a Falsity: But I would fain have the Actors never endeavour at Applause, by any Buffoonery, or debase the Dignity of Nature, by uncouth Grimace, and supply the Want of true Humour with farcical Face-making. *H.H.*

FANFLY.

At length, my Friends, at last is come the Day,
The long-expected, the long-talk'd of Day,
This Day of Days; and now we'll make a Night on't*.   [*Huzza.*

GAMBLE.

Permit me, Squire, to join this happy Cry,
And as I stand on Tiptoe with you joy.

FANFLY.

Tom Gamble, Friend, thy Merit's truly great,
Whether you crack a Joke, or break a Pate;   50
I've seen thy Stick high brandish'd o'er the Foe,
Flash on his Face, and bleed him at a Blow:
Then o'er the Midnight Glass, I have heard thee speak,
And Puns, like Hiccups, from thy Bosom break:
So like thy Wit, embottl'd Small-beer works,
Flies frothy up, and rumbling bursts the Corks.
And thou, my *Beverage*, I've seen,
Trip up the nimblest on the Green,
And heard thee in stentorean Sounds,
Out-roar the deep-mouth'd op'ning Hounds: 60
So have I heard, amidst the Shouts
Of Bonfires, Mobs on Powder Plots,
A snapping Cracker shake the Plain,
And bounce and burst, and bounce again.

BEVERAGE.

But you've done more, what's all that we can show,
To what the Squire has done, or what the Squire may do?

FANFLY.

What I have done? (but 'tis not fair to boast)
Can none remember, and yet sure all must,

* How to make Night of Day, I cannot reconcile this Line. I have often, indeed,
heard Persons talk of making a Night on't; and out of Curiosity, I once went to see
some Spirits perform; but they made nothing on't, unless making one another
drunk could be termed making any Thing. *P.P.*

How I disputed once with the fam'd *Henley*?*
When Folly, like a chatt'ring Magpye, sat   70
Full on my Forehead, thro' the whole Debate,
On Wings of Bats between us Dullness bore,
And common Sense stood trembling at the Door,
Words wav'd on Words, on Nonsense, Nonsense roll'd,
And I myself appear'd the greatest Scold.

ARIETTA *comes forward.*

O *Arietta*, O my warbling Dear,
Whose Voice is sweeter than the tuneful Sound
Of well-match'd Beagles, op'ning in full Cry;
Thy Eyes are brighter than the Glow-worms Light,
Thy Cheeks are redder than the ripen'd Peach,   80
Suffer thy Swain those fragrant Fruits to reach.

CAPRIOLA *goes between.*

CAPRIOLA.

That I forbid, nay, start not, Sir, 'tis I.

ARIETTA.

Turn this Way, Squire, this Way cast your Eye†.

* Vulgarly called Orator. *Vide* Dunciad. I have heard the Author of this Parody
several Times disputed with him. If so, I really think he has very truly depicted
himself. *H.H.*
     This is a Parody on the Speech of *Alexander* the Great.
               Can none remember? Yes sure all must.
                    When Glory, like a dazzling Eagle, stood
                    Perch'd on my Beaver, in the Granic *Flood,*
                    When Fortune's Self, my Standard trembling bore,
                    And the pale Fates stood frighted on the Shore,
                    When the Immortals on the Billows rode,
                    And I myself appear'd the leading God.
     † *This Way cast your Eye.*
     It will be very proper for the Gentlemen and Ladies of the Theatre, the younger
Sort I mean, to be very perfect in this Exercise of the Eye, and also in the verticular
Motion of the Head. For it is a common Practice among them, to talk to the Pit,
more than to the Performer that's along with them; and also, when they are spoke
to, it is proper for them to *seem* to mind what is said, and not, while a Description
is related to them, or any Story that affects the Personage they represent, be looking
round the Audience for their Acquaintance, &c. *P.P.*

SONG.

By the Joys of Embrace, when entwin'd in my Arms,
　While languishing Love fill'd our Eyes,
　　You murmuring swore, you'd be true to my Charms,
And sealed it with short-broken Sighs*.

FANFLY.

Bravo, my Life, my lovely *Arietta*,
There—there's my Purse, if you want Money, take it,
But take not me, for I am all *Arietta*'s.
Sooner shall Jews sly Jesuits become,
And Presbyterians kiss the Toe of *Rome*.
Wits follow† *Whitfield*, Whores adore plain Dealing.
St. *Giles*'s to St. *James*'s shall remove,
Sooner than I'll neglect this Lady's Love.

90

CAPRIOLA.

Squire, stand off, I'll—O thou saucy Slut,
E'er I bear this, I'll—Let me go, Sirrah.

ARIETTA.

What w'oud *Capriola*'s Mutton-Fist be at?

CAPRIOLA.

Your negro Nose, *Arietta*, that is flat.

---

* *Love fill'd our Eyes*—Nonsense—Loving filling the Eyes, and Murmurs, and *short-broken Sighs*. These are all unnatural Phrases, fit only for Novel-Writers, &c.
It is now several Years since my first Cohabitation with my Wedlock-joined Friend, and though Nature calls for a Satisfaction of carnal Appetite, Posterity for an Increase of Inhabitants, and even Marriage-Laws demand fulfilling, I never met with any of the above-mentioned Languishings. They are heterogeneous to the Improvement of our Species, and since we are commanded to increase, we should go about to obey that Precept, as Philosophers, as Scholars, and as wise Men ought to do, soberly and cooly, as we should take off a Glass of Wine, not madly and voraciously, as intoxicating Epicures swallow Pint-Bumpers. *P.P.*

† *Whitfield*, an itinerant Field-preacher, who was followed by Multitudes of both Sexes, whose weak Minds were startled by the terrible Anathemas he vociferously thundered against them. He set himself as a Refiner of the Christian Religion, in a Manner repugnant to all Rules of Decency, Morality, or good Manners.

N.B. These Things happened at a Time when the Works of *Boyle*, *Barrow*, *Lock*, and *Tillotson*, lay unheeded, on Dust-fill'd Shelves, and within a few Years of that remarkable Æra, called the Year of the Bottle-Conjurer.

FANFLY.

So pendant cross a Line, I've oft seen hung,   ICO
Two tail-ty'd Cats, and spitting as they swung;
Teeth gnash with Teeth, with Talons, Talons jar,
'Till scratching ends this caterwauling War.

CAPRIOLA.

Where shall the wretched *Capriola* waddle?
Upon Misfortunes now I sit a-straddle*.
Will you not kiss me, Squire?

FANFLY.

Fiddle faddle.

ARIETTA.

Your Absence, Madam, will prevent Reproach,
Will you walk off, or will you have a Coach?

CAPRIOLA.

Trollop, 'tis well, at length, my ebbing Pride
Returns again, swift as a high Spring-Tide: 110
And by this Box, this *Pinchbeck*-Box, I swear†;
Which never more this Pinch of Snuff shall share,
I, unconcern'd, Inconstancy can bear.
I'll take a Link myself and light you Home;
Nay, make your Bed, and sweep you out your Room:
But first a Pound of Gun-powder I'd buy,

---

* This is a very pertinent Simile, to sit a-straddle upon Misfortune, *i.e.* to ride the wooden Horse of Adversity.

† *Pinchbeck*—Pinchdeck'd Box it should be. It means to deck it with a Pinch of Snuff, or to be deck'd with a Pinch of Snuff. *H.H.*

Whether it should be *deck'd*, or no, I cannot tell certainly, since greater Men than me have been divided about using that Word: For in the *Tempest*, Act I. Scene the Second, there is the Word *deck'd*, according to Mr. *Theobalds*.
       Who deck'd with Tears the Sea.
Oxford Edit. *Brack'd with Tears the Sea*, *i.e.* made the Salt-water brackish.
Warburton. *Mock'd with Tears the Sea.*
Dr. Bentley. *Stock'd with Tears the Sea.*
   I say, *repugnantibus omnibus*, it should be, *flock'd i.e.* the Tears *flock'd* to the Sea. *P.P.*

---

111 *Pinchbeck*-Box] Box made of pinchbeck, a cheap metal somewhat resembling gold.

Under the Bed it secretly shou'd lye;
Then take a Match, and to repay this Evil,
I'll blow you both together to the Devil.

> [*Throws Snuff in* Arietta's *Face, and exit.*

ARIETTA.

O, Squire *Fanfly*, I am almost choak'd;   120
How cou'd you leave me for a Slut so saucy?
How did you get her? tell me; I'll forgive you.

FANFLY.

So I will.
Once on a Time, past Twelve o'Clock at Night,
When ev'ry Lamp was out, and at each Stand
The drowsy Watchman snor'd thro' the dark Street;
No Flambeaux-blazing Chariot flash'd along,
But gloomy Night in humdrum Silence mop'd;
Disguis'd with Drink, and for a Frolick fit;
By Help of Ladder raised to mend the Roof,
Hap'ly I stole, unheeded, to her Garret.   130

BEVERAGE.

'Twas lucky, tho' you did not break your Bones.

FANFLY.

So it was.
I found the sleepy, trapish, tipling, Fair,
Snoring, supinely, on a three-legg'd Chair.
A ragged Stocking hid one tawny Fist,
Drawn, like a Muffatee, a-down her Wrist.
Drop'd by her Side lay diff'rent colour'd Yarn,
With which the industrious Nymph was wont to darn.
A twinkling Light within the Socket gleam'd;
I reel'd to reach it, and the Damsel scream'd:
I snatch'd the Fair, half-walking, to my Breast;   140
And then; but mum, I must not tell the rest*.

ARIETTA.

O, the dear Rake, the lovely midnight Rogue;
O, I could jump into a Ditch to meet thee,
And wander with thee in a Winter's Rain.

* I think our Squire is something more modest than *Lothario* however. *P.P.*

Let pimpled Prudes on Citron Waters dote,
And may stale Maids their sleek-comb'd Lap-dogs love;
For thee, my Dear, Imperial Tea I'd spill,
Forgo the Fashion, and forget Quadrille.

FANFLY.

Here this Coquets, curse on your Constitutions,
My Heart dances a Hornpipe;   150
I am I know not how; but when 'tis Night
I will do—what I will.

ARIETTA.

And so you shall.
Go now, and take a Bottle with your Friends;
But stay not late, nor come not, Love, in Liquor.
Like the poor Turtle I shall sit forlorn,
Waiting to welcome you, and have the Bed warm'd.   [Exit.

Enter SYBILLA the Governess.

GOVERNESS.

Sir, if you please, a Word or two with you.

FANFLY.

Madam, your humble Servant; how do you do.

GOVERNESS.

Well, Sir, I thank you, and hope you're so too.

FANFLY.

Here! bring some Wine.

GOVERNESS.

I'll drink none as I live.   160

FANFLY.

Pray, Lady fair, one single Glass receive.

GOVERNESS.

No; pray excuse me.

FANFLY.

Pray excuse me, Ma'am.
One single Glass can never do you Harm.

GOVERNESS.

Well, Squire, I vow you're such another Man—!
I'm quite confounded; but, since here I am,
And I must drink, my Dear, I'll drink a Dram.   [*Drinks.*
But to the Purpose, Sir, you are to know,
Since my poor Husband's Death, who left me low; }
Tho', little did he think it wou'd be so;
I've kept a Boarding-School, 'tis now three Years,   170
To shew young Misses Plain-work, and their Pray'rs.
I form their female Minds, I mend their Tastes,
Teach them to read, and raise the various Pastes;
To knot the bordering Fringe, to whip the Seam,
The Lawn to flourish, and to skim the Cream.
Amidst the pretty, prattl'ing, playing, Fair,
(By their kind Parents trusted to my Care,)
There's one Miss *Languish*, handsome, on my Word,
And rich enough to make a Man a Lord*.

FANFLY.

For me, perhaps.

GOVERNESS.

Perhaps so—Lack-a-day.   180
Yet who knows that; for, as some Folks will say, }
We are gone To-morrow, tho' we're here To-day. }
All our first Bread we're certain where we eat; }
The Wisest knows not where his last he'll get; }
For tho' we're born we are not bury'd yet. }
But to my Purpose; tho', as I was saying,
Miss *Molly Languish*; well, a-lack-a-day;
Indeed, 'tis Pity; so, indeed, you'll say:
She pouts, she glouts, she moaps, she frets, she fumes,
And all for what? Why, for a Husband truly: 190

---

*To make a Man—then *Spunge* should say, *O Lord*! It is a natural Exclamation of a Man much indebted himself, upon hearing of a Woman who would make a Man, to break out into such a Surprize—*O Lord*— For the Future therefore it must be thus;

> *—handsome, on my Word,*
> *And rich enough to make a Man.*
> SPUNGE.   *——Oh Lord! P.P.*

But how do you think all this is brought about,
Why Love and Murder always will come out,
As my Spouse us'd to say—that's without Doubt*. }

FANFLY.

What's this to me, Ma'am?

GOVERNESS.

Why, Sir, you shall hear.
There is a Fellow that belongs to you,
Who, like a Peacock, struts and makes a Shew,
Has turn'd her Head, and makes her talk of Wedlock;
Of losing Maidenheads, and merry Christ'nings:
This Fellow follows us from Street to Street,
Winks thro' the Windows, ogles her incessant;   200
At Meals at Home, on *Sunday* at the Church;
No Place is free, he frights me with his Stares,
He spoils our Dinner, and disturbs our Prayers.

FANFLY.

What is his Name?

GOVERNESS.

Spunge, Sir, I think, he's call'd.

FANFLY.

Go, somebody, and seek him.

BEVERAGE.

Here he comes, unlook'd for.

Enter SPUNGE, *drunk.*

FANFLY.

O, come hither Scoundrel:
You spunging, shifting, sharking, shuffling Wretch,
Who, Spaniel-like, at well-fill'd Tables waits.—   210

GOVERNESS.

Ay, Mr. what d'ye call'm; marry come up—

* *Without doubt*—alluding to the Apothegm of *Pythagoras*'s Daughter, *sine dubitante. H.H.*

FANFLY.

Nay, give me Leave, Madam. Hark ye, Sirrah.
How dare you?

SPUNGE.

Be fuddl'd, I presume:
Why, I have been drinking Bumpers to your Health,
And, if you grudge it, Sir, why then, good-bye to you.

FANFLY.

Hold, Sir, take one Glass more before you go*.
[*Throws Wine in his Face.*

SPUNGE.

How soon you see a modest Man is dash'd†,
It's damn'd ungen'rous tho', to give me Wine‡,
And hit me in the Teeth with it.

FANFLY.

You'll go a Courting, will you, courting Ladies!   220

GOVERNESS.

Ay, and fine Ladies too! Meat for his Master.

SPUNGE.

Had I been sober, tho' you are a Squire,
You had not dared to strike me.

FANFLY.

Dared not, damn you.

SPUNGE.

Damn you; no, you dare not.

---

* Wit.   † More Wit.   ‡ Most Wit.
These are the three Degrees of Comparison in *Wit*. The first Degree is the
HUM, *i.e.* endeavouring to impose on the Credulous, *e.g.* He says, he will give him
another Glass of Wine; but, how does he give it? The other stands ready to take it;
but how does he take it?
The second Degree of Wit consists in the Action of throwing a Glass of Wine.
This may be properly called *Wit-pantomimical*, just like throwing Tobacco-pipes
out of a Joke, burning Waiters Wigs in Fun, scorching the Shoes of their sleepy
Companion, or blackening his Face, or hiding his Pocket-book.
The third is, the *Paranomasia*, or Pun, to dash and hit.

FANFLY.

Give me a Horsewhip, Cane, a Mop, or Beesom.

GAMBLE.

O Sir, have Patience*.

FANFLY.

Preach Patience to your Creditors, you Blockhead†:
Where is the Scoundrel?

SPUNGE.

Who is it you mean?

FANFLY.

Go to the Pump you Sloven, and get clean.
Go pump him, that will wash him, for he wants it‡.   230
                                    [*Hits a Mop in his Face.*

SPUNGE.

Be warn'd, ye Youths, ye ever-thirsty Souls,
Who fond of Frolicks, doat on midnight Bowls;
By my Example learn to shun my Fate,
How wretched is the Man who loves to prate:
If you can work; O! stick to what your Trade is,
Strong Liquors leave, and making Love to Ladies.   [*Carried off.*

FANFLY.

Wou'd ye, fair Maids, our secret Failings scan,
And as you pick your Laces chuse the Man,
Tho' Lace bespangled hides the strong clos'd Seam,
And the Paste Buckles o'er the Instep beam: 240
Tho' o'er the Hat the Milk-white Feather's spread,
The Plumy Play-Thing shades a brainless Head.
Did ye but know the gay embroider'd Coat
Oft cloaths a Coxcomb, oft conceals a Sot.
But 'tis in vain, fatally fond of Shew,
You see, and sigh in Secret—Heav'ns! a Beau
You wish to wed—and often after find
A rotten Carcase and a wretched Mind.
Splendid thus monumental Marbles shine,
Tho' foul Corruption fills the gorgeous Shrine.   250

* The Supplication.   † The Replication.   ‡ The Application.

BEVERAGE.

Now, if you please, Sir, we'll go in to Dinner.

FANFLY.

With all my Heart, *Tom Beverage*, make some Punch*:
Then, like a Thing, o'me the mad *Macedonian*,
Like *Caesar*, *Cyrus*, or like any other.
But why shou'd I of any other tell,
None but myself can be my Parallel†:
Then, like myself, exalted will I stand,
With a Pint Bumper in my lifted Hand;
Time, Life's worst Load, in Liquor shall be lost,
And at each Glass we'll sacrifice a Toast: 260
Nocturnal Rites, uncheck'd by saucy Care,
To Joy-inspiring *Bacchus* we'll prepare;
God of good Fellows, Vintage-blessing Power,
O beam propitious on our social Hour,
With smiling Bowls we'll laugh the Night away;
We'll love Tomorrow, but get drunk To-day.

End of the First ACT.

---

* *Punch*—from *Punic*—base, *treacherous*; because it often steals away our Reason. *P.P.*

† This borrowed Line is partly geometrical, partly mathematical, partly mechanical, and partly neither. *H.H.*

PREFACE

TO THE

Second ACT.

IN this Second Part, the Reader, if he will give himself the Trouble of looking over them, will find some Notes, which seem as if design'd to drole on Mr. *Warburton*'s Observations. They were so. For though Mr. *Warburton* is universal in Learning, he is not quite so perfect in Judgment and Taste; unless, like the great Mr. *Addison*, he suffers Prejudice to get the better of both.

EVERY Part of *Grammar* he is Master of, yet there is one Part of Speech he is sometimes deficient in; which is, *Good Manners*. This, I think, is obvious to every Reader, who will peruse his Notes on SHAKESPEAR; for he has, out of the Fulness of his Spleen, been pleas'd to load the *Players* with several gross, undeserved Epithets, throughout his Annotations.   11

FOR, whenever any Interpolation, by an ignorant Transcriber, has been foisted into the Text, he is not content with casting the Odium on the Players, but immediately adds the Epithets, *foolish*, *infamous*, *impertinent*, or *prophane*. Certainly he must forget SHAKESPEAR was a Player; if he does not, in regard to so great a Genius, he might treat his Brethren with a little more Lenity.

THE Usage the Actors have received from him, urged me;

> *The meanest in Renown;*
> *The poorest Trifler of the Town,*   20

to twirl a Sling against this *Classical Goliah*; for, I think, every Person belonging to the Theatres, has a Right to treat that Man with Ridicule, who endeavours to throw them into Contempt.

LIKE *Scaliger*, he quits the Gentleman when he takes up the Critic, and thinks a Multitude of Learning will attone for an Abundance of Rudeness;

---

3 Mr. *Warburton*'s Observations] William Warburton (1698–1779) was the fifth editor of Shakespeare's plays, his edition having appeared in eight volumes in 1747. Warburton abused not only the players, but his own predecessors, and most of his emendations were as spurious as Stevens implies. Thomas Edwards's *The Canons of Criticism* had poured earlier ridicule upon his editorial incompetence.

but, with Submission to his Scholarship, Good-nature is as far before great Learning, as the Actions of the Heart to the Intentions of the Head.

> *Good Nature and good Sense for ever join;*
> *To err is Human, to forgive Divine.*
>
> POPE.

ACT II.

SCENE *a Tavern, all sitting round.*

GOVERNESS *asleep on one Side.*

FANFLY.

HERE's to our noble Selves, and those that love us;
All drink it deep, and make the Welkin roar
With Undulation dire. Sound away.

Enter BEVERAGE, GAMBLE, *and* SPUNGE.

How now! Did I not order you shou'd pump that Fellow?

BEVERAGE.

So we wou'd, Sir, but for one cogent Reason.

FANFLY.

What was that?

BEVERAGE.

He would not let us.

FANFLY.

Oh, oh!

BEVERAGE.

Hear us with Patience, and we'll tell our Tale.

GAMBLE.

This memorable Day, to After-times,   10
Shall stand recorded as a Day of Wonders,
While Windows shall with Verse obscene be scratch'd:
While Thieves die sniv'ling in *Sternholdian* Rhymes;
While the luxurious Rich love *Ranelagh*;

13 *Sternholdian* Rhymes] I.e. doggerel.   14 *Ranelagh*] Gardens on the Thames at Chelsea, famous as a setting for entertainments and masquerades.

Or while the Poor on *Sunday* fill the Fields,
This Deed shall live in *Monthly Magazine*.

BEVERAGE.

Upright, amidst my Stable-Yard, firm-brac'd
With Iron Hoops; Spoils of well empty'd Casks,
Deep in the Ground transfixed, there stands a Pump,
Well known to Carriers, and to scolding Queans;   20
Whose Heads have oft beneath the Spout been drench'd*:
Salubrious Stream; for female Tongues a Cure;
At your Command he underneath was plac'd.
My Ostler ready at the Handle stood,
With out-stretch'd Arm; but as we sometimes see
The watching Cat leap on the Mouse surpriz'd,
And grasp her hard; so swift he sideway sprung,
And seized my Servant with athletic Gripe,
Trip'd up his Heels; then swung him swiftly round,
And souc'd him over Head within the Horse-pond.   30

---

* *Been duck'd*, it should be, for it implies their Heads were stooped, or bent,
under the Pump. Think not, Reader, this Emendation unnecessary, since our best
Critics seldom change Words to better Purpose, *e.g. Merchant of Venice*. Act IV.
Scene the Second.
Shakespear. *The Danger formerly by me rehears'd.* ⎫ Spoke
Warburton. *The Danger formally by me rehears'd.* ⎭ by *Portia*.
If you think fit, *vide Bentley*'s Note on the Words *sacred* and *secret* in MILTON.
Another Alteration here, I beg Leave to insert, of Mr. *Warburton*'s.
Mercutio's Speech of Queen *Mab*, he says she comes,
    In Shape no bigger than an Agate Stone set in a Ring.
Mr. *Warburton* will have it, *In Shade*, i.e. *like a Comet.*
Again, in *Coriolanus*:
A *Volscian* tells *Meninius*, that *Coriolanus* will front his Revenges with the *Groans
of old Women.*
        The virginal Palms of their Daughters, i.e. the held-up Hands.
        The palsied Intercessions of old Dotards.
That is, the Mothers may beg, the Children supplicate, the Fathers intercede in vain.
    Mr. *Warburton* will alter *Palms* to *Pasmes*, or *Pames*, from the *French Pasmer* or
Pamer, i.e. *Swooning Fits.*
    Was the learned Critic to be ask'd, What Occasion for Notes on these Places?
Could he tell us he made the Text better?—No; more intelligible—no. Why,
then all these learned, laborious Annotations—Why, for the same Reason Butchers
blow Veal, to make the Commodity swell, and sell better.

L

GAMBLE.

Then with a Look, fierce as Bumbailiff's Face,
He grasp'd, with raw-bone Fists, the deep-fixed Pump,
Squeezing it close, then writhed it too and fro,
From the Foundation loosening, by the Roots
Uplifting tore it, with *Herculean* Hurl,
Upon the flinty Pavement flung it down;
Horrid to see, and shiver'd it to Splinters.

FANFLY.

Tom Spunge, your Hand—you have been very silly;
But let that pass, no Man is wise at all Times*.
That Colt, got by Bay *Bolton*, I will give you: 40
In some frequented Inn, I'll set you up,
And for a Sign you shall hang out a Pump;
But now sit down. *Tom Beverage* sing a Song.
Shall I get drunk, or shall I not, my Friends:
Let me consider; 'tis a Point precarious.

To drink, or not to drink, that's the Question:
Whether 'tis nobler in a Man to suffer
From Gout, or Dropsy, by outrageous Drinking,
Or prudent arm our Reason 'gainst Debauch,
By Temperance to cure them. Let me think: 50
If by a social Glass or two, we cure
The Vapours, and elate the Woe-worn Mind;
'Tis a Prescription which ev'ry Wretch should take.
To thirst—to drink—to drink perhaps too much.
Ah! there's the Rub—the Fear of getting drunk
Adorns Sobriety with all its Charms:
Else, who'd Attendance and Dependance feel?
Who'd gloomy sit, on rainy Days, at Home?
By Weather mop'd: Who'd be by Spleen oppress'd?
Or, sorrowing, sigh for an ungrateful Fair?   60
Bad Luck at Hazard, or worse Luck at Law?

---

* *Nemo mortalium omnibus horis sapit.*—Here, Reader, please to observe by this, and several other Quotations, truly *classical*, our Author was a Man of great Learning. This I think proper to premise, lest After-ages should dispute whether he had any or no?

As by the famous Play-writer, SHAKESPEAR, we have an Example; who several will not allow to have been a Man of any Learning; tho' we must be Men of Learning; ay, and good Learning too, to read him. *P.P.*

When each, at once, might lay Remembrance dead*,
Did not the Dread of being sick next Day,
Or the worse Dread of not knowing how to pay,
Puzzle Desire, and make us rather choose
To stay at Home, in Poverty and Thirst,
Than run into Diseases, and in Debt?

Enter DRAWER.

DRAWER.

An'please your Worship, here's your Huntsman wants you.

FANFLY.

Let him come in.

Enter HUNTSMAN.

Well, what's the Matter, Sirrah?

HUNTSMAN.

As I sat smoking in my Landlord's Kitchen†,   70
I heard a mighty Hollooing in the Streets:

---

* *Lay Remembrance dead*—Ay, but how—Why, by drinking to be sure, that must
be his Meaning.
   There is a Line in SHAKESPEAR'S *As you like it*, of striking *dead*, spoke by the
Clown, which has been altered, and interpreted, I think, very oddly. The Line is,
It strikes a Man more dead than a great Reckoning in a little Room. The *Oxford*
Edition alters it to *a great Reeking in a little Room.* Mr. *W.* denies that, keeps to the
original Text, but says, *the Line means that the Bill was very extravagant, and every
Thing the Guests had, very bad and mean.*
   So in *Edgar*'s Description of *Dover* Cliff, *the Surge that o'er the idle Pebbles plays.*
Idle there, Mr. *W.* says, means *barren, uncultivated.* Now, would not it do, if we
considered them, as *idle*, to lie still, and let the Water pass over them?
   What Occasion for a Note there, and such a forced Interpretation?
   Another, as forced an Interpretation of this modern Scholiast, we find on a Line
in *Love's-Labour lost*, Act I. Scene 1.
   This Child of Fancy, Mr. *W.* says, *Shakespear* calls them, *Children of Fancy; not
for being beholden to Fancy for their Birth, but because Fancy has its Infancy as well
as Manhood.*
   Vide his Note on *Romances* at p. 260, at the End of the above mentioned Play.
   † This Description, I cannot say, requires any Explanation; but as I am not
willing the Reader should lose any Observation, especially those that are right-
worthy to be read, I shall here offer to his Consideration, one of Mr. *W.* on the
Entrance and Words of a Servant in the *Winter's Tale*, Act IV. Scene 7.
   A Servant tells his Master, that twelve Labourers have made themselves all Men

I left my Pipe, and ran to know the Matter.
I saw *Capriola* in a mighty Hurry,
Heading a Mob, and throwing Money to them:
She brib'd the mercenary Dogs to march
To *Charing-Cross*, and break Miss *Ary*'s Windows.

FANFLY.

Thus from the Glass, I rise to save my Love,
Go, call a Coach, on Wings of Windmills move;
Swift as the Bullet, bursting from the Gun,
Rattling like Thunder, thro' the Streets we'll run,
And when we'are there, we'll see what's to be done,

} 80

[*Exeunt.*

SCENE *a Bed-chamber.*

*ARIETTA asleep in a Chair, GHOST walks on with a Candle.

GHOST.

In dismal Ditty, doleful sounding Verse,
I'm sent thy Fall, *Arietta*, to rehearse.   [*Bell tolls.*

---

of *Hair* to dance. Mr. *W.* observes, that Men of Hair signifies Men nimble, and
that the Phrase is taken from Tennis-Balls, *because they are stuffed with Hair;* so
that the Sense is, *they are stuffed with Hair.*

Now when they enter, it happens they were all dressed like Satyrs, all in shaggy
Dresses made of *Hair*, which was what the Servant meant; but his Interpretation
is like the Foreigner's, who mistook the Words under a Sign, *Money for live Hair*,
to signify, *Money for living here.*

* The scrupulous Exactness that Mr. *W.* pays to the coming of *Hamlet*'s Ghost,
here must be remembered. *Hamlet* tells the Ghost, *Be thy Intents wicked or
charitable.*

Mr. *W.* will have it, *Be thy Advent wicked or charitable.* Now, be Judge, O
Reader, how nicely this is altered.

The Son says, *Be thy Intentions good or bad*, this is plain.

The Critic says, *Be thy Coming good or bad*, not quite so clear. *H.H.*

The Ghost says, according to *Shakespear, Confined fast in Fires.*

According to Mr. *Warburton, Confined too fast in Fires.*

To shew Mr. *W.* that I can alter as well as himself, nay, and amend his own
Edition, behold an Example.

O Buckingham, beware of yonder Dog,
His venom Tooth will rankle to the Death. Warburton.

    Q. Margaret, Richard III. Act I. Scene 3.

I say it should be.

His venom Tooth will rankle thee to Death.

But hark, the Bellman summons me away,
If I had Time, I had much more to say.   [*Exit.*

ARIETTA.   [*Wakes.*

Methought I heard a melancholy Tone;
Well, from henceforth I'll never lie alone:
I was a-dream'd, as how a Ghost was here,
My Cap stands right up, and I quake for Fear.   [*Noise.*
Oh me, what Noise is that?
Oh! 'Squire, 'Squire, 'Squire, 'Squire, 'Squire!   10
In Straw-fill'd Sty, thus have I heard a Swine
Sigh for her Mate, for her Companion pine;
Send thro' the senseless Pales, her snuffling Groans,
Eccho'd by squeaking Pigs in shriller Tones.
                        [*Goes to the Door, and shrieks.*

Enter CAPRIOLA, *with a Bottle in one Hand, and a Phial in t'other.*

CAPRIOLA.

At last she's found, now by my best Brocade,
I'll not depart 'till I have sluic'd the Jade*.
                        [ARIETTA *behind the Skreen.*
Come forth, thou Wretch, thou Robber of my Right,
Think not to skreen thee from thy Rival's Sight†.

---

* *Sluic'd the Jade.*—It should be; souc'd the Jade. *Sluic'd* is too indelicate a
Word for a fine Lady to make use of. I think it is the Business of every Com-
mentator, to be nice in regulating the Ideas of his Characters, or else we may
construe Expressions, put into the Mouths of nice Ladies, to very gross Meanings.
Well has Mr. *W.* shewed us an Example of that, by his Note in *King Lear*, Act I.
Scene 2, *Regan* says, *Which the most precious Square of Sense possesses.* On this,
he thus judiciously, delicately remarks:

By the Square of the Senses, we are here to understand, the *four* nobler Senses,
viz. Seeing, Hearing, Tasting, and Smelling; for a young Lady could not, with any
Decency, insinuate, she knew of any Pleasure which the fifth afforded.

He is so very nice, in respect of the Senses, that he will not allow them to be
pierced. It is not right, he thinks, so he alters a Line in *Lear*'s Curse,

From *A Father's Curse pierce every* Sense *about thee*,
To *A Father's Curse pierce every* Fence *about thee.*

† Here is a Piece of Wit, which may pass unnoticed by the Reader, if I do not
put him in Mind of it: It is this—
Think not to skreen thee.—Memorandum, she is gone behind the Skreen.

ARIETTA.

I hear a Voice, coarse as the Fish-Wife's Throat,
Whose Sound was loud as those who Flounders cry,   20
As harsh as Sand-Boys, or as Brick-Dust Sellers:
*Thy foul-mouth'd Tongue, all *Billingsgate* exceeding,
Declares you know not what belongs to Breeding.

CAPRIOLA.

Trollop, I scorn to force Discourse unto ye, ⎫
But hear, ye Slut, come do as I command ye, ⎬
Drink me this Bottle off of *British* Brandy? ⎭
Drink it all up, or else, by all my Woes,
Full in your Face this *Aquafortis* goes.
Be quick, be quick, immediately obey me,
I'll mark you else, Miss, tho' the Squire slay me.   30

ARIETTA.

What, wou'd you poison me? Sure, you're but jesting.

CAPRIOLA.

No Words, I charge you; but now pray be tasting.

* *Foul-mouth'd Tongue.*
In *As you like it*, you may meet with the Word *foul*.
Foul is most *foul*, being *foul* to be a Scoffer.
    This, I believe, is obvious to the meanest Capacity. Homeliness is made worse, if the Ugly pretend to rail at the Deformed.
    But the Sagacity of Mr. *W*. renders it,
    Foul is *foul*, being *found* to be a Scoffer.
And declares the Repetition of *foul* is too absurd to come from *Shakespear*.
    Playing upon Words was not *Shakespeare*'s greatest Beauty, but it was very much his Practice. Allow me, Reader, to give you a Specimen of Mr. *W*. playing upon Words himself.
    He, in his Notes on the Witches of *Macbeth*, their Charms, and Incantations, says, as extravagant shocking and absurd all this is, the Play has had the *Power* to *charm* and *bewitch* every Audience, from that Time to this.
    And since I have offered a Specimen of his Humour, give me Leave to exhibit one of his Wit.
    In the same Play he says, after some Account of the Sun, and its Rays, Optics &c. *a Rainbow is no more a Reflection of the Sun, than a Tune of a fiddle.*

---

21 Sand-Boys] Street-sellers of sand.

ARIETTA.

Let me conjure you, Madam, pray excuse me?
I never wrong'd you, why shou'd you abuse me?
I, like fair *Rosamond*, in *Woodstock* Bower,
Am sacrific'd to *Eleanor*'s fierce Power.

CAPRIOLA.

Not wrong'd me! O thou tinsel trapish Trull,
O give me Patience, all ye sheepish dull;
Ye hen-peck'd Husbands, and ye oft-kicked Cowards!
No rather give me Rage, remorseless Rage,   40
Fill with fell Hate, my Breast ye Prudes disgrac'd,
Ye antiquated Toasts, give me your Spleen?
Ye Gamesters, Goalers, and ye purse-proud Traders,
Give me your merciless stern Minds a Moment?
Now, by my Soul, you Jade, unless you drink it,
Upon thy white-wash'd Face this Phial flies,
Levels thy Nose, and burns out both thy Eyes.

ARIETTA.   [*Drinks.*

Oh! oh! oh!
I'm in a dismal Pickle.
Like a Tetotum, my poor Head is whirling.
As School-boys make the giddy Top run round,   50
So reels *Arietta* 'till she drops to Ground.

Enter Squire FANFLY.

FANFLY.

O Brimstone, thou shalt sleep to Night in Bridewell.
Thou Cinder-sifting, dirty, stroling Punk;
Oh *Arietta*—Oh ye Powers—she's drunk.

ARIETTA.

I am, indeed; I'm in a sad Condition.
Oh! I am sick. What's that which dances by me?
Behold, the Tea-Table is all a-float;
See Tea-Cups sailing, Tea-Spoons turn'd to Oars,
Chairs, Night-Gowns, Pillows, Lap-Dogs, Cards, and Counters,
Oh! Water, Water, Oh— Oh—   [*Sleeps.*

FANFLY.

At length she's dumb, her nimble Tongue stands still,   61
Her talking Faculties by Sleep are numb'd,
And ev'ry Sound has left her silent Lips.
O thou sweet-pleasing Sleep, whose ebon Wand,
With drowsy Poppies wreath'd, can slumb'rous charm
Ev'n Ladies Tongues, and at thy wond'rous Touch,
Silence is fix'd on tattle-loving Fair.

CAPRIOLA.

Since then, to Night, you can't this Lady see,
Come, my dear Squire, come along with me?

FANFLY.

Avaunt, get out, I'd rather see a Tipstaff.   70

CAPRIOLA.

Yes, I will go, curse on your steady Muscle.
Oh! I could hate myself for being kind
To savage Man, the only Beast untam'd.
Each Brute, from Instinct, feels a separate Taste,
But motley-minded Man mimics them all.
First, like a Spaniel, fawning, then puts on
An Ape's Grimace, and Monkey-like he plays,
Sly as the wily Fox, insidious plots,
Or rudely rushes, like the Mountain Bull,
And all to win poor, weak, defenceless Woman.   80
But when Desire by full Possession's cloy'd,
Like secret skulking Moles, they coward hide,
Or bray, like stupid Asses, of our Favours.
Woman to undeserving Man was given,
The last best Gift of ever-bounteous Heaven,
Fond, like a Child, at first the Play-Thing pleas'd,
But soon, too soon, the self-same Beauty teiz'd;
He cries to change, and sighs for other Toys,
Ideot-like dotes, or Savage-like destroys:
While wretched Woman-kind betray'd, like me,   90
Can only curse the Sex, as I do thee*.

                                        [*Spits at him, and exit.*

   * This *Tag* is in true Tragedy Taste. Here are a Parcel of trite Common Place
Similies crouded together, and Half a Dozen Verses at the End, which is on
Purpose, that the Heroine may make a graceful *Exit*. H.H.

FANFLY.

Put her to Bed, and let's go in to Supper,
And, in Despite of Grief, let us be merry*.
The Sweet-heart thus her bonny Sailor leaves,
And yields reluctant to the Wind-rais'd Waves,
Turns quick, and views the Vessel with a Fright,
Stretching away, and less'ning to her Sight,
Sighing, at last she sees it lose the Shore,
Then looks, and looks, till she can look no more.

A *Midnight* SCENE.

Enter SPUNGE.

SPUNGE.

'Tis now the Dead of Night; so much the better:
Lamp, by your Leave,—shew Light to read this Letter?

Honoured Sir,

HOPING these Lines in Health will find you well,
As I myself am, I make bold to tell,
If you, to Night, to our Back-door repair,
When it strikes Twelve, you'll surely find one there.

Now grizly Night, thy pitch'd Tarpaulin spread,
Black as the sooty Chimney-sweeper's Sack;
Snore, ye bed-wanting Bunters, on each Bulk;   10
Wake not, ye Watchmen, while I warn my Love,
Molly, Miss *Molly*, O Miss *Molly*, *Molly*—
But see the Casement opens, she appears,
And spreads a sparkling Light along the Lane.

MISS.

Who's there?

---

* This is right. *And in Despite of Grief*, &c. So *Antipholis*, in the *Comedy of Errors*,
Act III. Scene 1, says, *And in Despite of Wrath, mean to be merry*; for he has received
several Rebuffs from his Wife, and is resolved to go to another House.
  And in Despite of her Wrath, be merry.
  But Mr. *W.* renders it,
  And in Despite of Mirth, mean to be merry.

SPUNGE.

My dear, 'tis I, your True-love, *Spunge*.

MISS.

If I, poor Girl, do trust myself with you,
May I depend, Sir, you'll be always true?

SPUNGE.

By yon pale greasy Lamp that twinkling burns;
By the still Silence of this Tongue-ty'd Night;
By this sad Soul that snores, immers'd in Drink—   20

MISS.

O, do not swear—I do indeed believe,
So sweet a Tongue, sure, never can deceive.
Here, take this Bundle?

As he takes it, a Noise is heard within, of, Bring him along; *the 'Squire is carried across the Stage, and the Watchmen seize* Spunge, *and carry him off last.*

SCENE *the Watch-House.*

Constable asleep, Watch asleep, all asleep*.

Enter SPUNGE.

1st WATCHMAN.

An please your Honour's Worship, Mr. *Constable*, I have reprehended an suspicious Fellow, and made bold, as it is my Duty, an it please you, to bring him before your Worship.

CONSTABLE.

Where did you reprehend him?

2nd WATCHMAN.

Just by, he stood hiding himself as I and my Partner came by, and thought, as how it might be proper to take care of him: Whereby, least he should rob any Body, we took this Bundle from him.

* *All asleep.* A fine Instance and Emblem of Tranquility.

Enter SPUNGE] Together, presumably, with two more watchmen as custodians. The characters already present are 'all asleep'.

CONSTABLE.

Oh, oh; ay, ay, he's a Thief sure enough, and I know a Thief as well as the
Beggar knows his Dish, as the Song says. Come, Sirrah, who are you?

SPUNGE.

A Gentleman.   10

CONSTABLE.

Yes, yes, you shall be hang'd like a Gentlemen*. What's your Name?

SPUNGE.

Spunge.

CONSTABLE.

Spunge! Oh, Mr. *Spunge*, you shall be squeez'd dry enough before we
have done with you.   [*A great Laugh.*

1st WATCHMAN.

Ay, Master Constable's a parlous Man at a Joke. And how came you by
that Bundle, Sirrah? Did not you steal it?

SPUNGE.

No, Sir?

CONSTABLE.

No, Sir; no, Sir. But I say Yes, Sir, you did, Sir, and you'll be hang'd,
Sir. Here's a Rogue for you, first robs, and then denies it; telling me, his
Majesty's Representative, a Lye to my Face. But now you shall hear how I'll
prove him a Rogue: First and foremost, as I said before, he must be a Rogue,
because he denies it, for that's always the Trick of a Rogue: Next, he must
be a Rogue, because, at this Time, all honest People shou'd be in Bed: And
lastly, he must be a Rogue, because—because—Who did you belong to,
Sirrah? What Complices have you?   25

SPUNGE.

I belong to 'Squire *Fanfly*.

* This is quite in Nature: For it is common for an inferior Officer of Justice to
sentence every Man who is brought before him; to drole on the Distresses of his
Looks, or his Dress, and to make him out a Rogue by the Force of Physiognomy.

1st WATCHMAN.

O! he's gone to *Bedlam*; they carried him away To-night.

SPUNGE.

If he is mad, then I'm indeed undone.
Farewel the noble Treats, the nimble Race,
The eager Cockings, and all studious Whist;   30
No more shall I, the well-wax'd Cork unscrew:
Who'll now the noisy Dun's tumultous Voice,
With Pill-*Peruvian* stop?

CONSTABLE.

Carry him into the next Room, while we consult about him. Now,
Neighbours, as you were saying, the 'Squire was mad, I am a saying, this
Man is mad also. D'ye hear how he talks about a Cock and a Bull? So ye
that took him shall carry him to *Bedlam*, and I'll take Care of the Bundle,
and deliver it to the right Owner, when I can find one, and so let Justice take
Place, and good Morrow all.—Break up the Watch.

SCENE *the last*.

BEDLAM.

Enter the 'Squire's MAMMA, *and* PHLEBOTOME.

MAMMA.

Sir, tho' you have my Son, yet pray be gentle,
Let him be mildly brought again to Reason.

PHLEBOTOME.

Madam, will it please you, stand by, and observe him,
You then shall see my Method, and no Doubt,
You will approve the Medicines I prescribe.
[*A Noise is heard within, of Singing, ratling Chains, Roaring,* &c.

Enter a LADY.

LADY.

Your Grace's most devoted, my Lord, your humble; pray let me see you at
my Drum To-night; there will be Miss *Rout*, Madam *Racquet*, Lady *Hurri-
cane*, and the Dutchess of *Helter-Skelter*.

7 Drum] Informal evening party.

MAMMA.

Pray, who is this?

PHLEBOTOME.

A kept Mistress, who run mad because a Tradesman's Wife took the Wall
of her.   11

DANCING-MASTER.

Damn the *Dutch*, I say.   [*Within.*

PHLEBOTOME.

O! here comes the Dancing-Master: He lost his Senses studying Politics.

Enter DANCING-MASTER.

DANCING-MASTER.

I say, Sir, the *Dutch* can't dance, Sir. For, suppose, Sir, now all the
Princes in *Europe* at an Assembly, the Queen of *Hungary* opens the Ball, and
the King of *Prussia* puts her out. The *French* figure in and out just as they
please; the *Dutch* don't dance, Sir, but keep serving every Body with Tea
and Coffee.

PHLEBOTOME.

What do the *English* do, Sirrah?

DANCING-MASTER.

Oh, oh, the *English*—Why they pay the Fidlers.   20

Enter SHOEMAKER.

SHOEMAKER.

I'll pay no Body, Sir, I'm for Liberty and Property, and damn all Taxes.

PHLEBOTOME.

This was a mad Shoemaker; his Skull was crack'd at an Election.

SHOEMAKER.

Huzza, Liberty for ever—and *Old England* always. Friends and Fellow-
Craft, I am come among you to promote Peace and good Neighbourhood,
and I'll knock any one down that dares deny it. It's Time that all Taxes were
made an End of, for before Taxes, every poor Man was as good as a Lord;
we could have Liquor for nothing, and Meat without Money. Therefore, I
say, no Taxes.

10 took the Wall of her] Supplanted her.

Enter GAMESTER.

GAMESTER.

I say, done to you.

PHLEBOTOME.

This is a Gamester; he run mad after Religion.　　　　　　　30

GAMESTER.

What's the most Odds against a Man's going to Heav'n?

Enter BARBER.

BARBER.

The World wants Shaving.

PHLEBOTOME.

This is a Barber's 'Prentice, who run mad with Metaphysics.

GAMESTER.

What's the most Odds a Man goes to Heaven?

BARBER.

Heaven is immaterial, abstracted from infinite Space; for the World lies in the Clouds, as a Wash-Ball in a Bason of Suds: Therefore, Gravitation's consider'd as a Predicament of Matter, by the same Parity of Reason.

GAMESTER.

What's the most Odds against a Man's going to Heaven?

SHOEMAKER.

Sirrah, you are a Placeman; you want to make Int'rest at Court, Sirrah.

Enter POET.

POET.

And rumbling, grumbling, and I'm cold and queer.　　　　　40

PHLEBOTOME.

O! this is the Poet; his Play was damn'd, and he ran mad upon it.

POET.

This Play, Sir, is call'd, *The Deluge.* It opens with a Soliloquy of one of *Noah*'s Sons, who is lamenting the Loss of his Perriwig, which was spoil'd in the Rain.

36 Wash-Ball] Round ball of soap.

Now does the rumbling Thunder rend the Sky,
And crawling Caterpillars trembling fly.
Now purring Cats the nimble Mice pursue,
And boneless Ghosts turn twinkling Candles blue.
The Light'ning flashes, thro' the fiery Clouds,
Scare the bold *Titan*'s, and all *Homer*'s Gods,   50
And while the Combat lasts, all Heaven's at Odds.

GAMESTER.

I'll take the Odds, I say done first.

Enter Squire FANFLY.

MAMMA.

O my poor Child, my *Fanfly!*

FANFLY.

Who's that calls?
O, my Mother! Is it you? O let me out,
Release me from this Wretchedness, I'll promise
To offend no more; no more with Rakes to run,
But live your loving, your obedient Son.

MAMMA.

Come to my Arms, my rash, unthinking Child,
And let me fold ye. Thus the cackling Hen,
When the stray Chicken's found, with joyful Clucks,
The tender Nurseling laps beneath her Wing.

FANFLY.

Farewel all Drinking, and the Joys of Love,
By all the Gods, to study I'll remove;
I'll live by Book, and learn to think by Rule,
And quite forget that I was once a Fool.

PHLEBOTOME.

Well, since you both so well agree,
This is a Day of Jubilee;
Ye mad Inhabitants advance,
And, like yourselves, leap up a Dance.

DANCE.

FINIS.

THE ROVERS

George Canning

1770–1827

John Hookham Frere

1769–1846

George Ellis

1753–1815

The Rovers is a sort of closet burlesque—the only play in the present collection not intended for stage performance. Hence its somewhat fragmentary
nature, its indispensable mock-critical apparatus, and the casual abridge-
ment of its penultimate act into four lines. An amended version of the piece
was actually staged at the Haymarket in 1811: but a latter-day director
could decide for himself what modifications might be necessary in production,
and it is accordingly the original text which is here reprinted. Hence the
appearance of a plot-summary in between the acts, and of the two datelines—
which distinguish the successive issues of *The Anti-Jacobin* in which *The
Rovers* first appeared.

    The Rovers was just one (though the only one in dramatic form) of a long
series of political and literary burlesques included in *The Anti-Jacobin* during
its brief existence under William Gifford's editorship—an existence roughly
concurrent with the parliamentary session of November 1797 to July 1798.
And the collected *Poetry of the Anti-Jacobin*, published in the following year,
represented but one of the features of its weekly issues—albeit the one that
has proved most enduring. The political movement to which the journal
claimed eponymous allegiance has come to bear the taint of witch-hunting,
and of an extreme conservatism insensitive to the genuine grievances of the
people: akin to anti-communism in our own time, anti-jacobinism was thus
used as a stick with which to beat any and all liberal opposition to the policies
of Pitt's administration. So there is, at times, a reactionary flavour to the

Poetry of the Anti-Jacobin—poetry for which Gifford was jointly responsible with George Canning, John Hookham Frere, and George Ellis. Southey was a frequent butt of this collaborative satire, though the radical sympathies for which he was attacked were already waning. And in *The Rovers*, the target of the three authors was not only the sentimentality and moral self-indulgence of German drama, but also its egalitarian tendencies. The play is, nevertheless, unique in choosing this particular object of parody: and in variously paralleling Goethe's *Stella* and Schiller's *The Robbers*—not to mention several plays by Kotzebuë—it was serving a serious corrective purpose, however dubious the underlying political ethic.

The influence of German drama was particularly strong at this time. Not only were Lessing, Goethe, Schiller, and Schlegel the creators of the single worthwhile body of serious drama conceived in Europe during the eighteenth century, but the sympathies of Goethe and Schiller, in particular, were on the side of the revolutionary angels. *The Robbers* thus anticipated the melodrama in its proletarianism—and Goethe's *Stella* the liberalizing of sexual relationships, in that 'double arrangement' which *The Rovers* echoed in its sub-title and its intended climax. The burlesque ridiculed both the political and moral tone of the German drama—and, in its personation of William Godwin under the guise of the mock-author, Higgins, it also attacked the most prominent of jacobin sympathizers in England. More pertinently, from a contemporary point of view, *The Rovers* captures the feel of the parodied plays—their abundance of instant friendships, their gothick embellishments, their 'imprisonments, post-houses and horns', their complicated plots, and (a particular feature of the translations to which the collaborators were indebted) their declamatory rhetoric. That it does so with a harshness unusual in burlesque is a measure of the sincerity with which the authors confused sentimentalism and sedition.

POETRY

OF THE

ANTI-JACOBIN.

———

LONDON:

PRINTED FOR J. WRIGHT,
PICCADILLY.
1799.

THE ROVERS;

OR,

THE DOUBLE ARRANGEMENT.

June 4.

OUR ingenious Correspondent, Mr. HIGGINS, has not been idle. The deserved popularity of the Extracts, which we have been enabled to give from his two Didactic Poems, the PROGRESS OF MAN, and the LOVES OF THE TRIANGLES, has obtained for us the communication of several other works, which he has in hand, all framed upon the same principle, and directed to the same end. The propagation of the New System of Philosophy forms, as he has himself candidly avowed to us, the main object of all his writings. A system comprehending not Politics only, and Religion, but Morals and Manners, and generally whatever goes to the composition or holding together of Human Society; in all of which a total change and revolution is absolutely necessary (as he contends) for the advancement of our common nature to its true dignity, and to the summit of that perfection which the combination of matter, called MAN, is by its innate energies capable of attaining. 14

Of this System, while the sublimer and more scientific branches are to be taught by the splendid and striking medium of Didactic Poetry, or *ratiocination in rhyme*, illustrated with such paintings and portraitures of Essences and their Attributes, as may lay hold of the imagination, while they perplex the judgment;—the more ordinary parts, such as relate to the conduct of common life, and the regulation of social feelings, are naturally the subject of a less elevated style of writing;—of a style which speaks to the eye as well as to the ear,—in short, of Dramatic Poetry and Scenic Representation.

"With this view," says Mr. HIGGINS (for we love to quote the very words of this extraordinary and indefatigable writer), "with this view" says he in a letter dated from his study in St. Mary Axe, the window of which looks upon the parish pump—"with this view, I have turned my thoughts more particularly to the German Stage; and have composed, in imitation of the

---

3 the PROGRESS OF MAN] A parody of Payne Knight's *Progress of Civil Society.*
3 LOVES OF THE TRIANGLES] A 'mathematical and philosophical poem', parodying Darwin's *Loves of the Plants.* 6 the New System of Philosophy] The allusion is to Godwin's critical analysis of existing social institutions in his *Political Justice* (1793).

most popular pieces of that country, which have already met with so general reception and admiration in this,—a Play: which, if It has a proper run, will, I think, do much to unhinge the present notions of men with regard to the obligations of Civil Society; and to substitute in lieu of a sober contentment, and regular discharge of the duties incident to each man's particular situation, a wild desire of undefinable latitude and extravagance,—an aspiration after shapeless somethings, that can neither be described nor understood,—a contemptuous disgust at all that *is*, and a persuasion that nothing is as it ought to be;—to operate, in short, a general discharge of every man (in his own estimation) from every tie which laws divine or human, which local customs, immemorial habits, and multiplied examples impose upon him; and to set them about doing what they like, where they like, when they like, and how they like,—without reference to any law but their own will, or to any consideration of how others may be affected by their conduct.   41

"When this is done, my dear Sir," continues Mr. H. (for he writes very confidentially)—"You see that a great step is gained towards the dissolution of the frame of every existing community. I say nothing of *Governments*, as *their* fall is of course implicated in that of the Social System:—and you have long known, that I hold every Government (that acts by coercion and restriction—by laws made by the few to bind the many) as a *malum in se*,—an evil to be eradicated,—a nuisance to be abated,—by force, if force be practicable, if not,—by the artillery of reason—by pamphlets, speeches, toasts at Club-dinners, and though last, not least, by Didactic Poems.   50

"But where would be the advantage of the destruction of this or that Government, if the form of Society itself were to be suffered to continue such, as that another must necessarily arise out of it, and over it?—Society, my dear Sir, in its present state, is a *hydra*. Cut off one head,—another presently sprouts out, and your labour is to begin again. At best, you can only hope to find it a *polypus*;—where, by cutting off the *head*, you are sometimes fortunate enough to find a *tail* (which answers all the same purposes) spring up in its place. This, we know, has been the case in France;—the only country in which the great experiment of regeneration has been tried with any thing like a fair chance of success.   60

"Destroy the frame of society,—decompose its parts,—and set the elements fighting one against another,—insulated and individual,—every man for himself (stripped of prejudice, of bigotry, and of feeling for others) against the remainder of his species;—and there is then some hope of a totally new *order of things*,—of a *Radical Reform* in the present corrupt System of the World.

"The German Theatre appears to proceed on this judicious plan. And I have endeavoured to contribute my mite towards extending its effect and its popularity. There is one obvious advantage attending this mode of teaching;

—that it can proportion the infractions of law, religion, or morality, which it recommends, to the capacity of a reader or spectator. If you tell a student, or an apprentice, or a merchant's clerk, of the virtue of a Brutus, or of the splendour of a La Fayette, you may excite his *desire* to be equally conspicuous; but how is he to set about it? Where is he to find the tyrant to murder? How is he to provide the monarch to be imprisoned, and the national guards to be reviewed on a white horse? But paint the beauties of *forgery* to him in glowing colours;—shew him that the presumption of virtue is in favour of rapine, and occasional murder on the highway;—and he presently understands you. The highway is at hand—the till or the counter is within reach. These *haberdashers' heroics* come home to the business and the bosoms of men. And you may readily make ten *footpads*, where you would not have materials nor opportunity for a single *tyrannicide*.

"The subject of the piece, which I herewith transmit to you, is taken from common or middling life; and its merit, is that of teaching the most lofty truths in the most humble style, and deducing them from the most ordinary occurrences. Its moral is obvious and easy; and is one frequently inculcated by the German Dramas which I have had the good fortune to see; being no other than '*the reciprocal duties of one or more husbands to one or more wives, and to the children who may happen to arise out of this complicated and endearing connection.*' The plot, indeed, is formed by the combination of the plots of *two* of the most popular of these plays (in the same way as Terence was wont to combine two stories of Menander's). The characters are such as the admirers of these plays will recognize for their familiar acquaintances. There are the usual ingredients of imprisonments, post-houses and horns, and appeals to angels and devils. I have omitted only the *swearing*, to which English ears are not yet sufficiently accustomed.   96

"I transmit at the same time a *Prologue*, which in some degree breaks the matter to the audience. About the song of Rogero, at the end of the first Act, I am less anxious than about any other part of the performance, as it is, in fact, literally translated from the composition of a young German friend of mine, an *Illuminé*, of whom I bought the original for three and sixpence. It will be a satisfaction to those of your Readers, who may not at first sight hit upon the tune, to learn, that it is setting by a hand of the first eminence.— I send also a rough sketch of the plot, and a few occasional notes.—The *Geography* is by the young Gentleman of the *Morning Chronicle*."   105

---

91 *two* of the most popular of these plays] Schiller's *The Robbers*, and Goethe's *Stella*.

THE ROVERS;

OR,

THE DOUBLE ARRANGEMENT.

Dramatis Personæ.

PRIOR *of the* ABBEY *of* QUEDLINBURGH, *very corpulent and cruel.*

ROGERO, *a Prisoner in the Abbey, in love with* MATILDA POTTINGEN.

CASIMERE, *a Polish Emigrant, in Dembrowsky's Legion, married to* CECILIA, *but having several Children by* MATILDA.

PUDDINGFIELD *and* BEEFINGTON, *English Noblemen, exiled by the Tyranny of King John, previous to the signature of Magna Charta.*

RODERIC, *Count of* SAXE WEIMAR, *a bloody Tyrant, with red hair, and an amorous complexion.*

GASPAR, *the Minister of the Count; Author of* ROGERO'S *Confinement.*

Young POTTINGEN, *Brother to* MATILDA.

MATILDA POTTINGEN, *in love with* ROGERO, *and Mother to* CASIMERE'S *Children.*

CECILIA MÜCKENFELD, *Wife to* CASIMERE.

Landlady, Waiter, Grenadiers, Troubadours, &c. &c.

PANTALOWSKY *and* BRITCHINDA, *Children of* MATILDA, *by* CASIMERE.

JOACHIM, JABEL, *and* AMARANTHA, *Children of* MATILDA, *by* ROGERO.

Children of CASIMERE *and* CECILIA, *with their respective Nurses.*

Several Children; Fathers and Mothers unknown.

The Scene lies in the Town of WEIMAR, *and the Neighbourhood of the* ABBEY *of* QUEDLINBURGH

Time, from the 12th to the present Century.

PROLOGUE—in Character.

Too long the triumphs of our early times,
With civil discord and with regal crimes,
Have stain'd these boards; while Shakespeare's pen has shewn
Thoughts, manners, men, to modern days unknown.
Too long have Rome and Athens been *the rage;*   [*Applause.*
And classic Buskins soil'd a British Stage.

To-night our Bard, who scorns pedantic rules,
His Plot has borrow'd from the German schools;
—The German schools—where no dull maxims bind
The bold expansion of the electric mind.   10
Fix'd to no period, circled by no space,
He leaps the flaming bounds of time and place:
Round the dark confines of the forest raves,
With *gentle* Robbers* stocks his gloomy caves;
Tells how Prime Ministers† are shocking things,
And *reigning Dukes* as bad as tyrant Kings;
How to *two* swains‡ *one* nymph her vows may give,
And how *two* damsels‡ with *one* lover live!

---

* See the "Robbers," a German tragedy, in which Robbery is put in so fascinating
a light, that the whole of a German University went upon the highway in conse-
quence of it.

† See "Cabal and Love," a German tragedy, very severe against Prime Ministers,
and reigning Dukes of Brunswick.—This admirable performance very judiciously
reprobates the hire of German troops for the *American* War in the reign of Queen
Elizabeth—a practice which would undoubtedly have been highly discreditable to
that wise and patriotic Princess, not to say wholly unnecessary, there being no
American War at that particular time.

‡ See the "Stranger; or, Reform'd Housekeeper," in which the former of these
morals is beautifully illustrated;—and "Stella," a genteel German comedy, which
ends with placing a man *bodkin* between *two wives,* like *Thames* between his *two
banks,* in the Critic. Nothing can be more edifying than these two Dramas. I am
shocked to hear that there are some people who think them ridiculous.

---

5 Too long have Rome and Athens been *the rage*] An ironical inversion of Pope's plea in
his Prologue to Addison's *Cato,* for the use of classical rather than the fashionable French
and Italian models.   10 electric] Lively, far-ranging.   (†) "Cabal and Love"] By Schiller.
(‡) the "Stranger; or, Reform'd Housekeeper"] By Kotzebuë.

Delicious scenes!—such scenes *our* Bard displays,
Which, crown'd with German, sue for British, praise.   20

Slow are the steeds, that through Germania's roads
With hempen rein the slumbering post-boy goads;
Slow is the slumbering post-boy, who proceeds
Thro' deep sands floundering, on those tardy steeds;
More slow, more tedious, from his husky throat
Twangs through the twisted horn the struggling note.

These truths confess'd—Oh! yet, ye travell'd few,
Germania's *Plays* with eyes unjaundic'd view!
View and approve!—though in each passage fine
The faint translation* mock the genuine line,   30
Though the nice ear the erring sight belie,
For *U twice dotted* is pronounced like *I;**   [*Applause.*
Yet oft the scene shall nature's fire impart,
Warm *from* the breast, and glowing *to* the heart!

Ye travell'd few, attend!—On *you* our Bard
Builds his fond hope! Do you his genius guard!   [*Applause.*
Nor let succeeding generations say
—A British Audience *damn'd* a German play!
                               [*Loud and continued Applauses.*

Flash of Lightning.—The Ghost of PROLOGUE'S GRANDMOTHER *by the Father's
side, appears to soft music, in a white tiffany riding-hood.* PROLOGUE *kneels
to receive her blessing, which she gives in a solemn and affecting manner, the
Audience clapping and crying all the while.—Flash of Lightning.—*PROLOGUE
and his GRANDMOTHER *sink through the trap-door.*

* These are the warnings very properly given to Readers, to beware how they
judge of what they cannot understand. Thus, if the translation runs "*lightning of
my soul, fulguration of angels, sulphur of hell;*" we should recollect that this is not
coarse or strange in the German language, when applied by a lover to his mistress;
but the English has nothing precisely parallel to the original Mulychause Arch-
angelichen, which means rather *emanation of the archangelican nature*—or to
Smellmynkern Vankelfer, which if literally rendered, would signify *made of stuff
of the same odour whereof the Devil makes flambeaux.* See Schüttenbrüch on the
German Idiom.

THE ROVERS;

OR,

THE DOUBLE ARRANGEMENT.

ACT I. SCENE I.

Scene represents a Room at an Inn, at Weimar—On one side of the Stage the Bar-room, with Jellies, Lemons in Nets, Syllabubs, and part of a cold roast Fowl, &c.—On the opposite side a Window looking into the Street, through which Persons (Inhabitants of Weimar) are seen passing to and fro in apparent agitation—Matilda appears in a Great Coat and Riding Habit, seated at the corner of the Dinner Table, which is covered with a clean Huckaback Cloth—Plates and Napkins, with Buck's-Horn-handled Knives and Forks, are laid as if for four Persons.

Mat. Is it impossible for me to have dinner sooner?
Land. Madam, the Brunswick post-waggon is not yet come in, and the Ordinary is never before two o'clock.
Mat. [*With a look expressive of disappointment, but immediately recomposing herself.*] Well, then, I must have patience. [*Exit Landlady.*] Oh Casimere!—How often have the thoughts of thee served to amuse these moments of expectation!—What a difference, alas!—Dinner—it is taken away as soon as over, and we regret it not!—It returns again with the return of appetite.—The beef of to-morrow will succeed to the mutton of to-day, as the mutton of to-day succeeded to the veal of yesterday.—But when once the heart has been occupied by a beloved object, in vain would we attempt to supply the chasm by another. How easily are our desires transferred from dish to dish!—Love only, dear, delusive, delightful Love, restrains our wandering appetites, and confines them to a particular gratification!   13

Post-horn blows, Re-enter Landlady.

Land. Madam, the post-waggon is come in with only a single gentlewoman.
Mat. Then show her up—and let us have dinner instantly; [*Landlady going*] and remember—[*after a moment's recollection, and with great earnestness*]—remember the toasted cheese.   [*Exit Landlady.*

Cecilia enters, in a brown Cloth Riding-dress, as if just alighted from the Post-waggon.

Mat. Madam, you seem to have had an unpleasant journey, if I may judge from the dust on your riding-habit.

Cec. The way was dusty, Madam, but the weather was delightful. It recall'd to me those blissful moments when the rays of desire first vibrated through my soul.   22

Mat. [*Aside*] Thank heaven! I have at last found a heart which is in unison with my own [*to Cecilia*]—Yes, I understand you—the first pulsation of sentiment—the silver tones upon the yet unsounded harp. . . .

Cec. The dawn of life—when this blossom [*putting her hand upon her heart*] first expanded its petals to the penetrating dart of Love!

Mat. Yes—the time—the golden time, when the first beams of the morning meet and embrace one another!—The blooming blue upon the yet unplucked plum!—   30

Cec. Your countenance grows animated, my dear Madam.

Mat. And yours too is glowing with illumination.

Cec. I had long been looking out for a congenial spirit!—my heart was withered—but the beams of yours have re-kindled it.

Mat. A sudden thought strikes me—Let us swear an eternal friendship.

Cec. Let us agree to live together!

Mat. Willingly.   [*with rapidity and earnestness.*

Cec. Let us embrace.   [*they embrace.*

Mat. Yes; I too have lov'd!—you, too, like me, have been forsaken!
                         [*doubtingly, and as if with a desire to be informed.*

Cec. Too true!   40

Both. Ah these men! these men!

Landlady enters, and places a Leg of Mutton on the Table, with sour Krout and Pruin Sauce—then a small Dish of Black Puddings.—Cecilia and Matilda appear to take no notice of her.

Mat. Oh Casimere!

Cec. [*Aside*] Casimere! that name!—Oh my heart, how it is distracted with anxiety.

Mat. Heavens! Madam, you turn pale.

Cec. Nothing—a slight megrim—with your leave, I will retire—

Mat. I will attend you.
                         [*Exeunt Matilda and Cecilia. Manent Landlady and Waiter,*
                                           with the Dinner on the Table.

Land. Have you carried the dinner to the prisoner in the vaults of the abbey?

Waiter. Yes.—Pease soup, as usual—with the scrag end of a neck of mutton—the emissary of the Count was here again this morning, and offered me a large sum of money if I would consent to poison him.   52

Land. Which you refused?   [*with hesitation and anxiety.*

Waiter. Can you doubt it?   [*with indignation.*

Land. [*recovering herself, and drawing up with an expression of dignity*] The conscience of a poor man is as valuable to him as that of a prince. . . .

Waiter. It ought to be still more so, in proportion as it is generally more pure.

Land. Thou say'st truly, Job.

Waiter. [*with enthusiasm*] He who can spurn at wealth when proffer'd as the price of crime, is greater than a prince.   60

Post-horn blows. Enter Casimere (in a travelling dress—a light blue great coat with large metal buttons—his hair in a long queue, but twisted at the end; a large Kevenhuller hat; a cane in his hand).

Cas. Here, Waiter, pull off my boots, and bring me a pair of slippers. [*Exit Waiter*] And heark'ye, my lad, a bason of water [*rubbing his hands*] and a bit of soap—I have not washed since I began my journey.

Waiter. [*answering from behind the door*] Yes, Sir.

Cas. Well, Landlady, what company are we to have?

Land. Only two gentlewomen, Sir.—They are just stept into the next room—they will be back again in a minute.

Cas. Where do they come from?

All this while the Waiter re-enters with the bason and water, Casimere pulls off his boots, takes a napkin from the table, and washes his face and hands.

Land. There is one of them I think comes from Nuremburgh.

Cas. [*Aside*] From Nuremburgh [*with eagerness*] her name?   70

Land. Matilda.

Cas. [*Aside*] How does this idiot woman torment me!—What else!

Land. I can't recollect.

Cas. Oh agony!   [*in a paroxysm of agitation.*

Waiter. See here, her name upon the travelling trunk—Matilda Pottingen.

Cas. Ecstacy! ecstacy!   [*embracing the Waiter.*

Land. You seem to be acquainted with the lady—shall I call her?

Cas. Instantly—instantly—tell her lov'd, her long lost—tell her—

Land. Shall I tell her her dinner is ready?

Cas. Do so—and in the mean while I will look after my portmanteau.

                                                              [*Exeunt severally.*

Scene changes to a subterraneous Vault in the Abbey of Quedlinburgh;—with Coffins, 'Scutcheons, Death's Heads and Cross-bones.—Toads and other loathsome Reptiles are seen traversing the obscurer parts of the Stage.— Rogero appears, in chains, in a Suit of rusty Armour, with his beard grown, and a Cap of a grotesque form upon his head.—Beside him a Crock, or Pitcher, supposed to contain his daily allowance of sustenance.—A long silence, during which the wind is heard to whistle through the Caverns.—Rogero rises, and comes slowly forward, with his arms folded.

Rog. Eleven years! it is now eleven years since I was first immured in this living sepulchre—the cruelty of a Minister—the perfidy of a Monk—yes, Matilda! for thy sake—alive amidst the dead—chained—coffined—confined —cut off from the converse of my fellow-men.—Soft!—what have we here? [*stumbles over a bundle of sticks*] This cavern is so dark, that I can scarcely distinguish the objects under my feet. Oh!—the register of my captivity— Let me see, how stands the account? [*Takes up the sticks, and turns them over with a melancholy air; then stands silent for a few moments, as if absorbed in calculation*] eleven years and fifteen days!—Hah! the twenty-eighth of August! How does the recollection of it vibrate on my heart! It was on this day that I took my last leave of my Matilda. It was a summer evening—her melting hand seemed to dissolve in mine, as I prest it to my bosom— Some demon whispered me that I should never see her more.—I stood gazing on the hated vehicle which was conveying her away for ever.—The tears were petrified under my eyelids.—My heart was crystallized with agony. —Anon—I looked along the road.—The Diligence seemed to diminish every instant.—I felt my heart beat against its prison, as if anxious to leap out and overtake it.—My soul whirled round as I watched the rotation of the hinder wheels.—A long trail of glory followed after her, and mingled with the dust— it was the emanation of Divinity, luminous with love and beauty—like the splendour of the setting sun—but it told me that the sun of my joys was sunk for ever—Yes, here in the depths of an eternal dungeon—in the nursing cradle of hell—the suburbs of perdition—in a nest of demons, where despair in vain sits brooding over the putrid eggs of hope; where agony wooes the embrace of death; where patience, beside the bottomless pool of despondency, sits angling for impossibilities—Yet even *here*, to be- hold her, to embrace her—Yes, Matilda, whether in this dark abode, amidst toads and spiders, or in a royal palace, amidst the more loathsome reptiles of a Court, would be indifferent to me—Angels would shower down their hymns of gratulation upon our heads—while fiends would envy the eternity of suffering love. . . . Soft, what air was that? it seemed a sound of more than human warblings—Again [*listens attentively for some minutes*]—Only the wind—It is well, however—it reminds me of that melancholy air, which has so often solaced the hours of my captivity—Let me see whether the damps of this dungeon have not yet injured my guitar. [*Takes his Guitar, tunes it, and begins the following Air with a full accompaniment of Violins from the Orchestra.*

[*Air, Lanterna Magica.*]

SONG

BY ROGERO.

I.

Whene'er with haggard eyes I view
 This dungeon that I'm rotting in,
I think of those companions true
 Who studied with me at the U—
    —niversity of Gottingen,—   40
    —niversity of Gottingen.
  [*Weeps, and pulls out a blue kerchief, with which he wipes
   his eyes; gazing tenderly at it, he proceeds—*

II.

Sweet kerchief, check'd with heav'nly blue,
 Which once my love sat knotting in!—
Alas! Matilda *then* was true!
 At least I thought so at the U—
    —niversity of Gottingen—
    —niversity of Gottingen.
  [*At the repetition of this Line Rogero clanks his Chains
                in cadence.*

III.

Barbs! barbs! alas! how swift you flew
 Her neat post-waggon trotting in!
Ye bore Matilda from my view;   50
 Forlorn I languish'd at the U—
    —niversity of Gottingen—
    —niversity of Gottingen.

IV.

This faded form! this pallid hue!
 This blood my veins is clotting in,

ROGERO] This character lampooned Sir Robert Adair, a Whig politician educated at Göttingen, who had indeed fallen in love with his tutor's daughter.

My years are many—they were few
    When first I enter'd at the U—
                —niversity of Gottingen—
                —niversity of Gottingen.

V.

There first for thee my passion grew,   60
    Sweet! sweet Matilda Pottingen!
Thou wast the daughter of my Tu—
    —tor, Law Professor at the U—
                —niversity of Gottingen—
                —niversity of Gottingen.

VI.

Sun, moon, and thou vain world, adieu,
    That kings and priests are plotting in:
Here doom'd to starve on water-gru—
    —el* never shall I see the U—
                —niversity of Gottingen—   70
                —niversity of Gottingen.—

[*During the last Stanza Rogero dashes his head repeatedly against the walls of his Prison; and, finally, so hard as to produce a visible contusion. He then throws himself on the floor in an agony. The Curtain drops—the Music still continuing to play, till it is wholly fallen.*

* A manifest error—since it appears from the Waiter's conversation (p. 333), that Rogero was not doomed to starve on water-gruel, but on pease-soup; which is a much better thing. Possibly the length of Rogero's imprisonment had impaired his memory; or he might wish to make things appear worse than they really were; which is very natural, I think, in such a case as this poor unfortunate gentleman's.
                                                        Printer's Devil.

(*) *Printer's Devil*] A printer's errand boy, whose powers are here suggested to be suffi-cient for critical annotation

WE have received, in the course of the last week, several long, and to say the truth, dull letters, from unknown hands, reflecting, in very severe terms, on Mr. HIGGINS, for having, as it is affirmed, attempted to pass upon the world, as a faithful sample of the productions of the German Theatre, a performance no way resembling any of those pieces, which have of late excited, and which bid fair to engross the admiration of the British Public.

As we cannot but consider ourselves as the guardians of Mr. HIGGINS's literary reputation, in respect to every work of his which is conveyed to the world through the medium of our paper (though, what we think of the danger of his principles, we have already sufficiently explained for ourselves, and have, we trust, succeeded in putting our Readers upon their guard against them)—we hold ourselves bound not only to justify the fidelity of the imitation—but (contrary to our original intention) to give a further specimen of it in our present Number, in order to bring the question more fairly to issue between our Author and his calumniators.   15

In the first place, we are to observe, that Mr. HIGGINS professes to have taken his notion of German plays wholly from the Translations which have appeared in our language.—If *they* are totally dissimilar from the originals, Mr. H. may undoubtedly have been led into error; but the fault is in the translators, not in him. That he does not differ widely from the models which he proposed to himself, we have it in our power to prove satisfactorily; and might have done so in our last Number, by subjoining to each particular passage of his play, the scene in some one or other of the German plays, which he had in view when he wrote it. These parallel passages were faithfully pointed out to us by Mr. H. with that candour which marks his character; and if they were suppressed by us (as in truth they were) on our heads be the blame, whatever it may be. Little, indeed, did we think of the imputation which the omission would bring upon Mr. H. as in fact, our principal reason for it, was the apprehension, that from the extreme closeness of the imitation in most instances, he would lose in praise for invention, more than he would gain in credit for fidelity.   31

The meeting between Matilda and Cecilia, for example, in the First Act of the "Rovers," and their sudden intimacy, has been censured as unnatural. Be it so. It is taken *almost word for word*, from "Stella," a German (or professedly a German) piece now much in vogue; from which also the catastrophe of Mr. HIGGINS's play is in part borrowed, so far as relates to the agreement to which the Ladies come, as the Reader will see by and by, to share Casimere between them.

M

The dinner scene is copied partly from the published translation of the "Stranger," and partly from the first scene of "Stella." The song of Rogero, with which the first act concludes, is admitted on all hands to be in the very first taste; and if no German original is to be found for it, so much the worse for the credit of German literature.   43

An objection has been made by one anonymous letter-writer, to the names of Puddingfield and Beefington, as little likely to have been assigned to English characters by any author of taste or discernment. In answer to this objection, we have, in the first place, to admit that a small, and we hope not an unwarrantable, alteration has been made by us since the MS. has been in our hands.—These names stood originally Puddincrantz and Beefinstern, which sounded to our ears as being liable, especially the latter, to a ridiculous inflection—a difficulty that could only be removed by furnishing them with English terminations. With regard to the more substantial syllables of the names, our Author proceeded in all probability on the authority of Goldoni, who, though not a German, is an Italian writer of considerable reputation; and who, having heard that the English were distinguished for their love of liberty and beef, has judiciously compounded the two words *Runnymede* and *beef,* and thereby produced an English Nobleman, whom he styles *Lord Runnybeef.*   58

To dwell no longer on particular passages—the best way perhaps of explaining the whole scope and view of Mr. H.'s imitation, will be to transcribe the short sketch of the plot, which that Gentleman transmitted to us, together with his Drama; and which it is perhaps the more necessary to give at length, as the limits of our paper not allowing of the publication of the whole piece, some general knowledge of its main design may be acceptable to our Readers, in order to enable them to judge of the several Extracts which we lay before them.   66

PLOT.

Rogero, son of the late Minister of the Count of Saxe Weimar, having, while he was at college, fallen desperately in love with Matilda Pottingen, daughter of his tutor, Doctor Engelbertus Pottingen, Professor of Civil Law; and Matilda evidently returning his passion, the Doctor, to prevent ill consequences, sends his daughter on a visit to her Aunt in Wetteravia, where she becomes acquainted with Casimere, a Polish Officer, who happens to be quartered near her Aunt's; and has several children by him.   73

Roderic, Count of Saxe Weimer, a Prince of a tyrannical and licentious disposition, has for his Prime Minister and favourite, Gaspar, a crafty villain, who had risen to his post by first ruining, and then putting to death, Rogero's father.—Gaspar, apprehensive of the power and popularity which the young Rogero may enjoy at his return to Court, seizes the occasion of his

intrigue with Matilda (of which he is apprized officially by Doctor Pottingen)
to procure from his Master an order for the recall of Rogero from college,
and for committing him to the care of the Prior of the Abbey of Quedlinburgh, a Priest, rapacious, savage, and sensual, and devoted to Gaspar's
interests—sending at the same time private orders to the Prior to confine him
in a dungeon.   84

Here Rogero languishes many years. His daily sustenance is administered
to him through a grated opening at the top of a cavern, by the Landlady of
the Golden Eagle at Weimar, with whom Gaspar contracts, in the Prince's
name, for his support; intending, and more than once endeavouring, to
corrupt the Waiter to mingle poison with the food, in order that he may
get rid of Rogero for ever.   90

In the mean time Casimere, having been called away from the neighbourhood of Matilda's residence to other quarters, becomes enamoured of, and
marries Cecilia, by whom he has a family; and whom he likewise deserts
after a few years co-habitation, on pretence of business which calls him to
Kamtschatka.

Doctor Pottingen, now grown old and infirm, and feeling the want of his
daughter's society, sends young Pottingen in search of her, with strict
injunctions not to return without her; and to bring with her either her present
lover Casimere, or, should that not be possible, Rogero himself, if he can
find him; the Doctor having set his heart upon seeing his children comfort-
ably settled before his death. Matilda, about the same period, quits her
Aunt's in search of Casimere; and Cecilia having been advertised (by an
anonymous letter) of the falsehood of his Kamtschatka journey, sets out in
the post-waggon on a similar pursuit.   104

It is at this point of time the Play opens—with the accidental meeting of
Cecilia and Matilda at the Inn at Weimar. Casimere arrives there soon after,
and falls in first with Matilda, and then with Cecilia. Successive *éclaircisse-
ments* take place, and an arrangement is finally made, by which the two
Ladies are to live jointly with Casimere.

Young Pottingen, wearied with a few weeks search, during which he has
not been able to find either of the objects of it, resolves to stop at Weimar,
and wait events there. It so happens that he takes up his lodging in the same
house with Puddincrantz and Beefinstern, two English Noblemen, whom the
tyranny of King John has obliged to fly from their country; and who, after
wandering about the Continent for some time, have fixed their residence at
Weimar.   116

The news of the signature of Magna Charta arriving, determines Puddincrantz and Beefinstern to return to England. Young Pottingen opens his
case to them, and intreats them to stay to assist him in the object of his
search.—This they refuse; but coming to the Inn where they are to set off

for Hamburgh, they meet Casimere, from whom they had both received many civilities in Poland. [122]

Casimere, by this time, tired of his "DOUBLE ARRANGEMENT," and having learnt from the Waiter that Rogero is confined in the vaults of the neighbouring Abbey *for love*, resolves to attempt his rescue, and to make over Matilda to him as the price of his deliverance. He communicates his scheme to Puddingfield and Beefington, who agree to assist him; as also does Young Pottingen. The Waiter of the Inn proving to be a *Knight Templar* in disguise, is appointed leader of the expedition. A band of Troubadours, who happen to be returning from the Crusades, and a Company of Austrian and Prussian Grenadiers returning from the Seven Years' War, are engaged as troops.

The attack on the Abbey is made with success. The Count of Weimar and Gaspar, who are feasting with the Prior, are seized and beheaded in the Refectory. The Prior is thrown into the dungeon, from which Rogero is rescued. Matilda and Cecilia rush in. The former recognizes Rogero, and agrees to live with him. The Children are produced on all sides—and Young Pottingen is commissioned to write to his father, the Doctor, to detail the joyful events which have taken place, and to invite him to Weimar to partake of the general felicity. [139]

ACT II.

Scene—a Room in an ordinary Lodging-House, at WEIMAR.—PUDDINGFIELD *and* BEEFINGTON *discovered, sitting at a small deal Table, and playing at All-Fours. Young* POTTINGEN, *at another Table in the corner of the Room, with a Pipe in his Mouth, and a Saxon Mug of a singular shape beside him, which he repeatedly applies to his lips, turning back his head, and casting his eyes towards the Firmament—at the last trial he holds the Mug for some moments in a directly inverted position; then replaces it on the Table, with an air of dejection, and gradually sinks into a profound slumber.—The Pipe falls from his hand, and is broken.—*

Beef. I beg.
Pudd. [*deals three Cards to Beefington*] Are you satisfied?
Beef. Enough. What have you?
Pudd. High—Low—and the Game.
Beef. Damnation! 'tis my deal. [*deals—turns up a knave*] One for his heels! [*triumphantly.*

Pudd. Is king highest?

s.d. *All-Fours*] A card game, so called because four points were at stake.

Beef. No. [*sternly*] The game is mine. The knave gives it me.

Pudd. Are knaves so prosperous?

Beef. Ay marry are they in this world. They have the game in their hands. Your kings are but *noddies** to them.   10

Pudd. Ha! Ha! Ha!—Still the same proud spirit, Beefington, which procured thee thine exile from England.

Beef. England! my native land!—when shall I revisit thee?

       [*during this time Puddingfield deals and begins to arrange his hand.*

Beef. [*continues*] Phoo—Hang All-Fours; what are they to a mind ill at ease?—Can they cure the heartache?—Can they soothe banishment?—Can they lighten ignominy?—Can All-Fours do this?—O! my Puddingfield, thy limber and lightsome spirit bounds up against affliction—with the elasticity of a well bent bow; but mine—O! mine—

    [*falls into an agony, and sinks back in his Chair. Young Pottingen, awakened
      by the noise, rises, and advances with a grave demeanour towards
      Beefington and Puddingfield. The former begins to recover.*

Y. Pot. What is the matter, Comrades?†—you seem agitated. Have you lost or won?   20

Beef. Lost.—I have lost my country.

Y. Pot. And I my sister.—I came hither in search of her.

Beef. O, England!

Y. Pot. O, Matilda!

Beef. Exiled by the tyranny of an Usurper, I seek the means of revenge, and of restoration to my country.

Y. Pot. Oppressed by the tyranny of an Abbot, persecuted by the jealousy of a Count, the betrothed husband of my sister languishes in a loathsome captivity—Her lover is fled no one knows whither—and I, her brother, am torn from my paternal roof and from my studies in chirurgery; to seek him and her, I know not where—to rescue Rogero, I know not how. Com-

---

* This is an excellent joke in German; the point and spirit of which is but ill-*Rendered* in a translation. A NODDY, the Reader will observe, has two significations —the one a *knave at All-fours:* the other a *fool* or *booby.* See the translation by Mr. Render of Count Benyowsky, or the Conspiracy of Kamtschatka, a German Tragi-Comi-Comi-Tragedy; where the play opens with a Scene of a Game at Chess (from which the whole of this Scene is copied) and a joke of the same point, and merriment about Pawns, *i.e.* Boors being *a match for* Kings.

† This word in the original is strictly *fellow-lodgers*—"*Co-occupants of the same room, in a house let out at a small rent by the week.*"—There is no single word in English which expresses so complicated a relation, except perhaps the cant term of *chum,* formerly in use at our Universities.

(*) Count Benyowsky] By Kotzebuë.

rades, your counsel—my search fruitless—my money gone—my baggage
stolen! What am I to do?—In yonder Abbey—in these dark, dank vaults,
there, my friends—there lies Rogero—there Matilda's heart—   34

SCENE II.

Enter Waiter.

Waiter. Sir, here is a person who desires to speak with you.

Beef. [*Goes to the door, and returns with a Letter, which he opens—On
perusing it his countenance becomes illuminated, and expands prodigiously*]
Hah, my friend, what joy!   [*turning to Puddingfield.*

Pudd. What? tell me—let your Puddingfield partake it.

Beef. See here—   [*produces a printed Paper.*

Pudd. What?—   [*with impatience.*

Beef. [*in a significant tone*] A newspaper!

Pudd. Hah, what sayst thou!—A newspaper!

Beef. Yes, Puddingfield, and see here [*shews it partially*] from England.

Pudd. [*with extreme earnestness*] Its name!

Beef. The *Daily Advertiser*—

Pudd. Oh ecstasy!   10

Beef. [*with a dignified severity*] Puddingfield, calm yourself—repress those
transports—remember that you are a man.

Pudd. [*after a pause with suppressed emotion*] Well, I will be—I am calm—
yet tell me, Beefington, does it contain any news?

Beef. Glorious news, my dear Puddingfield—the Barons are victorious—
King John has been defeated—Magna Charta, that venerable immemorial
inheritance of Britons, was signed last Friday was three weeks, the third of
July Old Style.

Pudd. I can scarce believe my ears—but let me satisfy my eyes—shew me
the paragraph.   20

Beef. Here it is, just above the advertisements.

Pudd. [*reads*] "The great demand for Packwood's Razor Straps"—

Beef. 'Pshaw! what, ever blundering—you drive me from my patience—
see here, at the head of the column.

Pudd. [*reads*]

"A hireling Print, devoted to the Court,
"Has dared to question our veracity
"Respecting the events of yesterday;
"But by to-day's accounts, our information
"Appears to have been perfectly correct.

18 Old Style] According to the Julian, not Gregorian calendar.

"The Charter of our Liberties receiv'd
"The Royal Signature at five o'clock,   30
"When Messengers were instantly dispatch'd
"To Cardinal Pandulfo; and their Majesties,
"After partaking of a cold collation,
"Return'd to Windsor."—I am satisfied.

Beef. Yet here again—there are some further particulars [*turns to another part of the Paper*] "Extract of a Letter from Egham—'My dear Friend, we " 'are all here in high spirits—the interesting event which took place this " 'morning at Runnymede, in the neighbourhood of this town' "—

Pudd. Hah! Runnymede—enough—no more—my doubts are vanished— then we are free indeed!—   41

Beef. I have, besides, a Letter in my pocket from our Friend, the immortal Bacon, who has been appointed Chancellor.—Our outlawry is reversed!— what says my Friend—shall we return by the next packet?

Pudd. Instantly, instantly!

Both. Liberty!—Adelaide!—revenge!

[*Exeunt—Young Pottingen following, and waving his Hat, but obviously without much consciousness of the meaning of what has passed.*

Scene changes to the outside of the Abbey. A Summer's Evening—Moonlight.
Companies of Austrian and Prussian Grenadiers march across the stage, confusedly, as if returning from the Seven Years' War. Shouts and martial Music.
The Abbey gates are opened. The Monks are seen passing in procession, with the Prior at their head. The Choir is heard chaunting Vespers. After which a pause. Then a Bell is heard, as if ringing for supper. Soon after, a noise of singing and jollity.

Enter from the Abbey, pushed out of the gates by the Porter, a TROUBADOUR, *with a bundle under his cloak, and a* LADY *under his arm.* TROUBADOUR *seems much in liquor, but caresses the* FEMALE MINSTREL.

Fem. Min. Trust me, Gieronymo, thou seemest melancholy. What hast thou got under thy cloak?

Trou. 'Pshaw, women will be inquiring. Melancholy! not I.—I will sing thee a song, and the subject of it shall be thy question—"what have I got under my cloak?" It is a riddle, Margaret—I learnt it of an Almanac-maker at Gotha—if thou guessest it after the first stanza, thou shalt have never a drop for thy pains. Hear me—and, d'ye mark! twirl thy thingumbob while I sing.

Fem. Min. 'Tis a pretty tune, and hums dolefully.

> *[Plays on her Balalaika.**
> *Troubadour sings.*

> I bear a secret comfort *here*,　　　　　　　10
> *[putting his hand on the bundle, but without shewing it.*
> A joy I'll ne'er impart;
> It is not wine, it is not beer,
> But it consoles my heart.

Fem. Min. [*interrupting him*] I'll be hang'd if you don't mean the bottle of cherry-brandy that you stole out of the vaults in the Abbey cellar.

Trou. I mean!—Peace, wench, thou disturbest the current of my feelings—

> [*Fem. Min. attempts to lay hold on the bottle. Troubadour pushes her aside,*
> *and continues singing without interruption.*

> This cherry-bounce, this lov'd noyau,
> My drink for ever be;
> But, sweet my love, thy wish forego;
> I'll give no drop to thee!　　　　　　　20

> [*Both together.*]

Trou. {This}
F. M. {That} cherry-bounce {this}{that} loved noyau,

Trou. {My}
F. M. {Thy} drink for ever be;

Trou. {But, sweet my love, {thy wish forego!
F. M. {　　　　　　　　　{one drop bestow.

Trou. {I　　}
F. M. {Nor} keep it all for {me!
　　　　　　　　　　　　{thee!

> [*Exeunt struggling for the bottle, but without anger or animosity, the Fem.*
> *Min. appearing by degrees to obtain a superiority in the contest.*

END OF ACT II.

Act the Third—contains the eclaircissements and final arrangement between Casimere, Matilda, and Cecilia; which so nearly resemble the concluding Act of "Stella," that we forbear to lay it before our Readers.

* The Balalaika is a Russian instrument, resembling the guitar.—See the Play of "Count Benyowsky," *Rendered* into English.

9, s.d. *Troubadour sings*] The following song parodies one by Sheridan interpolated into the London production of Kotzebuë's *Stranger*.

ACT IV.

*Scene—the Inn door—Diligence drawn up. Casimere appears superintending
the package of his Portmanteaus, and giving directions to the Porters.*

Enter Beefington and Puddingfield.

Pudd. Well, Coachey, have you got two inside places?

Coach. Yes, your Honour.

Pudd. [*seems to be struck with Casimere's appearance. He surveys him earnestly,
without paying any attention to the Coachman, then doubtingly pronounces*]
Casimere!

Cas. [*turning round rapidly, recognizes Puddingfield, and embraces him.*

Cas. My Puddingfield!

Pudd. My Casimere!

Cas. What, Beefington too! [*discovering him*] then is my joy complete.

Beef. Our fellow-traveller, as it seems?

Cas. Yes, Beefington—but wherefore to Hamburgh?

Beef. Oh, Casimere*—to fly—to fly—to return—England—our Country—
Magna Charta—it is liberated—a new æra—House of Commons—Crown
and Anchor—Opposition—   11

Cas. What a contrast! you are flying to Liberty and your home—I driven
from my home by tyranny—am exposed to domestic slavery in a foreign
country.

Beef. How domestic slavery?

Cas. Too true—two wives—[*slowly, and with a dejected air—then after a
pause*]—you knew my Cecilia?

Pudd. Yes, five years ago.

Cas. Soon after that period I went upon a visit to a Lady in Wetteravia—
my Matilda was under her protection—alighting at a peasant's cabin, I saw
her on a charitable visit, spreading bread and butter for the children, in a
light blue riding habit. The simplicity of her appearance—the fineness of the
weather—all conspired to interest me—my heart moved to hers—as if by a

---

* See "Count Benyowsky: or, the Conspiracy of Kamschatka," where Crustiew,
an old gentleman of much sagacity, talks the following nonsense.

Crustiew. [*with youthful energy and an air of secrecy and confidence*] "To fly, to
"fly, to the isles of Marian—the island of Tinian—a terrestrial paradise. Free—
"free—a mild climate—a new-created sun—wholesome fruits—harmless inhabi-
"tants—and Liberty—tranquillity."

---

10 Crown and Anchor] A tavern in Arundel Street, Strand, where the Whig Club was in
the habit of holding its meetings.

magnetic sympathy—we wept, embraced, and went home together—she became the mother of my Pantalowsky. But five years of enjoyment have not stifled the reproaches of my conscience—her Rogero is languishing in captivity—if I could restore her to *him!*   27

Beef. Let us rescue him.

Cas. Will without power,* is like children playing at soldiers.

Beef. Courage without power,† is like a consumptive running footman.

Cas. Courage without power is a contradiction.‡—Ten brave men might set all Quedlinburgh at defiance.

Beef. Ten brave men—but where are they to be found?

Cas. I will tell you—marked you the Waiter?   34

Beef. The Waiter?—   [*doubtingly.*

Cas. [*in a confidential tone*] No Waiter, but a *Knight Templar.* Returning from the Crusade, he found his Order dissolved, and his person proscribed. He dissembled his rank, and embraced the profession of a Waiter. I have made sure of him already. There are, besides, an Austrian and a Prussian Grenadier. I have made them abjure their national enmity, and they have sworn to fight henceforth in the cause of Freedom. These, with young Pottingen, the Waiter, and ourselves, make seven—the Troubadour, with his two attendant Minstrels, will complete the ten.   43

Beef. Now then for the execution.   [*with enthusiasm.*

Pudd. Yes, my boys—for the execution.   [*clapping them on the back.*

Waiter. But hist! we are observed.

Trou. Let us by a song conceal our purposes.

RECITATIVE ACCOMPANIED.§

   Cas. Hist! hist! nor let the airs that blow
        From Night's cold lungs, our purpose know!
Pudd. Let Silence, mother of the dumb,   50
Beef. Press on each lip her palsied thumb!
Wait. Let Privacy, allied to Sin,
        That loves to haunt the tranquil inn—

---

* See "Count Benyowsky," as before.

† See "Count Benyowsky."

‡ See "Count Benyowsky" again. From which Play this and the preceding references are taken word for word. We acquit the Germans of such reprobate silly stuff. It must be the translator's.

§ We believe this song to be copied, with a small variation in metre and meaning, from a song in "Count Benyowsky; or, the Conspiracy of Kamschatka,"—where the conspirators join in a chorus, *for fear of being overheard.*

> *Gren.*⎫ And Conscience start, when she shall view,
> *Trou.*⎭ The mighty deed we mean to do!

GENERAL CHORUS—Con spirito.

> Then Friendship swear, ye faithful Bands,
>   Swear to save a shackled hero!
> See where yon Abbey frowning stands!
>   Rescue, rescue, brave Rogero!
> *Cas.* Thrall'd in a Monkish tyrant's fetters   60
>   Shall great Rogero hopeless lie?
> *Y. Pot.* In my pocket I have letters,
>   Saying, "help me, or I die!"

Allegro Allegretto.

> *Cas. Beef. Pudd. Gren.*⎫ Let us fly, let us fly,
> *Trou. Waiter, and Pot.* ⎬ Let us help, ere he die!
> *with enthusiasm.*   ⎭

> [*Exeunt omnes, waving their hats*

Scene—the Abbey Gate, with Ditches, Drawbridges, and Spikes. Time—about an hour before Sunrise. The Conspirators appear as if in ambuscade, whispering, and consulting together, in expectation of the Signal for attack. The WAITER *is habited as a Knight Templar, in the dress of his Order, with the Cross on his breast, and the Scallop on his shoulder.* PUDDINGFIELD *and* BEEFINGTON *armed with Blunderbusses and Pocket-pistols; the* GRENADIERS *in their proper Uniforms. The* TROUBADOUR *with his attendant Minstrels, bring up the rear—martial Music—the Conspirators come forward, and present themselves before the Gate of the Abbey.—Alarum—firing of Pistols—the Convent appear in Arms upon the Walls—the Drawbridge is let down—a Body of Choristers and Lay-brothers attempt a Sally, but are beaten back and the Verger killed. The besieged attempt to raise the Drawbridge—* PUDDINGFIELD *and* BEEFINGTON *press forward with alacrity, throw themselves upon the Drawbridge, and by the exertion of their weight, preserve it in a state of depression—the other besiegers join them, and attempt to force the entrance, but without effect.* PUDDINGFIELD *makes the signal for the battering ram. Enter* QUINTUS CURTIUS *and* MARCUS CURIUS DENTATUS, *in their proper Military Habits, preceded by the Roman Eagle—the rest of their Legion are employed in bringing forward a battering ram, which plays for a few minutes to slow time, till the entrance is forced. After a short resistance, the besiegers rush in with shouts of Victory.*

Scene changes to the interior of the Abbey. The inhabitants of the Convent are seen flying in all directions.

The Count of Weimar *and the* Prior, *who had been found feasting in the Refectory, are brought in manacled. The* Count *appears transported with rage, and gnaws his chains. The* Prior *remains insensible, as if stupified with grief.* Beefington *takes the keys of the Dungeon, which are hanging at the* Prior's *girdle, and makes a sign for them both to be led away into confinement—* Exeunt Prior *and* Count *properly guarded. The rest of the Conspirators disperse in search of the Dungeon where* Rogero *is confined.*

END OF ACT THE FOURTH.

BOMBASTES FURIOSO

William Barnes Rhodes

1772–1826

William Barnes Rhodes had little claim to distinction besides his authorship of *Bombastes Furioso*: he was a clerk at the Bank of England for twenty-four years, enjoying promotion to the office of chief teller for a further three immediately before his death. There is a suggestion of the plodding pace of such a life about this single excursion into playwriting—an occasional heaviness to the humour and something correct and clerkly about the tone of his archetypally-titled *Bombastes Furioso*.

The processes which were to transform burlesque into extravaganza during the nineteenth century can already be seen at work in Rhodes's play. But the mere presence of punning and of over-assertive colloquialism doesn't matter in itself: what does matter is the attendant vulgarizing and dilution of satiric content, and the continuing attempt—less and less precise in its aim—to hit a target long since pock-marked with scars inflicted by earlier writers. For by 1810, when *Bombastes Furioso* was first performed, there were few new jokes to be made about heroic drama or its even hoarier bombastic hero. Rhodes nevertheless chose soldierly love and valour as his theme, only to lose sight of his generic pedigree, and to drop into the debased couplets—one is reluctant to dignify them as mock-heroics—which were to become the stock-in-trade of that master of Victorian extravaganza, J. R. Planché. In this sense, the faults of *Bombastes Furioso* are symptomatic of a general decline. Granted its deficiencies, the play is not an unworthy or unamusing specimen of its kind: but the kind is one which exploits easier effects than those on which the vintage burlesques relied.

If the total impact of *Bombastes Furioso* is therefore slight, it does have particular turns of phrase, particular moments of bathos, which are happy enough. There is its opening discourse on the subject of Artaxominous's hangover. There is Bombastes's momentary double-take on discovering that his rival is the King, and his later soliloquy, neatly blending the principled and the pragmatic, on the relative advantages of suicide and madness. Such moments—and there are enough of them to keep one's interest alive—are distinguished by that purposeful incongruity between action and idiom which is at the heart of burlesque. And perhaps Rhodes sensed his own limitations: his play is a mere one-act in length, brief enough to keep its initial momentum from flagging, and to prevent the reworking of limited resources from becoming obtrusive. Staged anonymously at the Haymarket in 1810, an accredited text of *Bombastes Furioso* under the author's own name did not appear till 1822. In reprinting it here, my intention is not to assert its intrinsic merit so much as to demonstrate the diminishing force of the burlesque form in a century less sympathetic to its *critical* kind of creativity.

BOMBASTES FURIOSO;

A

Burlesque Tragic Opera,

IN ONE ACT:

FIRST PERFORMED

AT THE

THEATRE ROYAL, HAYMARKET,

AUGUST 7, 1810.

BY WILLIAM BARNES RHODES.

London:

PRINTED FOR THOMAS RODD,

2, GREAT NEWPORT STREET.

1822.

ADVERTISEMENT.

THE very powerful effect produced by the inimitable acting of the several Performers in the following dramatic trifle, is sufficiently known by the highly flattering reception it met with; and had the Author considered his part equally deserving the applause so liberally bestowed upon it, an edition long before this would have been given to the public: yet, however deficient it may be in point of composition, the very objectionable light in which the spurious copies lately issued from the press have placed it, will, he trusts, be deemed a sufficient apology for its now being printed as it was first performed.

Lyons Inn,
October 21, 1822.

Dramatis Personæ.

Artaxominous, King of Utopia	Mr. MATTHEWS
Fusbos, Minister of State	Mr. TAYLOR
General Bombastes	Mr. LISTON
Attendants	{ Mr. TREBY { Mr. NORRIS
Distaffina	Miss H. KELLY.

Drummer, Fifer, and Soldiers.

---

*⁂ The lines to which an inverted comma is prefixed,
were omitted after a few nights' repetition.*

BOMBASTES FURIOSO.

𝔖𝔠𝔢𝔫𝔢 𝔍.—*Interior of the Palace.*

ARTAXOMINOUS *in his Chair of State; a Table set out with Bowls, Glasses, Pipes, &c.; Attendants on each side.*

TRIO—*Tekeli.*

1st ATT.   What will your Majesty please to wear?
    Or blue, green, red, black, white, or brown?
2d ATT.   D'ye choose to look at the bill of fare?
ARTAX.   Get out of my sight, or I'll knock you down.
2d ATT.   Here is soup, fish, or goose, or duck, or fowl, or
    pigeons, pig, or hare;
1st ATT.   Or blue, or green, or red, or black, or white, or brown.
    What will your Majesty, &c.
ARTAX.   Get out of my sight, &c.

              [Exeunt Attendants.

Enter FUSBOS, *and kneels to the King.*

FUS.   Hail, Artaxominous! ycleped the Great!
   I come, an humble pillar of thy state,   10
   Pregnant with news—but ere that news I tell,
   First let me hope your Majesty is well.
ART.   Rise, learned Fusbos! rise, my friend, and know
   We are but middling—that is, but *so so.*
FUS.   Only *so so!* O monstrous, doleful thing!
   Is it the mulligrubs affects the king?
   Or, dropping poisons in the cup of joy,
   Do the blue devils your repose annoy?
ART.   Nor mulligrubs, nor devils blue, are here,
   But yet we feel ourself a little *queer.*   20
FUS.   Yes, I perceive it in that vacant eye,
   The vest unbutton'd, and the wig awry;
   Ungarter'd hose, with slippers down at heel,
   And beard unconscious of the biting steel:

16 mulligrubs] Depression of spirits. 18 blue devils] Delirium tremens.

	So sickly cats neglect their fur-attire,	
	And sit and mope beside the kitchen fire.	

ART.   Last night, when undisturb'd by state affairs,
Moist'ning our clay, and puffing off our cares,
Oft the replenish'd goblet did we drain,
And drank and smok'd, and smok'd and drank again;   30
Such was the case, our very actions such,
Until at length we got a drop too much.

FUS.   'So when some donkey on the Blackheath road
'Falls, overpower'd, beneath his sandy load;
'The driver's curse unheeded swells the air,
'Since none can carry more than they can bear.

ART.   'The sapient Doctor Muggins came in haste,
'Who suits his physic to his patients' taste;
'He, knowing well on what our heart is set,
'Hath just prescrib'd "to take a morning whet;" '   40
The very sight each sick'ning pain subdues,
Then sit, my Fusbos, sit and tell thy news.

FUS.   Gen'ral Bombastes, whose resistless force
Alone exceeds by far a brewer's horse,
Returns victorious, bringing mines of wealth!

ART.   Does he, by jingo? then we'll drink his health.

FUS.   'In vain their numbers faced our gallant few!
'Scarce had your *sable*-guards appear'd in view,
'When all the crowd of *scarecrow-onians* yield,
'And leave their ragged banners in the field.   50
'So, when a debtor whose exploring eyes
'Afar in some high street a dun espies,
'Through lanes and courts he takes his well-known way,
'Nor stops to parley when he cannot pay.'
But hark! with loud acclaim, the fife and drum
Announce your army near; behold, they come!

Enter BOMBASTES, *attended by one Drummer, one Fifer, and two Soldiers, all very materially differing in size.*

BOM.   (*to Army*) Meet me this ev'ning at the Barley-Mow;
I'll bring your pay, you see I'm busy now:
Begone, brave army, and don't kick up a row.

                                  [*Exeunt Soldiers.*

    (*to the King*) Thrash'd are your foes—this watch and silken string
Worn by their chief, I as a trophy bring;   61
I knock'd him down, then snatch'd it from his fob;

          "Watch, watch," he cried, when I had done the job:
          "My watch is gone," says he—says I "Just so;
          "Stop where you are—watches were made to go."

ART.   For which we make you Duke of Strombelo;

> [*Bombastes kneels; the King dubs him with a pipe, and then
> presents the bowl.*

          From our own bowl here drink, my soldier true;
          And if you'd like to take a whiff or two,
          He whose brave arm hath made our foes to crouch,
          Shall have a pipe from this our royal pouch.   70

BOM.   Honours so great have all my toils repaid!
          My Liege, and Fusbos, here's "Success to trade."

FUS.   Well said, Bombastes! since thy mighty blows
          Have given a quietus to our foes,
          Now shall our farmers gather in their crops,
          And busy tradesmen mind their crowded shops;
          The deadly havock of war's hatchet cease;
          Now shall we smoke the *calumet* of peace.

ART.   I shall smoke short-cut, you smoke what you please.

BOM.   Whate'er your Majesty shall deign to name,   80
          Short cut or *long*, to me is all the same.

BOM. &
FUS.   In *short*, so *long* as we your favours claim,
          Short cut or *long*, to us is all the same.

ART.   Thanks, gen'rous friends! now list whilst I impart
          How firm you're lock'd and bolted in my heart:
          So long as *this here* pouch a pipe contains,
          Or a full glass in *that there* bowl remains,
          To you an equal portion shall belong;
          This do I swear, and now—let's have a song.

FUS.   My Liege shall be obey'd.

BOM.   Fusbos, give place,   90
          You know you haven't got a singing face;
          Here, nature smiling, gave the winning grace.

          SONG, BOMBASTES—*Hope told a flatt'ring Tale.*

>   Hope told a flattering tale,
>   Much longer than my arm,
>   That love and pots of ale
>   In peace would keep me warm:

78 *calumet*] Indian pipe of peace.

The flatt'rer is not gone,
She visits number one:
In love I'm monstrous deep,
Love! odsbobs, destroys my sleep.   100

Hope told a flattering tale,
  Lest love should soon grown cool;
A tub thrown to a whale,
  To make the fish a fool:
Should Distaffina frown,
Then love's gone out of town;
And when love's dream is o'er,
Then we wake and dream no more.

[*Exit.*

[*The King evinces strong emotions during the song, and at the*
conclusion starts up.

FUS.   What ails my Liege? ah! why that look so sad?
ART.   (*coming forward*) I am in love! I scorch, I freeze, I'm mad!   110
       O tell me, Fusbos, first and best of friends,
       You, who have wisdom at your fingers' ends,
       Shall it be so, or shall it not be so?
       Shall I my Griskinissa's charms forego,
       Compel her to give up the regal chair,
       And place the rosy Distaffina there!
       In such a case, what course can I pursue?
       I love my Queen, and Distaffina too.
FUS.   And would a King his General supplant?
       I can't advise, upon my soul I can't.   120
ART.   'So when the vessel man is toss'd about
       'Upon that ocean call'd the "sea of doubt,"
       'Now safe he rides, and then on danger's brink;
       'Nor can he tell if he's to swim or sink.
FUS.   'So, when two roads a weary trav'ller spies,
       'And knoweth not on which his journey lies,
       'At once he stops, and seems in doubtful plight,
       'Since *this* may lead him wrong, and *that* not right.'
ART.   So when two feasts, whereat there's nought to pay,
       Fall unpropitious on the self-same day,   130
       The anxious Cit each invitation views,
       And ponders which to take or which refuse:

	From *this* or *that* to keep away is loth,

From *this* or *that* to keep away is loth,
And sighs to think he cannot dine at both.   [*Exit.*

Fus.   So when some school-boy, on a rainy day,
Finds all his playmates will no longer stay,
He takes the hint himself—and walks away.   [*Exit.*

Scene II.—*Another Apartment in the Palace.*

Enter ARTAXOMINOUS.

Art.   I'll seek the maid I love, though in my way
A dozen gen'rals stood in fierce array!
Such rosy beauties nature meant for kings;
Subjects have treat enough to see such things.

⁎ *The comic Song introduced in this place by Mr.* MATTHEWS, *not
being written by the author of the Piece, he is under the necessity of
apologizing for its omission.*

Scene III.—*Inside of a Cottage.*

Enter DISTAFFINA.

Dis.   This morn, as sleeping in my bed I lay,
I dreamt (and morning dreams come true, they say),
I dreamt a cunning man my fortune told,
And soon the pots and pans were turn'd to gold!
Then I resolv'd to cut a mighty dash;
But, lo! ere I could turn them into cash,
Another cunning man my hear betray'd,
Stole all away, and left my debts unpaid.
                                      [*Enter Artaxominous.*
And pray, sir, who are you I'd wish to know?
Art.   Perfection's self! O smooth that angry brow!   10
For love of thee I've wander'd thro' the town,
And here have come to offer half a crown.
Dis.   Fellow! your paltry offer I despise;
The great Bombastes' love alone I prize.
Art.   He's but a Gen'ral—damsel, I'm a King;

Dis.   O Sir! that makes it quite another thing.
Art.   And think not, maiden, I could e'er design
            A sum so trifling for such charms as thine.
            No! the half crown that ting'd thy cheeks with red,
            And bade fierce anger o'er thy beauties spread,   20
            Was meant that thou shouldst share my throne and bed.
Dis.   (aside) My dream is out, and I shall soon behold
            The pots and pans all turn to shining gold.
Art.   Here on my knees, (those knees which ne'er till now
            To man or maid in suppliance bent), I vow
            Still to remain, till you my hopes fulfil,
            Fixt as the Monument on Fish-street hill.
Dis.   And thus I swear, as I bestow my hand,
            As long as e'er the Monument shall stand,
            So long I'm your's——
Art.   Are then my wishes crown'd?   30
Dis.   La! Sir, I'd not say no for twenty pound:
            Let silly maids for love their favours yield,
            Rich ones for me—a king against the field.

            SONG, Distaffina—*Paddy's Wedding.*

                    Queen Dido at
                    Her palace gate
            Sat darning of her stocking O;
                    She sung and drew
                    The worsted through,
            Whilst her foot was the cradle rocking O.
                    (For a babe she had   40
                    By a soldier lad,
            Though hist'ry passes it over O;)
                    "You tell-tale brat,
                    "I've been a flat,
            "Your daddy has proved a rover O.

                    "What a fool was I
                    "To be cozen'd by
            "A fellow without a penny O;
                    "When rich ones came,
                    "And ask'd the same,   50
            "For I'd offers from never so many O.

44 *flat*] Dupe, fool.

"But I'll darn my hose,
"Look out for beaus,
"And quickly get a new lover O;
"Then come, lads, come,
"Love beats the drum,
"And a fig for Æneas the rover O."

ART. So Orpheus sung of old, or poets lie,
   And as the Brutes were charm'd, e'en so am I.
   Rosey-cheek'd maid, henceforth my only queen,   60
   Full soon shalt thou in royal robes be seen;
   And through my realm I'll issue this decree,
   None shall appear of taller growth than thee:
   Painters no other face pourtray—each sign
   O'er alehouse hung shall change its head for thine.
   Poets shall cancel their unpublish'd lays,
   And none presume to write but in thy praise.
           [Distaffina produces a bottle and glass.

DIS. And may I then, without offending, crave
   My love to taste of this, the best I have?

ART. Were it the vilest liquor upon earth,   70
   Thy touch would render it of matchless worth;
   Dear shall the gift be held that comes from you;
   Best proof of love, [*drinks*] 'tis full proof Hodges too:
   Through all my veins I feel a genial glow,
   It fires my soul——

BOM. *(within)*   Ho, Distaffina, ho!

ART. Heard you that voice?

DIS.   O yes, 'tis what's his name,
   The General; send him packing as he came.

ART. And is it he? and doth he hither come?
   Ah me! my guilty conscience strikes me dumb:
   Where shall I go? say, whither shall I fly?   80
   Hide me, oh hide me, from his injur'd eye!

DIS. Why, sure you're not alarm'd at such a thing!
   He's but a Gen'ral, and you're a King.
          [Artax. secretes himself in a closet.

Enter BOMBASTES.

BOM. Lov'd Distaffina! now by my scars I vow,
   Scars got—I haven't time to tell you how;
   By all the risks my fearless heart hath run,

Risks of all shapes from bludgeon, sword, and gun,
Steel traps, the patrole, bailiff shrewd, and dun;
By the great bunch of laurels on my brow,
Ne'er did thy charms exceed their present glow!   90
O let me greet thee with a loving kiss—
Hell and the devil!—say who's hat is this?

DIS.   Why help your silly brains, that's not a hat.

BOM.   No hat?

DIS.   Suppose it is, why what of that?
A hat can do no harm without a head!

BOM.   Whoe'er it fits, this hour I doom him dead;
Alive from hence the caitiff shall not stir—

                                        [*Discovers the King.*

Your most obedient, humble servant, sir.

ART.   O General, O!——

BOM.   My much-loved master, O!
What means all this?

ART.   Indeed I hardly know——   100

DIS.   You hardly know!—a very pretty joke,
If kingly promises so soon are broke!
Arn't I to be a Queen, and dress so fine?

ART.   I do repent me of the foul design;
To thee my brave Bombastes I restore
Pure Distaffina, and will never more
Through lane or street with lawless passion rove,
But give to Griskinissa all my love.

BOM.   No, no, I'll love no more; let him who can
Fancy the maid who fancies ev'ry man.   110
In some lone place I'll find a gloomy cave,
There my own hands shall dig a spacious grave,
Then all unseen I'll lay me down and die,
Since woman's constancy is——all my eye.

TRIO—O Lady Fair!

DIS.   *O cruel man! where are you going?*
       Sad are my wants, my rent is owing.

BOM.   *I go, I go, all comfort scorning;*
       Some death I'll die before the morning.

DIS.   *Heigh O, Heigh O! sad is that warning:*
       O do not die before the morning!   120

ART.   *I'll follow him, all danger scorning;*
       He shall not die before the morning.

BOM.	*I go, I go, &c.*
DIS.	*Heigh O, Heigh O, &c.*
ART.	*I'll follow him, &c.*

[Exeunt.

𝔖𝔠𝔢𝔫𝔢 𝔍𝔙.—*A Wood.*

Enter FUSBOS.

FUS. This day is big with fate: just as I set
   My foot across the threshold, lo! I met
   A man whose squint terrific struck my view;
   Another came, and, lo! he squinted too:
   And ere I'd reach'd the corner of the street,
   Some ten short paces, 'twas my lot to meet
   A third who squinted more—a fourth, and he
   Squinted more vilely than the other three.
   Such omens met the eye when Cæsar fell,
   But caution'd him in vain; and who can tell   10
   Whether those awful notices of fate
   Are meant for Kings, or Ministers of State?
   For rich or poor, old, young, or short or tall,
   The wrestler Love trips up the heels of all.

SONG—My Lodging is on the cold Ground.

My lodging is in Leather-lane,
 A parlour that's next to the sky;
'Tis expos'd to the wind and the rain,
 But the wind and the rain I defy:
Such love warms the coldest of spots,
 As I feel for Scrubinda the fair;   20
O she lives by the scouring of pots,
 In Dyot-Street, Bloomsbury-square.

O was I a quart, pint, or gill,
 To be scrubb'd by her delicate hands,
Let others possess what they will
 Of learning, and houses, and lands;
'My parlour that's next to the sky
 'I'd quit, her blest mansion to share;

'*So happy to live and to die*
  '*In Dyot-street, Bloomsbury-square.*   30

'*And O would this damsel be mine,*
  '*No other provision I'd seek;*
'*On a* look *I could breakfast and dine,*
  '*And feast on a* smile *for a week.*'
But, ah! should she false-hearted pro ve,
  Suspended, I'll dangle in air;
A victim to delicate love,
  In Dyot-street, Bloomsbury-square.

                                                              [*Exit.*

Enter BOMBASTES, *preceded by a Fifer, playing*
"*Michael Wiggins.*"

BOM.   Gentle musician, let thy dulcet strain
            Proceed—play Michael Wiggins once again,—   40
            Music's the food of love; give o'er, give o'er,
            For I must batten on that food no more.
            My happiness is chang'd to doleful dumps,
            Whilst, merry Michael, all thy cards were trumps.
            So, should some youth by fortune's blest decrees
            Possess at least a pound of Cheshire cheese,
            And bent some favour'd party to regale,
            Lay in a kilderkin, or so, of ale;
            Lo! angry fate, in one unlucky hour
            Some hungry rats may all the cheese devour,   50
            And the loud thunder turn the liquor sour.
                                   [*Forms his sash into a noose.*
            Alas! alack! alack! and well-a-day,
            That ever man should make himself away;
            That ever man for woman false should die,
            As many have, and so, and so——wont I;
            No, I'll go mad! 'gainst all I'll vent my rage,
            And with this wicked wanton world a woful war I'll wage.

            [*Hangs his boots to the arm of a tree, and, taking a scrap of*
            paper, with a pencil writes the following couplet, which he
            attaches to them, repeating the words

            "Who dares this pair of boots displace,
            "Must meet Bombastes face to face."
            Thus do I challenge all the human race.   60
                           [*Draws his sword, and retires up the stage.*

Enter ARTAXOMINOUS.

ART. Scorning my proffer'd hand he frowning fled,
   Curs'd the fair maid, and shook his angry head.
            [*Perceives the boots and label.*
   "Who dares this pair of boots displace,
   "Must meet Bombastes face to face."
   Ha! dost thou dare me, vile obnoxious elf;
   I'll make thy threats as *bootless* as thyself:
   Where'er thou art, with speed prepare to go
   Where I shall send thee—to the shades below!
            [*Knocks down the boots.*

BOM. (*coming forward*) So have I heard on Afric's burning shore,
   A hungry lion give a grievous roar;   70
   The grievous roar echo'd along the shore.

ART. So have I heard on Afric's burning shore
   Another lion give a grievous roar,
   And the first lion thought the last a bore.

BOM. Am I then mock'd? Now by my fame I swear
   You shall soon have it——There!   [*They fight.*

ART.   Where?

BOM.   There and there.

ART. I have it sure enough—Oh! I am slain,
   I'd give a pot of beer to live again;
   Yet, ere I die, I something have to say:
   My once lov'd Gen'ral, prithee come this way!   80
   Oh! Oh! my Bom——   [*Falls on his back.*

BOM.   bastes he would have said;
   But ere the word was out his breath was fled.
   Well, peace be with him, his untimely doom
   Shall thus be mark'd upon his costly tomb:—
   "Fate cropt him short—for be it understood,
   "He would have liv'd much longer—if he could."
          [*Retires again up the stage.*

Enter FUSBOS.

FUS. This was the way they came, and much, I fear,
   There's mischief in the wind—what have we here?
   King Artaxominous bereft of life!
   Here'll be a pretty tale to tell his wife.   90

BOM. A pretty tale, but not for thee to tell,
   For thou shalt quickly follow him to hell;

There say I sent thee, and I hope he's well.

Fus. No, thou thyself shalt thy own message bear;
   Short is the journey, thou wilt soon be there.

             [They fight.

     DUETT—*Weippert's Fancy.*

Bom.   '*I'll quickly run you through,*
Fus.   '*No hang me if you do,*
   '*I think I know a trick can equal two of that;*
    '*My sword I well can use,*
    '*So mind your Ps and Qs:*   100
Bom. '*I thank you, Sir, but I must caution you of that.*

    (*Lord Cathcart's Favourite.*)

Fus.   ' '*Tis a pleasure to fight*
      '*With a man so polite,*
   '*Then hear in return what I'll do, Sir;*
    '*I'll take down aught you'll say*
    '*In the will-making way,*
   '*And be your Executor too, Sir.*

Bom.   '*O, Sir, there's no need*
      '*For so friendly a deed,*
   '*But I hope for yourself you're provided;* 110
    '*Since your worldly affairs*
    '*Will devolve to your heirs,*
   '*As soon as the point is decided,*
    '*Then come on while you can,*
    '*Meet your fate like a man—*
   '*Bombastes shall ne'er be derided.*'

Bom. O Fusbos, Fusbos, I am diddled quite,
   Dark clouds come o'er my eyes, farewell, good night!
   Good night! my mighty soul's inclin'd to roam,
   So make my compliments to all at home.   120

          [Lies down by the King.

Fus. And o'er thy grave a monument shall rise,
   Where heroes yet unborn shall feast their eyes;
   And this short Epitaph that speaks thy fame,
   Shall also there immortalize my name:—
   "Here lies Bombastes stout of heart and limb,
   "Who conquer'd all but Fusbos—Fusbos him."

 117 diddled] Done for, mortally wounded.

Enter DISTAFFINA.

DIS.   Ah, wretched maid! O miserable fate!
        I've just arriv'd in time to be too late:
        What now shall hapless Distaffina do?
        Curse on all morning dreams, they come so true.   130
FUS.   Go, beauty, go, thou source of woe to man,
        And get another lover where you can:
        The crown now sits on Griskinnissa's head;
        To her I'll go——
                        But are you sure they're dead?
DIS.
FUS.   Yes, dead as herrings—herrings that are red.

                        FINALE.

DIS.   *Briny tears I'll shed,*
ART.   *I for you shall cry too;*
FUS.   *Zounds! the King's alive;*
BOM.   *Yes, and so am I too.*

DIS.   *It was better far*   140
ART.   *Thus to check all sorrow;*
FUS.   *But, if some folks please,*
BOM.   *We'll die again to-morrow.*

DIS.   *Tu ral, lu ral, la,*
ART.   *Tu ral, lu ral, laddi;*
FUS.   *Tu ral, lu ral, la,*
BOM.   *Tu ral, lu ral, laddi.*
        [*They take hands and dance round, repeating tu ral, &c.*

                        FINIS.

Selected Bibliography

Editions

George Villiers, Duke of Buckingham, *The Rehearsal*, ed. Montague Summers (Stratford-on-Avon: Shakespeare Head Press, 1914)

John Gay, *The Poetical Works*, ed. G. C. Faber, Oxford Standard Authors (London: Oxford University Press, 1926)

John Gay, Alexander Pope, and John Arbuthnot, *Three Hours After Marriage*, ed. John Harrington Smith (Los Angeles, Calif.: Publications of the Augustan Reprint Society, 1961)

Henry Fielding, *The Tragedy of Tragedies*, ed. James T. Hillhouse (New Haven, Conn.: Yale University Press, 1918)

Authorities

Richmond F. Bond, *English Burlesque Poetry* (Cambridge, Mass.: Harvard University Press, 1932)

V. C. Clinton-Baddeley, *The Burlesque Tradition in the English Theatre after 1660* (London: Methuen, 1952)

Malcolm Goldstein, *Pope and the Augustan Stage* (Stanford, Calif.: Stanford University Press; London: Oxford University Press, 1958)

Leo Hughes, *A Century of English Farce* (Princeton, N. J.: Princeton University Press; London: Oxford University Press, 1956)

George Kitchin, *A Survey of Burlesque and Parody in English* (Edinburgh: Oliver and Boyd, 1931)

John Loftis, *The Politics of Drama in Augustan England* (Oxford: Clarendon Press, 1963)

Archibald B. Shepperson, *The Novel in Motley* (Cambridge, Mass.: Harvard University Press, 1936)

George Sherburn, 'The Fortunes and Misfortunes of *Three Hours After Marriage*', in *Modern Philology* XXIV (1926–7), 91–109

Dane Farnsworth Smith, *Plays About the Theatre in England* (London: Oxford University Press, 1936)

James Sutherland, 'Satire in the Theatre', in *English Satire* (London: Cambridge University Press, 1958), pp. 133–52